Donation for:
Hayden Janney's Birthday
2003
© IF4473

Multi-
media
The Complete Guide

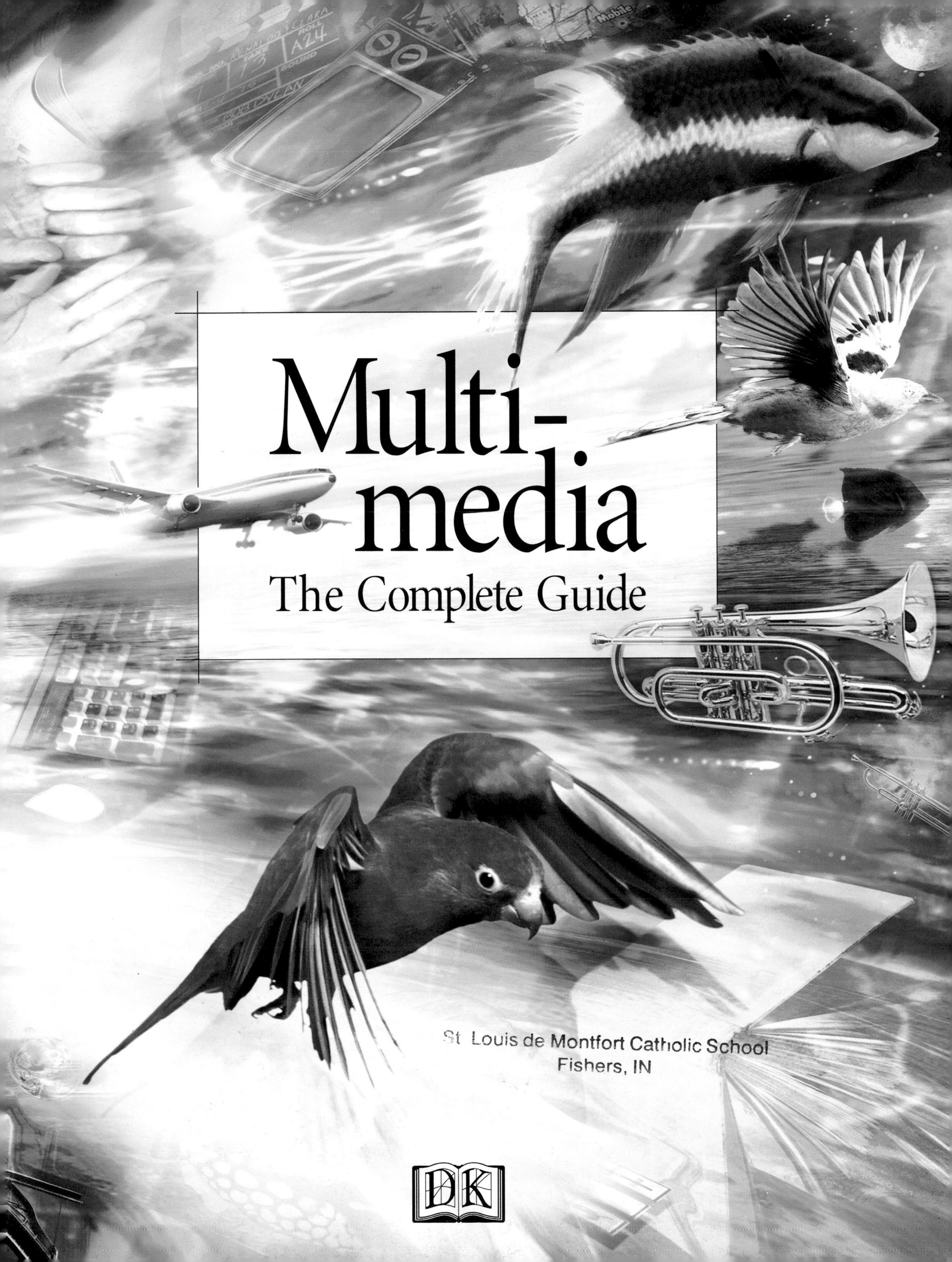

Multi-media

The Complete Guide

DK

A DK PUBLISHING BOOK

CONCEIVED, EDITED, AND DESIGNED BY DK DIRECT LIMITED

Project Editors Joe Elliot, Tim Worsley

US Editor Constance M. Robinson

Project Art Director Nigel Coath

Editors Brian Cooper, Susan Schlachter, John Watson

Editor-in-Chief Anthony Whitehorn

Senior Designer Stephen Cummiskey

Designers Tim Mann, Trond Wilhelmsen

Illustrators Coneyl Jay, Peter Scott, Matthew Wallis

Additional Illustrators Nigel Coath, Stephen Cummiskey, Tim Mann, Trond Wilhelmsen

Photographers Tony Buckley, Gary Ombler, Steve Gorton, Andy Crawford

Text Contributors David Bowen, George Cole, Brian Cooper, Joe Elliot, Paul Glancey, Rupert Goodwins, Nina Hathway, Peter Jackson, Graeme Kidd, Damien Noonan, Penelope Ody, Susan Schlachter, Steve Shipside, John Watson, Sid Wells, Tim Worsley

Picture Researchers Ingrid Nilsson, Sam Ruston

Production Manager Ian Paton

Editorial Director Reg Grant

Design Director Tony Foo

Publisher Jonathan Reed

First American Edition, 1996
2 4 6 8 10 9 7 5 3 1

Published in the United States by
DK Publishing, Inc.,
95 Madison Avenue,
New York, New York 10016

Library of Congress Cataloging-in-Publication Data

Multimedia, the complete guide.
p. cm.
ISBN 0-7894-0422-2
1. Multimedia systems.
QA76.575.C66 1996
006.6—dc20 95-30090
CIP

Color Reproduction by Triffik Technology, UK
Printed and bound in Italy by A. Mondadori Editore, Verona

PREFACE

WE ARE LIVING IN THE MILLENNIUM OF the book, the century of cinema, and the decade of multimedia. The consequences of this are staggering. Our world is awash with information. We are confronted with a constant stream of new information and also a constant stream of new information technologies: multimedia, on-line multimedia, interactive television, virtual reality, the Internet, and so on.

Despite the rush of technology, however, multimedia may hold the key to simplifying the information age. By presenting words, sounds, pictures, animation, and film in an interactive way it allows us to choose our own paths through information. In this respect, it is similar to the natural ways we learn as young children. When we come into this world we are beautifully programmed – to crawl around, to touch things, to look at things, to hear things, to feel things. We do not need words, concepts, or a curriculum: we explore. It is said that in our first year we learn more than at any other time in our lives. This total interaction with information is what multimedia offers: in a multimedia environment you can learn naturally. And because multimedia creates worlds you can control, its potential to entertain and educate is enormous.

Multimedia, the Complete Guide is a comprehensive and detailed exploration of the entire multimedia phenomenon. It contains over 1,000 images, which reveal how multimedia works, how it is used, and how it is made. It examines the full range of multimedia applications – encyclopedias, interactive movies, in-flight entertainment, and so on – as well as the range of multimedia machines – computers, home consoles, and virtual reality equipment. The book reveals how multimedia text, sound, graphics, animation, and video are created and how they are built into an interactive whole. In addition, it explores the world of on-line multimedia, the Internet, and interactive television – as it is today and as it will be in the future.

Today, a child exploring a multimedia encyclopedia can discover – through words and sounds and moving pictures – how the agricultural revolution brought civilization to humankind. The same encyclopedia will illustrate interactively how the Industrial Revolution took us into the modern world. And future editions will reveal how the closing decades of this millennium marked the beginning of the information revolution.

Peter Kindersley

Contents

Multimedia Software

How Multimedia Computers Work

Multimedia Machines
VIRTUALITY

Chapter 4

Chapter 5

Reference

INTRODUCTION

MULTIMEDIA MAY WELL BE THE most powerful educational tool yet invented, and it has the potential to become the ultimate in entertainment. The reason for this is twofold. First, as its name conveys, multimedia has the supreme advantage of combining many different types of media into one: text, pictures, animation, narration, video, and music. Second, it is interactive: the user does not receive the information passively, as when reading a book or watching television, but controls it, deciding which of the various avenues to explore and being able to jump forward, backward, or from one to another at will. This information can be controlled, accessed, and cross-referenced in a way that suits the user. In the business world, companies are using multimedia to set up information kiosks for customers, or to train staff at a level and pace that suits each individual; in the home, both young and old are using multimedia software, delivered on a CD-ROM, as a source of entertainment and knowledge. Multimedia is all set to change our lives for good.

MULTIMEDIA
In 1985, Microsoft called multimedia "the new papyrus."

A MULTIMEDIA REVOLUTION

There is another definition of multimedia, usually spoken of in the same breath as the "information superhighway."

This involves the merging of communications media industries such as telephone, cable television, and movie companies. It is a vision of a network that will bring multimedia software – and assorted other services – into the home through a cable. This vision is fast becoming reality as interactive services start to appear.

However you define it, multimedia is having a huge impact on our lives. It might have been premature to label it "the new papyrus," as Microsoft did a decade ago, but few now doubt that multimedia technology is set to play an equally revolutionary role.

DIGITAL DAYS

The key to this multimedia revolution is digitization – which means the conversion of all types of information, such as words, sound, pictures, video, and numbers, into a special code that electronic machines can recognize and understand.

The first type of machine to make use of digital information was the computer. "Information processors," which filled whole rooms, began to appear in large organizations in the 1950s; they were used to perform complex calculations, and could display only text and figures on screen.

Soon, simple digital graphics were appearing on computers; inevitably, the first programs to be run on the graphics-capable systems were games.

Technology moved on, and by the late seventies, video arcades were offering interactive multimedia that combined graphics and computer-generated sound in games such as *Space Invaders*.

EARLY GRAPHICS
Computer graphics as they looked in 1972 in Atari's *Pong* tennis game.

DIGITAL DISTRACTIONS
Early arcade games such as *Battlezone* were the public's first taste of digital graphics.

Soon hobbyists were buying the first home computers and games consoles. Then, in 1981, IBM unveiled its first PC (personal computer), and the business world bought into computing wholesale. Few people, however, predicted the breakneck pace of growth and development that has characterized the computer industry ever since.

Today just about anything can be converted into digital code. A computer simply processes numbers and does not know or care whether those numbers represent a Mozart symphony, a Rembrandt self-portrait, or an accounting firm's five-year business plan. Multimedia home computers can now produce stunning 3-D graphics, photo-realistic pictures, movie footage, hi-fi sound, and breathtaking animation, while all the time they are just pushing figures.

Today's multimedia computers are at the forefront of a much bigger multimedia revolution, however – they are leading the move away from analog media machines towards digital ones.

PAINT BY NUMBERS
A digitized masterpiece is just another set of electronic code to a multimedia computer.

FROM A TO D
Today's analog media machines will probably be superseded by digital ones.

ANALOG INTO DIGITAL

Most of the media machines in homes today – such as TV sets, video recorders, radios, and most telephones – are analog. They deal with information that has been transmitted as varying electrical voltages, not as electronic code.

This is changing fast. Some cordless and cellular telephones already use digital technology. Radio stations are testing out digital broadcasting, and the VCR (videocassette recorder) is under threat from digital video. And so, while the thought of connecting your telephone to your TV set or your computer to your VCR may seem absurd now, one day they may all be in the same box. As the digitization of media proceeds apace, and as the technology advances, so the foundations of the multimedia revolution are being laid.

At the forefront of progress is the CD (compact disc), which was invented to hold digital music, but now, as the CD-ROM, carries multimedia information.

CD-ROM DELIVERS

CD-ROM (Compact Disc Read-Only Memory) sprang directly from the music CD, and from the same set of parents – Sony and Philips. It was a logical step; after all, music CDs store a stream of electronic code that represents sound waves. Replace that code with one that conveys digital pictures, text, animation, and so on, attach a modified CD player to a computer, and you have CD-ROM.

When CD-ROM first appeared in the mid-1980s, the storage capacity it offered the computer world seemed truly awesome. It could hold about 20 times more information than the hard disk of a typical desktop computer. To put that into perspective, a single CD-ROM can hold more than two complete sets of the *Encyclopaedia Britannica*, which is just the sort of quantity you need to produce high-quality multimedia. In fact, CD-ROM has been so successful a way to deliver multimedia products that now no home computer can be called truly complete without a CD-ROM drive.

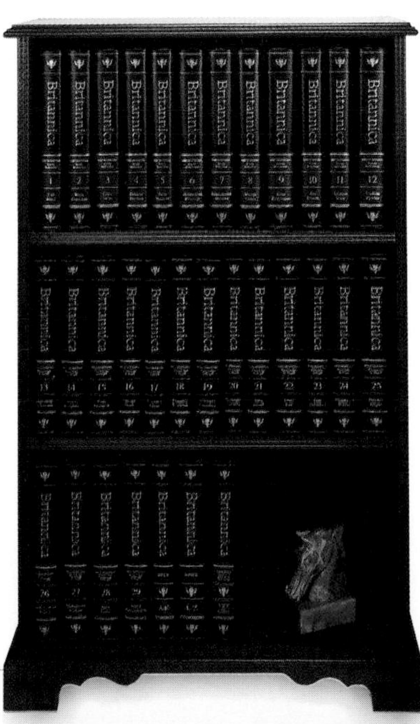

COMPACT KNOWLEDGE
The entire *Encyclopaedia Britannica* would fit twice on one CD-ROM.

WORLDS TO EXPLORE

Just as you can flip from track to track on a music CD, with simple computer software you can navigate the data on a CD-ROM so that it becomes an interactive experience. Instead of paging through the information in a linear way, as you would with a book, you can jump directly from one related entry to another, as your interest takes you. And with the addition of sound, graphics, and video, you can experience the full potential of multimedia.

YOUR OWN JOURNEY

Multimedia enables you to make your own way through information. This example from Dorling Kindersley's *Eyewitness Encyclopedia of Nature* shows how it is possible to jump between related topics at will.

Start Here
The naturalist's console is the control center of the program. To explore the world of nature, click on any image, such as the Mammals poster on the wall.

Mammals Poster
Clicking on the "Catlike Carnivores" image on the poster takes you to a page containing detailed information on the subject.

Back Home
To return to the main console, click outside the open window.

Video Clip
To watch a video clip about tigers and cubs, click on the play button. The clip plays in a window and then returns to the page.

Making a Link
Click on the "Prehistoric Mammals" image in the "See Also" box to jump to a page on the saber-toothed Smilodon.

See Also
The "See Also" box displays a list of related topics.

1995
140 million

1994
54 million

1993
17 million

1992
6 million

1991
2 million

ESCALATING SALES

CD-ROM was hardly an overnight success. Software companies would not risk the high costs of developing CD-ROM titles until more people had drives, but people were not buying drives until they saw more software. Once the deadlock eased, however, sales of CD-ROMs took off, as these estimated worldwide figures show.

INTERACTIVE ADVENTURES

Multimedia lets you explore information at your own pace. You can wander through an art gallery and choose which pictures to look at, what level of detail you require, and whether or not you want an expert spoken commentary. Or you could listen to a Beethoven symphony bar by bar, with the musical score shown on-screen and with extra annotations to point out the imagery and the repeated themes.

Multimedia does not stop at the edges of the real world either – from the cockpit of a jet aircraft or an X-Wing spacecraft you can fly through the virtual terrain of today's interactive games. Once information, real or imaginary, has been digitized and put on a CD-ROM, it can form part of a spectacular interactive world of discovery.

A Stopgap Measure...

At the present time, CD-ROM is unrivaled as the best way to deliver multimedia. Software companies like it because once a title has been developed, the discs are cheap to mass-produce. And consumers like it because it gives them access to new, exciting software.

However, CD-ROM is not quite perfect. The CD's musical roots mean that jumping from track to track and reading data off the disc both happen at a laid-back pace better suited to a music center than to the needs of interactive multimedia. Compared to the hard disk of any desktop computer, a CD-ROM drive is many times slower, and its capacity seems less dramatic than it once did. While it is true that one disc can hold a huge amount of text, the figures are not as impressive for graphics or video, since in the digital world the old saying about a picture being worth a thousand words is far from true. One full-screen, photographic-quality image takes up as much storage space as about 150,000 words. As we reach the limits of the single disc – some games titles occupy up to seven discs – experts are questioning the future of CD-ROM. For some, the compact disc is just a stopgap measure that will disappear the instant the information superhighway is in place.

Questionable Future
Will the CD-ROM survive, or will it be eclipsed by the information superhighway?

On-line Services
Services currently on trial include video-on-demand, video games, and on-line shopping.

...on the Road to the Highway

The information superhighway is a proposed communication network that will bring you multimedia through a socket in the wall. You will not need to find space in your home for videos, games cartridges, music CDs, newspapers, or CD-ROMs, because with the aid of a little black box you will be able to dial up a remote computer that will provide any of these services for you – interactive multimedia on-line.

You will have a much wider choice of up-to-date material available for instant access, from video-on-demand to virtual reality shopping malls, and from news broadcasts tailored to your personal interests to vast on-line research libraries. The service will be fully interactive too – you will be able to play video games against opponents on the other side of the world, control the course of interactive movies, and choose your own path through the world of on-line services. Furthermore, the service will revolutionize the way we communicate personally, by combining the power of electronic mail and the Internet with fax technology and videophones.

While we will not know for some time the exact direction the superhighway will take, this is the vision of our digital future that is driving the multimedia industry foward. The incredible capacity of fiber-optic cables will make it possible to transmit huge amounts of digital data into and out of our homes. The possibilities for what we do with it are endless.

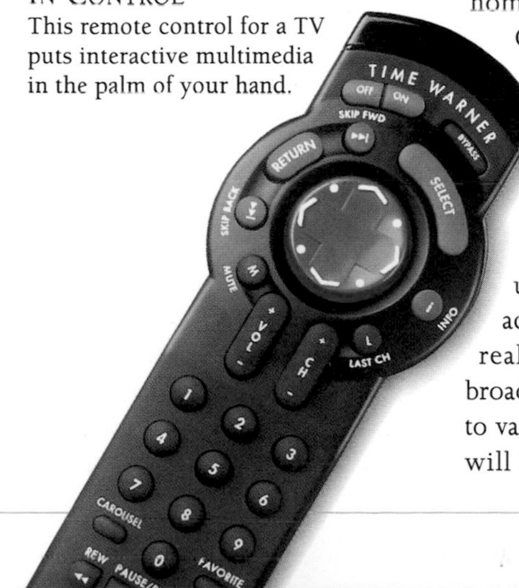

In Control
This remote control for a TV puts interactive multimedia in the palm of your hand.

THE NOT-SO-SUPER HIGHWAY?

The wide range of promised interactive multimedia services is an exciting prospect, and there is no wonder it is stirring up such media interest. To forge the superhighway and the "traffic" that will flow down it, new alliances are rapidly being formed between the cable and telephone companies that will build the highway, and the TV, film, and software companies that will supply the traffic. Yet, although the deals and promises are there, most of the infrastructure has still to be built – and it will not be easy.

Every home will need a high-capacity fiber-optic cable to link up with a network of even higher-capacity fiber-optic cables. To get there from today's arrangements for cable TV, where homes are connected by old-fashioned copper telephone wire to a network of standard fiber-optic cable, will require huge investment. It will be a good five or ten years before today's state-of-the-art interactive multimedia becomes widely available in most homes.

OUR MULTIMEDIA FUTURE
In the not too distant future, many people will get their multimedia through a TV set and set-top box signal decoder.

TOO MUCH EQUIPMENT?

While the superhighway is still some way off and its exact nature is not yet clear, the one thing today's TV, telecommunications, and computer companies are all sure of is that their survival depends on being part of the action. With so many players all trying to get ahead and set the standard that the rest have to follow, it is possible that the home of the future will not have a single, all-in-one on-line multimedia system but will instead have multiple sources of digital information – the game cartridge, CD-i titles, CD-ROM, Video CD, and a host of interactive TV services – along with a stack of decoder boxes, one for each type. If the digital media machines of the future are as incompatible as today's analog machines – so that you have to dial up one system to watch a movie, and another to find out more about an idea the film sparks off in your mind – perhaps the whole point of the digital revolution will have been missed.

Still, while the media companies of today rush to be the multimedia companies of tomorrow, all fighting for their own lane on the information superhighway, we may as well sit back and enjoy the ride – the interactive ride, that is – in the knowledge that, whatever it looks like when the dust finally does settle, multimedia is here to stay.

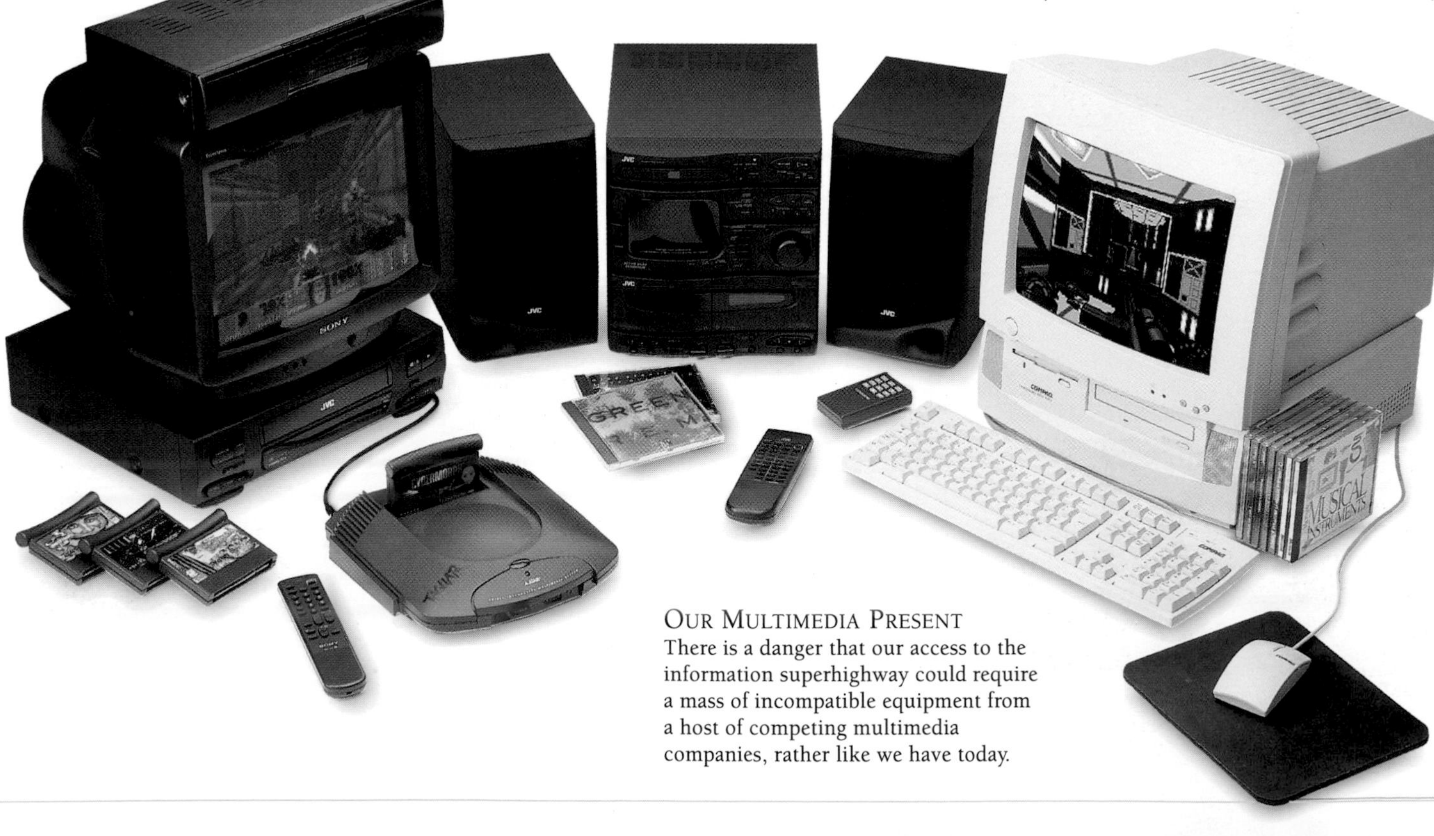

OUR MULTIMEDIA PRESENT
There is a danger that our access to the information superhighway could require a mass of incompatible equipment from a host of competing multimedia companies, rather like we have today.

How To Use This Book

This book is designed for browsing rather than reading from cover to cover. The book's five chapters cover everything from multimedia software and what you can do with it to the wide range of multimedia machines and how they work, from a behind-the-scenes look at how multimedia titles are made to how on-line multimedia and the information superhighway will affect our lives. At the back of the book you will find a detailed glossary of terms, a comprehensive index, and a list of the multimedia titles featured in the book. As an extra help, throughout the book certain key terms are highlighted as hotspots. Hotspots point you toward another section of the book where you will find more detailed information on the subject.

Hotspots point you to more information

To get you started, the outline below tells you what each chapter contains.

1 Multimedia Software
The first chapter looks at the different types of multimedia software and what you can do with them – from education, training, and reference titles to the games and entertainment classics.

2 How Multimedia Computers Work
This chapter takes the lid off a multimedia computer to show how it works, following the passage of digital data from the CD-ROM, the mouse, and the keyboard to the screen and speakers.

3 Multimedia Machines
This chapter compares the major multimedia players, from the PC and the Apple Macintosh to the home consoles: CD-i, 3DO, the Saturn, and the PlayStation – and on to the imaginary worlds of virtual reality machines.

4 How Multimedia is Made
From the secrets of 3-D animators to the workings of the sound studio, this chapter gives you a guided tour of how today's state-of-the-art multimedia titles are made.

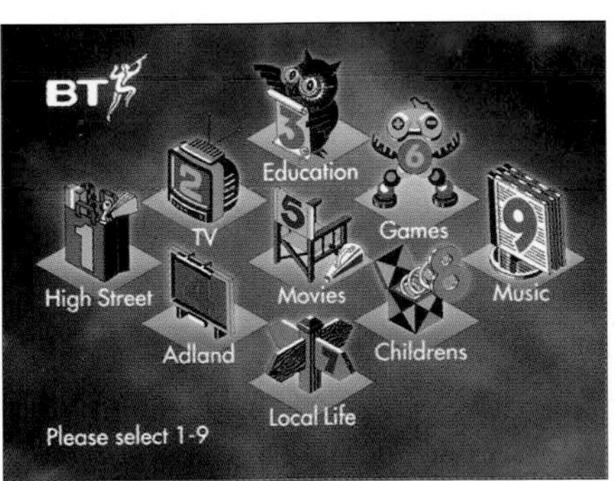

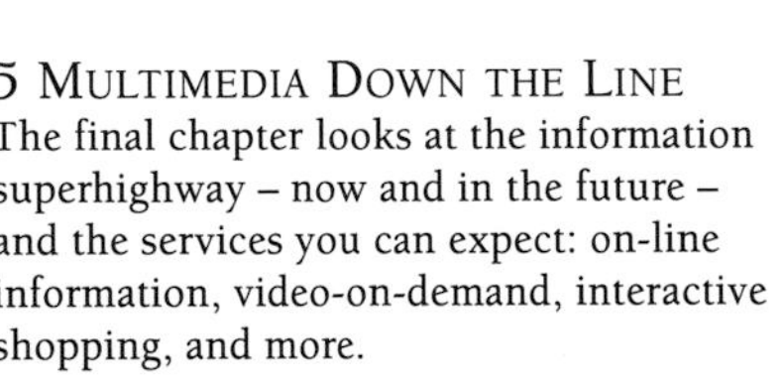

5 Multimedia Down the Line
The final chapter looks at the information superhighway – now and in the future – and the services you can expect: on-line information, video-on-demand, interactive shopping, and more.

Find
Countries
Antarctica
Antarctica
Antigua and Barbuda
Argentina
Armenia
Aruba (Neth.)
INFORMATION
INFORMATION

Multimedia Software

What is interactive multimedia – and what can it do? This chapter explores what is meant by "interactivity" and looks at the many different kinds of multimedia software: encyclopedias, interactive museums, math teachers, animated storybooks, games, interactive movies, in-flight entertainment, and more.

The World of Multimedia

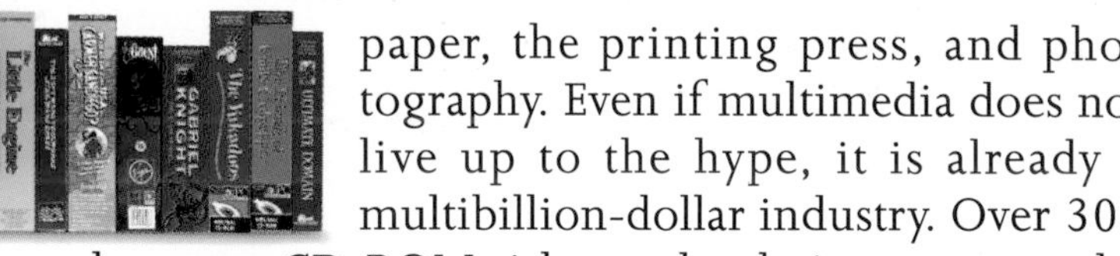

Multimedia software arrived in the mid-eighties, in the form of the CD-ROM. By the early nineties, the multimedia phenomenon was gathering momentum and had attracted great journalistic interest. The invention of the CD-ROM, with its capacity to store vast amounts of information, was being compared in significance to the invention of paper, the printing press, and photography. Even if multimedia does not live up to the hype, it is already a multibillion-dollar industry. Over 300 new CD-ROM titles make their way onto the shelves of computer and book stores every month. And many of them put computers to uses that could not possibly have been anticipated when multimedia first took off.

Software for Everyone

Most of the multimedia titles produced today are designed for home use. These titles fall into three broad categories: reference, which brings the resources of the public library into the home; education, which supplements classroom schooling; and entertainment. Within each category, certain genres have been established: the cartoon adventure and the interactive movie, for example, are both well-defined strands of entertainment software. A fourth category, services, covers wider multimedia applications: in workplaces, public galleries, shopping malls, and even airplanes.

In retrospect, it is not hard to see why multimedia has been put to so many uses. Computers have become powerful enough to process enormous quantities of almost any type of information held on CD-ROMs, from databases of statistical data to full-screen movie sequences. And hundreds of millions of people worldwide – all with different tastes and interests – have access to computers, either at home or at work. These factors have led to the rich variety of multimedia titles shown here. On the pages that follow, each multimedia genre is explored in more detail.

Reference

Encyclopedias
Atlases
Leisure Titles
Museums
Magazines

Home Library

Reference is the oldest and still the most popular use for CD-ROM-based multimedia. Traditional reference books – such as encyclopedias and atlases – adapt well to multimedia. And, although early claims that multimedia heralded the "death of the book" now seem exaggerated, multimedia encyclopedias now outsell printed ones.

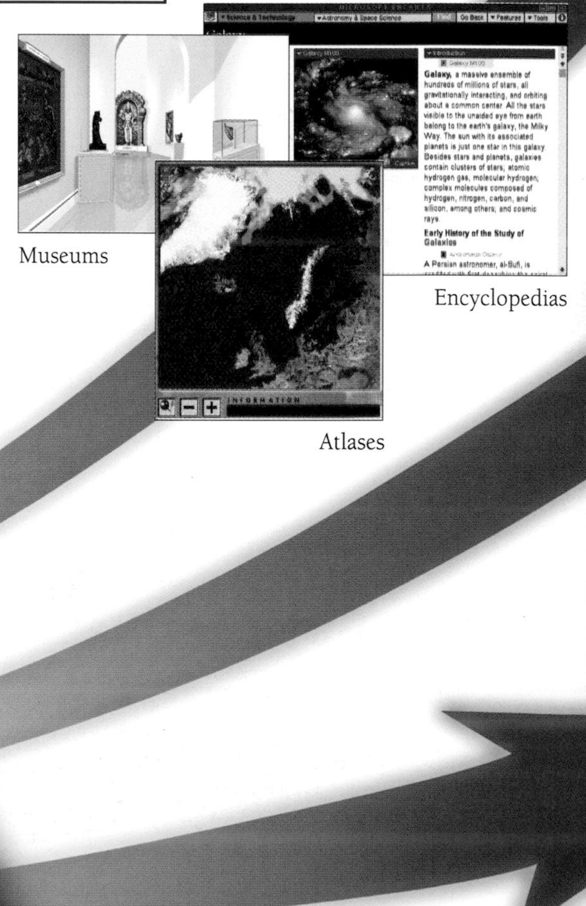

Museums

Encyclopedias

Atlases

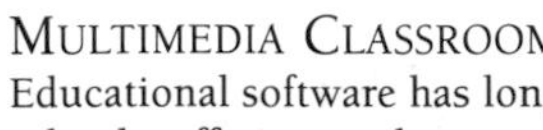

Multimedia Classroom

Educational software has long had a role in schools, offering students structured learning exercises that they can carry out at their own pace. Multimedia's potential for entertainment has led to a new breed of software – known as "edutainment" – that promotes learning through play, creative activities, and adventure games.

Education

- Early Learning
- Storybooks
- Math
- Creativity Tools
- Language Learning
- Science

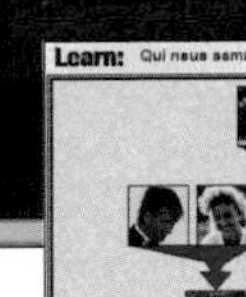

Math

Language Learning

Creativity Tools

Storybooks

Cartoon Adventures

Interactive Movies

Puzzle Games

Games and Entertainment

A CD-ROM typically costs twice as much as a board game, and four times as much as a music CD. Nevertheless, entertainment is multimedia's biggest growth area. Computer games developers now have million-dollar budgets; and in recent years, big-name music publishers, television companies, and movie studios have brought their backing and skills into the multimedia entertainment industry.

Entertainment

- Puzzle Games
- 3-D Action Games
- Cartoon Adventures
- Interactive Movies
- Multimedia Music
- New Directions

3-D Action Games

Multimedia Music

Information

In-flight Services

Training

Services

- Training
- Information
- Point-of-sale
- In-flight Services

Multimedia at Work

Outside the home, multimedia is taking on new and varied roles. In businesses, CD-ROMs are used to train the staff, while in stores, multimedia kiosks sell products. In museums and public places, information booths act as local guides. And in the skies, multimedia is transforming the concept of in-flight services.

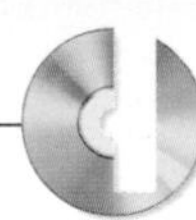

HOW INTERACTIVITY WORKS

A CD-ROM is a durable way of storing a large amount of multimedia information (text, narration, music, pictures, animation, video) that can be retrieved and presented by a computer. But the most important part of the multimedia experience is interactivity; not merely accessing the available information but having the opportunity to navigate through it, play with it, and sometimes even create something new from it. The way a multimedia title presents information and enables you to interact with it is called the title's "user interface." The interface must do two things. First, it must tell you what is available and what it can do. Second, it must provide you with a way of making a choice from the options presented; in most multimedia titles, this is achieved through the use of what is known as "hypermedia."

HYPERMEDIA

Many reference titles open with a main control screen, which is the heart of the user interface. From here you can explore the title. This might involve reading text, listening to music, watching movie clips, and so on. When these words, sounds, and pictures become interactive, they become hypermedia. Hypermedia is recognized by two characteristics. First, it enables you to respond to it, and it will then respond to you. For example, if you choose a word you might be taken to other, related words, or if you choose a picture you might be switched to another part of the title. Second, hypermedia has choices that are multilinear – it offers you many paths through the same information. The two forms of hypermedia most commonly used in multimedia are hypertext and hotspots.

INTERACTIVE BOOKS
Voyager's *Expanded Book* series takes popular novels and adds simple interactivity to the text. Although not strictly multimedia – they do not include sound or moving pictures – they are good examples of how hypertext can be used.

HYPERTEXT

A text-based title provides the widest opportunity to make use of hypertext. With hypertext, every word is "live" – when you choose it, you can instantly see a list of all the pages where that word occurs and jump straight to any of those pages. You can also highlight any word or passage that interests you or type notes into the margin without defacing the text for another reader. And you can copy whole passages for inclusion in a word processor document.

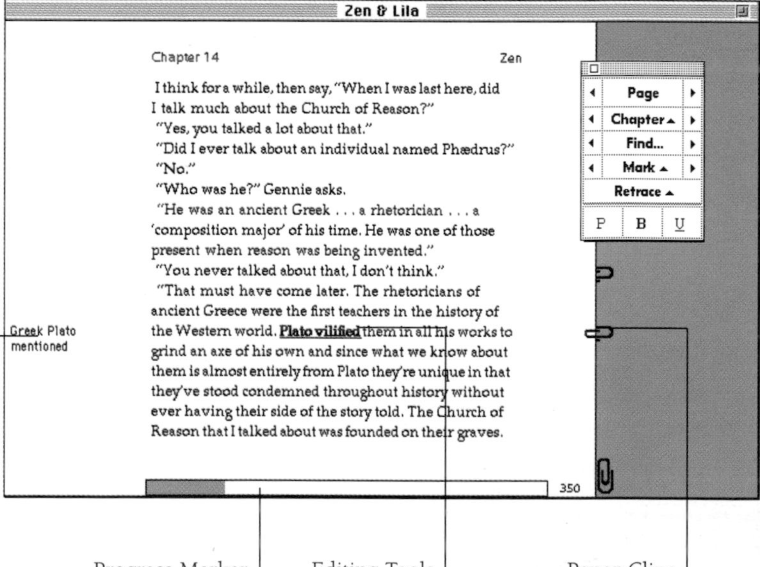

Marginal Notes
You can jot down your own comments instantly – and erase them just as quickly.

Progress Marker
The Progress Bar lets you see how far into the book you are.

Editing Tools
You can mark text as bold, underlined, or both, to make it stand out.

Paper Clips
These act as temporary bookmarks that you can flip to instantly.

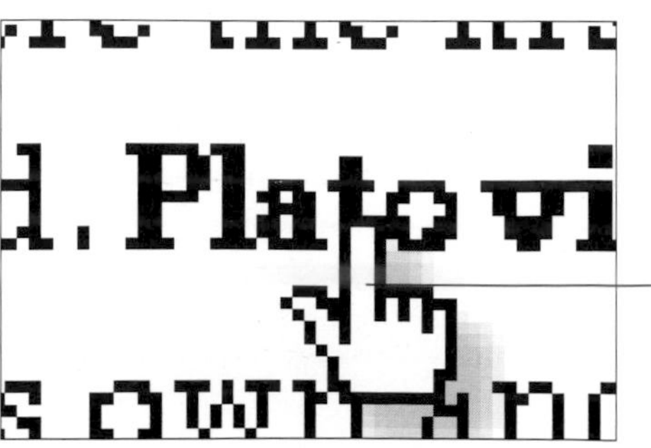

Live Text
Selecting text with the mouse pointer enables you to jump to other instances of that word or phrase.

Point and Click

The single most useful tool for the multimedia computer user is the mouse and its on-screen pointer, or cursor. In most multimedia titles a small pointer on the screen – most often in the shape of a hand or an arrow – follows the movements of the mouse. Choices are presented on-screen as words or pictures, and choosing between them is simple: you just point with the mouse and click the mouse button. Home console owners generally use a joypad to control the pointer instead, but the principle is the same.

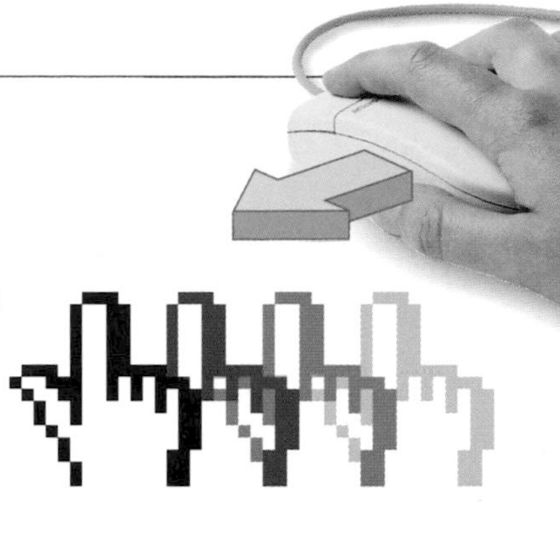

Bioforge
The robot hero's hand in Origin's Bioforge becomes the pointer for menu selections.

Pointer Power

Pointers take many forms, even within the same program. Different pointer shapes are used to indicate, for example, when the pointer is over a hotspot, or when the program is pausing to load new data. This gives the user important feedback about his or her actions.

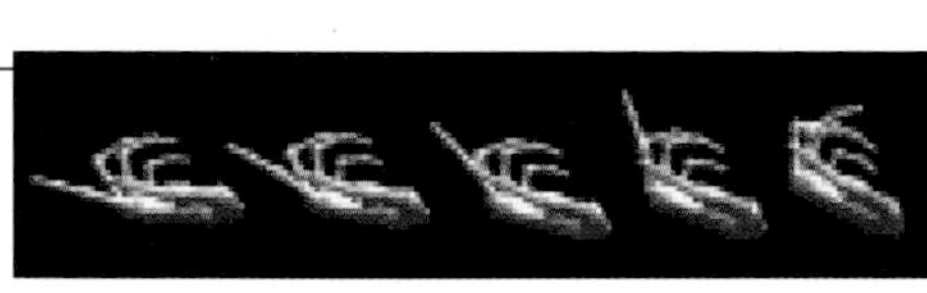

Moving Pointers
Some titles have animated cursors, such as this beckoning skeletal hand from Trilobyte's 7th Guest, *used to indicate a direction.*

Hotspots

Voyager's *Making Maus*, like almost all multimedia titles, makes extensive use of hotspots. A hotspot is usually an on-screen button or picture that reacts when you select it – by taking you to another part of the title, for example. Hotspots can also be invisible: they are revealed only by exploring the screen with the pointer and observing where the pointer changes shape. Another type of hotspot is hot text – a word or phrase that appears on screen in a different color from the main text to show that it is live.

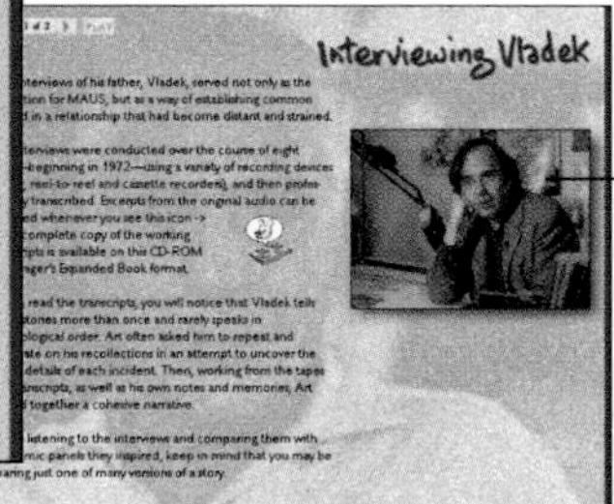

Dynamic Link
Hotspots often jump you to another screen. This action is known as a dynamic link. Here, one of the hotspots leads to a video and a transcript of an interview.

New Depths to the Page
The contents page is presented as a set of hotspot pictures. Each of these rectangles takes you to a different section of the title.

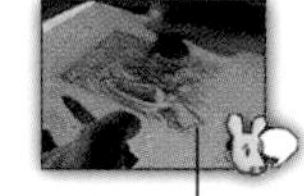

Introduction

Background Research

Page Layout

Pencil Artwork

Multimedia Conversion

Interfacial Differences

A given subject presents different opportunities for interactive multimedia. Here, four titles that show how the human body works reveal some of the many different approaches possible.

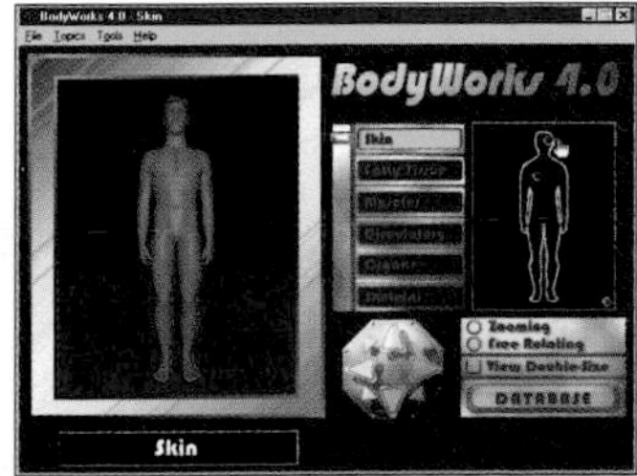

Softkey's *Body Works*

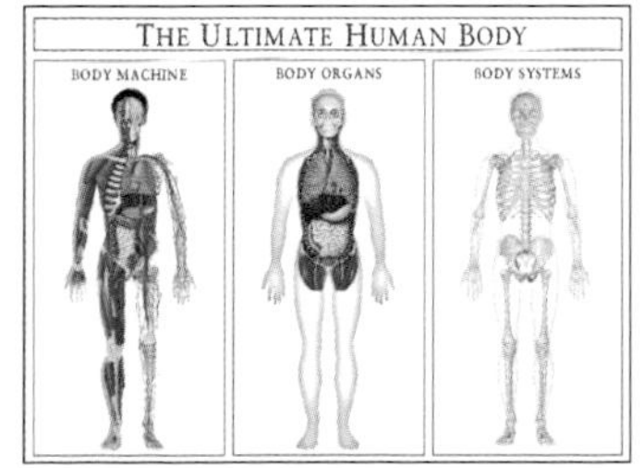

Dorling Kindersley's *The Ultimate Human Body*

IVI Publishing's *What is a Bellybutton?*

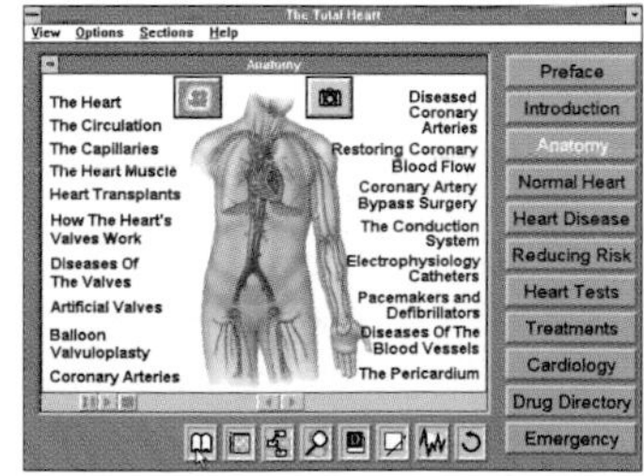

Mayo Clinic's *The Total Heart*

THE HOME LIBRARY

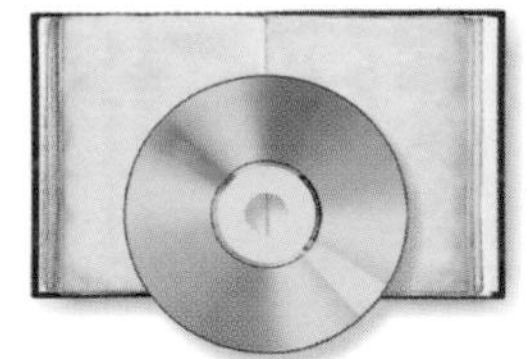

MULTIMEDIA REFERENCE TITLES can be used to access information in ways that would be impossible with printed books. Not only can the designers incorporate animations, videos, sound, and speech to enhance the presentation of written information, they can also provide hypertext and hypermedia links that allow the user to search for specific information or explore a topic more generally. The sophisticated "search engines" that allow you to embark on a voyage of discovery in multimedia reference titles are continually being refined and developed to allow easier access to the wealth of knowledge stored on these discs.

DIGITAL ENCYCLOPEDIAS

Encyclopedias have existed for almost 2,000 years. The Roman scholar Pliny the Elder's *Historia Naturalis* was the first, completed in AD 97. Multivolume printed editions, such as those published by Encyclopaedia Britannica or the *Academic American Encyclopedia*, have been used in schools and homes as reference sources throughout the 20th century. But the power of CD-ROM to store enormous amounts of information that can be searched in an almost infinite number of ways was quickly harnessed by encyclopedia publishers. As the CD-ROM revolution got under way, encyclopedia publishers stepped in, and by the mid-1990s all the major printed encyclopedias had been released as multimedia CD-ROMs.

MICROSOFT ENCARTA
Encarta uses menus that slide down onto the screen when the pointer is moved toward buttons or toolbars. When the Pinpointer search tool is first opened, it contains an alphabetical listing of all the articles on the disk. *Encarta* also offers an adventure-style quiz game in which you travel through a maze in search of a princess, making progress by answering questions correctly.

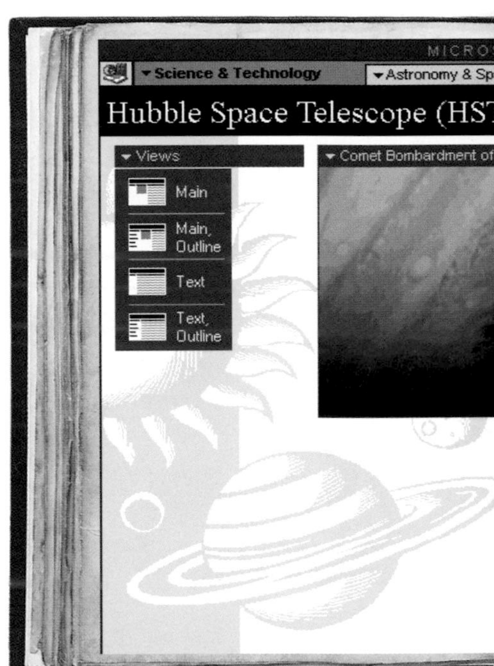

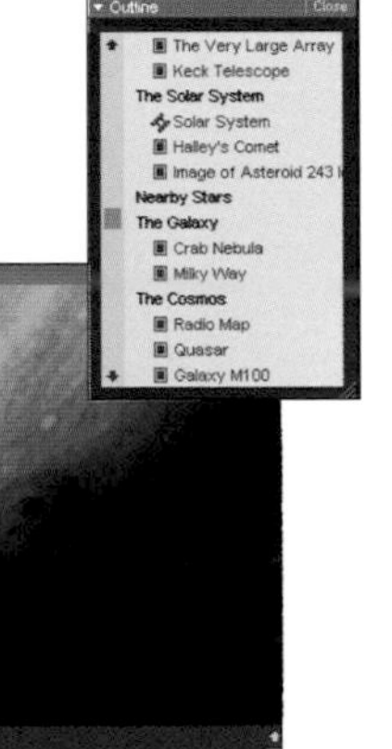

Outline
The Outline panel shows the main headings of an article together with the media elements it contains.

Photographs and Illustrations
There are over 8,000 photographs and illustrations included in Encarta. At right is a photograph of Jupiter taken by the Hubble Space Telescope, which shows the dark impact marks made on the planet by fragments of Comet Shoemaker-Levy 9.

Related Articles
The Related Articles button shows a list of articles that will widen the scope of your search.

Immediate Access
Once you have made a selection from the Related Articles list, the new article is displayed immediately.

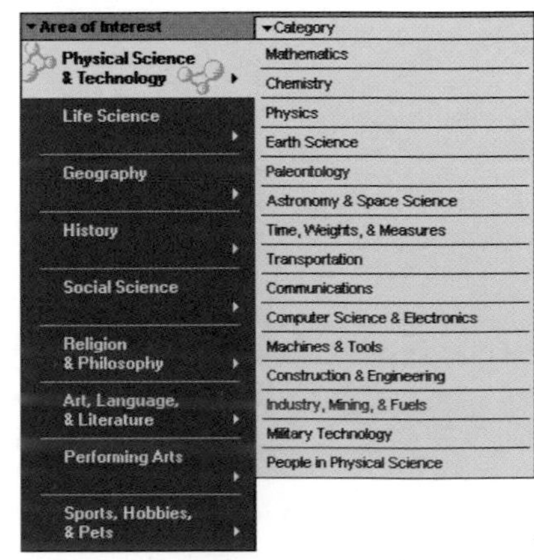

Areas and Categories
All Encarta's information is classified into Areas of Interest and Categories. When you select an Area of Interest, Pinpointer lists all the Categories for you.

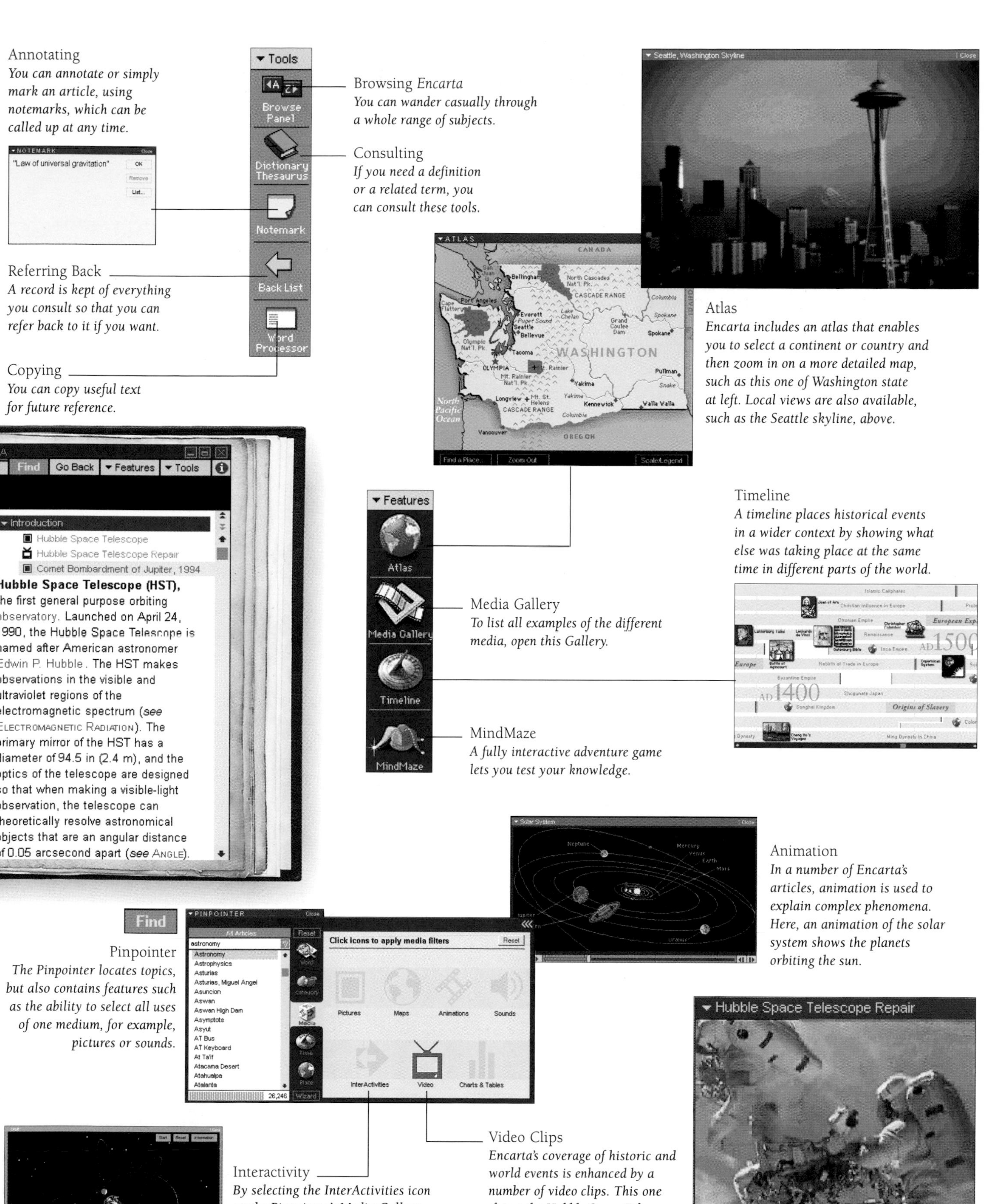

Annotating
You can annotate or simply mark an article, using notemarks, which can be called up at any time.

Browsing *Encarta*
You can wander casually through a whole range of subjects.

Consulting
If you need a definition or a related term, you can consult these tools.

Referring Back
A record is kept of everything you consult so that you can refer back to it if you want.

Copying
You can copy useful text for future reference.

Atlas
Encarta includes an atlas that enables you to select a continent or country and then zoom in on a more detailed map, such as this one of Washington state at left. Local views are also available, such as the Seattle skyline, above.

Timeline
A timeline places historical events in a wider context by showing what else was taking place at the same time in different parts of the world.

Media Gallery
To list all examples of the different media, open this Gallery.

MindMaze
A fully interactive adventure game lets you test your knowledge.

Animation
In a number of Encarta's articles, animation is used to explain complex phenomena. Here, an animation of the solar system shows the planets orbiting the sun.

Pinpointer
The Pinpointer locates topics, but also contains features such as the ability to select all uses of one medium, for example, pictures or sounds.

Interactivity
By selecting the InterActivities icon on the Pinpointer's Media Gallery, you can experiment with several interactive screens. One, for example, enables you to change the position and orbital velocity of the moon.

Video Clips
Encarta's coverage of historic and world events is enhanced by a number of video clips. This one shows the Hubble Space Telescope undergoing repairs. The sound track records conversations between the astronauts and the ground-control center.

One-subject Encyclopedias

General encyclopedias have long been a multimedia standard, but now an increasing number of titles cover just one subject – everything from anatomy to zoology is represented. Single-subject encyclopedias have two advantages over the general sort: first, being narrower in scope, they can go into much more detail; and second, they often present information in a more interesting way. The way a title presents information, its "look and feel," is known as its interface. General encyclopedias include so many different types of information that they have to use all-purpose interfaces, which are often fairly bland. One-subject titles, however, can build information into a graphical world specially created to entice the user into it. The example shown here is Dorling Kindersley's *Eyewitness Encyclopedia of Nature*, where you can find out about the natural world by looking through a microscope, tapping on a barometer, opening specimen drawers, and spinning a globe.

Fish Menu

From the main console (see below) you choose a subject area – in this example, a wall poster displays a menu of topics relating to fish. Each fish points toward a different entry in the encyclopedia – the five main types of fish and the question "What is a fish?" From here you begin a journey into the body of the encyclopedia.

Graphical
For more on graphics, see page 132

Pick Your Subject
Choosing one of the fish on the poster calls up an encyclopedia entry on this type of fish.

Information Center

The main screen of the *Encyclopedia of Nature* is a naturalist's console, complete with spinning globe, desk drawers, barometer, reference books, and other artifacts. This acts as a pictorial contents page – every object represents a different subject area. The graphical interface encourages exploration and offers many ways into the encyclopedia's body of information.

Fossil
This takes you to a timeline of the prehistoric era and subject entries about life before humans.

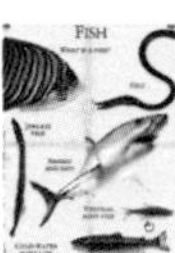

Wall Posters
Two of the main classes of animals – fish and mammals – are represented by wall posters. From these you can find out more about each kind of animal shown.

Barometer
Tapping on different sections of the barometer gives you information on the seasons, oceans, climatic regions, and the natural elements.

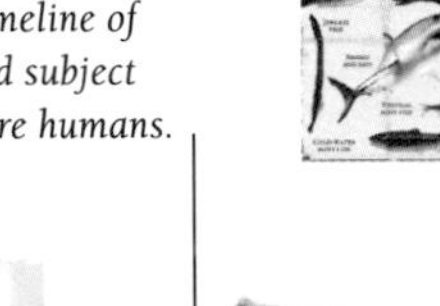

Microscope
The world of miniature life is revealed by looking through this microscope.

Globe
You can rotate the globe and zoom in to explore different habitats – American savanna, for example, or a coral reef in the Pacific Ocean.

Index
You can look up subjects in the index, which takes you to the relevant entries.

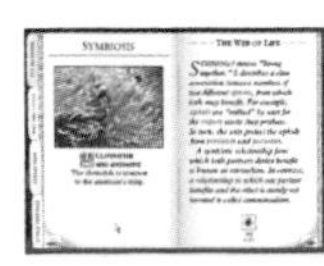

Green Book
This book opens to tell you about environmental issues. From any of its pages, you can move to related entries in the rest of the encyclopedia.

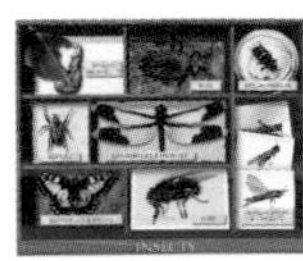

Specimen Drawers
These drawers pull out to reveal specimens of different animal and plant species. When you choose one, the program takes you to the main entry for that species.

Quiz Master
Inside this box is a game that tests your knowledge of the natural world. If one of the questions really interests you, you can jump to the entry for that subject in the encyclopedia.

Main Entry
Much of the information in the Encyclopedia of Nature *is contained in the subject entry pages, which combine written and spoken information with pictures, sound recordings, animation sequences, video clips, and cross-references to other parts of the encyclopedia.*

Cross-references
The See Also box points to a set of related but distinct topics – from here you can learn about the nature of fish, their habitat, and how they coexist with other forms of life.

Underwater Habitat
This coral reef scene shows a number of plant and animal species in their natural habitat. You can move about the habitat to explore it in more detail. The screen also acts as a starting point for further exploration.

Video Clip

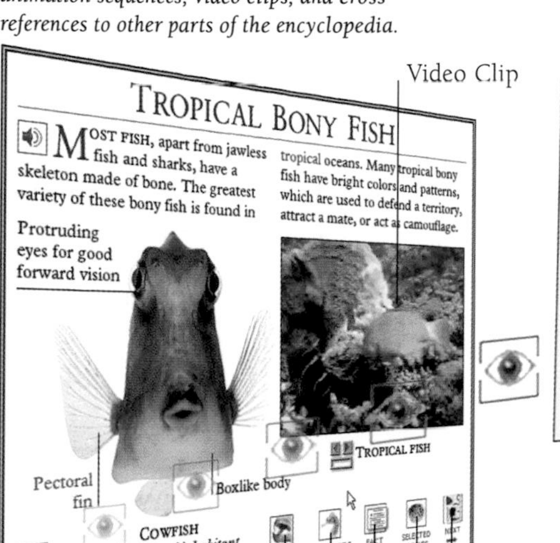

Scrolling Bar
The underwater seascape is several screens deep – this panel enables you to move through it.

Cross-reference Buttons
These buttons enable you to jump to entries for closely related subjects, such as other species from the same family.

Magnifying Glass
You can look more closely at part of the habitat with this magnifying glass.

More Information
From the coral reef scene, you can choose any of the undersea species to find out more about them.

BROWSE THE WORLD

One of the most common reference books in the home is the atlas. Multimedia atlases present the same information in a more dynamic and involving way. Navigating around the world is made easy and every country is brought to life with multimedia features such as sound, animations, satellite and time-lapse photography, and video clips. With a good multimedia atlas you search for a place-name and find yourself at its map location in seconds. Alternatively, you might find yourself taking a trip from Andorra to Australia or from Zagreb to Zaire simply because desktop traveling can be so addictive.

MULTIMEDIA ATLASES

Like the book atlas, the multimedia version contains maps, illustrations, tables, and statistical data relating to the whole world, as well as to regions and countries. Multimedia's unique twist is that it uses sound, video, and animation to present this information more vividly. It also allows the user to make a large number of choices about the way each map is displayed.

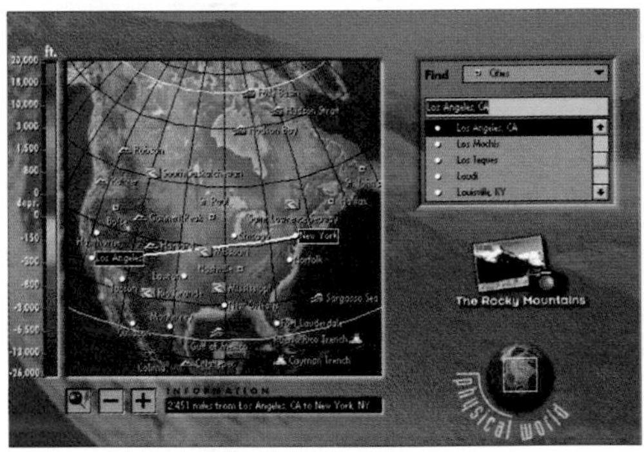

How Many Miles?
It takes no time at all to discover the distance between any two locations. The number of miles appears in the caption box.

CONTROL THE WORLD

With many titles, you can decide how much detail and what kind of details you want to see on screen. The scale of maps can be adjusted using zoom buttons. You can also choose the features that appear on the maps, or you can add new locations.

Most multimedia titles contain large databases of statistical information. This information can be very wide-ranging – from data on total urban populations to the number of radios per thousand people in any country. You can usually display and print the answers to any query in a number of different ways.

Navigate the Globe
The main screen gives you several ways of navigating the globe. You can point to any area and zoom in via the plus button.

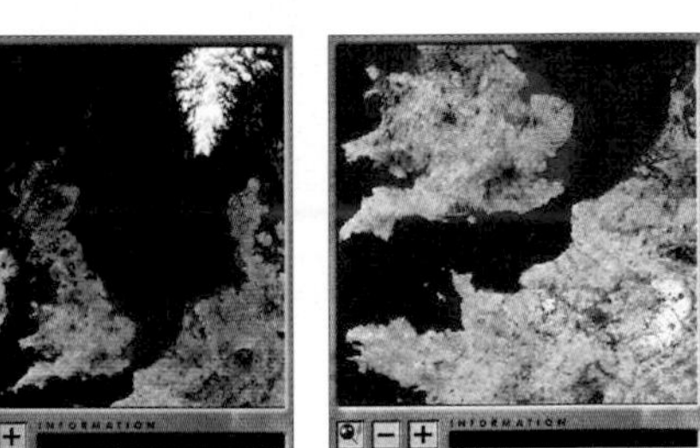

Presenting Complex Statistics

Presentation can affect how one absorbs statistical information. Here you see examples of a scatter chart, ranking table, line chart, and globe chart – all relating to the world's population since 1950.

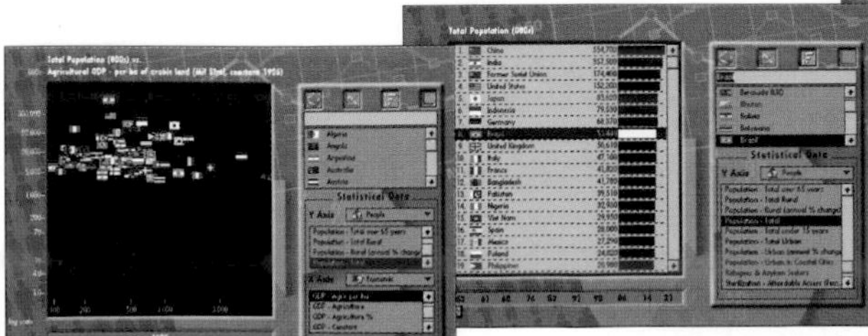

Scatter Chart

Ranking Table

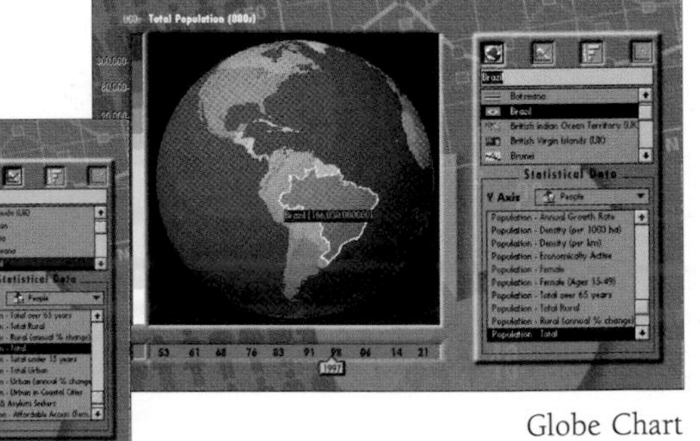

Line Chart

Globe Chart

Using the 3D Atlas

The main screen of Multimedia Corporation's *3D Atlas* features a globe and a find box. You can rotate the three-dimensional globe about any axis and zoom in to see individual countries or regions in more detail. You can also specify the type or amount of details to be displayed: for example, grid lines for latitude and longitude, cities, mountains, ocean depths. In addition, you can mark places that are significant to you with map pins and include text and pictures that you can view whenever you come back to the location in future.

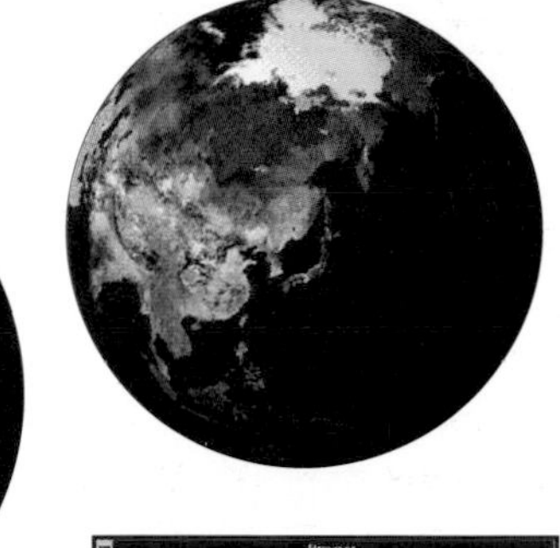

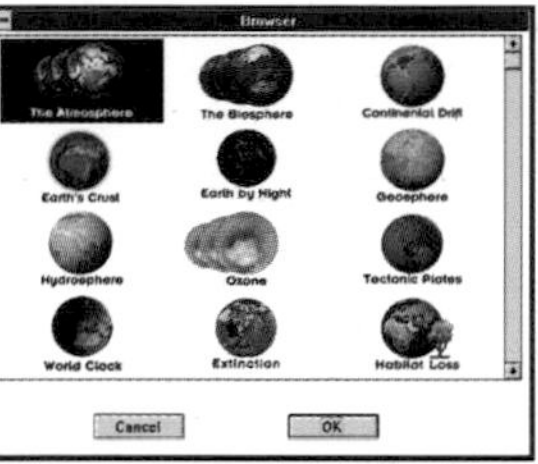

Browse for Information
From the Browser window, you can play any of the video and animation clips on the CD-ROM.

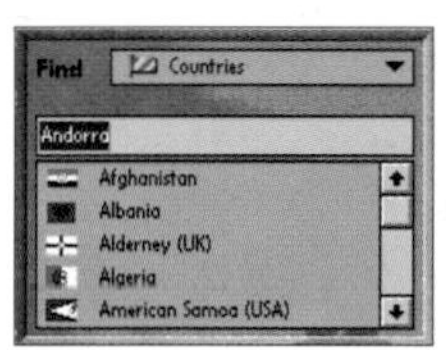

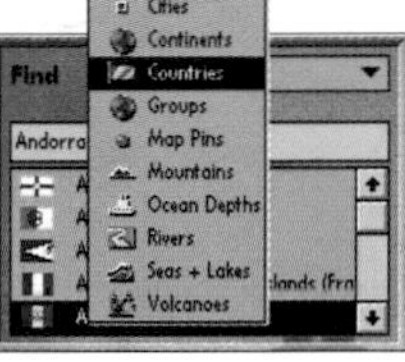

"Find" Feature
As well as instituting a search for any location you type, you can specify features to be displayed in the list: for example, rivers or volcanoes.

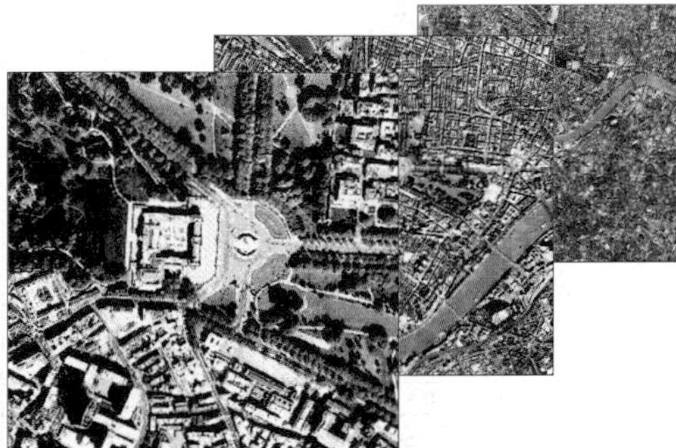

Focus on Major Cities
You can zoom in on satellite images of six major cities: Bombay, London, Moscow, New York, San Francisco, and Tokyo. This example shows London, with Buckingham Palace in the center.

Other Globes
On the main screen, you can display one of three different globes, featuring environmental, physical, or political information. You can also look at nine other globes that focus on various physical characteristics of the earth, such as the hydrosphere globe or the continental drift globe.

Video Clips
3D Atlas contains a large number of additional related video clips and animation. These clips include documentary videos about major environmental issues, such as acid rain and overfishing, and animated fly-throughs of different biomes, such as rain forest and tundra.

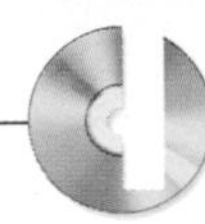

Leisure Pursuits

Leisure titles are among the fastest expanding multimedia sales areas. Books for the hobbyist and the enthusiast have always comprised a large part of publishing, and this strong market is being tapped for its multimedia potential. Books can offer a great deal, but more through the range of information they cover on any one subject than through flexibility and presentation, and it is precisely in this area of presentation that multimedia has the advantage.

Title Fight

It is in the area of leisure or lifestyle titles that multimedia is beginning to emerge as a viable alternative to traditional publishing. The range of subjects now available includes massage, beauty, and food; sports from golf to basketball; more practical pursuits such as carpentry; and hobbies such as photography, guitar playing, and astrology. As demand increases, so will the supply and variety of titles. Increasing specialization will also occur as the market grows. and costs come down. Here, we take a look at Microsoft's *Cinemania, Complete Baseball*, and *Wine Guide*.

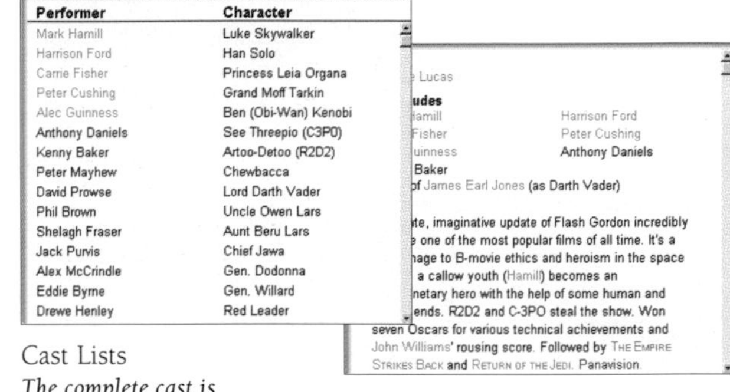

Cast Lists
The complete cast is available for the more important movies.

Reviews
Each movie listed by Cinemania is accompanied by at least one review to provide an idea of the quality and subject of the production.

Microsoft Cinemania '95

The features of *Cinemania* are accessed by first selecting from the categories: Movies, People, or Topics. In addition to the functions illustrated here, there is also a Gallery option that lists all the films for which either stills, clips, music, or dialogue are available; a Listmaker to record films for future viewing; a Movie Suggestions function that produces a list of recommended films; and an Award List option showing all Academy awards and nominations made since the prizes were established in 1927.

Dialogue Option
A short piece of dialogue is available for a number of movies included in Cinemania.

Movie Clip
For the major movies, a short clip lasting about 60 seconds can be viewed.

Biographies
More than 4,000 people connected with movies are included in Cinemania's biographical section. A photograph and a filmography is usually provided for the actors.

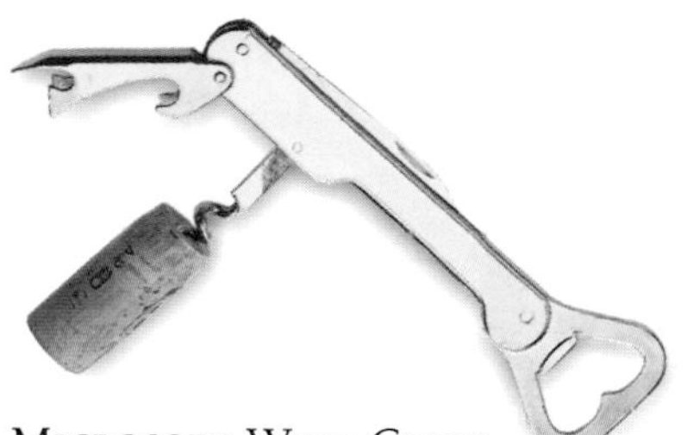

MICROSOFT WINE GUIDE
The *Wine Guide* covers all aspects of wine. Its pivotal feature is the extensive use of video clips of wine expert Oz Clarke, who lightheartedly presents the sometimes overserious world of wine.

Grape Profiles
Several hundred grape varieties are covered; and the characteristics of the 12 classic varieties are described in detail.

Worldwide Wine
The World Atlas of Wine contains maps of the 12 major wine producing areas. The maps are interactive and contain information about geography, history, and grape varieties.

Reading the Label
A number of different wine labels are included; each one has several different areas highlighted, for which detailed explanations are available.

MICROSOFT COMPLETE BASEBALL
Complete Baseball presents a comprehensive picture of the game of baseball. It also goes one step further than most CD-ROM titles: it allows you to subscribe to an on-line service from which you can download the latest data and news about the current season.

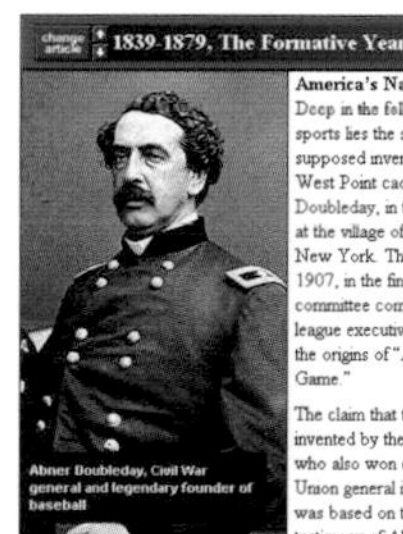

Chronicle
The history of baseball is covered in nine articles, beginning with this one dealing with the controversy over the invention of the game.

Players
Over 2,500 biographies of major figures in baseball are presented in the Players section.

Almanac
The Almanac consists of season summaries for the selected year. The articles include images, sound, and video clips.

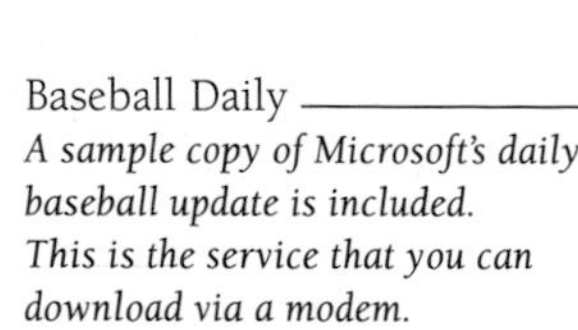

Baseball Daily
A sample copy of Microsoft's daily baseball update is included. This is the service that you can download via a modem.

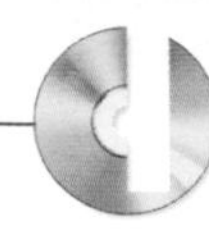

INTERACTIVE MUSEUMS

Visiting a modern museum or art gallery is perhaps the original multimedia experience – a combination of many of the elements that have made CD-ROM-based multimedia so successful. The exhibits in a museum are accompanied by written information, visual displays, and sometimes video presentations, and you can listen to expert commentary from a tour guide or on cassette. In addition, the exhibits are so arranged that you can browse through them and explore the information in your own way. Because museums so successfully combine various media in this way, they have given multimedia producers a useful model on which to base one-subject encyclopedia titles.

THE MUSEUM COMES TO YOU

Museums house the world's finest collections of antiquities and art treasures – their one disadvantage is the need for travel. With multimedia, however, you can see the Mona Lisa in the Louvre in Paris and the Smithsonian's dinosaur collection in Washington, DC, during the same afternoon. By combining photographs of the exhibits with detailed written and spoken information in a setting that imitates the real museum building, a multimedia museum can give the user a sense of actually visiting a collection.

ARTIFICIAL MUSEUMS

A multimedia title does not have to be based on a real museum, however. Using 3-D graphics, multimedia architects can construct a "virtual" museum building that exists only inside the computer. The user can wander through the imaginary building, stopping to take in and interact with the exhibits along the way. The example shown here, Dorling Kindersley's *Eyewitness Virtual Reality Cat*, combines a realistic museum interior with interactive exhibits to re-create the experience of visiting a museum.

3-D graphics
For more on 3-D graphics, see page 138

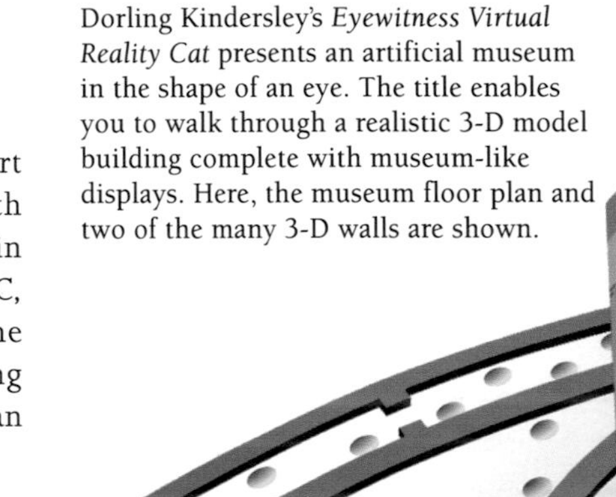

VIRTUAL MUSEUM
Dorling Kindersley's *Eyewitness Virtual Reality Cat* presents an artificial museum in the shape of an eye. The title enables you to walk through a realistic 3-D model building complete with museum-like displays. Here, the museum floor plan and two of the many 3-D walls are shown.

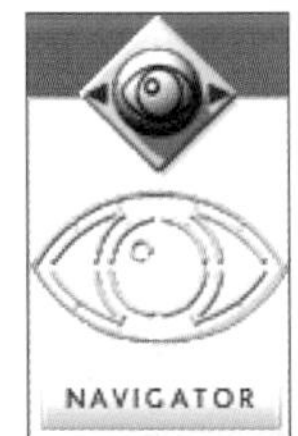

Instant Navigation
The navigator shows you a map of the museum (right) from which you can jump instantly to any exhibit.

Walking Through
As in a real museum, you can wander through the rooms and corridors to choose the exhibits you want to look at.

Cheetah Wall
This display contains several exhibits that all relate to cheetahs.

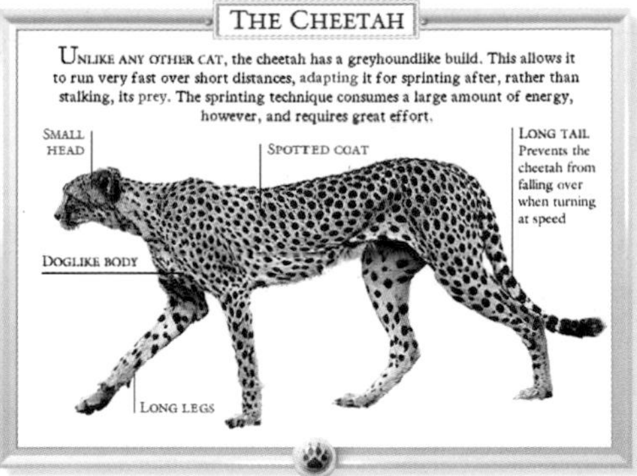

Information Panel
You can zoom into the main panel to see general information on cheetahs.

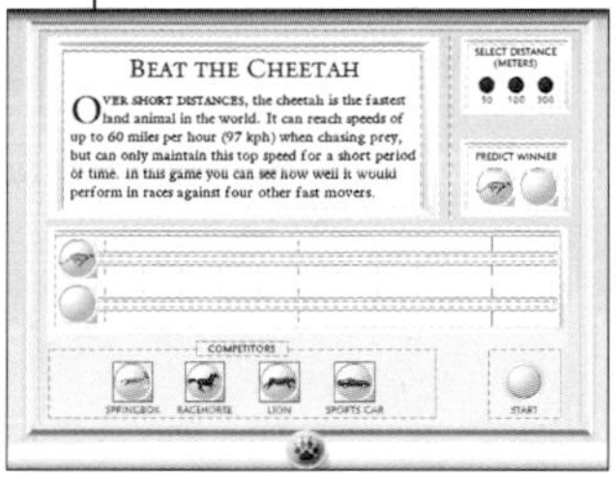

Beat the Cheetah
In this racing game you predict how well a cheetah will do against a racehorse, a puma, and a sports car.

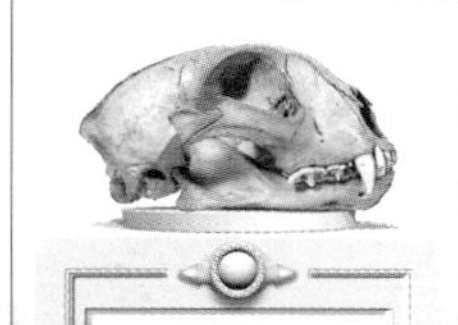

3-D Skull
You can rotate this cheetah's skull to see it from all sides.

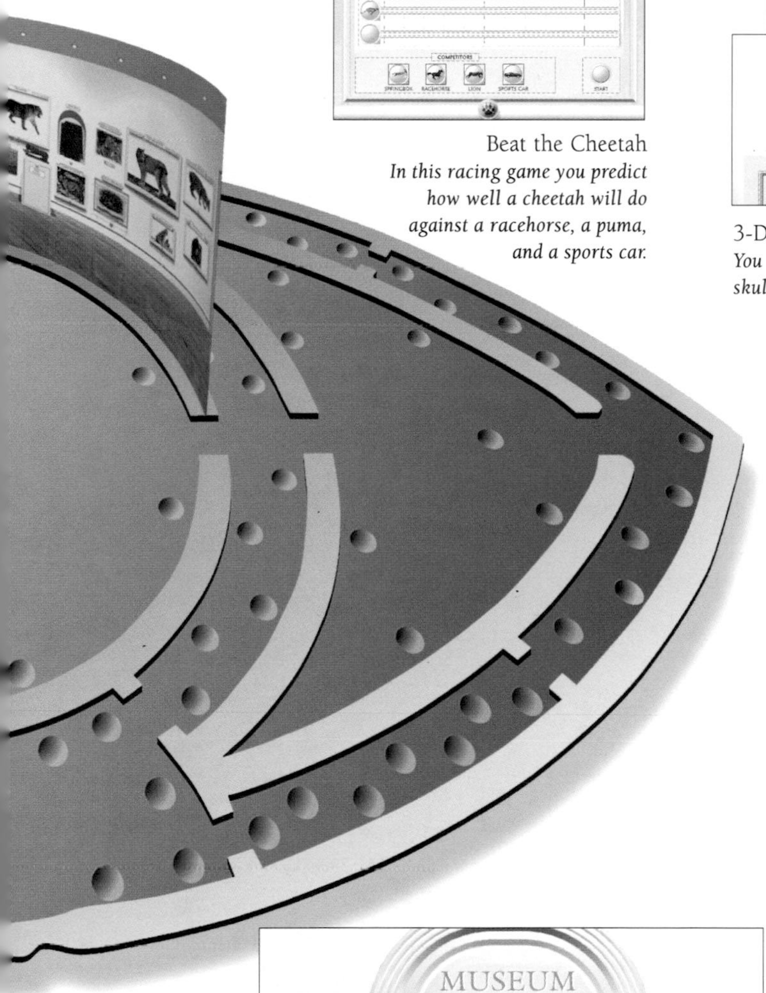

Le Louvre

BMG's *Le Louvre* focuses on 100 of the Parisian museum's most famous and significant paintings. Timelines are used to put paintings into their historical context, and commentaries, both spoken and written, on the selected works of art add to the viewer's understanding and enjoyment of them.

Museum Map
From the maps of each section of the museum, you can select which paintings to view – or you can choose to see an entire school of painting.

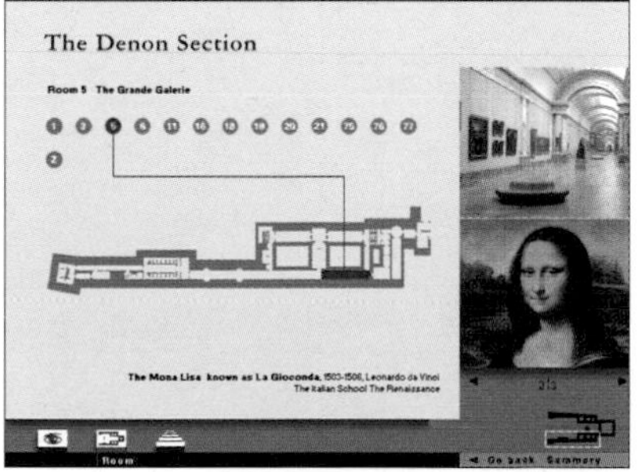

A School of Painting

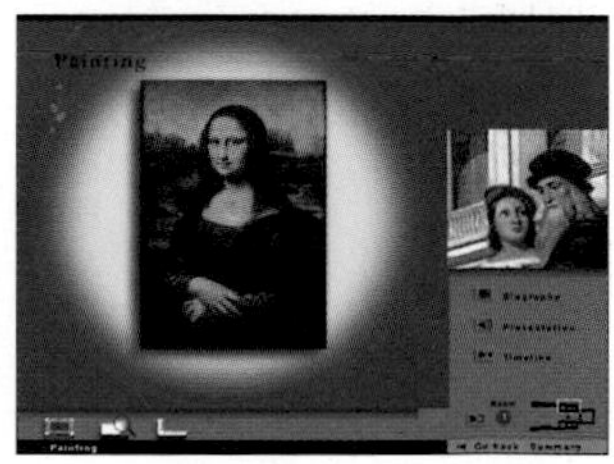

One Painting in Detail

Museum Store
Here you can use images or sounds from the museum to create your own stationery, screen-savers, or sound effects.

THE MULTIMEDIA MAGAZINE

It could be many years before daily or even weekly news can be supplied in an interactive form on CD-ROM, but multimedia publishers have already begun producing several magazines. These multimedia magazines each arrive on a single CD-ROM every one or two months and present their information via a graphical interface, using the full range of multimedia techniques. They offer the reader a completely new way to interact with a magazine's contents.

MAGAZINES FOR ALL SEASONS

Multimedia magazines range from titles such as *Blender* – youth culture and style journalism with a glossy interface that concentrates on music, movies, and fashion – to the cover-mounted CD-ROMs that come with computer and style magazines. Existing publications, for example *Time* and *Newsweek*, have also created interactive CD-ROM editions using the content of their printed publications, such as an almanac-style round up of a specific year, or an edition concentrating on a recent, significant event such as the Gulf War.

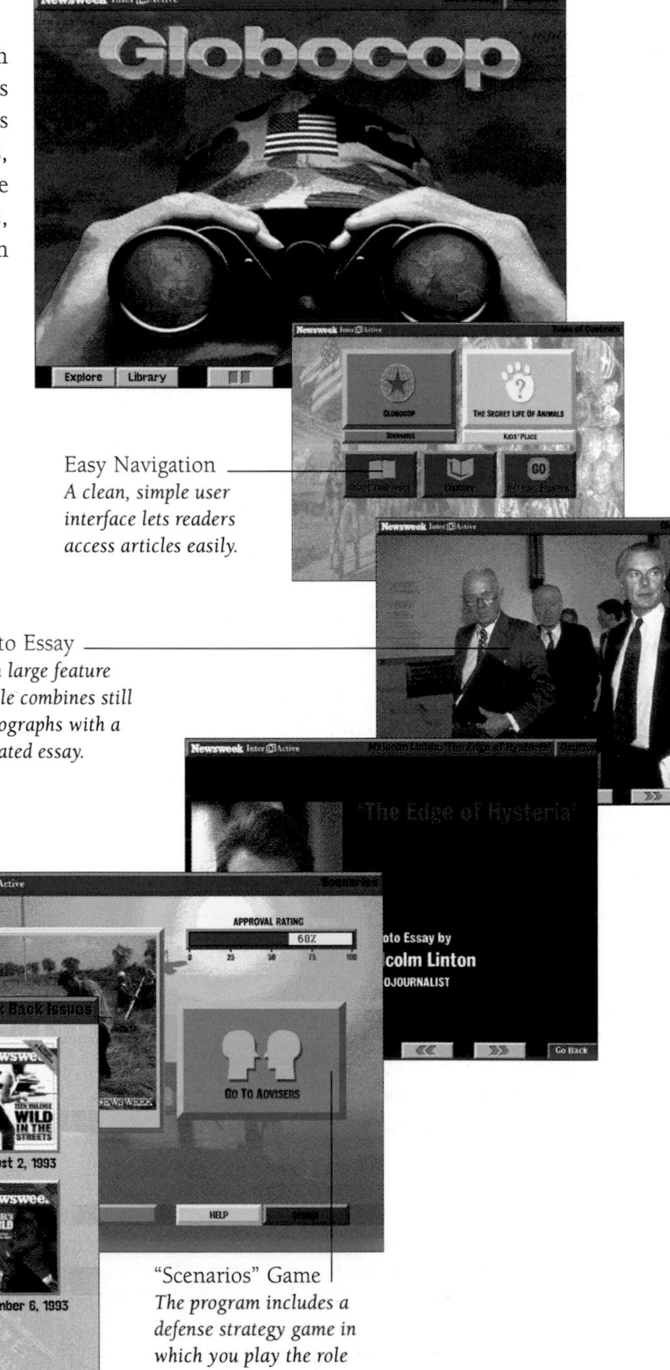

NEWSWEEK INTERACTIVE
Claiming to be the world's first interactive news magazine, *Newsweek Interactive* combines an archive of three months' worth of *Newsweek* (almost half a million words) with four hours of radio interviews from the weekly program "*Newsweek* on Air." Each edition also contains two large feature articles, which combine the journalistic and analytical expertise of the *Newsweek* team with multimedia and hypertext elements.

Easy Navigation
A clean, simple user interface lets readers access articles easily.

Photo Essay
Each large feature article combines still photographs with a narrated essay.

Back Issues
Readers can access and perform searches on the text of 13 back issues.

"Scenarios" Game
The program includes a defense strategy game in which you play the role of commander-in-chief.

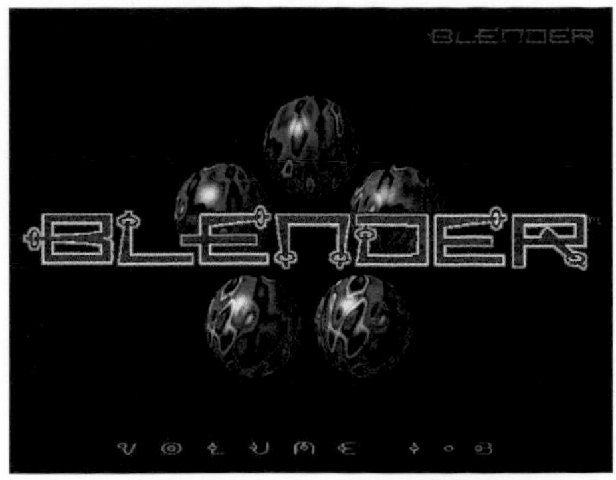

BLENDER

Dennis Publishing in New York is taking style and youth culture journalism into the multimedia age with *Blender*, a bimonthly magazine that comes on a CD-ROM and makes full use of multimedia interactivity. Its regular features include games, movie and music reviews, a fashion section, a horoscope page, electronic cartoons, and a digital gallery for computer-made art.

Contents Page
The contents page lets the reader choose an area of the magazine to explore.

MUSIC REVIEWS

Unlike a printed magazine, *Blender* contains sample audio tracks and the latest music videos.

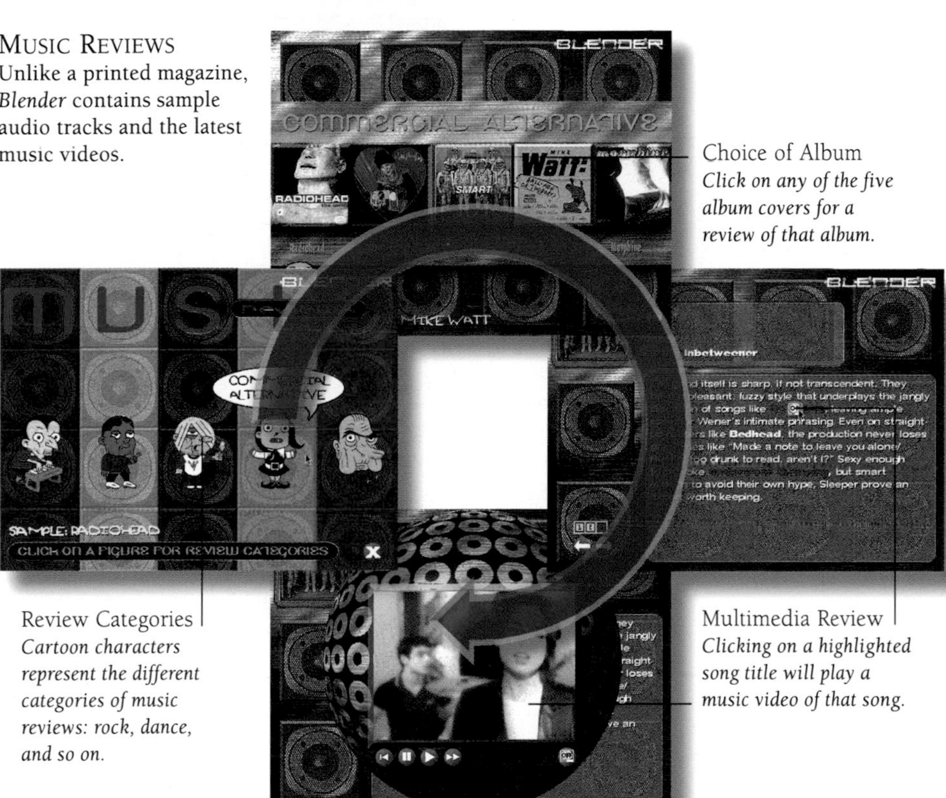

Choice of Album
Click on any of the five album covers for a review of that album.

Review Categories
Cartoon characters represent the different categories of music reviews: rock, dance, and so on.

Multimedia Review
Clicking on a highlighted song title will play a music video of that song.

Interactive Horoscopes
Each sign of the zodiac has a video clip of an astrologer reading your fortune.

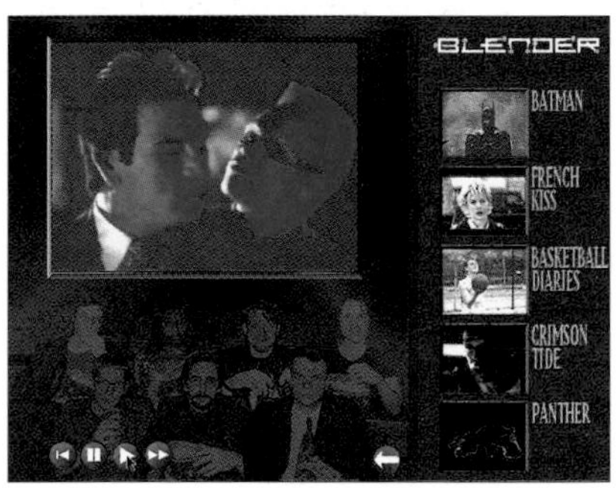

Movie Reviews
The movie reviews page contains video clips from the latest movie releases.

Cover-mounted CD-ROMs

Computer magazines and even some style magazines are mounting CD-ROMs on their covers that work with and complement the printed pages that they produce each month. The cover disc for the UK's *CD-ROM Magazine* not only contains demos of the latest CD-ROM titles and clips from digital movies, but also features multimedia work created by its readers and sent in as the modern equivalent of "letters." It also contains an extensive database that holds the text of all the product reviews the magazine has run since it was first published.

Different Levels
To explore the contents of the disc, readers enter a virtual elevator. To watch digital video clips, for example, they click on the word "Videodrome."

Fashion Showcase
In the fashion area, models display the latest designs. Clothing details are listed in the box on the left.

THE MULTIMEDIA CLASSROOM

ALL WORK AND NO PLAY makes Jack a dull boy, so the saying goes – but with many current educational multimedia titles, Jack would have difficulty telling the two activities apart. Many of the most popular "edutainment" titles combine elements of entertainment and education so effectively that younger children are unaware that they are learning. The best educational titles have learned some valuable lessons from games titles – they are packed with colorful animations, sound, video, and humor. Such titles are equally accessible to very young children, if they are helped by an adult, and to older children, who can explore the new worlds on-screen at their own pace. Edutainment is now an important consideration when a family buys a multimedia computer.

PLAYING AND LEARNING

Much of a young child's learning takes place through the interactivity of play: amusing himself or herself with toys and other objects, and experimenting with them, and taking part with others in games. This is well known by the producers of educational multimedia software for young children, and they have fashioned their products accordingly. Titles in this area fall into two broad groups. Some help to build skills in a specific subject area, such as spelling or math. Others are more open-ended and help children to develop their thinking skills; this kind of program is often described as "a gymnasium for the mind."

PRESCHOOL ACTIVITIES

Jumpstart Kindergarten from Knowledge Adventure is a collection of three kinds of preschool educational activities which can be broadly categorized as simple learning, problem solving, and developing creativity. Simple learning activities present essential, basic information, such as the letters of the alphabet, simple sequences of numbers, and the days of the week. Problem-solving activities usually require the child to recognize relationships between objects; for example, the child may be asked to place in order a number of dolls according to their relative size, or a series of numbered blocks in ascending or descending order. Creative activities invite the child to express himself or herself – for example, by constructing simple sentences or by choosing colors for the pictures in the paint-box exercise.

JUMPSTART KINDERGARTEN
Like many multimedia titles for the preschool age group, the on-screen environment of Knowledge Adventure's *Jumpstart Kindergarten* is very lively, with sounds and animation working to keep the child's attention at all times. The main screen represents a classroom. By clicking on the relevant parts of the screen, the child can take part in a variety of activities. These teach telling the time, basic counting and geometry, reading, and language skills.

See How They Run
Choosing a number on the mat will bring the same number of mice scurrying from the mouse hole. This activity teaches simple counting.

An Exercise in Size
This activity involves placing a set of Russian dolls in order of size. A star appears below any doll that is placed in the correct position.

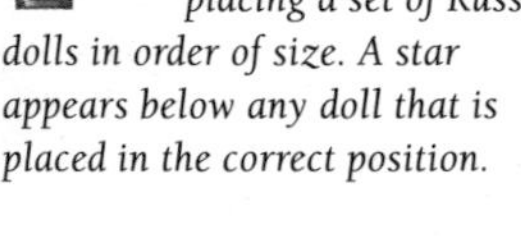

Learning by Numbers
Here the task is to arrange the blocks in numerical order. This teaches the child about number relationships.

Perfect Teacher

Mr. Hopsalot – the cartoon rabbit who acts as guide and teacher figure for the kindergarten – regularly offers instructions and advice on how to use the program and its activities. He also provides plenty of encouragement and praise when it is needed.

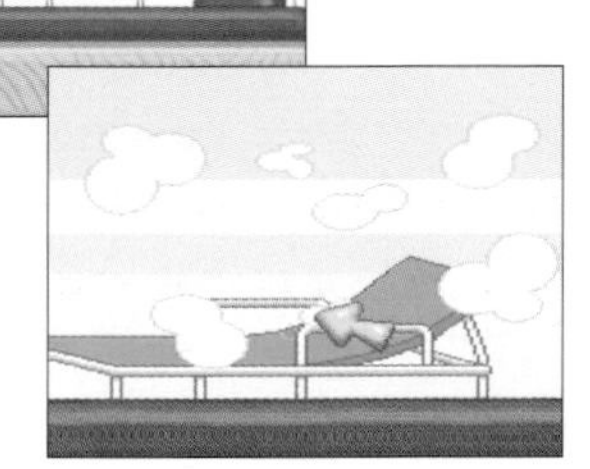

Follow That Hamster
Inside the cage, a hamster sunbathes – but not for long. Soon he disappears, leaving a clue behind him. By following this clue, the child will find him within one of the other activities.

Telling the Time
"10 o'clock AM: I play in the schoolyard." The animated clock teaches the relationship between the time and daily activities.

Pick a Flower
This door leads outside to the garden where Mr. Hopsalot is planting flowers. Here the activity is to name the next flower in a simple sequence.

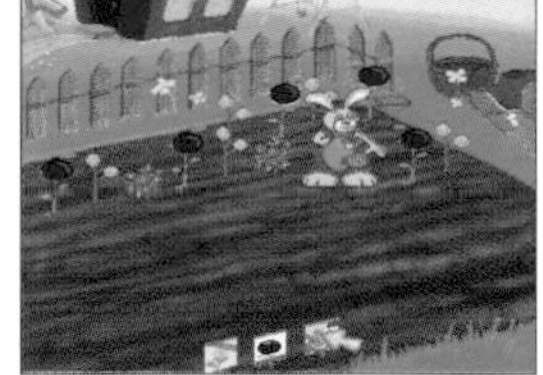

Just for Fun
Under the sink lurks a plumber – some animations and sounds just make the kindergarten a lively place in which to be.

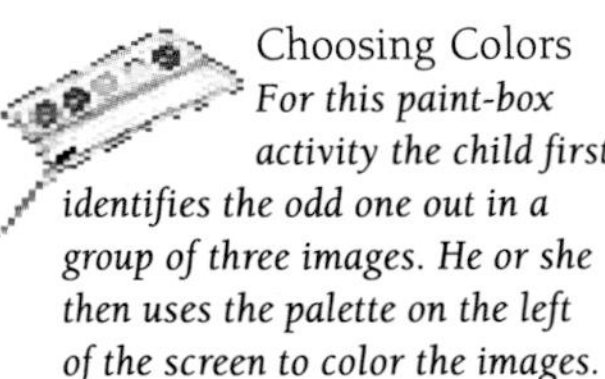

Choosing Colors
For this paint-box activity the child first identifies the odd one out in a group of three images. He or she then uses the palette on the left of the screen to color the images.

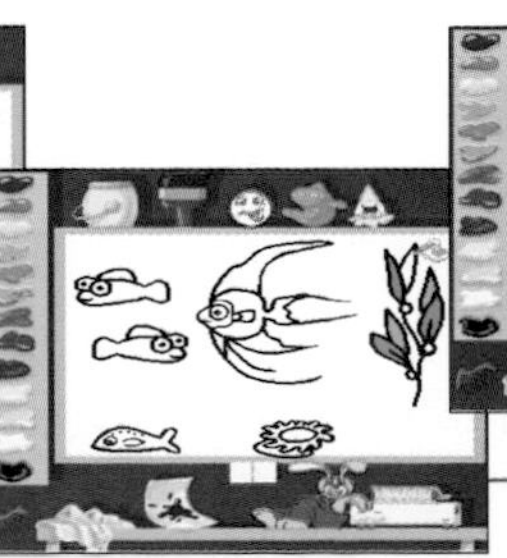

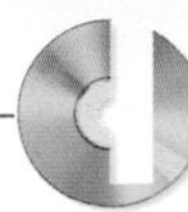

Children's Stories

Stories for children will never be the same again thanks to multimedia and the interactivity of CD-ROM. Multimedia children's storybooks are interactive versions of printed children's books, offering their users new worlds to explore and enjoy. They are simple to use, let children progress through a story at their own pace, and, best of all, can be very effective in helping a child learn to read.

Learning to Read

Most multimedia children's storybooks work on the principle that entertainment and education can make a powerful combination: children usually encounter a variety of humorous characters who pop up to embellish the main story with amusing diversions; and at the same time children learn to read by following the text on the screen as it is read out by a narrator, and by watching short animations that illustrate the meaning of different words or phrases.

Living Books

Broderbund's Living Books is one of the best children's series on CD-ROM. Each title is based on a popular story and consists of a series of animated screens that take children through the tale. The opening screen offers children two options: "Read to Me" lets them sit passively through the story as it is narrated; "Let Me Play" means they can play interactively with the characters on screen. Apart from their entertainment value, the titles also help children to recognize words. You can see how it all works here, with a screen from *The Tortoise and the Hare*. The scene opens with the tired Hare slowing down and taking a rest under a tree.

Secret Password
Choose the door in the tree and a young mouse walks up, knocks on the door, and asks "Can I come in?" But she needs a secret password. After three wrong guesses she realizes the password is "Can I come in, please?"

The Tortoise and the Hare
Based on Aesop's fable, Broderbund's *The Tortoise and the Hare* takes this classic story and enhances it with multimedia interactivity. After hearing a part of the story read aloud, children can click on almost anything on the screen to discover a hidden surprise.

Grammar Lessons

Two of the screens concentrate on verbs and prepositions. The Hare performs a series of actions, while the Tortoise encounters some obstacles he has to get over. Children can click on each word, hear it spoken, and see the relevant meaning through an animated sequence.

Skipping
With typical energy, the Hare illustrates the word "skip."

Uphill
The Tortoise sweats as he struggles to demonstrate the meaning of the word "uphill."

Highlighted Words

Whether a child chooses to listen passively to the story or to play with it interactively, the words on each screen are read out by a narrator. Each word can be highlighted using the cursor, allowing the child to hear it read aloud again.

THE TORTOISE

As the hero of the story, the Tortoise defies all odds by winning the race through slow but steady progress.

Tarzan in the Trees

Click in the trees, and a young bear swings through the branches, yodeling like Tarzan. He crashes through the treehouse window, reappears at the front door with a saucepan jammed firmly over his head, then reels down the stairs before disappearing out of the left-hand side of the screen.

Dinosaur Antics

The right bank of the river is home to a dinosaur who tramps noisily around the river, calls out in an unexpected soprano, then smiles sheepishly before disappearing off the screen.

SIMON THE STORYTELLER

The story is narrated by Simon, a crow in red sneakers. He appears in each scene to read the text, and even adds his own asides to the story.

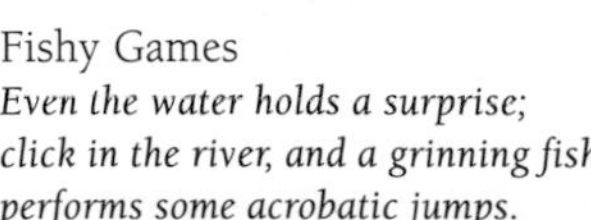

Fishy Games

Even the water holds a surprise; click in the river, and a grinning fish performs some acrobatic jumps.

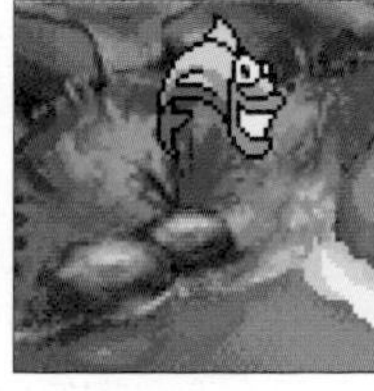

Timid Mouse

If the child clicks on the hole in the riverbank, a mouse appears and proceeds to wash herself, until she sees the viewer watching. Now bashful, she grabs her towel and runs back into her house.

Fun with Numbers

Some children love playing with numbers, but many find mathematics too difficult or just plain boring. Edutainment software can make learning math fun – or at least a lot less painful – by incorporating solid math practice work into a multimedia combination of animation, problem-solving exercises, learning games, and sometimes an adventure plot too. The majority of math edutainment titles also employ the perfect teachers – cartoon characters – who are friendly, patient, encouraging, and instantly forgiving.

Adventures with Math

Different multimedia titles teach math in very different ways. Some present activities that are no different from answering problems set by a teacher at a blackboard – but they are presented in a lively way by animated characters who offer encouragement and perform tricks, so the whole experience is made a lot more entertaining. Other titles present math as interactive games or puzzles that stretch the player's math skills to solve problems and win the game. And yet other titles weave math problems into animated adventures; because the problems are pivotal to the plot, the player has an added incentive to get stuck into playing with numbers.

Math Made Fun
In Humongous Entertainment's adventure game *Freddi Fish and the Case of the Missing Kelp Seeds* you meet the exuberant Mr. Starfish, whose animated antics inject excitement into a series of otherwise straightforward math problems.

Math Activities

Broderbund's *Math Workshop* is a mathematical activity center with a series of puzzles and games that present traditional math tasks in a new way. Here, a game of shapes teaches players about working with fractions. The aim of the game is to divide a whole bar into pieces (fractions) and rejoin them in a certain combination using three tools.

Cutting Tool
This tool can cut the bar or any piece of the bar into a number of same-sized fraction pieces.

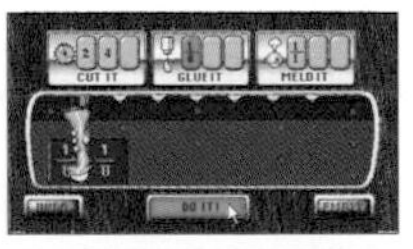

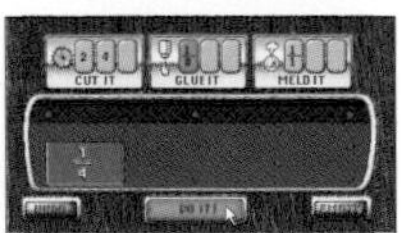

Glueing Tool
This tool rejoins pieces of the same size.

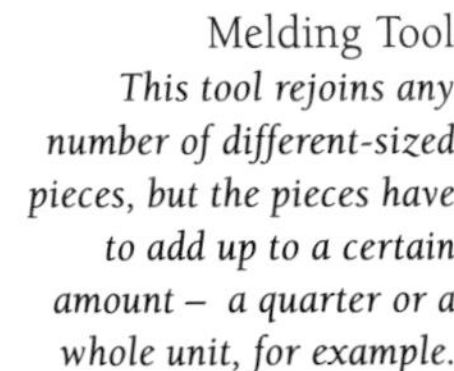

Melding Tool
This tool rejoins any number of different-sized pieces, but the pieces have to add up to a certain amount – a quarter or a whole unit, for example.

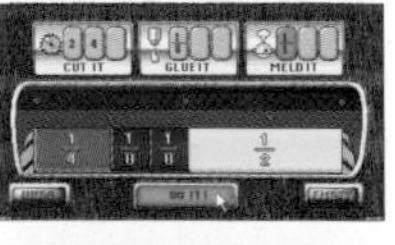

Math Detectives

Counting on Frank from Electronic Arts is an adventure game whose plot revolves entirely around number skills. Henry is the math hero; Frank is his dog. Together they explore their neighborhood looking for clues to help them win a local competition. To earn clues, Henry has to answer math problems and play math games that he finds hidden along the way.

The Race Is On
The adventure starts when Henry learns that he can win a trip to Hawaii by deducing the number of jelly beans in a jar. The competition gives young players an incentive to complete the math adventure.

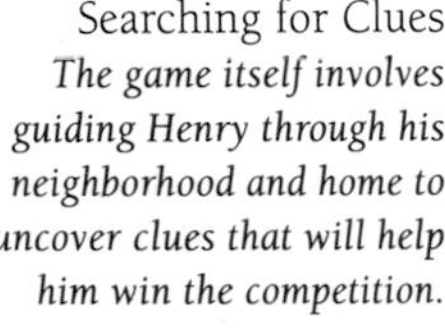

Searching for Clues
The game itself involves guiding Henry through his neighborhood and home to uncover clues that will help him win the competition.

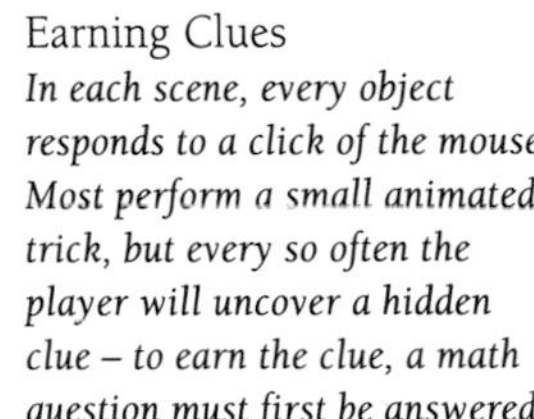

Earning Clues
In each scene, every object responds to a click of the mouse. Most perform a small animated trick, but every so often the player will uncover a hidden clue – to earn the clue, a math question must first be answered.

Notepad and Calculator
The question appears in Henry's notepad. The calculator can be used to work out the answer. Each correct answer earns a clue to the number of jelly beans – the number is not divisible by three, for example.

Math Games
Hidden in some scenes are math-based games that are fun to play and exercise math skills at the same time.

Magic Numbers
In this game the player plays against Frank the dog. The two roll a fraction die in turns, and then fit the fractions into the board. The winner is the first person to make a row that adds up to two.

The Reward
When the player has enough clues, he or she can enter the competition. Players who deduce the correct number are rewarded with copious praise and an entertaining animation.

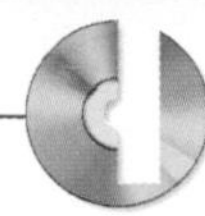

Developing Creativity

A typical multimedia title is the product of the creative energies of dozens of writers, designers, animators, sound engineers, and technicians. Some multimedia titles offer children the chance to take part in a similar creative process. These products lend a new dimension to the traditional school activities of creative writing, art, and drama by encouraging the child not just to interact but also to create. Many titles develop skills that will benefit the user in a practical way in future employment, and at the same time they help him or her to experience the creative processes involved in planning, organizing, and presenting work effectively.

Creative Activities

In the workplace, "productivity" software, such as desktop publishing software, is used to produce business letters, documents, and presentations. By adapting productivity tools for children, multimedia developers produce "creativity" titles, in which the emphasis is on having fun while acquiring new skills. A typical multimedia creativity title will offer the child a simple and welcoming framework within which to experiment.

House of Creativity
The activities in Creative Writer *are organized by using the floors of a building to represent different creative activities. It is as easy to move between different activities as it is to move between floors of a building.*

Working with Multimedia

Creativity titles usually provide "libraries" of images, sounds, animations, and text that the child can use in any combination. Once the child is familiar with the on-screen setup and the way the various tools interrelate (for example, how to integrate a sound and an image into a newsletter), the child will begin to add his or her own words, images, and sounds. With more advanced titles, he or she may soon be producing and directing animated cartoons or even "programming" computer games.

Creative Writer

Microsoft's *Creative Writer* offers activities such as making a newsletter or creating a family history album. It also introduces basic typography and page layout in a lively, jargon-free style (for example, italic text is described as "slanty"). One of the most useful features is called the "ideas workshop." This aims to stimulate ideas for creative writing.

Ideas Workshop
This area contains two machines designed to clear junior writer's block by providing a "wacky sentence" or an "inspirational picture."

Splot Machine
Three images or phrases appear every time the fish-shaped handle is pulled. These elements produce a "wacky sentence."

Picture Window
After choosing a suitable picture, the child can call up a crayon easel and make changes to the illustration.

Formatting the Text
Drop-down menus help the child add color and special effects to text, and to include images to illustrate the text or to represent words.

Writing a New Story
The image, imported directly from the Ideas Library, encourages the child to begin writing a new story immediately.

Background Library
The child can choose backgrounds from this library for each scene of the movie.

Stamp Library
Static objects from this library can be dropped onto the background screen.

Animation Library
These figures become animations when the user drags them across the screen.

Spider-man Cartoon Maker

This Knowledge Adventure title enables children to make their own cartoons featuring the Marvel Comics superhero, using animations and artwork from the Spider-man television series. The child can choose from a large selection of backgrounds, static objects, animations, and sounds. He or she can also record new narration and sounds.

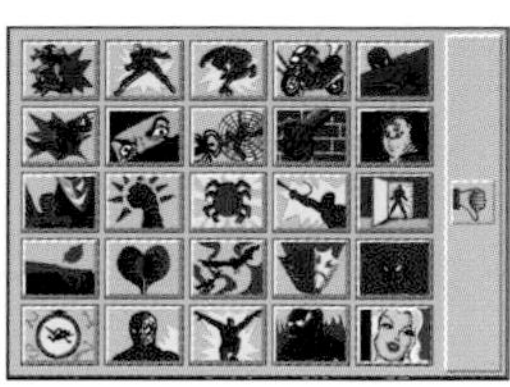

Music Library
Each icon represents a musical theme that the child can assign to the scenes in the movie.

Klik & Play

Europress's *Klik & Play* is a sophisticated games creator that helps the user construct a wide variety of Windows games. He or she can adapt any of the ten games supplied with the title or design a completely new game. To create a new game, the user chooses a background, then places static and animated objects on it, then finally defines how each object moves and behaves in certain circumstances (such as collision with another object).

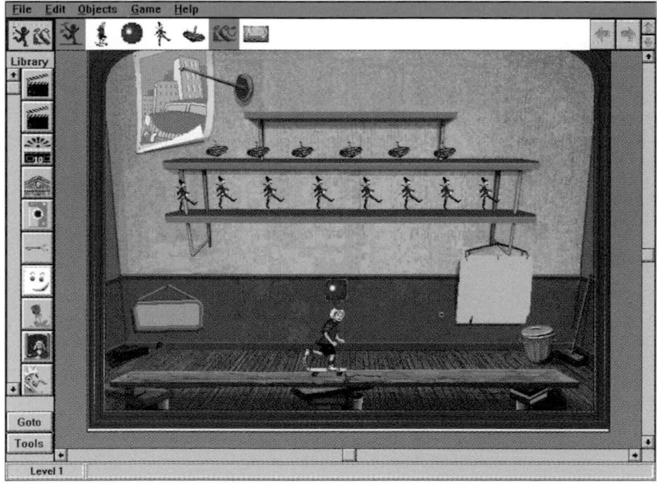

Simple Game
In the very simple example shown here, the object of the game is to move the skateboarder so that he deflects a bouncing ball onto the moving targets above until they have all disappeared. This game took just a few minutes to compile.

Animation Editor
This enables the user to determine many aspects of the animated soldier's movement – such as its type, speed, direction, and overall pattern. The animation sequence, which can be edited, appears in the boxes at the bottom.

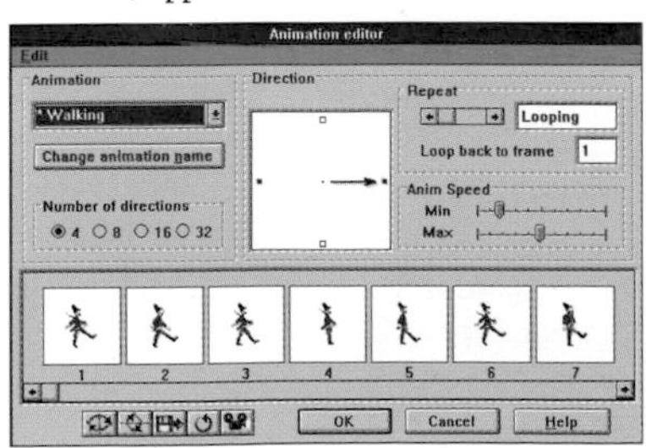

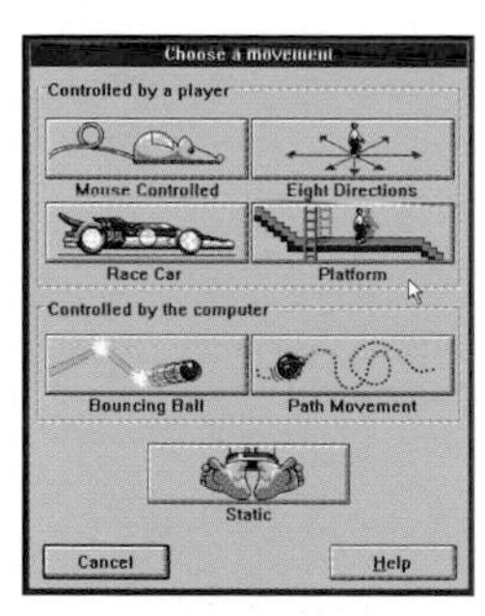

Choice of Movement
The user defines the movement patterns of the skateboarder and the method of control – in this case, by mouse.

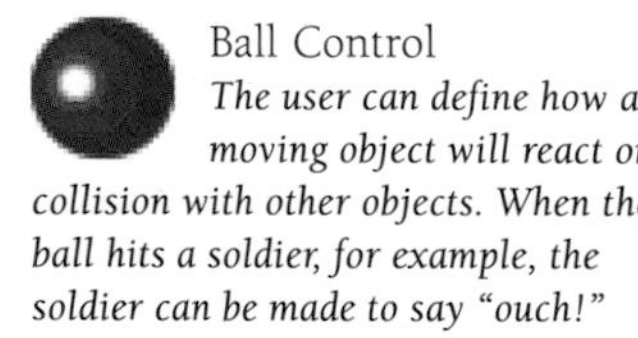

Ball Control
The user can define how a moving object will react on collision with other objects. When the ball hits a soldier, for example, the soldier can be made to say "ouch!"

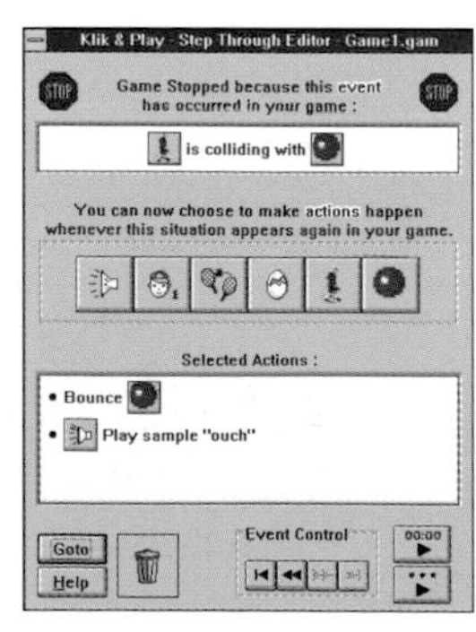

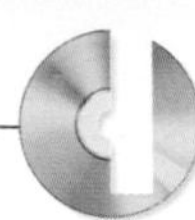

Learning New Languages

As part of growing up, we all learn our native language by hearing speech in a context that provides clues about the meaning of the words. Research has shown that people learn a language four to five times faster with this "natural" approach than with conventional instruction. Multimedia can provide an interactive and involving learning system that parallels the way we all learned our first language, and anyone with a multimedia PC now has ready access to what was once possible only with expensive language-laboratory equipment.

FRANCAIS | LA TRADUCTION | LE PROFESSEUR

Translation Windows
At any time you can see the English text and teacher's notes by choosing these buttons.

Absorbing Activities

Multimedia language titles use many of the techniques of the traditional audiovisual language laboratory. Vocabulary, for example, is built up by associating words and phrases with images: the learner sees the image of a cat, hears the word "cat," and is then invited to repeat the word. Multimedia's great advantage over traditional systems, however, is that it employs extra teaching tools, makes the learning process more fun, and allows users to set their own timetable. For instance, as well as looking and listening, learners can record themselves, then play back the recording to check their pronunciation, and they can test their comprehension by playing games or answering quizzes – all at their own pace and in any order they choose.

Building Basic Vocabulary

EuroTalk's *Jeux d'Images Multimédia* is an interactive flash card system for teaching basic French. Children (with help from a teacher or parent if necessary) can play language games in French and record their own words and sentences. Each exercise gains marks toward a bronze, silver, or gold medal – a simple but effective device that encourages the child to return to exercises at which he or she is weaker.

Listen and Locate
All the learner needs to do is listen to the word and then point at the corresponding image. A wrong answer loses points.

Going for Gold
Each exercise is marked, and the points earned go toward earning the learner a medal.

Choosing Favorite Words
The learner chooses favorite frames and sounds from the reels of film to play back in a movie theater, and in so doing absorbs more vocabulary.

Learning from a Comic Strip

EuroTalk's *Apprenez le Français avec le Fils d'Astérix* presents a story in strip format using the familiar cartoon characters but with all the advantages of multimedia. At any time, learners can choose which part of the story to access, and whether they want narration and/or text. This title uses modern, colloquial language and will best suit those who have mastered basic vocabulary and grammar.

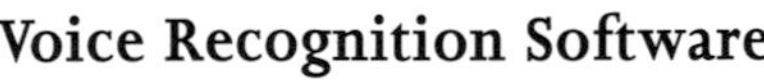

Translation Options
You can change the language of translation from English to Italian, German, Spanish, Portuguese, or Arabic.

Test Yourself
As with most learning titles, there is a quiz that tests your new skills.

Turning the Page
Access any page of the comic book from this screen.

Practicing Pronunciation
On this screen, you can record and play back your own voice to practice your pronunciation.

Voice Recognition Software

Most multimedia language learning titles allow a learner to practice pronunciation by recording and playing back his or her voice, then comparing it with that on the CD-ROM. The Learning Company's *French Vocabulary Builder* takes this a stage further. This title features voice recognition software that assesses the learner's pronunciation on a scale ranging from Tourist to Native.

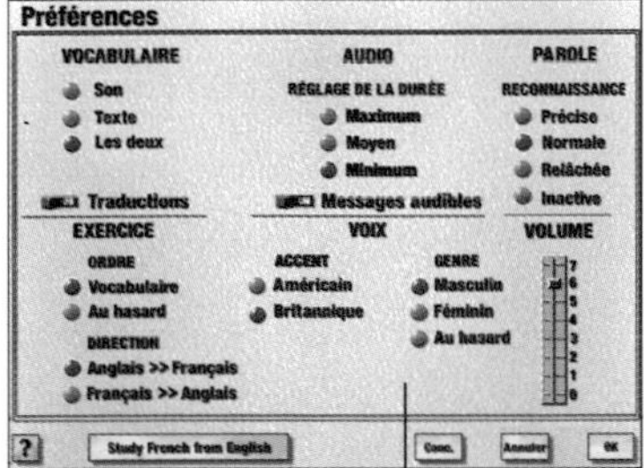

Record and Play
On this screen you choose exactly how you want the program to present speech.

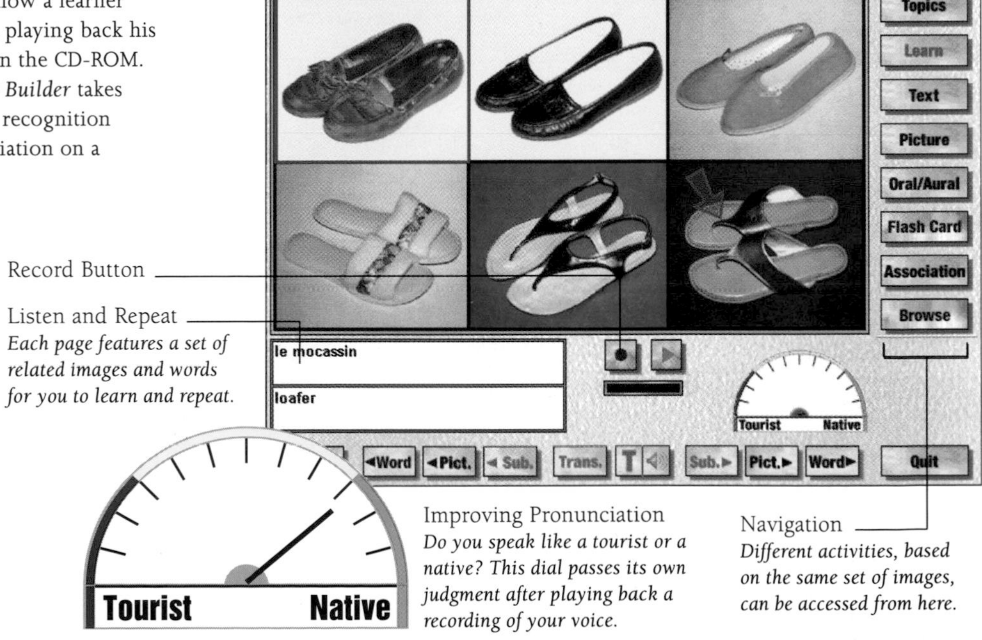

Record Button

Listen and Repeat
Each page features a set of related images and words for you to learn and repeat.

Improving Pronunciation
Do you speak like a tourist or a native? This dial passes its own judgment after playing back a recording of your voice.

Navigation
Different activities, based on the same set of images, can be accessed from here.

Scientific Discovery

The world of science is fascinating, but to many it appears complex and difficult. In an attempt to explain science to the layman, multimedia publishers have created CD-ROMs that are solely devoted to making the subject readily accessible and fun to learn about. These titles use multimedia not just to present facts but to provide a highly interactive experience that encourages learning by exploration.

Bringing Science to Life

Science titles aim to bring the subject to life in the same way that a good science teacher would in a school laboratory. They combine factual information with a multitude of practical demonstrations to keep the student interested. Furthermore, they can offer insights into subjects that would be difficult to create at school or at home, such as showing a close-up view of the moon's surface, or how it feels to walk around the ancient site of Stonehenge in England. Some titles are based on "rooms" that you walk through and explore; others adopt an interactive book approach, in which you can look up topics that interest you and jump to related subjects.

Isaac Asimov Science Adventure II

Knowledge Adventure's *Isaac Asimov Science Adventure II* takes you into a virtual world crammed with exhibits and experiments: you step into a laboratory and wander around, examining the things that interest you or following a line of inquiry.

HyperGallery
One door leads into the HyperGallery. The images in each room have annotations for extra information.

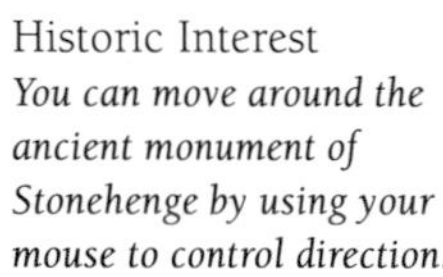

Historic Interest
You can move around the ancient monument of Stonehenge by using your mouse to control direction.

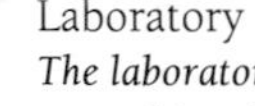

Laboratory
The laboratory walls are covered in exhibits that come alive when approached.

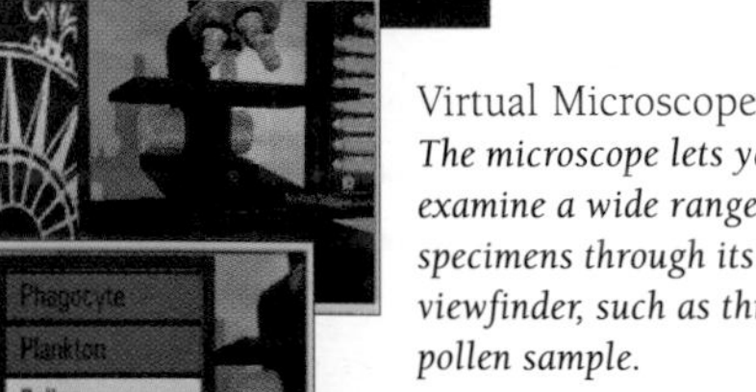

Virtual Microscope
The microscope lets you examine a wide range of specimens through its viewfinder, such as this pollen sample.

Pollen Sample

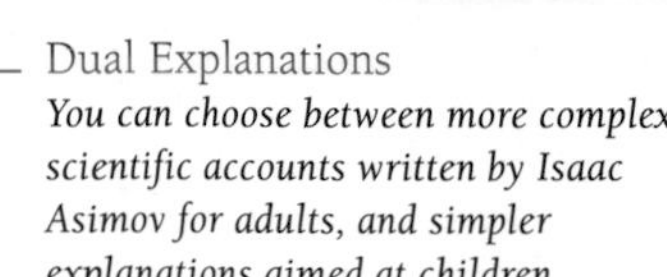

Dual Explanations
You can choose between more complex scientific accounts written by Isaac Asimov for adults, and simpler explanations aimed at children.

Movie Theater
One of the doors in the laboratory leads into a theater where you can watch scientific movies.

The Way Things Work

Dorling Kindersley's *The Way Things Work* centers on an inventor's workshop and explores the workings of a wide variety of machines and other inventions. It also has special sections on the scientific principles behind these inventions, and the stories of their inventors. An animated Woolly Mammoth acts as a guide and does his best to explain things.

Historical Timeline
A timeline, split into historical periods such as "The Steam Age," shows each invention's place in history.

Workshop
The workshop is full of inventions that perform short animations if you click on them.

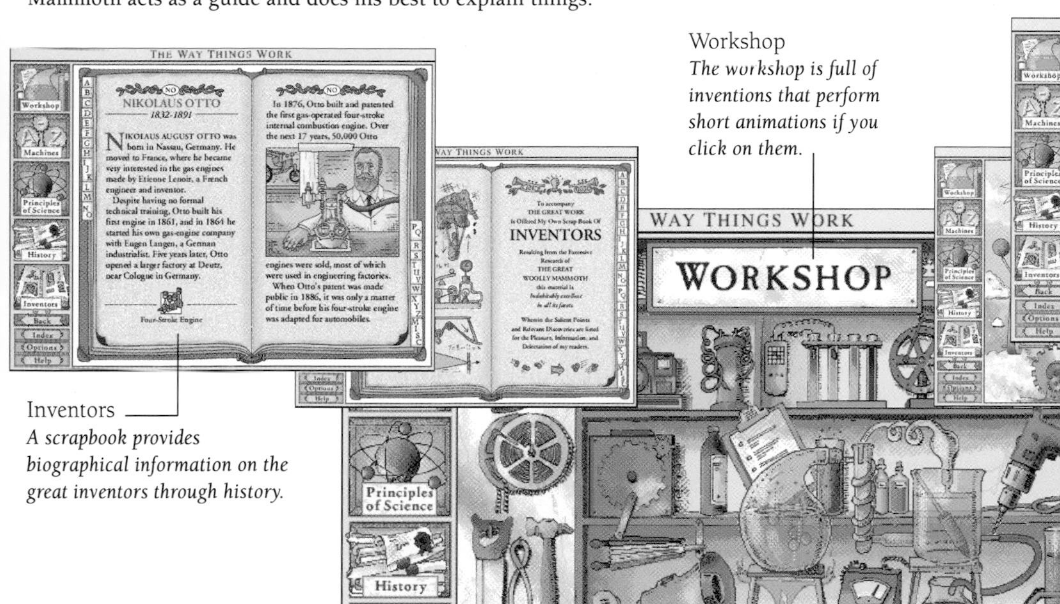

Inventors
A scrapbook provides biographical information on the great inventors through history.

A–Z of Machines
Each machine can be located by choosing a letter on the wheel. They are ordered alphabetically.

Principles of Science
This area of the program enables the user to explore such scientific fundamentals as pressure, friction, and heat.

Cross-reference
Each topic is cross-referenced to other, related areas of the program.

Mammoth Movies
The Woolly Mammoth stars in a series of short movies that illustrate scientific principles, such as heat, shown here.

More Information
Important words are explained in detail inside pop-up windows.

Animation Clip
In a book it is difficult for pictures and text alone to explain how a machine works. Multimedia animations can convey this information explicitly.

Games and Entertainment

Computer games have developed almost as rapidly as computers themselves. Over the last 25 years or so, such games have progressed from relatively simple versions of card or board games to today's spectacular and involving games: games based on realistic simulations of airplane flying, car racing, and so on; fast and sometimes violent action games (often called shoot-'em-ups); and adventure, puzzle, and strategy games (in which the player can adopt a role and explore vast fictional worlds). All this has been made possible by CD-ROM, which has led to improved production values in computer-based entertainment and the creation of larger, more realistic, and ever more impressive electronic worlds.

Puzzle Games

Board games were a source of inspiration for the designers of early computer games. Computerized versions of tabletop war-games appeared, and fantasy role-playing games such as *Dungeons and Dragons* were soon adapted by designers. In such games, pictures were used to support the text that described a location, and graphics were used to represent the pieces in a war-gaming simulation. But it required a real feat of the imagination to gain a sense of "being there." Multimedia has changed this. Over the last few years, the presentation of multimedia puzzle games has reached new heights as programmers have combined real-world video sequences with incredibly realistic, rendered graphics. CD-ROM has given rise to new kinds of puzzle games, such as Broderbund's *Myst*, which places the player in a realistic three-dimensional environment.

To the Clock Tower
From the library, a path leads down to the shore. Across a small stretch of sea lies the clock tower. But how do you get in?

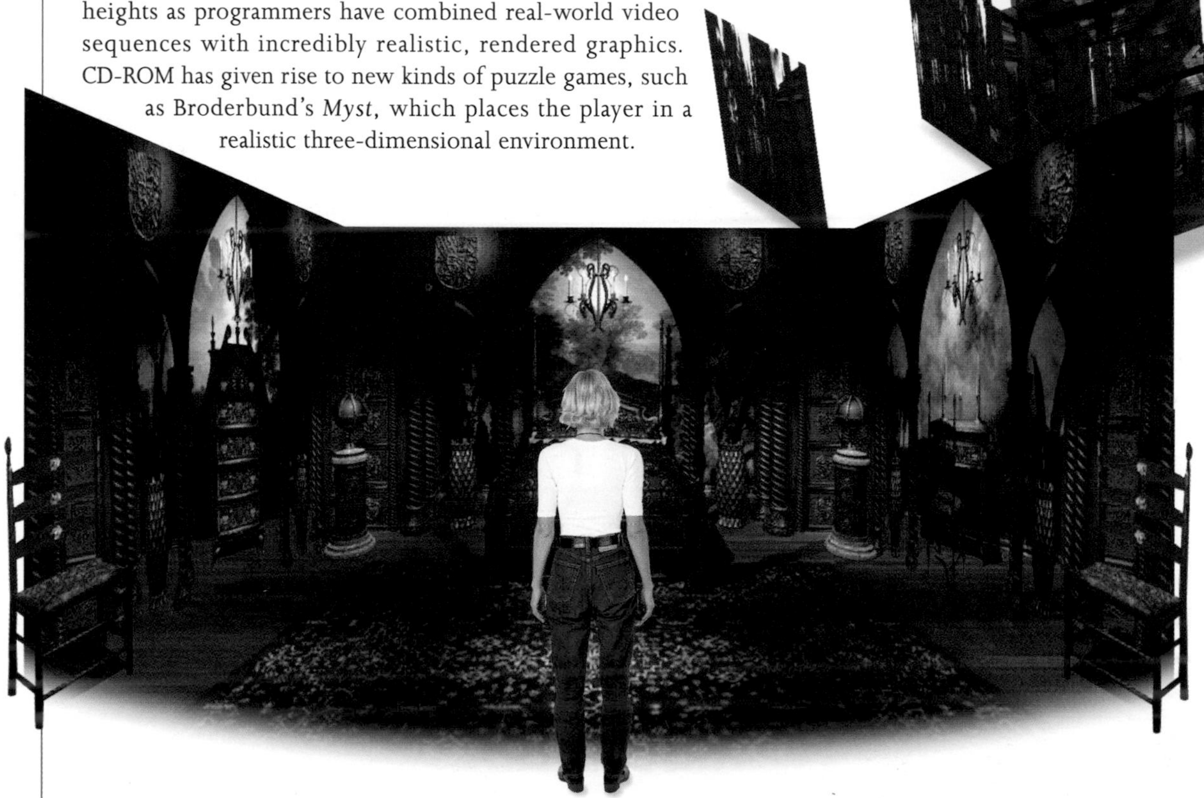

Puzzle of the Furnace
Once you have lit the furnace in the log cabin, you can hear the fire roar; but what is all the energy being used for?

Navigation
Getting around the world of Myst *could not be simpler – just pointing the hand-shaped cursor and clicking the mouse button takes you to a new location.*

Myst

With sales of over half a million, Broderbund's *Myst* is one of the most popular computer games of all time and has won acclaim from experienced and novice computer gamers alike. *Myst* takes you to a surreal island and leaves you there. As you begin the game, you will see no controls on the screen, no hints, no instructions, no tasks or missions to embark on. Even the manual supplied with the game is little more than an empty notebook. The single page of instructions simply suggests that you note down every clue and keep a record of every observation that you make.

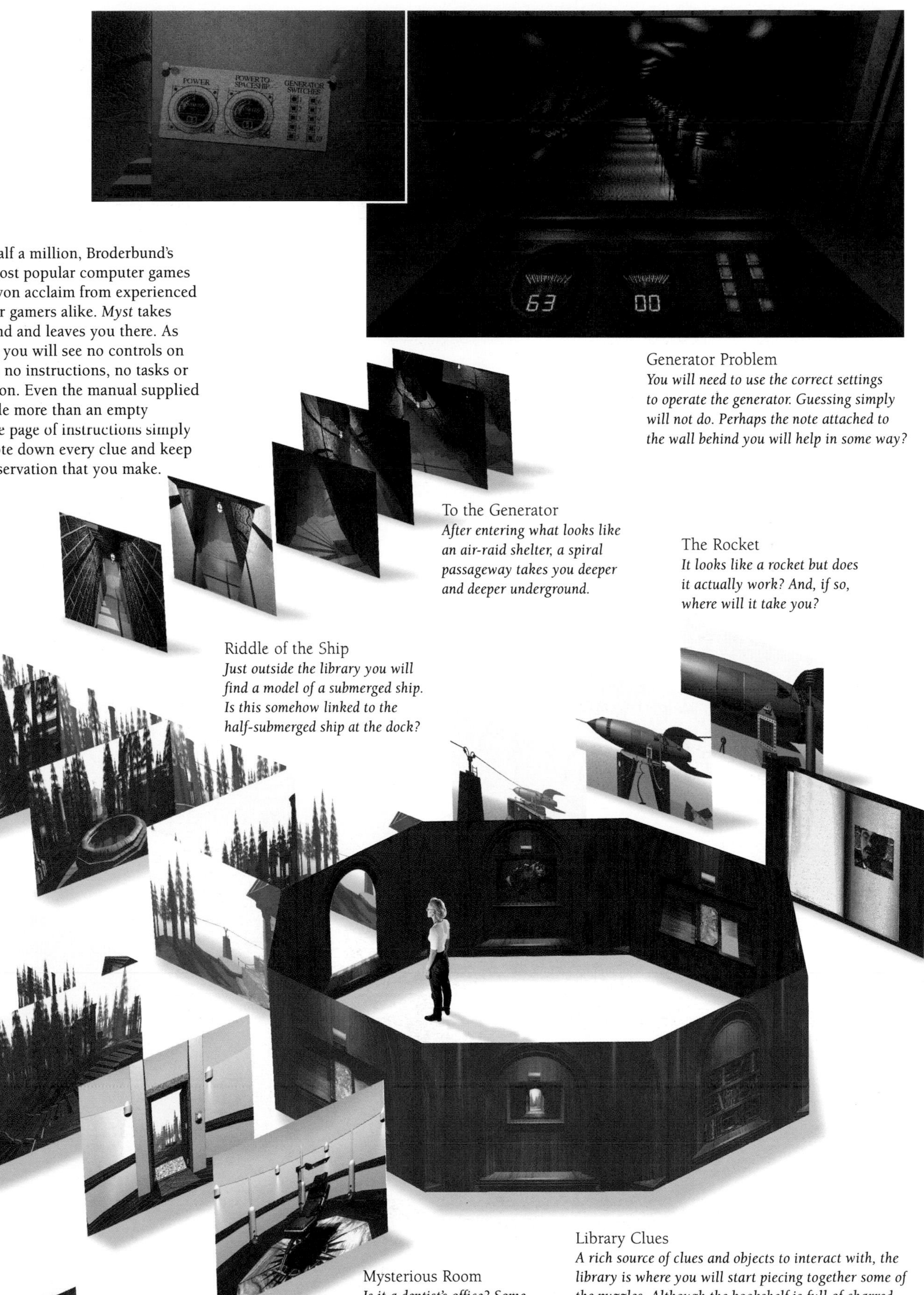

Generator Problem
You will need to use the correct settings to operate the generator. Guessing simply will not do. Perhaps the note attached to the wall behind you will help in some way?

To the Generator
After entering what looks like an air-raid shelter, a spiral passageway takes you deeper and deeper underground.

The Rocket
It looks like a rocket but does it actually work? And, if so, where will it take you?

Riddle of the Ship
Just outside the library you will find a model of a submerged ship. Is this somehow linked to the half-submerged ship at the dock?

Mysterious Room
Is it a dentist's office? Some kind of torture chamber? A closer look is required.

Library Clues
A rich source of clues and objects to interact with, the library is where you will start piecing together some of the puzzles. Although the bookshelf is full of charred and burned books, some diaries are still legible. Will you find something in their pages to help you?

3-D Action Games

Yesterday's game was the platform game, in which you moved around a two-dimensional world. Today's games, however, have entered the third dimension. Multimedia machines are now powerful enough to produce realistic 3-D environments in which you can drive, kill, fly, and die. Consoles have specialized graphics chips to handle the new games, and many console buyers now choose machines purely on the basis of what they can run in 3-D. In fact, some console manufacturers become seriously concerned if they do not have at least two major 3-D titles for their platform. Now that PCs have also become powerful enough to run 3-D games software, a serious hardware battle is being fought out on the field of 3-D combat.

3-D environments
For more on 3-D environments, see page 148

Combat Games

Among entertainment titles that have come to be regarded as classics, 3-D combat games such as *Doom* by id Software hold an unchallenged position. These games are often set in hostile underground labyrinths on distant planets or in vast space stations in imminent danger of being turned into a galaxy of neutrinos. With these complex settings, nonstop action, instant results, and sudden death around every corner, 3-D combat has taken the games market by storm, gaining devotees ranging from children as young as nine to middle-aged marketing directors. The core idea is essentially simple – it amounts to little more than killing around corners, using awesome firepower. But it is this simplicity of action within complex and highly convincing settings that gives the games their unrivaled ability to involve the player. When you are moving fast through an unknown land, encountering aliens who are strangers to civilized conversation, there is neither the opportunity nor the need to sit back and think.

Doom Daddy
Few games have achieved the impact of *Doom* by id Software. The somber dark gray settings give a solid background to one of the more popular shoot-'em-ups.

Simple but Convincing
These still images show how economically yet effectively the stormtroopers in Dark Forces *have been drawn. The speed of movement compensates for the primitive drawing.*

Martial Arts

The legendary *Doom* spawned a number of clones that developed variations on its settings, movement, weaponry, and player's opponents. However, another breed of game has emerged for people who prefer the intricacies and more contact-intensive rewards of martial arts action. Rather than having the perspective of the first-person gun, these games give you a figure that you manipulate, using the keyboard or joystick, to take on an opponent in weapon-free physical combat. The camera angle is controlled by the program: the camera appears to swoop and float around the action, taking whichever position shows the most mayhem.

A martial arts variation on 3-D combat is provided by *FX Fighter* from Argonaut/GTE. You select one fighter from eight cybermorphs and play against the program or another human player. The combat areas are varied, the animation is fast, the air is thick with flying kicks, and secret moves have to be found by rapid random moves of the joystick.

Skillful Play
Each of the combatants in *FX Fighter* has unique skills that can be accessed by the player, using concealed key or joystick commands.

Camera Shots
The camera view changes, often to show the best angle for the player to select an attacking shot.

Light and Dark Forces

One of the best games to follow *Doom's* blazing trail was *Dark Forces* by LucasArts. Whereas *Doom* is set entirely in gloomy surroundings, *Dark Forces* alternates these with light-colored settings; you are also given the added advantage of being able to look up and down as well as from side to side. Based on the *Star Wars* movies, it intercuts scenes between the action sequences, which gives the title a more cinematic quality than its predecessor.

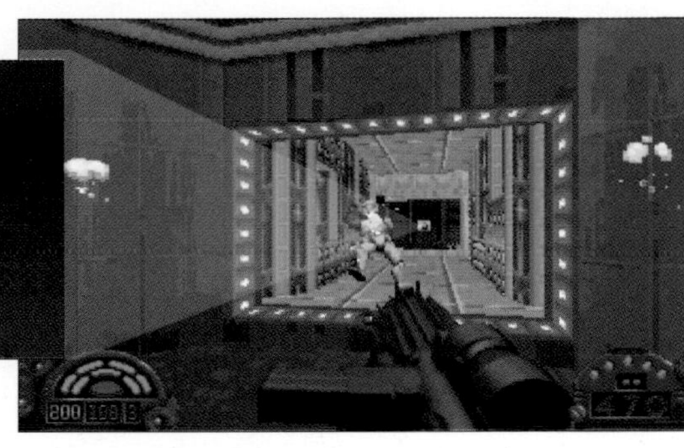

Finding the Key
To fulfill a mission in Dark Forces, *you often need to find a key – in a hazardous, heavily guarded area – that will enable you to progress to the next stage of the game.*

Your Objective
Beyond the stormtroopers is a room. You need to overcome them to enter it.

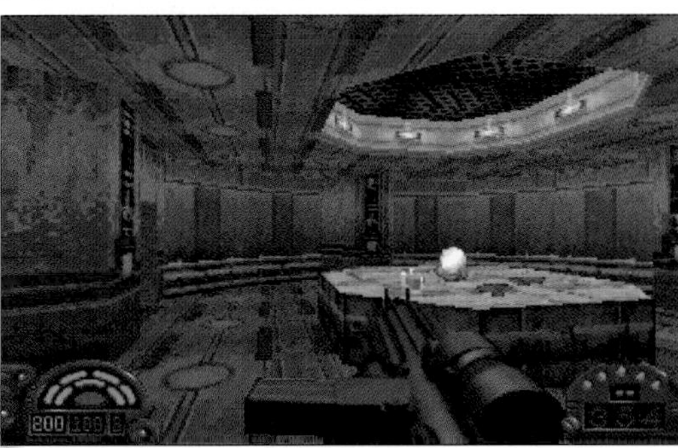

Scene Shifting
Dark Forces uses a variety of different "sets," such as the inside of a spaceship, shown here.

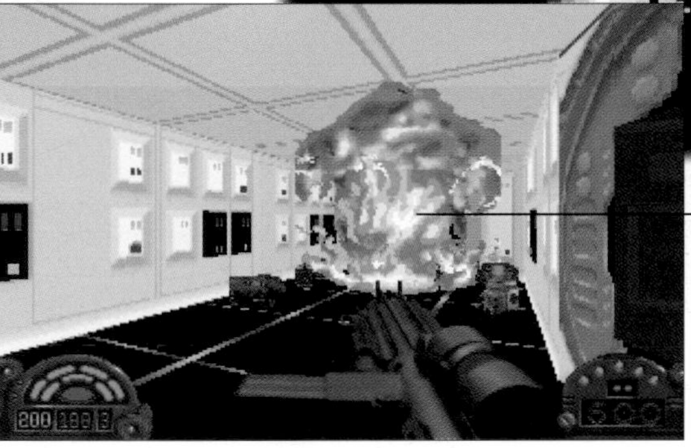

Big Bangs
The interactive sequences are heightened by some highly dramatic detonations.

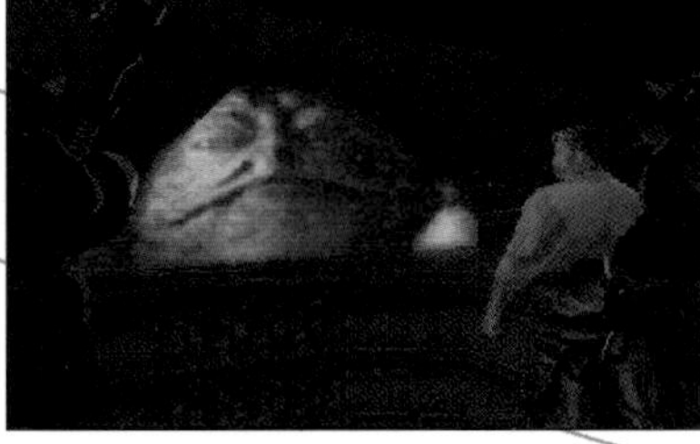

Animated Storylines
Noninteractive animations develop the plot, which you follow as you progress through the game.

Marathon II

Another title in the *Doom* mold is *Marathon II* by Bungie. In addition to mutual slaughter when played as a multiplayer game on a network, this title features cooperative levels of play – players help one another to escape. These screen shots show scenes from a network game.

Possessing a Skull
In one of the network games in Marathon II, *you have to find and hold on to a skull for as long as possible to win the game.*

3-D Flying and Driving

Flying and driving titles make heavier demands on hardware than any other form of multimedia game. This is because they have a complex combination of essential requirements: high-speed movement; instant reaction to the player's control; and constant feedback so that the player can assess his or her degree of skill and success. In addition, because these games provide only one activity – flying or driving – they must add variety: a choice of cars or airplanes with different characteristics, and a number of different settings in which the action can take place.

Increasing Realism

Driving simulations first appeared on arcade machines in the 1970s, but their lack of processing power meant that the first games employed only two-dimensional graphics and sprites (small animated characters). The illusion of motion perspective was created by enlarging the sprites as they moved toward the edges of the screen.

The more powerful processors that appeared in the early 1980s enabled designers to use 3-D graphics for the first time. These early 3-D titles used wireframe shapes, where only the edges of the shapes are drawn according to the rules of perspective. However, these shapes did at least allow the first flying simulations to be produced. These included the more complicated moves involved in flying an aircraft, such as climbing or descending to different altitudes and lateral airplane movements. The first simulations were set in outer space, filled with rudimentary planets, spacecraft, and missiles. When today's more powerful computers arrived, it became possible to simulate the experience of flying over a terrestial landscape.

Magic Carpet 2

The innovative *Magic Carpet 2*, by Bullfrog Productions, ignores airplanes in favor of a flying carpet. The convincing flying simulation places a great deal of control in the hands of the player, and the changes from fast-forward to hover to speedy retreat are smooth and instantaneous. You cannot crash, but the game is still not easy.

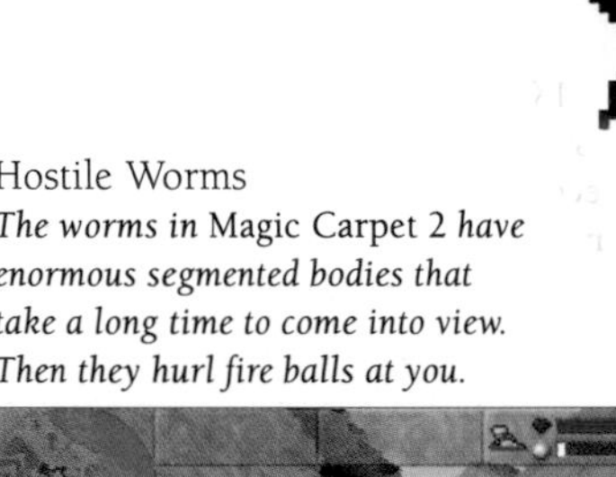

Hostile Worms

The worms in Magic Carpet 2 *have enormous segmented bodies that take a long time to come into view. Then they hurl fire balls at you.*

Stinging Bees

These monsters sting if they can get close enough to you, but they do not die when they have struck – they live to sting again.

Balloon and Castle

When you kill a monster, its "life force" is transported to your castle by balloon for safekeeping. This life force gives you the power to cast spells.

FLIGHT UNLIMITED

One of the outstanding features of *Flight Unlimited*, by Looking Glass Technologies, is the naturalistic appearance of the terrain as you fly over it. The landscape was created from digitized photographs, and as it unfolds below it can have a mesmerizing effect. The user can perform aerobatics – rolls and spins are simulated with a realism that some might find dizzying.

Surrounding Landscape
As you take off and climb over the hills beyond the airfield, this is your first sight of the surrounding countryside.

Grounded or Airborne
When starting a flying mission, you can decide whether the plane is stationary at the end of the runway, or airborne, or ready to taxi to the runway.

Landing the Airplane
Learning to line up the runway and land the airplane is not the least of the challenges that you will face.

FORMULA ONE GRAND PRIX 2

Microprose built on the success of the first version of their race game with this second release. A form of artificial intelligence determines how the different built-in race drivers respond to the changing conditions of the race – these drivers are based on the actual Formula One driver lineup.

Lifelike Models
The cars are realistically modeled on Formula One machines. They are texture-mapped and light-sourced for extra realism.

Changing Perspective
The game lends distance and perspective to its settings by graying out buildings as they recede into the background.

Grand Prix Manager
Microprose have also released a racing team manager game, Grand Prix Manager. *The car setup can be customized in every detail, and the races take place on accurate representations of 16 race tracks from around the world.*

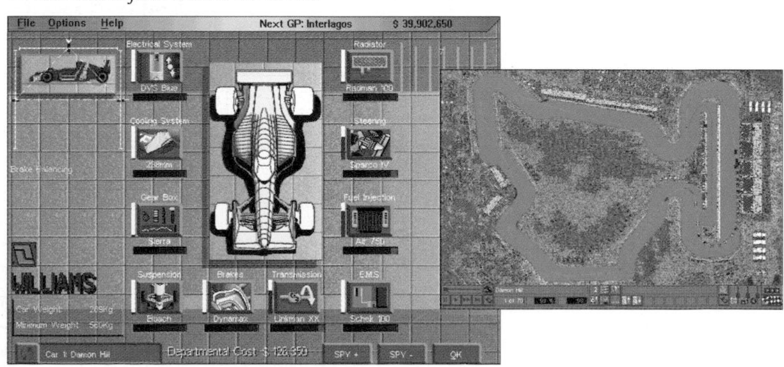

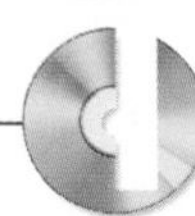

Cartoon Adventures

Twenty years ago, when the mouse was a rare accessory and the average computer's processing power was a mere fraction of that of today's computers, one of the earliest kinds of games available was the text-only adventure game. Players of these early adventure games relied heavily on their imagination since the games contained no graphics. The genre was very popular, however, and, with the introduction of graphics, has developed at an astonishing rate: today, adventure games often take the form of interactive cartoons on CD-ROM that combine stereo sound with stunning graphics and animations. Many titles have a soundtrack recorded by professional actors and musicians, and a story developed by a whole team of scriptwriters, animators, and designers.

Full Throttle
Full Throttle, by LucasArts, is an animated movie you can control. You need to steer Ben, the main character, through a series of adventures and encounters. The vibrant rock sound track, the explosive action sequences, and the use of cinematic techniques (such as unusual camera angles) give this title considerable impact.

Graphic Developments

Early graphic adventure games depended on keyboard input to move the story along. If simple graphics were used, they were there mainly to illustrate the story. The player typed instructions at the keyboard, usually consisting of simple sentences such as "go North," "open blue door with iron key," and so on, using a vocabulary of sometimes only a few hundred words.The first graphic adventures began to appear early in the 1980s. Modern CD-ROM adventure games contain elements similar to those found in the first simple text-only games. In a typical adventure game, the player makes progress by picking up and using objects, interacting with other characters, exploring the game's world, and solving puzzles of varying complexity. In modern graphic adventures, the player controls a character's movements with a mouse or joystick, by using a pointer either to indicate the required direction for movement or to access a control panel or toolbar to carry out various actions.

Problem Solving in *Full Throttle*
Full Throttle *consists of a number of stages that are seamlessly integrated into the storyline. Each stage contains a series of interrelated puzzles which you have to solve before progressing to the next stage of the game.*

Finding the Way In
Here, Ben needs to find a way into the junkyard. When he pulls the chain, the rolling door on the left opens.

Each time Ben lets go of the chain and tries to reach the door, it closes too quickly for him to enter.

Obviously, just pulling the chain does not work. Maybe Ben needs to find help somewhere else in the area.

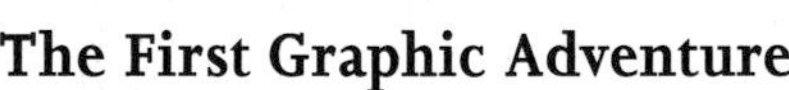

The First Graphic Adventure

The first graphic adventure game, *Mystery House*, was developed by Sierra OnLine and the first copies were sold in 1980. Players needed to type commands at the keyboard, but simple graphics were used to illustrate the story. All text appeared at the bottom of the screen. *Mystery House* proved very popular.

Text Commands
After reading a brief description of the location, players typed appropriate commands.

Arcadelike Action

Full Throttle *features sections of "arcadelike" action: game elements where timing and manual dexterity are more important than problem-solving skills. Here, Ben has to remove the other biker from his seat. The box in the lower left-hand corner shows his chosen method.*

High-quality Animation

The quality of animation in this title compares favorably with the best animated movies. This sequence shows Ben successfully unseating his rival.

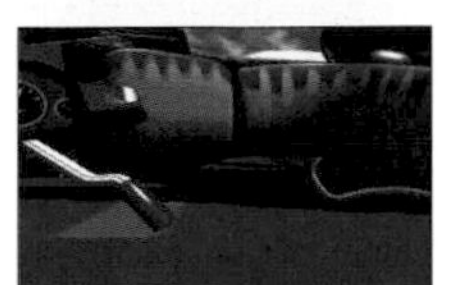

Choosing Ben's Words

Most dialogue in Full Throttle *is spoken by the characters during the course of the action. Occasionally, you need to participate actively in a dialogue by choosing a suitable question or response from a list.*

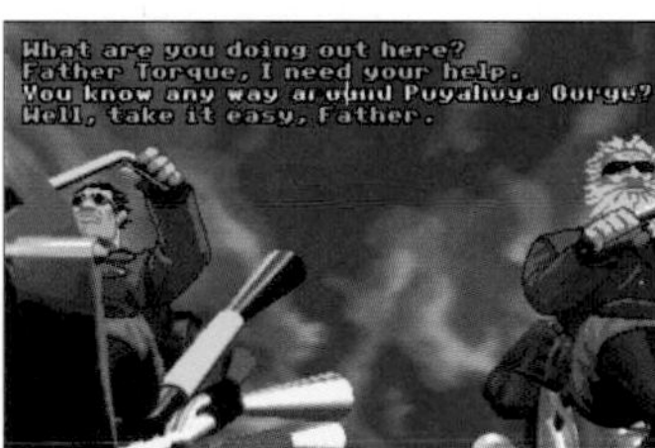

Cut Scenes

Many animated sequences simply move the story along and are not interactive. These sequences are usually action-packed and often involve Ben roaring off somewhere on his bike.

Actions and Objects

Full Throttle's normal screen contains no icons (apart from the crosshair pointer) until you click a mouse button. The left button brings up an actions icon labeled with the object you are attempting to use. The right button reveals Ben's inventory – the objects that he is currently carrying and can use – in a large skull icon.

Actions Icon

Moving the pointer around the icon lets you choose Ben's actions. For example, moving the cursor over the hand allows him to touch, pick up, or punch an object.

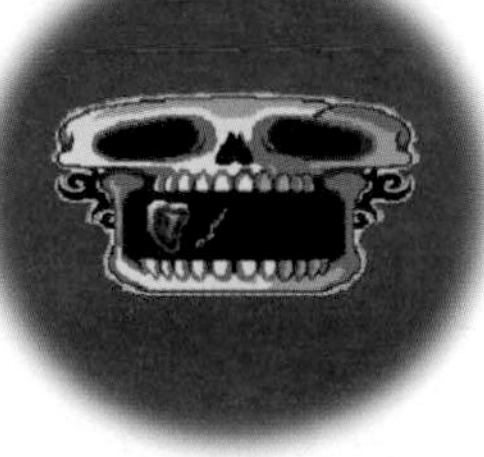

Inventory Icon

Any object that you pick up during the course of the game is held here. You can use any of these obects by clicking on them.

Mixed-genre Adventure Games

To complete a typical adventure game successfully, the player needs to explore a series of locations thoroughly, examine everything carefully, and question any characters (usually nonhuman) encountered along the way. Some titles, however, extend the range of such games by borrowing elements from other multimedia genres. Spectrum Holobyte's *Star Trek: The Next Generation "A Final Unity"* sets a typical cartoon adventure within a wider scenario containing elements usually found in management games and flight simulations. Players looking for more of a challenge than simply exploring the galaxy can opt to control every operational aspect of the starship USS Enterprise; beginners and adventure-game purists can delegate the navigation and combat tactics to one of the crew.

Television Tie-in
Based on the popular television series Star Trek – The Next Generation, *the game uses the familiar opening sequence, titles, theme music, and closing credits. The voices of the real actors add a further touch of authenticity.*

The Bridge of the Enterprise
This is the main screen of the game. Here you take on the role of Captain Picard – consulting the crew, communicating with the game's other characters, and interrogating the ship's computer before making decisions and issuing commands. Clicking on certain areas of the screen will allow you to access other important areas or functions of the ship.

Conference Lounge
For talking to any visitors to the ship.

Tactical Computer
For controlling the Enterprise during combat.

Turbolift
For access to engineering, the transporter, and the holodeck.

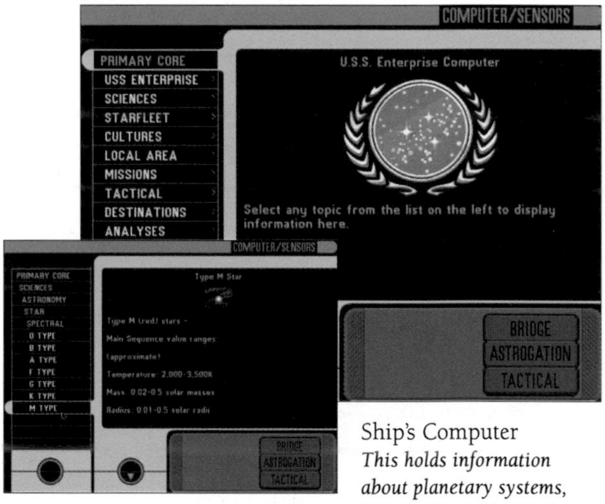

Ship's Computer
This holds information about planetary systems, historical records, combat tactics, and so on. You may wish to access this database regularly.

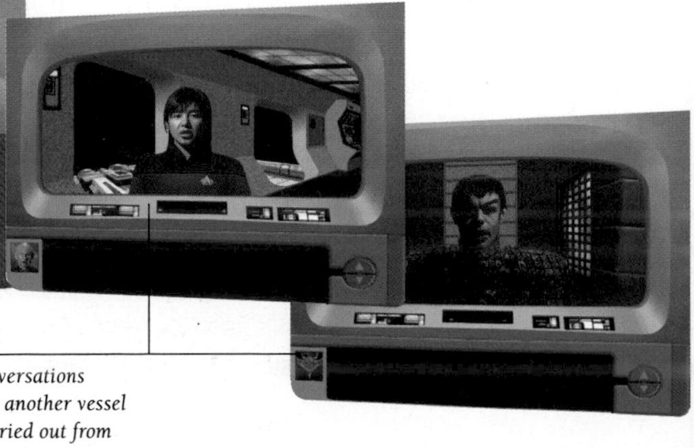

Astrogation Terminal
For plotting the course of the Enterprise.

Viewscreen
Face-to-face conversations with someone on another vessel or planet are carried out from the bridge via the viewscreen.

Controlling the USS Enterprise

If you opt to take full control of the Enterprise (rather than delegate control to crew members) you will need to familiarize yourself with the three main control areas – Engineering, Astrogation, and Tactical.

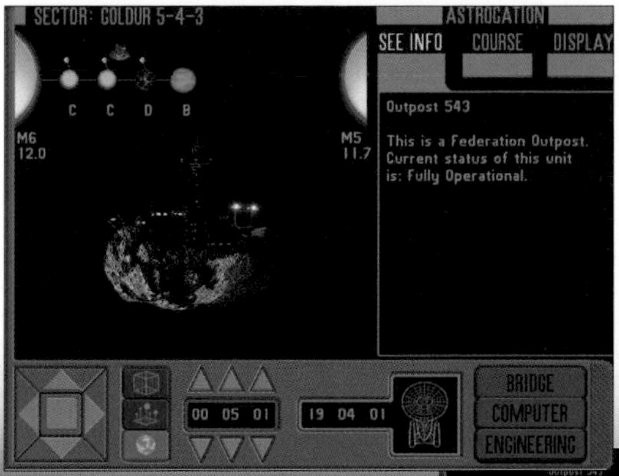

Astrogation

Here you plot the course of the Enterprise, using a number of screens. You can access detailed information about planets and star systems before working out and inputting your destination coordinates. You also control the speed of the ship.

The Art of Delegation

If you delegate functions to crew members, they will often guide you toward the best decisions at key stages.

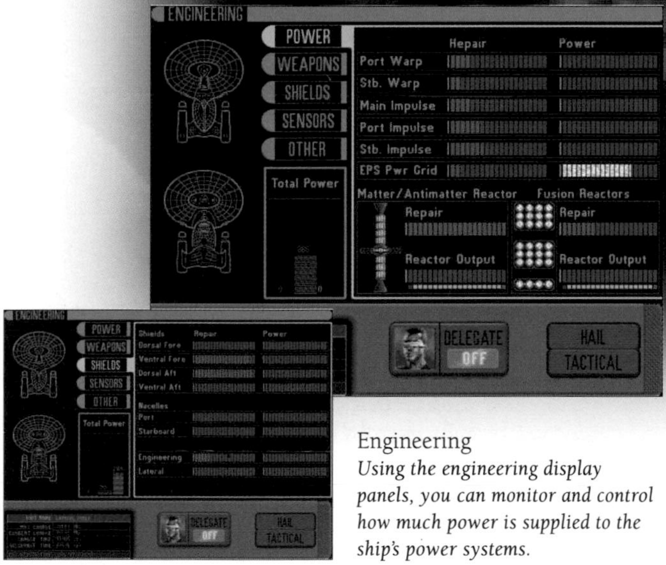

Tactical

From this area you can fire weapons, operate sensors, raise and lower shields, engage in combat, and even control the flight of the Enterprise, using your keyboard's number pad.

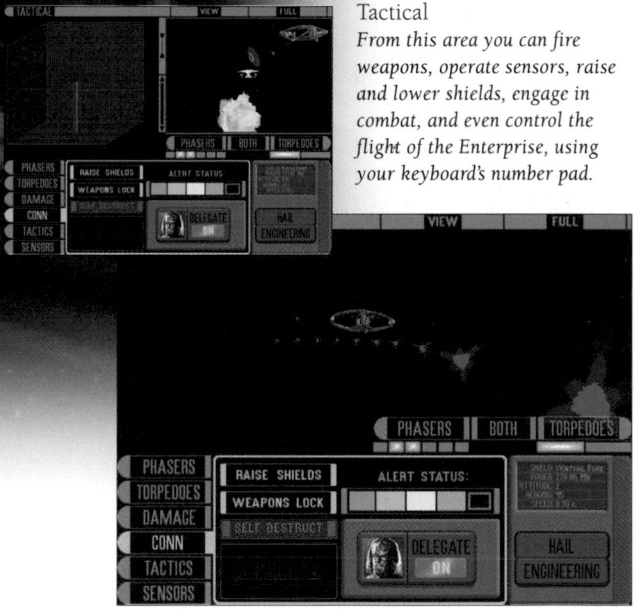

Engineering

Using the engineering display panels, you can monitor and control how much power is supplied to the ship's power systems.

Away Team Missions

At the heart of the adventure game *"A Final Unity"* is a role-playing element. You can assign up to four crew members to an "away team mission." After beaming them down to a planet's surface, you explore the alien environment with each team member, solving problems by interrogating any of the planet's inhabitants you meet.

Transporter Room

Alien Worlds

Two possible locations to be visited by your away teams in "A Final Unity."

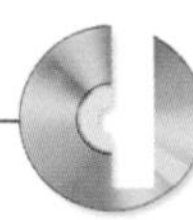

INTERACTIVE MOVIES

The idea of directing and taking part in their own movie has instant appeal for most people. And, with interactive movies, multimedia has made this possible for the games player. An interactive movie involves the player on several levels: he or she can watch the movie unfold, and direct the sequence of events. The essential feature that makes this level of involvement possible is the use of video sequences showing actors playing roles in the game. The quality of an interactive movie will depend on how much video is included, the way it is used, and how much opportunity it provides for player input.

MAKING IT INTERACT

In an ideal world, the player of an interactive movie would be able to completely determine the movie's outcome; in practice, due to the limitations of space on a CD-ROM, players are presented with predetermined options. One approach is to provide the player with long sequences of video, and then allow him or her to choose from various courses of action until the solution to a problem is found, and the game can continue. These movies effectively have a single plot through which the player travels. A second technique is to use multiple plots. With this approach, the player's actions alter the flow of the storyline and the video that appears will depend on the choice the player has made. This makes for a more truly interactive movie.

The Great Outdoors
Not all of the action takes place inside the increasingly claustrophobic house: some key scenes happen outdoors.

Moving Image
The video footage of Adrienne moving through the house is superimposed on rooms created using 3-D computer graphics.

The Daedalus Encounter

In this Mechadeus game, the player has two human accomplices on video, (one shown below). The player remotely controls an airborne probe to explore regions into which the actors are unable to go, and translates alien languages so that new areas can be opened up and vital controls operated.

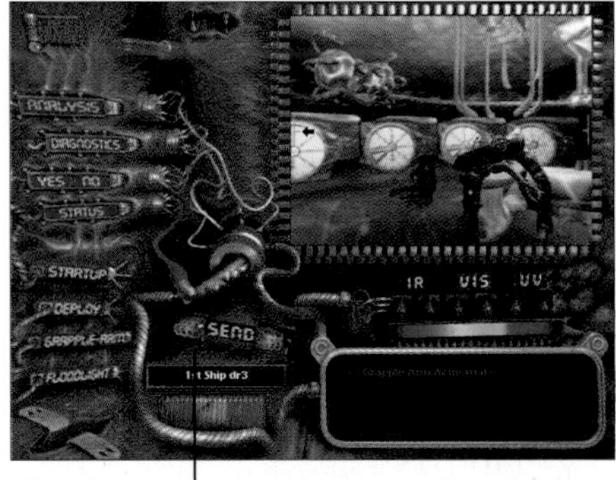

Player's View
The interface consists of a set of controls notionally wired into the player's brain.

Logic Puzzle
The player encounters puzzles such as this one, where a logic circuit has to be set up by manipulating binary switches on color-coded components of the circuit.

Intercutting
Phantasmagoria uses many standard film-making techniques, including intercutting close-up shots in the footage to heighten elements of the drama.

Phantasmagoria

These richly colored shots from Sierra's *Phantasmagoria* show the main setting for this interactive movie. Adrienne and Don have bought a vast rambling house that once belonged to an illusionist but has remained empty and undisturbed for years. The player directs Adrienne as she explores the house and its surroundings and slowly begins to discover its dark secrets. The title also includes noninteractive footage that contains important developments in the story.

Labyrinth
The main house is a labyrinth of stairs, passages, and rooms that each contain different surprises and clues.

Close-up Corner
The most significant parts of the house are shown in close-up and vivid detail.

Opening Doors
Some rooms require the imaginative use of found objects before they can be entered. Here, Adrienne is using a poker – found in the dining room – to open a trapdoor.

Awaiting Developments

This complete game screen shows Adrienne waiting patiently to be given a direction to follow or an object to examine.

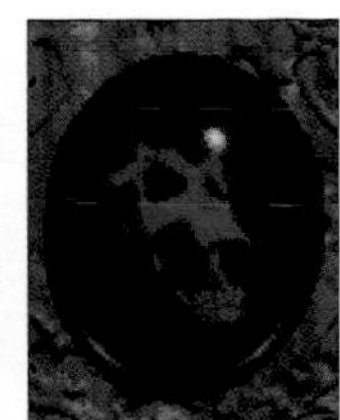

The Hint Keeper
Hints are available from an irascible crimson skull that watches your every move.

Pointer
The normal single yellow pointer turns red when moved over a "hot" object, or becomes an arrow to indicate a possible direction. Either can be chosen by clicking the mouse button.

Collecting Objects
An inventory stores found objects for later use; they can be viewed in rotating 3-D by moving them over the eyeball.

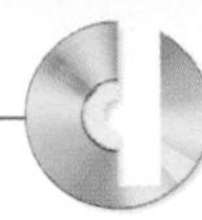

INTERACTIVE MUSIC

Interactive CD-ROM has already opened up new avenues for artists, such as David Bowie, who are actively exploring multimedia for themselves. Music companies, too, are aiming to provide enhanced versions of audio CDs and music videos by releasing them on CD-ROM and adding multimedia elements. It may not be too long before the CD Plus (a type of CD containing both audio and multimedia information) replaces the audio CD as the most common recorded-music format in most homes.

CD Plus
For more on CD Plus, see page 81

MUSIC WITHOUT INSTRUMENTS

Most multimedia music CD-ROMs include interactive elements of some kind. Some titles simulate the experience of working in a recording studio, allowing you to mix your own tracks using a number of prerecorded samples or by adding your own recorded samples. Other titles promote the creative output of a musician or group – perhaps centered on a new album – by inviting you to explore a virtual world created from sound, images, and video clips relating to their life, work, and backlist. Some artists are now producing work specifically for multimedia.

ROCK 'N ROLL YOUR OWN
This title from Compton's NewMedia presents eight prerecorded songs that can either be played as they were recorded or be remixed and saved to disk. *Rock 'n Roll Your Own* is not intended to replace "serious" musical sampling and sequencing software. It is more a tool kit introducing some of the concepts that lie behind the digital editing of music.

Record the Session
You can use this button to record and play back sessions you are especially pleased with.

Add Your Own Samples
Using a microphone and your computer's sound card, you can record new sounds or vocals and use them to enhance – or replace – elements of the songs provided.

Keyboard Sampling
A keyboard facility lets you construct your own tunes.

Using the Vib-a-tron
After choosing a sound from the Vib-a-tron's drop-down menu, you can add "scratch" effects to the sound by dragging the mouse back and forth over this area.

Watch a Video
Each song section is accompanied by a video clip.

Vocalizer
Click on these buttons at any time during playback to insert a vocal sample.

Control Screens
Each song has its own control screen. You can choose instrumental and vocal segments from this, combine them, and play them in sequence.

Songalizer
To choose the sequence in which your samples will be played, you need to drag the buttons (labeled I through X) from the left of the screen into the free spaces on the Songalizer.

Major Rock Stars on CD-ROM

In Ion's *Jump, the David Bowie Interactive CD-ROM*, you explore a virtual world based on a skyscraper. By following the corridors, you find rooms containing material related to the *Black Tie, White Noise* album. Pointing and clicking your mouse reveals photographs, interviews, and video clips – including four music videos. You can also take take an active role by editing an audio track and a video track, saving your favorite mixes to play back later.

Transport Controls

Video Screen

Edit Your Own Video
You can edit a master video by mixing video sequences from five different sources to accompany the audio playback. Clicking on a preview screen makes it appear in the main video screen. This sequence can be played back or saved to disk.

Track Sliders

Mix Your Own Track
You can mix your own version of the audio track Black Tie, White Noise *by moving the track sliders to alter the volume of voices and instruments during playback.*

Preview Screens

Transport Controls

The Editing Suite
Audio and video remixing takes place in the editing suite.

Video Screen

Choose a Topic
To view a video clip of David Bowie revealing his thoughts on such topics as "fulfillment" and "the universe," choose a topic from the videocassette.

Discussion Topics

Audio CD and CD-ROM Combined

Sarah McLachlan, The Freedom Sessions is an eight-track audio CD from Arista with an additional CD-ROM multimedia track. The multimedia track contains samples of more than 30 songs, speeches, photographs, and video clips promoting the work of the artist.

Trip to Thailand
Words, music, and video document a visit organized by the World Vision charity.

Touring Scrapbook
This contains photographs and spoken descriptions of the tour venues on the map.

CD+MM
When this CD was produced in 1995, the makers described their title as CD+MM. They advised listeners to avoid track 1 (the multimedia track) when playing the CD on conventional audio equipment, since they would hear only static or silence. Later titles have avoided this problem.

New Directions

Although the cost of producing a state-of-the-art game, reference, or edutainment title can be extremely high, the decreasing cost of hardware and software is now enabling some new multimedia producers to create titles relatively cheaply. The work of this "second wave" of producers often does not fall into easily definable categories. For example, although each of the three titles featured here shares the common link of humor, each one also has its own unique quality.

Games of Many Rewards

Multimedia games, like other multimedia genres, have their origin in traditional forms, but the endless opportunities for technical innovation offered by CD-ROM have enabled multimedia games to become much more inventive than their nonelectronic predecessors. To take one example, traditional games have a single well-defined goal, or "reward" – such as achieving checkmate in a game of chess or scoring 21 at blackjack – whereas CD-ROM games can offer "rewards" regularly, making the need for a final goal less important.

Three games are illustrated here: *Take Your Best Shot* offers the user a way of relieving stress; *P.A.W.S* is an interactive, cartoon-based interpretation of a dog's life; and *Monty Python's Complete Waste of Time* is part-nostalgia, part-game, but mostly a determinedly pointless exploration of inspired nonsense.

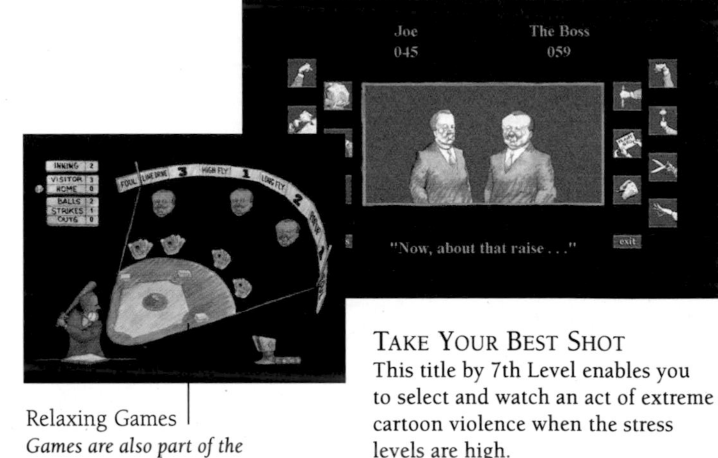

Relaxing Games
Games are also part of the title, including this bizarre version of baseball.

Take Your Best Shot
This title by 7th Level enables you to select and watch an act of extreme cartoon violence when the stress levels are high.

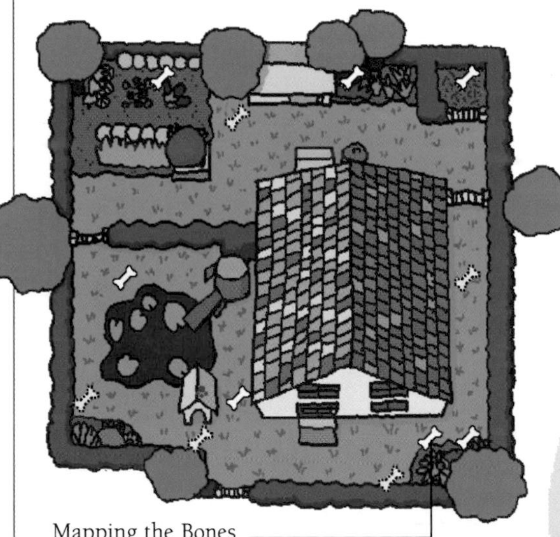

Mapping the Bones
Bones are the secret energy source in a dog's life, and finding them provides a delightful diversion. Like all sensible dogs, the one in P.A.W.S keeps a full-scale map of where bones have been buried.

P.A.W.S
Domestic Funk Products have produced a truly unique title in *P.A.W.S* (Personal Automated Wagging System). You live a "dog's life," finding bones, chasing cats, and exploring your garden territory. This gentle, whimsical title contains over 35,000 frames, which means that it is almost impossible to repeat any experience in this engaging dog's life.

Dog's Eye View

Bone Meal
The major reward for a dog – and for the player – is locating and uncovering a well-preserved bone for that all-important energy level.

Cats Are a Problem
Gentle dogs are popular with humans but unfortunately they are also popular with cats. When this cat appears, trouble follows.

Monty Python's Complete Waste of Time

Classic comedy dating from the earliest days of the computing revolution has been transferred onto CD-ROM by 7th Level. When you play the game, you enter the surrealistic world of Monty Python where insanity is a virtue and reason is a crime. The game explores the contents and thought processes of Mrs. Zambesi's brain. The makers claim that this exploration leads to a larger game and that if you complete this successfully you might win a real prize of a Pentium PC.

Watchdog
An old-time British "bobby" ensures that law and order is observed.

Portrait Gallery
In the world of Monty Python, walls do not have ears, they have mouths.

Loonatorium
In this part of the brain you can play "Spot the Loony," a game that is allegedly very important in learning about the larger game.

Corridor
Banners festoon the corridor soon after you enter it. When you have discovered how to remove them, you can enjoy a pinball game.

Chicken Man
A chicken with a mustache and a severe expression frequently appears. Its main role is to be used as target practice.

Pig Game
In this you play the part of a cowboy who tries to shoot flying piggy banks out of the sky. The consequences of failure are deadly.

MULTIMEDIA AT WORK

IN THE WORLD OF BUSINESS AND public service, the role being assumed by multimedia is now becoming increasingly important. From international corporations to small stores, the task of presenting information to clients, trainee staff, and the general public is being handed over to interactive multimedia, which can teach, inform, promote, and sell in new ways that are both more effective for the organization and more entertaining for the user. In the business world, the vast majority of successful companies recognize that a large investment in staff training pays dividends, and more and more of them are using multimedia for this purpose.

DESKTOP TRAINING

Large companies were among the first users of multimedia training aids – even before the advent of CD-ROM. Early interactive training programs used expensive laser disc players linked to computers. The cost of this equipment meant that interactive training had to be carried out in central company training centers. As a result of this inflexibility, training sessions had to be booked in advance, staff had to travel to them, and the training resources had to be shared. However, today's multimedia computers are cheap enough for workers to have them on their own desks, and today's training programs enable trainees to work unsupervised and at their own pace. What is more, the disc is always on hand if a staff member wants to revise a topic later. Even training videos – for many years a mainstay of corporate training departments – are now being produced on CD-ROM and are combined with interactive training exercises that can tailor the training to each individual's needs.

LEARNING MANAGEMENT
Leading Teams, from Xebec, is a highly interactive training program for trainee managers. The trainee views simulations and takes part in management decision exercises. The program evaluates these and assesses the trainee's performance.

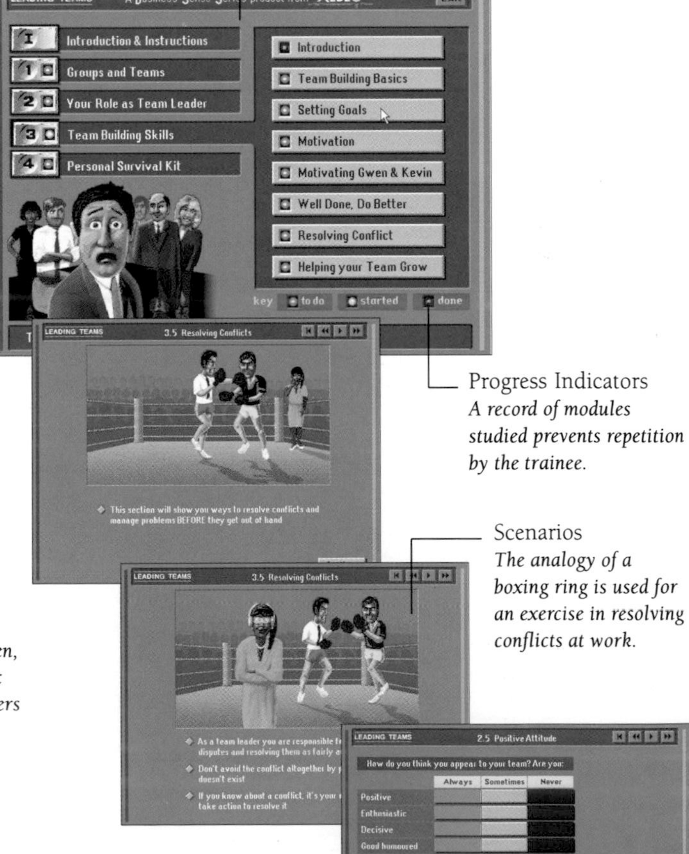

Responsible Choices
The title is module-based, which gives the trainee the responsibility for the choice of learning area.

Progress Indicators
A record of modules studied prevents repetition by the trainee.

Scenarios
The analogy of a boxing ring is used for an exercise in resolving conflicts at work.

Questions and Answers
The user's answers to a series of questions are evaluated and the software provides comments.

EXTENDING THE BOOK
Adobe's *Classroom in a Book* is designed to be used in conjunction with a training manual. It teaches graphic artists how to use Adobe's image manipulation program *Photoshop*.

Demonstrations
From the main menu screen, the user chooses one of six demonstrations. Each covers a different aspect of how Photoshop is used.

Models
The demonstration combines video clips and commentary to give the trainee step-by-step instruction.

System Training

CRT Multimedia's *EasyTutor Learn Windows 95* is an example of a training title designed to be used by trainees working alone and at their own pace. The title emphasizes the personal tutor approach: a high degree of flexibility of use, a choice of learning levels from beginner to in-depth, and continual assessment through testing and progress monitoring.

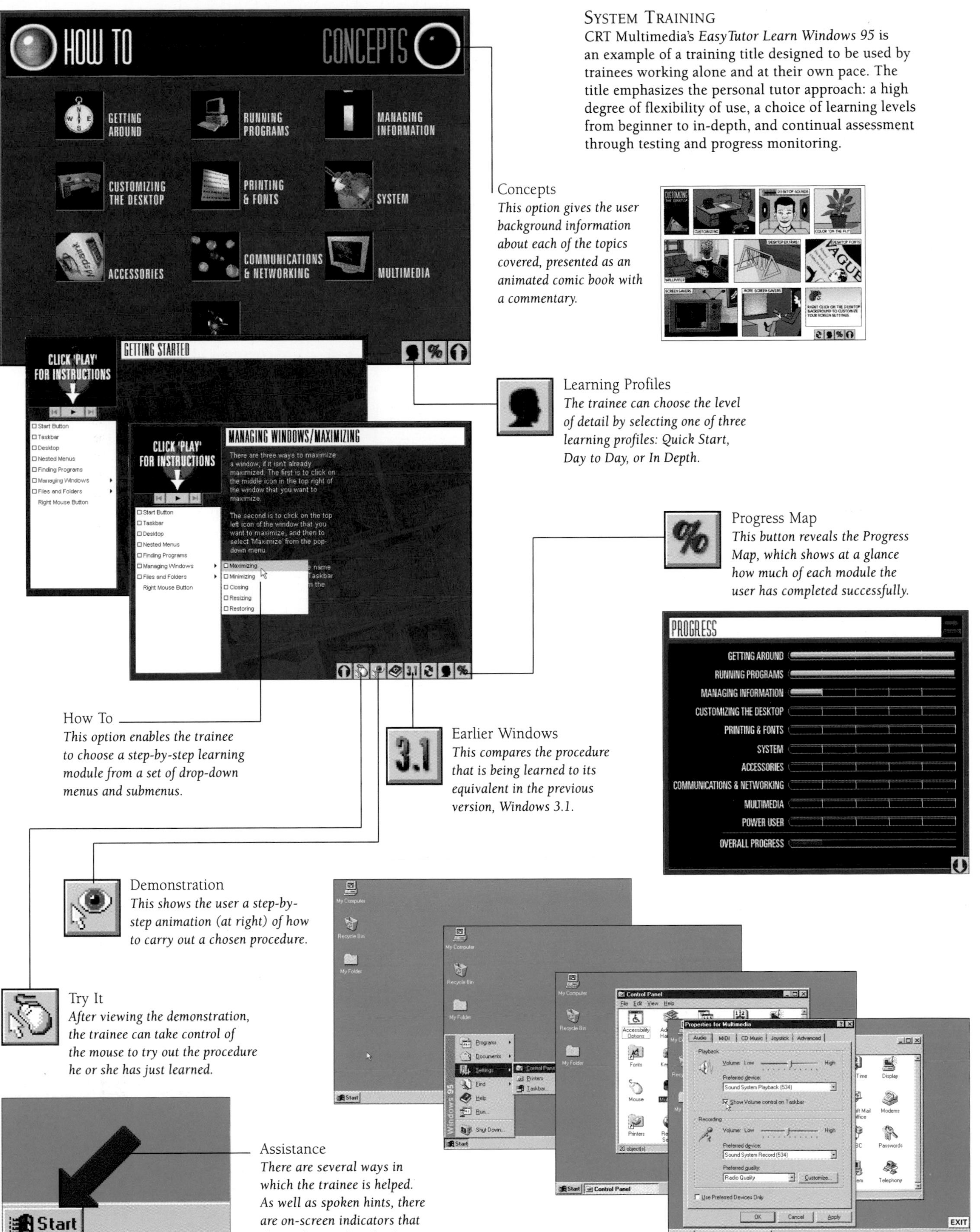

Concepts
This option gives the user background information about each of the topics covered, presented as an animated comic book with a commentary.

Learning Profiles
The trainee can choose the level of detail by selecting one of three learning profiles: Quick Start, Day to Day, or In Depth.

Progress Map
This button reveals the Progress Map, which shows at a glance how much of each module the user has completed successfully.

How To
This option enables the trainee to choose a step-by-step learning module from a set of drop-down menus and submenus.

Earlier Windows
This compares the procedure that is being learned to its equivalent in the previous version, Windows 3.1.

Demonstration
This shows the user a step-by-step animation (at right) of how to carry out a chosen procedure.

Try It
After viewing the demonstration, the trainee can take control of the mouse to try out the procedure he or she has just learned.

Assistance
There are several ways in which the trainee is helped. As well as spoken hints, there are on-screen indicators that show what needs to be done.

Public Information

Interactive multimedia software has been used in shopping malls since the early 1980s, providing customers with information about goods and services, and actually carrying out sales. Most systems run on a computer inside a kiosk and use the latest developments in multimedia to improve and increase their functions. It is now common to find kiosks that use touch screens, graphical interfaces, and video telephones, and they can be found in an increasing number of locations – not only in stores, but in museums, offices, and even aircraft.

Information at Your Fingertips

Today, retail kiosk systems are growing rapidly in number. They can be divided into two main groups: those primarily concerned with providing information, called point-of-information systems, and those involved in selling something, known as point-of-sale. Increasingly, many kiosks combine both functions. They can offer a wide range of information, record customer names and addresses for use in direct mail, and guide customers through the credit card payment process when making a purchase.

Kiosks are very well suited to selling entertainment goods such as CD-ROMs, music CDs, or videos. Many video rental stores have systems that take promotional clips from videos and let shoppers view these in the store before buying or hiring the movies to watch at home. There are similar systems to help customers choose a book or a recording of music.

Multimedia kiosks in museums can help visitors find their way around without recourse to an attendant, and they can also provide details about the museum's range of exhibitions and facilities. The illustrative sequence on this page shows some of the kiosk services provided at the Smithsonian Institution in Washington, DC.

Dinosaurs
Visitors can watch a full-motion video of museum highlights, such as the dinosaur exhibit.

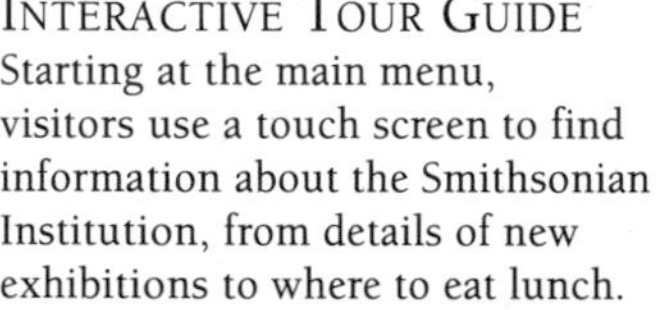

Interactive Tour Guide
Starting at the main menu, visitors use a touch screen to find information about the Smithsonian Institution, from details of new exhibitions to where to eat lunch.

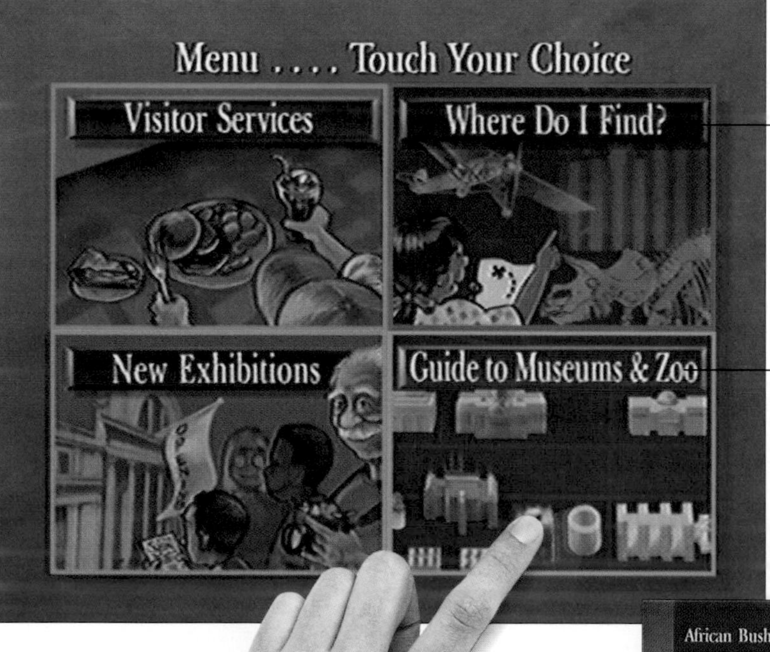

Where Do I Find?
Touching this button allows visitors to find out where a specific exhibit is located.

Building Contents
Touching one of the buildings on the museum map provides visitors with options for more information on the museum's attractions and services.

Choice of Language
The system operates in several languages.

Inside the Kiosk

Many retail kiosk systems initially used 12-inch laser discs to play information to their customers, but most quickly switched to personal computers, which use a hard disk to store the video clips, graphics, and sound needed to present multimedia information. Using a PC makes it easy to update information on a regular basis – for example, retailers can download (transfer from a larger computer) the latest prices of their goods via a satellite link or a data network to keep their kiosks completely up to date.

CD-ROM Systems

Retail outlets that sell items with a long shelf life, such as clothing, can run their point-of-sale systems from a CD-ROM rather than a hard disk. As a clothing company's product range changes, it can update its point-of-sale system by sending out CD-ROMs to outlets every six months – managers just replace the old disc with the new one.

Advanced Features

The features inside a multimedia kiosk vary enormously. Basic systems contain only a PC and a screen, whereas more advanced kiosks offer features such as printers, card readers, and even video telephones.

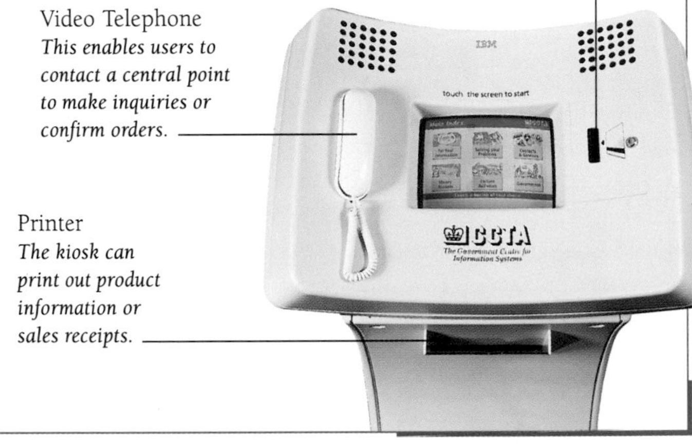

Card Reader
Point-of-sale units often have a slot or swipe reader for payment cards.

Video Telephone
This enables users to contact a central point to make inquiries or confirm orders.

Printer
The kiosk can print out product information or sales receipts.

Touch Screens

Many multimedia kiosks use a touch screen. The system software displays various graphical buttons or numbered options on screen, and users can move through the system simply by touching the relevant button or option. Touch screens are widely used because they require no computer experience or typing ability from the user.

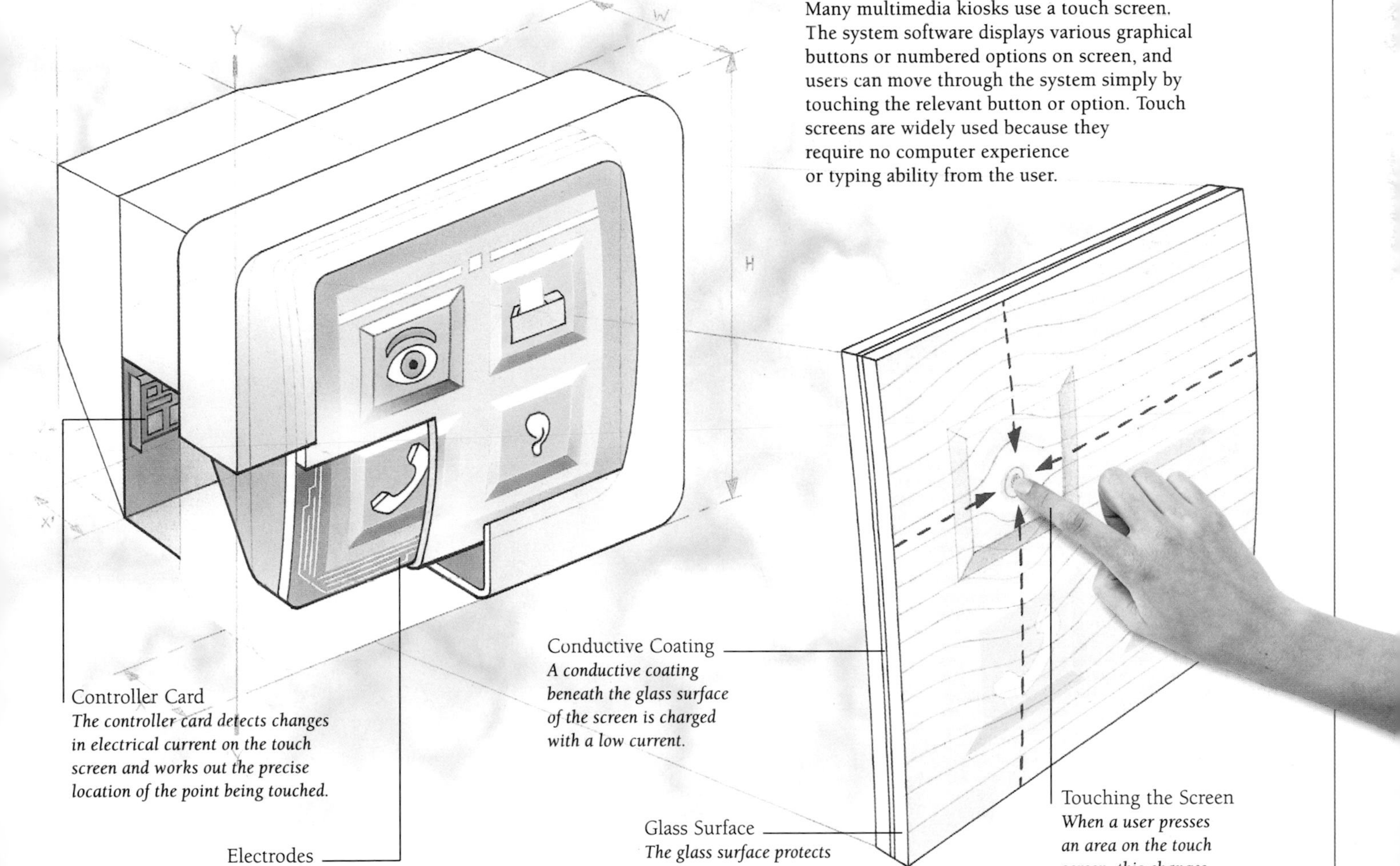

Controller Card
The controller card detects changes in electrical current on the touch screen and works out the precise location of the point being touched.

Electrodes
These supply current to the conductive coating.

Conductive Coating
A conductive coating beneath the glass surface of the screen is charged with a low current.

Glass Surface
The glass surface protects and seals the conductive layer beneath it.

Touching the Screen
When a user presses an area on the touch screen, this changes the electrical pattern.

Guiding the Customer

Retailers put a great deal of effort into designing a suitable interface for their point-of-sale kiosks – the system must be easy to use, especially for people who have never used a computer before. Many systems use a touch screen with on-screen prompts to help users navigate through the program. Most systems also have a high degree of visual sophistication. Some early kiosk screens consisted solely of text-based menus, which failed to attract many shoppers, but interfaces that show the user familiar pictures or icons to represent different choices are now becoming widespread.

Graphical Interface
An interface in a kiosk lets shoppers search for items by touching pictures or buttons on a screen.

Familiar Image
On this kiosk screen the image of a bookshelf starts the customer off on a book search.

Reaching a Wider Audience

Retailers have devised several ways of reaching as many customers as possible. Point-of-sale kiosks have been used to offer "big ticket" items – furniture, washing machines, and so on – in stores that would be too small to carry the physical stock of these goods for shoppers to examine. Such schemes have been especially useful in rural areas where customers live a long way from the nearest shopping center.

Another innovation is the use of "through the glass" technology – a touch screen or keypad is embedded in a store window, allowing customers to order goods or make inquiries outside normal business hours.

Retail kiosks have proved effective, but they reach only a limited number of people, and many companies see such stand-alone units as merely an interim measure before they can offer similar services to an even greater audience via the Internet or home-shopping channels on television.

Colorful Buttons
Large, pictorial buttons on this screen allow customers to search through video titles.

On-screen Keyboard
Users can type the title of a book or video they want by touching letters on an on-screen keyboard.

The Internet
For more on the Internet, see page 162

In-flight Movies
The aircraft has a selection of movies stored on the onboard computer. Passengers choose from a menu-driven interface.

On-screen Options
Choosing option B will display more details about the movie.

More Movies
Select this arrow to see details about the other available movies.

Services in the Sky

The British Airways in-flight entertainment system featured here is just one example of the advanced systems used by many airlines today. Services vary between carriers, but most include a range of films, games, and communications facilities.

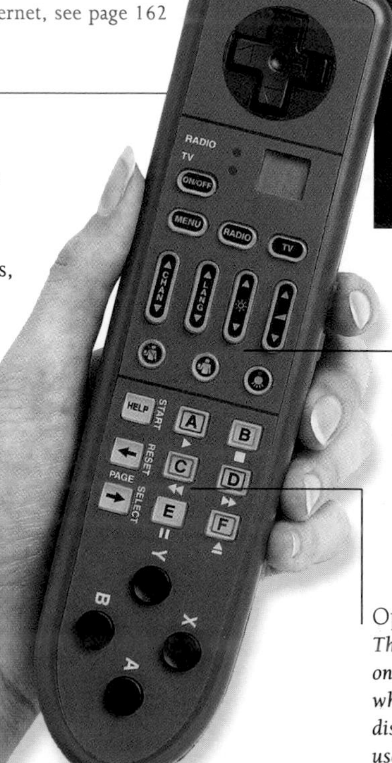

Multipurpose Controller
Passengers use a multipurpose control unit to navigate the entertainment system. The unit is housed in the armrest of the seat, but pulls out to reveal its more advanced features. This single unit is used to select movies, play games, make telephone calls, and read credit cards.

Basic Controls
While in the armrest, the unit can still be used to switch channels, regulate the volume, or turn on the overhead light.

Option Keys
These keys represent the buttons on the screen – for example, when the menu on the right is displayed, press the B button to use the in-flight shopping mall.

In-flight Multimedia

Sitting in an airline seat with nothing to do for nine hours and only the scheduled movie to watch spells boredom for many passengers. Airlines such as British Airways are using in-flight multimedia to make the journey more enjoyable. Seat-back interactive modules enable passengers to view movies on demand, play computer games, or "shop" from a selection of malls.

The modules are controlled from an onboard computer that stores details of programs for 24 film and entertainment channels. These can be viewed whenever the passenger chooses, thus suiting his or her needs rather than the flight attendants' schedule.

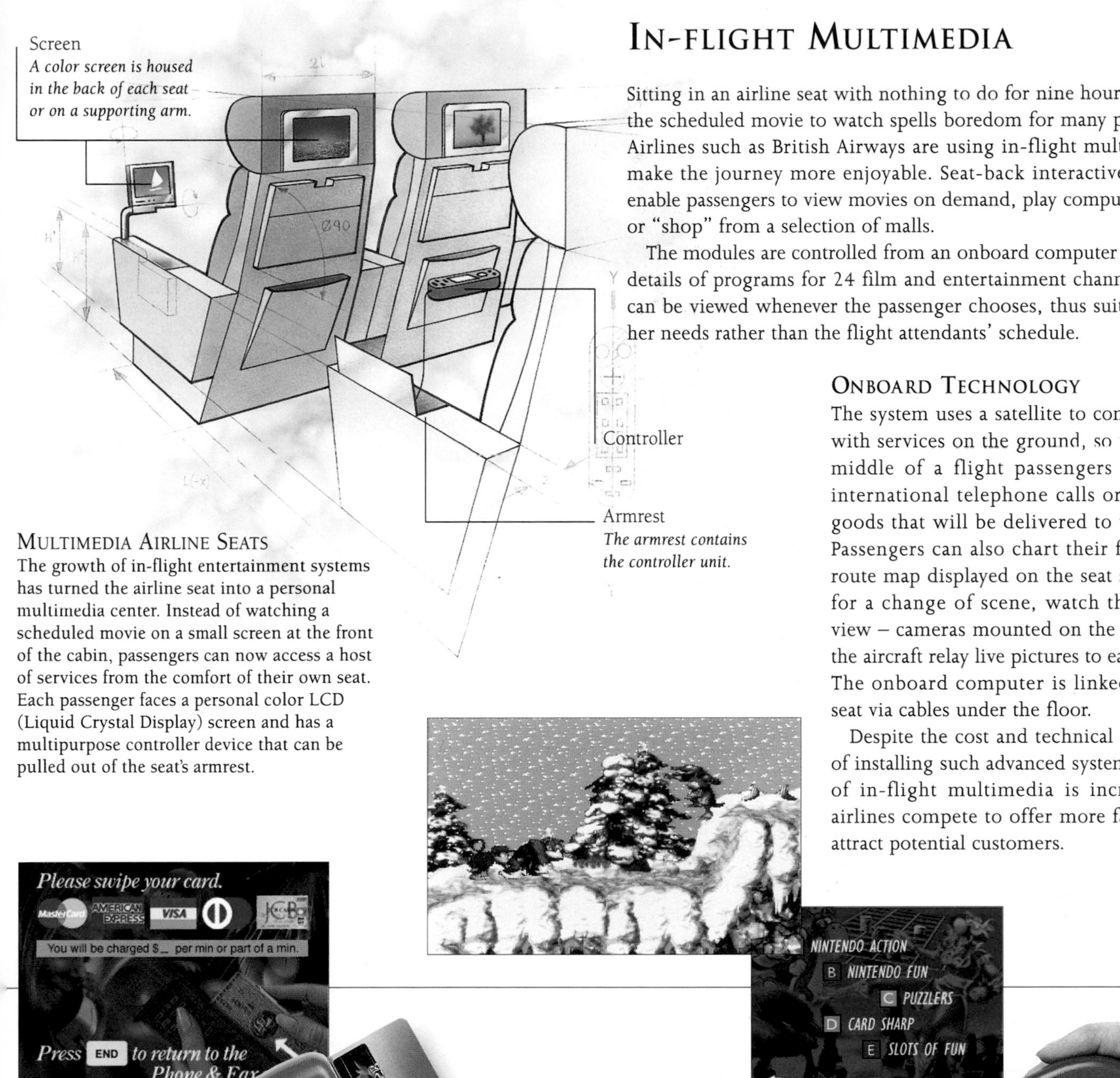

Multimedia Airline Seats

The growth of in-flight entertainment systems has turned the airline seat into a personal multimedia center. Instead of watching a scheduled movie on a small screen at the front of the cabin, passengers can now access a host of services from the comfort of their own seat. Each passenger faces a personal color LCD (Liquid Crystal Display) screen and has a multipurpose controller device that can be pulled out of the seat's armrest.

Onboard Technology

The system uses a satellite to communicate with services on the ground, so that in the middle of a flight passengers can make international telephone calls or purchase goods that will be delivered to the home. Passengers can also chart their flight on a route map displayed on the seat screen, or, for a change of scene, watch the passing view – cameras mounted on the outside of the aircraft relay live pictures to each screen. The onboard computer is linked to every seat via cables under the floor.

Despite the cost and technical challenges of installing such advanced systems, the use of in-flight multimedia is increasing as airlines compete to offer more facilities to attract potential customers.

Please swipe your card.

You will be charged $_ per min or part of a min.

Press END to return to the Phone & Fax

NINTENDO ACTION
B NINTENDO FUN
C PUZZLERS
D CARD SHARP
E SLOTS OF FUN
previous

Credit Card Swipe
The card is read by sliding it down the side of the unit.

Earpiece

Numeric Keypad

A–Z Keypad
This is used to type in names or addresses for in-flight purchases.

Mouthpiece

Game Controls

Making Calls

One side of the controller resembles a mobile telephone. To make a call, passengers first swipe their credit card, and then dial the number as normal.

Playing Games

Turn the unit over and sideways and it becomes a games controller with joypad-style buttons. A variety of electronic games is offered, from Nintendo titles to more traditional card games.

How Multimedia Computers Work

Today's multimedia computer is the product of several decades of extremely rapid advances in computer technology. This chapter looks inside a computer to show how the many components work – from mouse to monitor, from CD-ROM drive to speakers – and how they work together to bring multimedia from a compact disc to you.

INSIDE A PERSONAL COMPUTER

TO ENJOY MULTIMEDIA IT IS NOT necessary to understand how computers work – but, as with any technology, it can be fascinating to find out what is going on. Examining the components of a multimedia computer provides an insight into the computer's role both in storing the images, sounds, and words of the real world in digital format and the process of playing it back in the analog form we understand. As the world's most popular multimedia player, the IBM-compatible PC is used for illustration, but most processes also apply to other desktop computers. Information travels into and out of the computer via the keyboard, mouse, CD-ROM drive, screen, and speakers, while the processor, the "brain" of the computer, manages the overall flow of information both ways.

THE MULTIMEDIA PC

PCs consist of three main parts: an input device (such as a keyboard or mouse), an output device (such as a monitor), and the system unit, which houses the main electrical components. This cross section shows the system unit of a typical multimedia PC – that is, a PC that comes with a CD-ROM drive and sound facilities.

Expansion Slots
Expansion slots can be fitted with different expansion cards to add to a PC's capabilities.

Expansion Cards
Each expansion card consists of a fiberglass board equipped with chips and other electronic components. An expansion card is used to add certain functions to a computer – for example, a sound card dramatically improves the PC's sound capabilities.

I/O PORTS

The Input/Output ports at the back of the computer facilitate the transfer of data into and out of the computer. Keyboards, printers, and modems are all examples of I/O devices. Most expansion cards have I/O ports on the back of the board.

Joystick Port
When playing games, it is much easier to control movements with a joystick than with a keyboard or a mouse.

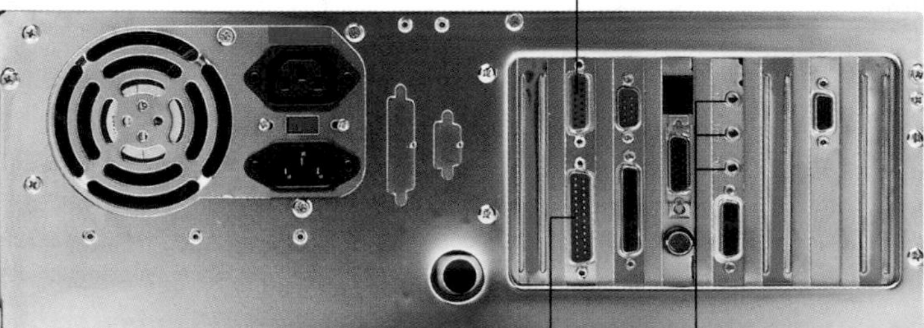

Modem Port
By plugging in a device called a modem, a computer can be linked via a telephone line to the multimedia network known as the information superhighway.

Sound Jacks
The jacks and the port on the back of the sound card are used for plugging in a microphone, speakers, or electronic instruments.

Motherboard
This is where most of the electronic units of a computer reside; they are connected by metallic tracks (called the bus) printed on the motherboard.

Bus
The bus is the network of metallic connectors that carries data, in the form of electrical pulses, from one component to another. A PC has several different types of buses.

Hard Disk Drive
Hard disks (seen above and below) are used for the permanent storage of programs and data. Their storage capacity is measured in megabytes (a megabyte is approximately a million bytes).

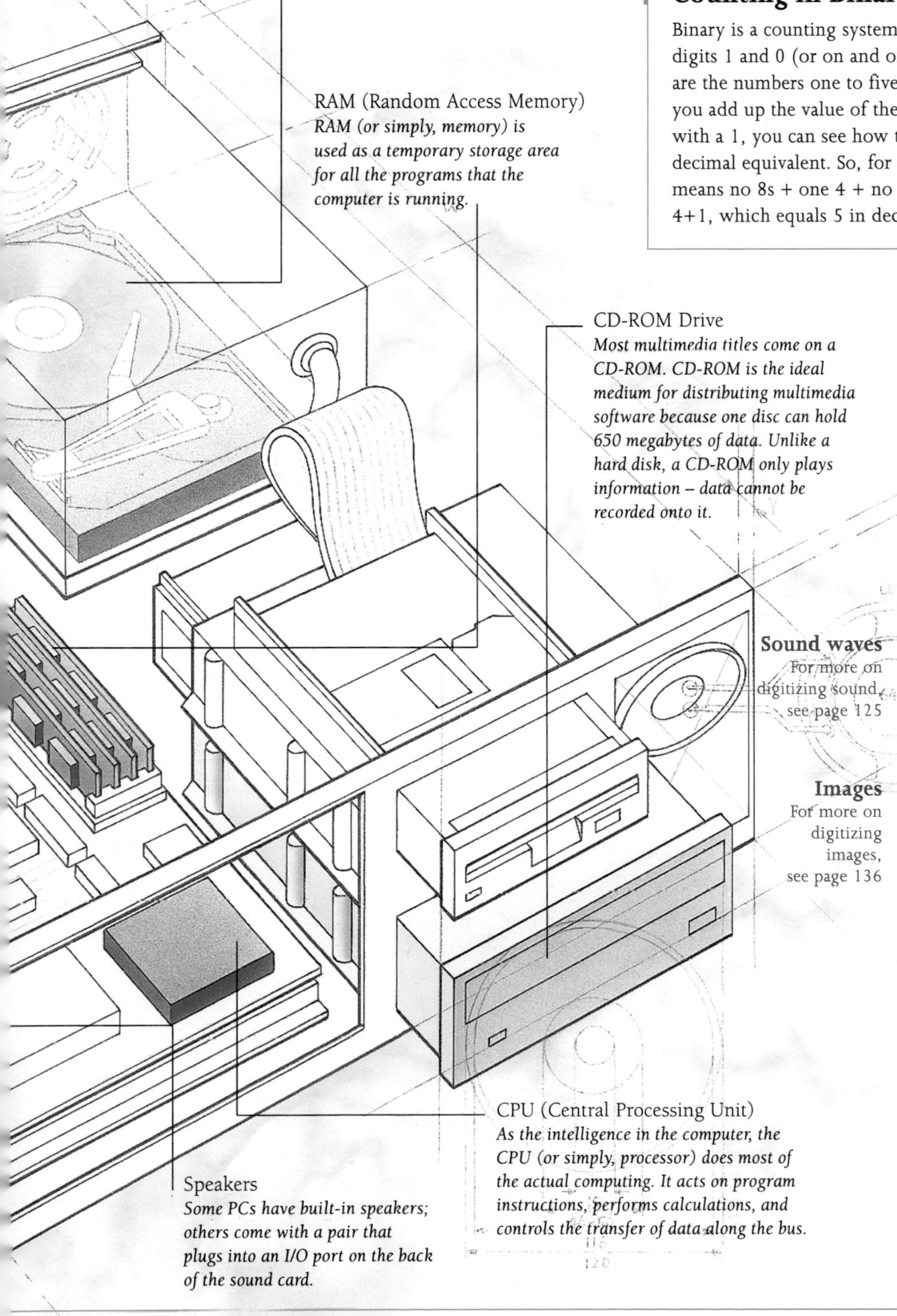

RAM (Random Access Memory)
RAM (or simply, memory) is used as a temporary storage area for all the programs that the computer is running.

CD-ROM Drive
Most multimedia titles come on a CD-ROM. CD-ROM is the ideal medium for distributing multimedia software because one disc can hold 650 megabytes of data. Unlike a hard disk, a CD-ROM only plays information – data cannot be recorded onto it.

CPU (Central Processing Unit)
As the intelligence in the computer, the CPU (or simply, processor) does most of the actual computing. It acts on program instructions, performs calculations, and controls the transfer of data along the bus.

Speakers
Some PCs have built-in speakers; others come with a pair that plugs into an I/O port on the back of the sound card.

The Binary System

Computers store and manipulate all data and information – programs, pictures, and so on – in the form of numbers. These numbers are not the same as decimal numbers; instead, the computer uses the binary system, which contains only two digits: 1 and 0 (somewhat like the dot and dash of Morse code). Each digit (1 or 0), called a bit, is represented in the computer by alternative electrical states – an electrical current (on) represents the number 1, and no current (off) stands for 0. By stringing bits together, the computer can express any number as a sequence of electrical pulses. In computers, bits are usually grouped in eights, and each group is known as a byte.

Counting in Binary

Binary is a counting system based on the two digits 1 and 0 (or on and off). On the right are the numbers one to five in binary – if you add up the value of the places marked with a 1, you can see how they add up to the decimal equivalent. So, for example, 0101 means no 8s + one 4 + no 2s + one 1, or 4+1, which equals 5 in decimal.

Binary Place 8	4	2	1	Decimal Equivalent
0	0	0	1	=1
0	0	1	0	=2
0	0	1	1	=3
0	1	0	0	=4
0	1	0	1	=5

Coding and Filing

Text is turned into binary code by assigning a specific number to each individual letter, and then representing that number in bits (for example, the capital letter A is given the number 65, and this is represented as 01000001 in binary). Additional coding is used to distinguish between letters and decimal numbers.

Sounds and pictures can be turned into numbers, and thus into binary code, using broadly similar methods. To digitize sound waves, the computer first divides them into thousands of tiny sections; then each section is measured for the strength of the signal at that point in time and the measurement is converted into a binary number. Images, too, are divided into parts – a grid of thousands of tiny colored dots – and then each part is assigned a number that corresponds to its color.

Sound waves
For more on digitizing sound, see page 125

Images
For more on digitizing images, see page 136

Whatever type of information has been digitized, it can then be stored as a block of binary code on a storage medium such as a hard disk, floppy disk, or CD-ROM. This block of code is known as a file. As well as containing the numbers that represent the actual data, each file has additional coding to signify the name of the file, what type of information the numbers represent, and how the information is organized.

THE HARD FACTS ABOUT SOFTWARE

The key to understanding how computers work is knowing the difference between hardware and software. Hardware comprises all the internal and external elements that you can see and touch; software is a set of instructions that tells the hardware what to do and how to interact with the user. Software can be divided into two main categories: operating systems and programs.

OPERATING SYSTEMS

The operating system is the computer's master control software – it manages the keyboard, screen, and disk drives, and it runs programs. When you switch on a PC, the operating system is automatically loaded into RAM (memory).

On the PC, the operating system is usually either Microsoft Windows or IBM's OS/2. Like the Macintosh operating system, these examples of the picture-based GUI (Graphical User Interface) have made PCs much simpler to use than when commands were typed onto a blank screen.

GUI
For more on the Graphical User Interface, see page 85

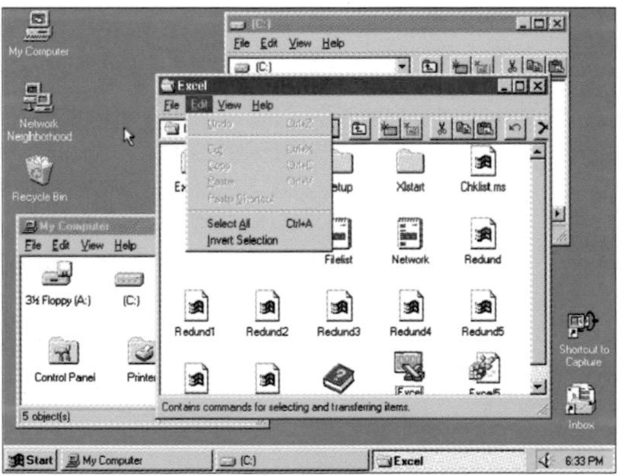

MICROSOFT WINDOWS
As the most popular operating system in the world, Windows controls over 80 percent of the world's PCs.

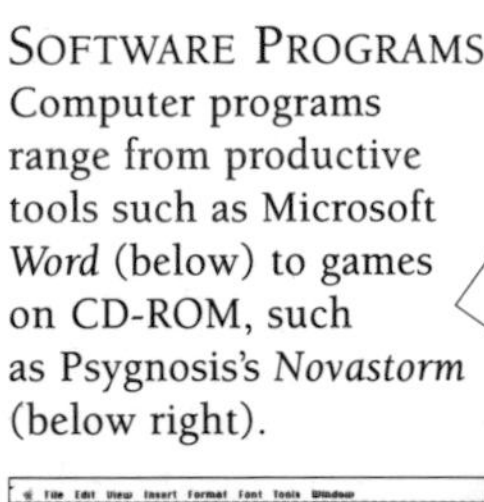

SOFTWARE PROGRAMS
Computer programs range from productive tools such as Microsoft *Word* (below) to games on CD-ROM, such as Psygnosis's *Novastorm* (below right).

PROGRAMS

Programs can be classified in several ways. Some are used as productive tools (such as word processors), and are known as applications. Others (such as multimedia titles) are made for information and entertainment.

Programs are written to work with a specific operating system; for example, a CD-ROM title written for Microsoft Windows cannot be understood by the Macintosh operating system.

Programs are stored on disk – the PC's hard disk, a floppy disk, or a CD-ROM. When you use a program, some of the program data is loaded into RAM, where it sits alongside the operating system. This gives the CPU (Central Processing Unit) easy access to the data.

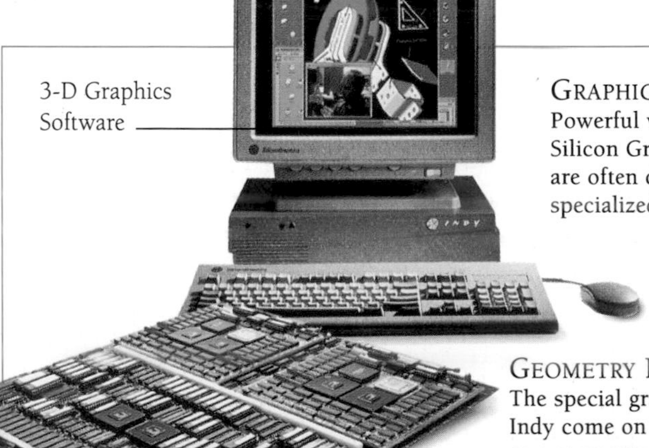

GRAPHICS COMPUTER
Powerful workstations such as this Silicon Graphics "Indy" computer are often dedicated to running specialized graphics software.

GEOMETRY ENGINE
The special graphics chips inside the Indy come on an expansion card known as a geometry engine. The card is designed to carry out the calculations that graphics software uses most often.

Workstations

Multimedia titles (especially games) often contain exquisite graphics produced with specialized 3-D graphics applications – software that only works on a powerful breed of computer known as a workstation.

Workstations were originally developed specifically for graphics applications such as CAD (Computer-Aided Design). They are far more powerful and much more expensive than PCs, and many use a notoriously unfriendly operating system called Unix. Because 3-D graphics software needs to make thousands of complex geometrical calculations, graphics workstations contain special-purpose graphics hardware – designed to speed up the math – and vast amounts of RAM.

The Processor

The CPU, usually known simply as the processor, controls the computer and takes decisions based upon the information it receives. Modern processors such as the Pentium make about 100 million decisions a second, and most of the rest of the computer is dedicated to relaying information to and from the processor.

The processor receives two types of information: instructions and data. The instructions come from programs and consist of orders such as "add these figures together." The data are the binary numbers, text, pictures, or sound; the processor interprets these and moves them about the computer.

The processor receives instructions from the program in RAM; it also uses RAM as a sort of "scratchpad" on which to perform calculations.

Brainy Chip
The processor chip is the true brain of the computer.

RAM Chips and Processor

A computer's performance is governed by the speed of its processor and the amount of RAM it has. Both can be "upgraded" – in the case of RAM, by slotting more chips in, and in the case of the processor, by replacing it with a newer, more powerful chip.

Processor
To handle the amount of information involved in playing animated sequences, video clips, and sound tracks, a multimedia computer requires a fast and powerful processor.

RAM Chips
The computer's memory, RAM, consists of rows of chips that serve as a temporary storage area for the operating system and any programs that are running.

Heat Sink
The latest processors operate at such high speeds that they can overheat. A heat sink helps to cool the processor down – some heat sinks even have built-in fans.

Upgrade Socket
Many PCs come with a processor upgrade socket on the motherboard. When a new, more powerful processor is manufactured, it can be fitted into this socket to replace the existing one.

Lever
The small lever arm makes it easy to remove the processor chip when upgrading.

Inside a Processor Chip
This magnified section of the inside of a processor chip shows the integrated circuits imprinted on its surface. The circuits carry the electrical currents that make up the on/off pulses of binary code.

More and More Bits

Like everything else in the computer, the processor deals with binary data. The instructions and data it receives are just a sequence of bits, and the number of bits it can handle at once allows its performance to be measured.

Each new generation of processors is marked by a huge leap in processing power. The 8088 in the first IBM PC was 8-bit, which meant that it could manipulate only one byte of information at a time. The next generation of processor, the 80286, was 16-bit, and the latest, the Pentium, is 64-bit. In a little more than a decade, data processing abilities have increased eightfold.

Clock Speed

Data handling is only one measure of processor performance, however. The clock speed, quoted in MHz (megahertz), units of frequency, is a measurement of how quickly the processor can act on an instruction.

If you think of one hertz as being equivalent to one clock tick, then one megahertz equals one million ticks per second. Early PCs ran at about 5 MHz – that is, they could process about five million instructions per second. An average PC these days runs at about 75 MHz.

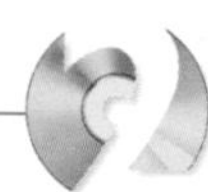

FROM MOUSE TO MONITOR

Multimedia computers receive their instructions and data from software stored on a CD-ROM. But software does not act on its own – it requires input from the user, via an input device such as a mouse or a keyboard. And when the processor has followed the software instructions and processed the multimedia data, it also needs some means of presenting the output – a monitor and speakers. Here we follow the passage of data from mouse to monitor.

MOUSE MOVES

When you use multimedia software and you want to access a point on the screen – a hotspot, for example – you move the mouse across a flat surface until the pointer is at the desired position and click the mouse button. As you move the mouse, the ball on its underside drives two rollers. Via the mouse cable, these rollers send information about the movement of the mouse to the processor, so that it always knows where to position the mouse pointer on screen.

Hotspot
For more on hotspots, see page 19

PLUG-AND-PLAY

The processor uses a part of the operating system called the mouse driver to interpret the signals from the mouse. Similarly, the keyboard, screen, sound card, and CD-ROM drive all have their own driver software.

To add a new device to a PC, the owner has to install its driver software. Before the introduction of modern operating systems, this task was often fraught with difficulty, as the settings for the new driver frequently clashed with those of an existing one.

Fortunately, the latest operating systems include "plug-and-play" capabilities. With these, the computer can install new drivers itself. Plug-and-play has made it easy for users to attach multimedia components such as sound cards and CD-ROM drives to a PC.

THE MOUSE
With its "point and click" action, the mouse is ideally suited to multimedia software. These days most CD-ROM titles require a mouse, although an alternative input device, the joystick, is often used for games.

Tracking Ball
When you move the mouse, the ball turns the two internal rollers.

Horizontal Roller
This roller picks up the side-to-side movements of the mouse.

Button
Clicking a mouse button sends a signal to the processor, which alerts the program to the action.

Vertical Roller
This roller picks up the backward and forward movements of the mouse.

Processing Circuitry
This transmits the roller movements to the computer.

The Computing Process

Computing tasks involve a complex set of operations, most of which are controlled and monitored by the processor. Here you can follow, in simplified form, the journey data takes from input to output. The following pages describe the process in more detail.

MOUSE
When you click the mouse button to initiate an action (for example, starting a video sequence), a signal is sent to the processor.

PROCESSOR
The processor sends a message to the program, indicating the area of screen where the action was performed.

PROGRAM
The processor checks through the instructions of the program stored in RAM (memory) to see what action should be taken in response. In this example it discovers that a particular video clip must be launched.

PROCESSOR
The processor sends a request for the relevant video file to the CD-ROM.

Bus Operations

The bus is the network of thin metallic tracks that transports data around the motherboard of the computer. There are a number of different buses inside a PC. For a start, three separate buses connect the processor to the rest of the computer – the data bus, the address bus, and the control bus, collectively known as the system bus.

Integrated Circuit

Data Bus
The data bus carries data between the disk drives, processor, and RAM.

Address Bus
The address bus carries information about where in RAM (memory) the data is going to or coming from.

Control Bus
The control bus is used to signal the direction of the flow of data.

The System Bus

This illustration shows the three buses that make up the system bus. In reality all bus tracks look identical – they have been colored here to highlight the difference.

The Expansion Bus

Another type of bus is the expansion bus, which connects expansion cards, such as the graphics and sound cards, to the computer's motherboard. The size of the expansion bus, known as its width, is critical to multimedia because it determines the speed at which sound and graphics are delivered. Bus width is measured in bits – the expansion bus in early PCs was 8-bit, the electronic equivalent of an eight-lane freeway. This matched the capacity of the processor.

When processor capacity increased to 16-bit, so did the data bus. To avoid making 8-bit cards redundant, the expansion bus was redesigned to take both 8- and 16-bit cards. This system is known as ISA (Industry Standard Architecture).

The Expansion Bus

The connectors of an expansion card fit into the expansion slot as shown on the right. The expansion slots are an extension of the system bus.

ISA Extension
An extension was added to make it a 16-bit slot.

Original 8-bit Expansion Slot

The Local Bus

ISA expansion slots were fine for 16-bit processors, but they became a bottleneck when 32- and 64-bit processors arrived. These processors can communicate with expansion cards at much higher speeds than the ISA bus will allow.

The solution is local bus expansion slots. These slots transfer data 32 bits at a time, and match the speed of the processor, so that the processor does not have to wait for data that has been held up by the bus. The result is that multimedia titles run much faster, with fewer pauses.

CD-ROM

When the video clip is located on the CD-ROM, its data is delivered into RAM.

Operating System

The processor follows instructions in the operating system stored in RAM to identify the data as it is delivered, separating graphics from sound. It then sends the data to the graphics and sound cards.

Graphics/Sound Card

The graphics and sound cards change the received data from digital to analog and output the result.

Screen and Speakers

The monitor displays the video clip, and the speakers play the sound.

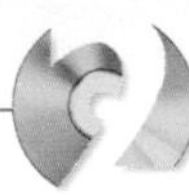

THE CD-ROM

A very simple idea led to the invention of the CD-ROM – it was to store computer data instead of sound on a CD. The disc itself consists of a wafer-thin aluminum layer sandwiched between two protective layers of plastic. During manufacture, data is stamped into the disc in the form of pits (hollow areas) and lands (flat areas), which represent the 1s and 0s of binary data. The pits and lands form a spiral running from the center of the disc to its edge.

Manufacture
For more on how CD-ROMs are made, see page 81

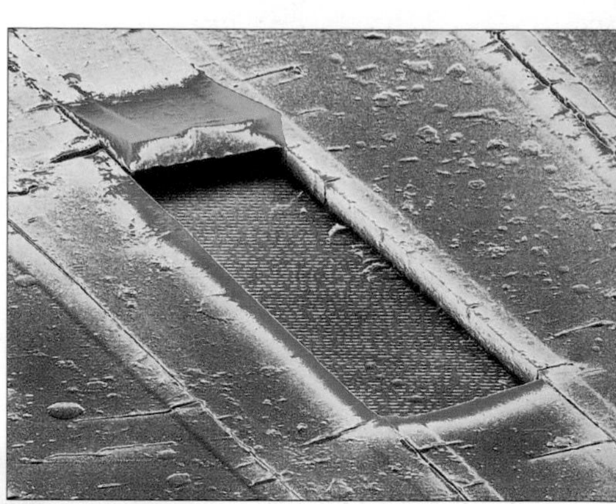

PITS AND LANDS
This magnified image shows the plastic coating of a compact disc peeled back to reveal the aluminum layer with its lands and pits.

REFLECTED LIGHT

During playback, a read head containing a laser beam is passed over the spinning CD-ROM via a system of prisms and mirrors. The beam passes through the plastic coating to the aluminum layer. Most of the beam is absorbed when it hits a pit, so that only a little light is reflected. When a land is encountered, most of the light is bounced back.

The reflected light is directed back – again, via a prism – to a light-sensitive photo diode, which translates the light patterns back into binary data.

INSIDE A CD-ROM PLAYER

CD-ROM players contain finely tuned components that direct a laser beam onto the disc and back again. All that touches the disc surface is light, so discs do not deteriorate when played.

5 Variable Rotation
The disc rotates to bring new data in front of the laser. To keep the rate at which data is accessed constant, the disc rotates more slowly when the read head is nearer the center.

6 Return Journey
The light is reflected by the surface of the disc and returns through the read head, the mirror, and the prisms. On the return journey, the prisms redirect the beam to the photo diode.

4 Read Head
The read head moves across the radius of the disc, directing the laser beam to the relevant area.

3 Mirror
The mirror redirects the incoming light to the read head.

2 Prisms
The laser beam passes through a system of prisms that refine the beam.

Speed Restrictions

While no one doubts that CD-ROM is a revolutionary technology, finding and transferring data at speed is not one of its outstanding features. Computers need to access chunks of data that are stored on various parts of a disc, and with CD-ROM it can take a long time for the laser head to move across the disc and reach the relevant data.

The amount of time it takes the laser head to locate data on the disc is known as the seek time. A typical CD-ROM drive has a seek time of about 150 milliseconds – about 20 times more than the seek time of a fast hard disk. This appears to be the physical limit for present CD-ROM technology.

Data Transfer Rates

Speed considerations don't end with seek times – the data must still be transferred from the disc to the PC's memory at an acceptable speed. This is known as the data transfer rate.

Early CD-ROM drives transferred data at 150 Kb/s (kilobytes per second). These drives are now virtually extinct, and most owners of multimedia computers have at least a double-speed drive with a data transfer rate of 300 Kb/s. Recent purchasers probably have quad-speed drives; these transfer data at a rate of 600 Kb/s.

Despite the steady increase in data transfer rates (six-speed drives are available), CD-ROM drives are still about ten times slower at transferring data than an average hard disk. The struggle to get data to the screen becomes especially apparent with video, although new video compression technologies have reduced the amount of data needed to produce good-quality, full-screen video sequences.

Video compression
For more on video compression, see page 156

Data Difficulties

Compared with hard disks, CD-ROM drives are slow at transferring data from the disc to the processor. This is especially noticeable with video, which often looks jerky, or can only be displayed in a tiny window.

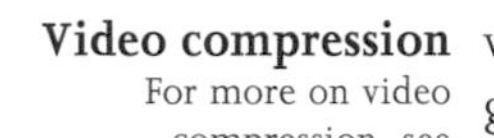

7 Photo Diode
This light-sensitive component translates the light reflected back from the disc into binary code and then passes it on to the processor.

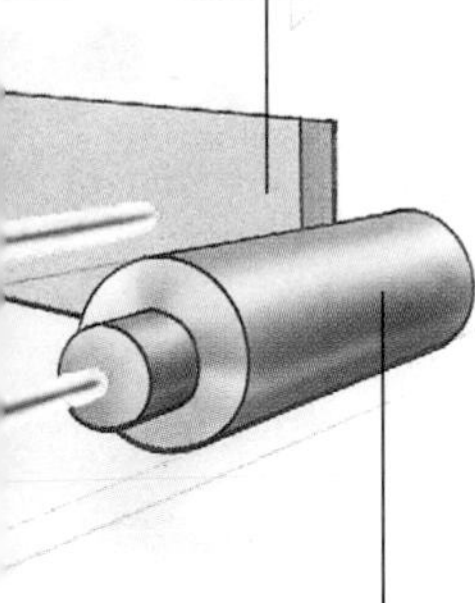

1 Laser Diode
This produces a highly accurate laser beam that can be targeted to within 1/25,000th of an inch (0.001 mm).

Stacking Them Up

This Pioneer stack system can carry up to six discs at a time, taking about five seconds to change between them.

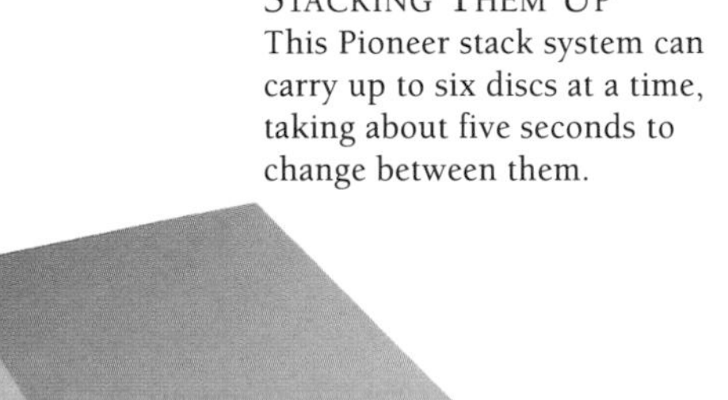

The Future Is Almost Here

Although CD-ROM drives have become much faster since they first appeared in the late 1980s, one aspect of their performance has not changed at all – the storage capacity of a CD. This remains at a stable 650 Mb (megabytes).

However, a coalition of major CD manufacturers has developed a high-density CD that can store over 9 Gb (9 gigabytes, or 9,000 Mb) on one disc. This is over 14 times the capacity of present CDs. The new technology features a dramatic increase in the number of pits and lands on the disc, coupled with an improved focusing mechanism for the laser beam. The other major advance is that both sides of the disc can be used: each double-sided disc can hold more than four hours of digital video.

Today, however, the ordinary CD-ROM is still the multimedia industry standard, and it will be some time before high-density CDs take over completely. The only other method of accessing more than the standard 650 Mb of data at once is the CD-ROM stack system. Stack systems have a multilayered caddy that takes up to six discs at a time, offering access to about 4 Gb of data.

THE MONITOR

The display area of a monitor is divided into a grid of pixels (short for picture elements). Every pixel is made up of three tiny dots of phosphor (a substance that glows when stimulated by electrons); one dot is red, one green, and one blue. By varying the brightness of each dot, electron beams within the monitor can make any pixel produce any color – and by combining patterns of pixels, on-screen graphics are made. Not all displays are equal, however. The resolution (sharpness) of the picture, measured as the number of pixels across by the number of pixels down, depends on the monitor and the graphics card that runs it. So does the number of different colors each pixel can display – the color depth – which ranges from two (black and white) to 16 million (photo-quality color).

Graphics
For more on graphics, see page 132

GRAPHICS CARD
The processor calculates what should appear on the screen – the graphics card converts it from a digital signal into an analog one for the monitor.

Graphics Controller

Video Buffer

THE GRAPHICS CARD

The CPU (processor) is constantly working out digital maps of what should appear on the screen – it delegates the task of actually displaying them to the graphics card, which has its own set of processors. The CPU sends each new map to the video buffer, an area of temporary memory on the card.

The graphics controller chip on the card reads the maps as they arrive in the buffer, and changes them into analog signals – patterns of varying voltages. These voltages power three electron beams at the back of the monitor, which give each pixel on the screen the right mix of red, green, and blue to make the required color.

INSIDE THE MONITOR
The monitor turns patterns of voltages from the graphics card into the patterns of light that make up the final image on the screen. Inside the monitor, beams of electrons are cleverly controlled to color every point on the screen.

1 Electron Beams
Three guns fire electrons at the screen. The strength of each beam is controlled by the incoming signal from the graphics card.

2 Shadow Mask
This thin sheet of metal contains tiny holes so arranged that as one beam passes through, it hits only red pixel dots at the front of the screen, the second hits only green, and the third only blue.

3 Path of Electron Beams
The beams sweep left to right across the screen, one row at a time. The entire screen is scanned at least 60 times a second.

4 Grid of Pixels
A closer look at the screen shows the gridlike pattern of pixels that makes up the picture. An average monitor "colors in" up to 750,000 pixels to draw each image on the screen.

5 Pixels in Close-up
A pixel is a group of three colored dots of phosphor, which glow when the electron beams hit them. Different colors are produced by varying the strength of each beam.

Sound System

Without a sound card, the PC has slightly less of a voice than the trashcan-sized robot R2D2 from the movie *Star Wars*. The sound card became the first essential multimedia add-on when CD-ROM drives were still an expensive luxury. Today's cards offer sophisticated, CD-quality music, speech, and sound effects.

Recording sound
For more on recording sound, see page 126

A sound card has two basic purposes. The first is recording sound – taking analog sound signals from a microphone and music from an electronic instrument, and converting them into sound files for storage on a computer disk. Second, it can take sound files from a disk or CD-ROM and play them back as analog sound through headphones, powered speakers, or even a surround-sound stereo system.

Two Machines in One

There are two types of sound files that can be stored on a disk or CD-ROM, and each one is dealt with by a different chip on the sound card. The first, a sampler chip, plays digital sound files – digitized recordings of real sound waves – by changing them into an analog signal that can be played through speakers or headphones.

Digital sound
For more on digital sound, see page 124

Also on the card is a synthesizer chip that works like the electronic synthesizers used by musicians. This chip deals with MIDI (Musical Instrument Digital Interface) files, which contain information similar to the notes in sheet music – "play B-flat using a piano voice," for example. To make MIDI music, the synthesizer chip follows the score, playing each note from a bank of over a hundred prerecorded musical instrument samples stored on the chip.

MIDI
For more on MIDI, see page 130

From CD to Speaker

To make multimedia sound, a sound card converts CD-ROM sound files (which may be digital sound or MIDI) into signals for the speakers, as shown here.

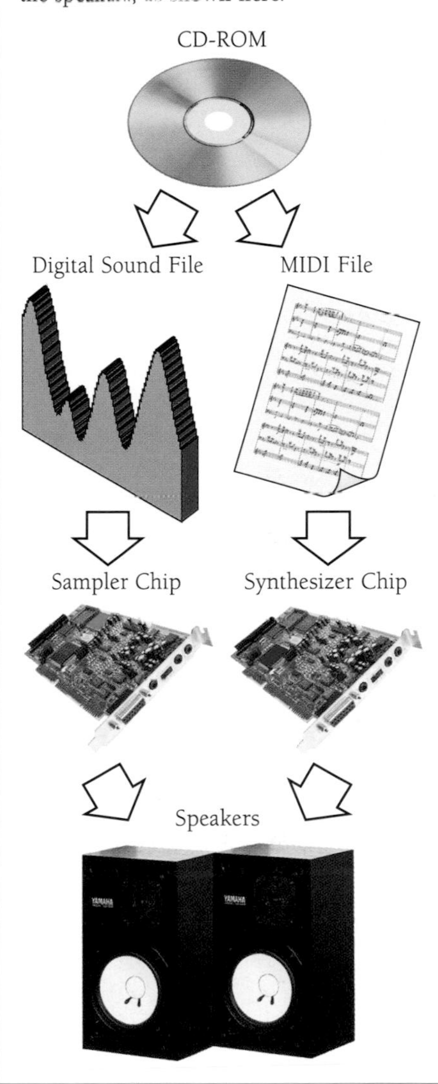

Sound Card

One of the sound card's jobs is to play back sound from a disk or a CD-ROM. It does this by converting digital and MIDI sound data into the traditional analog sound signals of headphones and speakers.

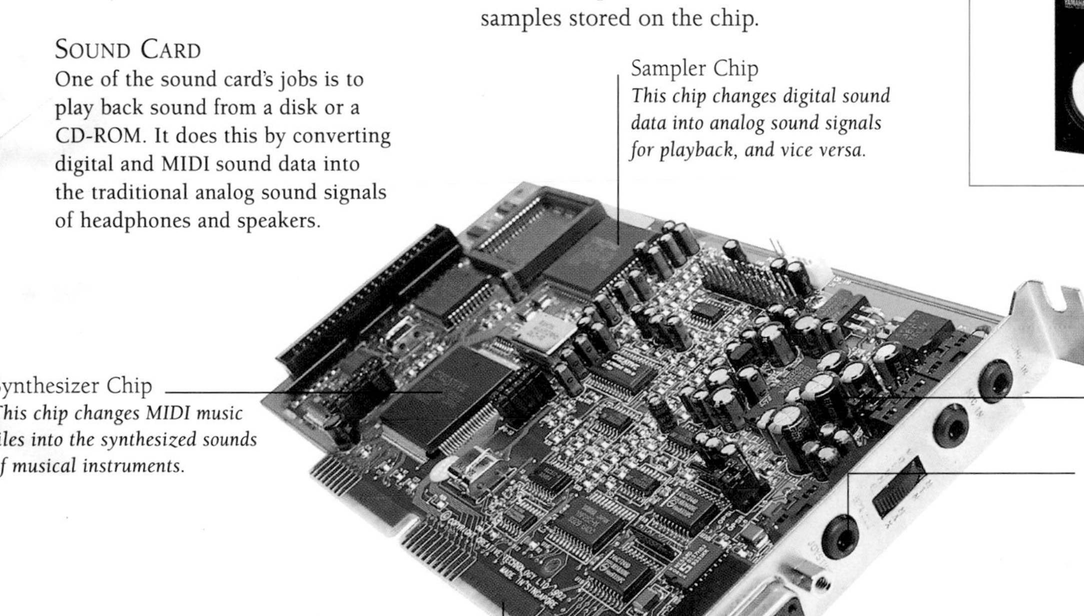

Sampler Chip
This chip changes digital sound data into analog sound signals for playback, and vice versa.

Amplifier
A small amplifier boosts the analog signal so it is loud enough for headphones or small speakers.

Synthesizer Chip
This chip changes MIDI music files into the synthesized sounds of musical instruments.

Speaker Out
The amplified signal is fed to headphones or powered speakers, which turn it into sound waves we can hear.

Expansion Slot Connectors
The sound card plugs straight into an expansion slot on the PC motherboard.

MIDI/Joystick Port
The sound card can record and output sound through an electronic keyboard or drum machine. Games players can also use the socket to connect a joystick.

Panasonic
Panasonic
VIRTUALITY

Multimedia Machines

Multimedia is made possible by the machines that play it and made better by advances in computer technology. This chapter traces the story of home multimedia players – desktop computers and home consoles – and looks at the major players of each kind. It goes on to explore the heightened realism and interactivity offered by virtual reality machines.

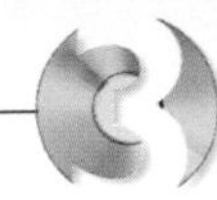

PLATFORMS AND PLAYERS

THE STORY OF MULTIMEDIA IS THE story of the machines that make multimedia happen. It was the ever-increasing pace of progress in computer technology during the last two decades coupled with the huge growth in popularity of desktop computing and digital entertainment that made multimedia possible. For software developers, keeping up with the machines is a frenetic race against time – making quality titles for today's machines before tomorrow's devices arrive. For the machine makers, the battle is to produce tomorrow's hardware today, or at least before their rivals do. And for the rest of us, the result is a vast and sometimes bewildering selection of multimedia players, or platforms, and the many different types of CDs that can be used with them.

THREE KINDS OF MACHINES

It is not surprising that, on average, one multimedia title in three is returned to the store because the software does not match the owner's hardware. There are dozens of multimedia platforms, but essentially they come in three varieties. The first of these, the desktop computers, are the direct descendants of the room-sized valve monsters of the 1940s. No longer the drab workhorses they once were, computers can offer dazzling multimedia performance.

By far the most popular multimedia machines, however, are the consoles – home entertainment systems that plug right into a television set. Because the console market is worth billions of dollars every year, the competition between manufacturers is extremely fierce. Most consoles are dedicated games machines, but some offer a range of educational and reference titles – these machines tend to be called simply "multimedia players" to avoid the games-only tag.

The third type of multimedia player is the virtual reality machine, which brings a new degree of new realism and new kinds of interaction to multimedia entertainment. The leading edge of virtual reality, however, is in its serious applications – in architecture, industry, medicine, and the armed forces – where the high-tech equipment in use points toward the future of multimedia machines.

Desktop computers
For more on desktop computers, see page 82

Consoles
For more on consoles, see page 92

Virtual reality
For more on virtual reality, see page 104

Console
Home consoles play CD-based multimedia on a television set.

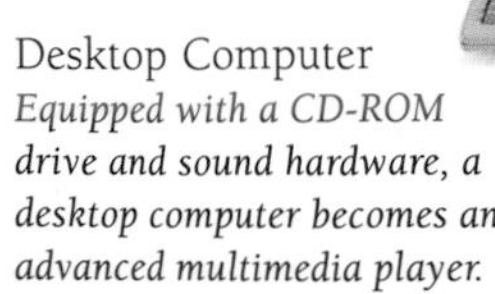

Desktop Computer
Equipped with a CD-ROM drive and sound hardware, a desktop computer becomes an advanced multimedia player.

Virtual Reality Machine
The expensive machines of the digital entertainment industry, such as this virtual reality machine, offer a new type of multimedia experience.

CD Formats

While the sophisticated machines of the amusement arcades have their multimedia software built in, multimedia for consoles and computers comes on compact discs. Multimedia CDs are physically the same as audio CDs, but the information they carry is different. With one exception, all multimedia players use CD-ROM (Compact Disc Read-Only Memory). The odd one out is the CD-i player, which has its own disc format – CD-interactive. The others might as well have their own formats, however, because although a CD-ROM drive can read any CD-ROM, each player uses different computer software.

CD-ROM drive
For more on CD-ROM drives, see page 74

AUDIO CD
The original compact disc was invented to hold over 75 minutes of digital music. Most multimedia players can play audio CDs.

PHOTO CD
The Photo CD is a format designed by Kodak to hold high-quality photographic images only. Few players can use Photo CDs.

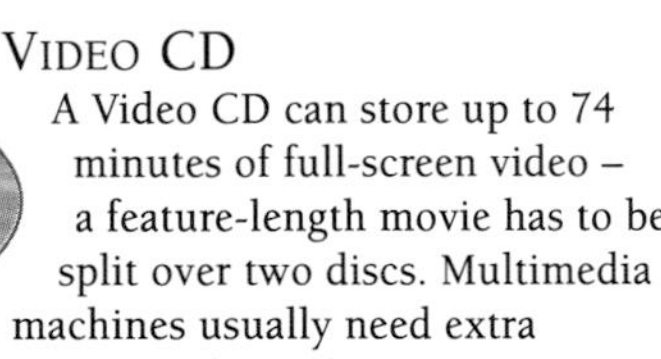

VIDEO CD
A Video CD can store up to 74 minutes of full-screen video – a feature-length movie has to be split over two discs. Multimedia machines usually need extra hardware to play Video CDs.

CD PLUS
CD Plus (also known as CD+Graphics, or CD+G) is mostly a music CD with a small amount of multimedia added – usually lyrics and band photos. A hi-fi will play it as a normal music CD, but a compatible multimedia player can show the graphics as the music plays.

CD-ROM AND CD-I
Both the CD-ROM and Philips' own-brand multimedia disc the CD-i can store sound, text, still and moving pictures, and computer software.

Cross-platform Multimedia

Some types of CDs can be used on a range of machines, but they do not offer full multimedia. Besides the original audio CD there are two other single-medium formats – Photo CD and Video CD. There is also a hybrid format – CD Plus – which is a cross between a music CD and a CD-ROM.

Meanwhile, the race is on to reengineer the compact disc from scratch so it can hold more information. These high-density CDs will eventually make today's CD and its many formats obsolete and will usher in new formats of their own.

High-density CDs
For more on high-density CDs, see page 75

How a CD Is Made

Every type of CD is made in the same way. First, the digital data is fed to a laser, which burns the data into the photographic coating of a spinning glass disc. Next, the glass master is dipped in acid to etch the data in, and then a metal imprint is made. On the production line, the imprint is used to stamp heated plastic blanks. The pressed discs are coated with a layer of reflective aluminum, which takes the shape of the stamped data. Then each disc is given a protective lacquer coating to make the final CD.

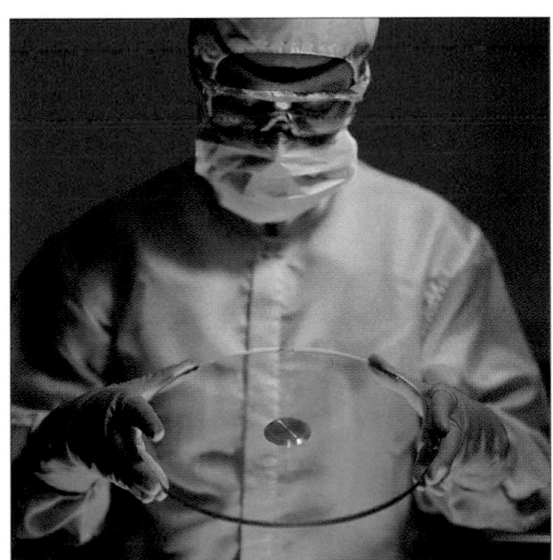

CHECKING THE GLASS MASTER
Because one speck of dust can ruin a CD, the master disc is handled in conditions that are hundreds of times cleaner than in an operating room.

THE FUTURE OF THE COMPACT DISC
Several companies are developing high-density CDs that can store over 14 times as much as today's compact discs.

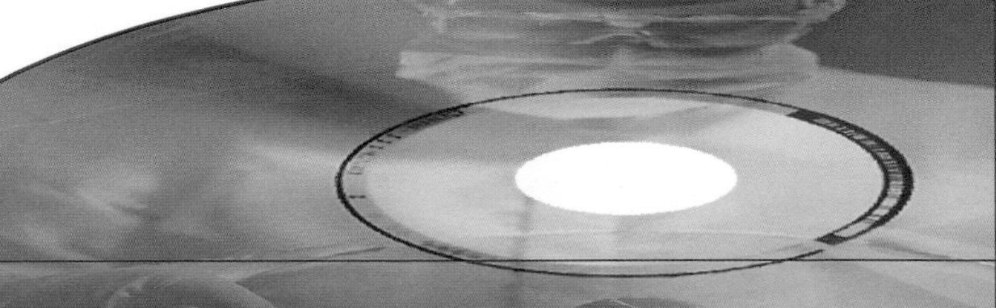

THE COMPUTER STORY

THE EARLIEST PROGRAMMABLE computer was conceived by Charles Babbage, an English mathematician (1792–1871). Babbage hit on the idea while building a mechanical calculating machine called the Difference Engine (inset). As this was 1823, the technology of the time did not allow his plans for a computer to bear fruit, but the ideas behind it – a device that would perform a variety of calculations according to a program that was input using punch cards – embodied many of the principles later used in the design of modern computers.

EARLY HISTORY

It was not until the invention of the vacuum tube in 1904 that the elements for building an electronic computer became available.

The vacuum tube, made of glass, encases a filament that produces electrons (subatomic particles that carry electricity) when heated. Depending on its construction, a vacuum tube can act as an amplifier, a signal detector, or a simple on/off switch. In early computers vacuum tubes were used mostly as amplifiers, but by about 1940 their function as on/off switches was used to represent binary code, with off standing for 0 and on standing for 1. Data was input via punch cards, and the various parts of the system had to be connected manually by cable, one at a time, as they were required.

Programming them was excruciatingly slow – a program that took five minutes to run could take several days to set up.

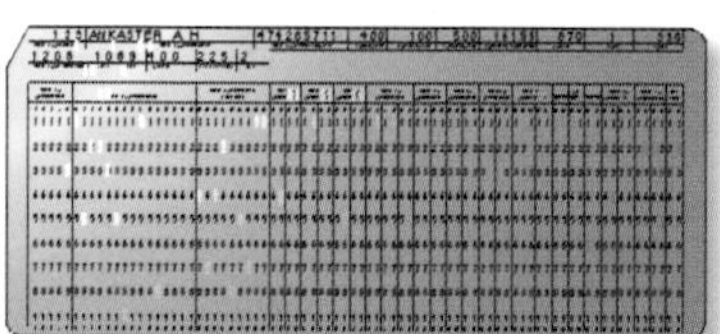

PUNCH CARDS
Data was fed into early vacuum tube computers via sheets of cardboard punched with holes.

Binary code
For more on binary code, see page 69

VACUUM TUBES TO TRANSISTORS

These early computers were used primarily by the military. World War II caused a spurt of innovation, and when the war ended, government departments began finding additional uses for the computer.

Vacuum-tube computers had many drawbacks, however. They were large, because vacuum tubes are bulky glass devices. They were unreliable, because the heating filaments could "blow," and the filaments also made the computers very hot. They were also limited in processing power, because the number of tubes that could reliably be used together was small.

These problems were solved in 1947, when Bell Telephone Laboratories in the United States invented the transistor. Transistors do the same things as vacuum tubes, but they use a small lump of a semiconducting material such as silicon to act as an on/off switch.

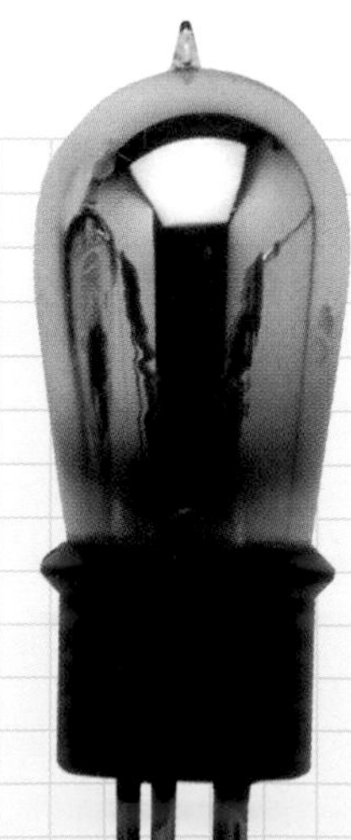

1940s

VACUUM TUBES
Vacuum tubes were the first electronic components. They were used initially in radios to amplify the received signal, but by the early 1940s their ability to transfer or block electric current was being exploited to represent binary code in computers.

1946

ENIAC COMPUTER
The ENIAC (Electronic Numerical Integrator and Computer) was a war baby, created to solve problems with ballistics during World War II. It was really a giant calculator, since it could not store programs or data. Although it was finished too late to help with the war effort, the 30-ton machine remained in use by the US army for many years.

1950s

TRANSISTORS
When vacuum tubes in computers were replaced by transistors in the early 1950s, computers became smaller and cheaper. A transistor consists of a pinhead-sized piece of semiconducting material enclosed in a metal case about half an inch (12 mm) long.

Mainframe Computers

With small, reliable, cool-running transistors replacing vacuum tubes, computers became smaller, more powerful, and much cheaper. The new machines (known as mainframe computers) found their niche in large corporations such as banks, where their processing power – roughly equivalent to that of an average modern PC – was shared by many users at the same time.

By today's standards, mainframes were huge, sometimes filling several rooms. Programs were usually input using punch cards, and data was stored on reels of magnetic tape (the equivalent of today's hard disk drives).

By the start of the 1960s the familiar names of the mainframe computer world – such as IBM (International Business Machines) and Sperry Univac – controlled the computer market worldwide.

Magnetic Tape
Transistor computers used plastic tape coated with metal to store data in the form of magnetic fields.

Down to Chip Level

In 1959, an American firm named Texas Instruments showed that it was possible to etch multiple transistors on one piece of silicon using photographic techniques. The transistors could then be connected by metal tracks etched into the silicon. This arrangement became known as an integrated circuit, or silicon chip, and from this moment on technology moved inexorably toward cramming the maximum number of transistors into the minimum area of silicon.

In 1971, an integrated circuit manufacturer named Intel was asked to supply all the main components of a computer on one integrated circuit for a new electronic calculator being designed by a Japanese company. The result, the 4004 chip, was billed by Intel as a "computer on a chip." It was about the size of a baby's fingernail.

The 4004 was the world's first microprocessor. Its invention set the stage for the arrival of the microcomputer – which, after all, is essentially a calculator with improved processing power and a few extra parts.

Microprocessor
For more on processors, see page 71

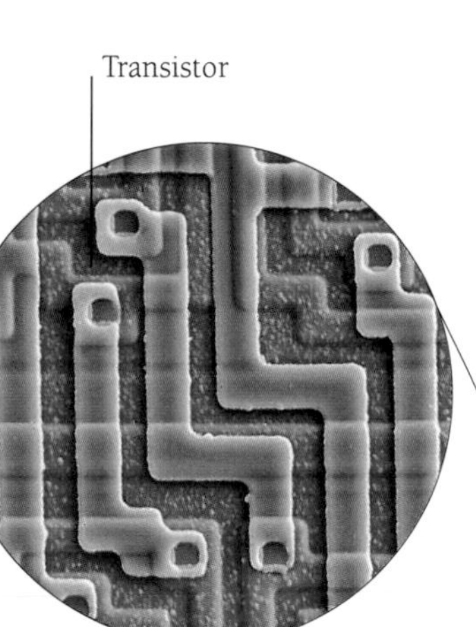

The Silicon Chip
The chips you see inside a computer are built up in layers; each layer is drawn onto a sheet of transparent film that is miniaturized before its patterns are photographically etched onto a thin slice of silicon.

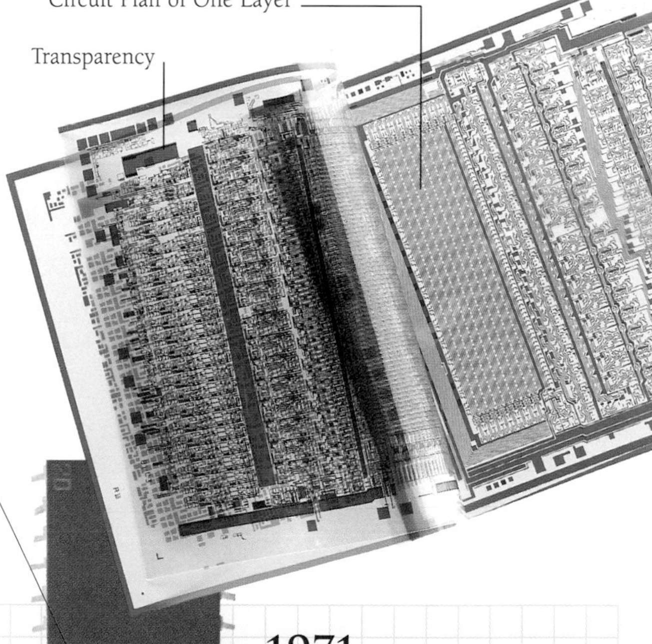

1960s

Mainframes
During the 1960s, mainframe computers were common in the scientific and business communities. Companies such as IBM, the best-known supplier of mainframes (such as that shown here, belonging to the System/360 series), introduced the concept of compatibility – all the members of this series could run the same software programs.

1971

Microprocessors
The personal computer revolution began with the invention of an integrated circuit known as a microprocessor. This "computer on a chip" is encased in a ceramic or plastic capsule for protection. A set of metal pins sticking out of the capsule connects the chip to the rest of the computer.

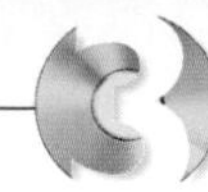

Intel's 8-bit Chip Family

Intel's 4004 processor was four bits wide – that is, it processed data four binary digits at a time. Intel soon improved the chip design to work with eight bits at a time; the result was the 8080 processor.

4-bit chip
For more on processor widths, see page 71

With the 8080 processor, all you needed to build a personal computer was some RAM (memory) and a way to get information into and out of the system. In January 1975, the American magazine *Popular Electronics* ran a feature on the "World's First Microcomputer Kit." The subject of the article, the Altair, was an instant hit with electronic engineers and programmers. All over the United States groups of enthusiasts met to build personal computers and exchange notes on circuitry and machine code.

RAM
For more on RAM, see page 71

These first personal computers would be unrecognizable to anyone using a PC or Macintosh today. The only storage media were paper tape or audiocassettes, and they used adapted electronic typewriters as their input and output device. It was a world of kits, where you had to solder the various parts together, build your own casing, and then struggle to make the limited machine do anything useful at all. Computing was confined strictly to enthusiasts.

Jobs, Wozniak, and Apple
In one year, Apple's founders went from the wooden-cased Apple I to the hugely successful Apple II.

Apple Hits the Market

Three companies changed all this, introducing personal computing to a much wider public. One was Commodore, which built a complete system with keyboard, screen, and cassette storage, called the Pet. Another was Tandy Radio Shack, with the TRS-80. But the most influential was Apple Computer.

Apple Computer was founded by two members of the California-based "Homebrew Computer Club," Steve Jobs and Steve Wozniak. Wozniak was the hardware engineer, Jobs the marketing man whose passionate vision of putting computers into the hands of ordinary people secured the necessary capital to fund Apple.

Apple II

By late 1976, the Apple I – nothing more than a circuit board and optional keyboard – was selling in several American stores. But it was the Apple II, introduced in 1977, that made the company its first million dollars. This was the first personal computer made for the mass market, a machine that required no knowledge of electronics or programming.

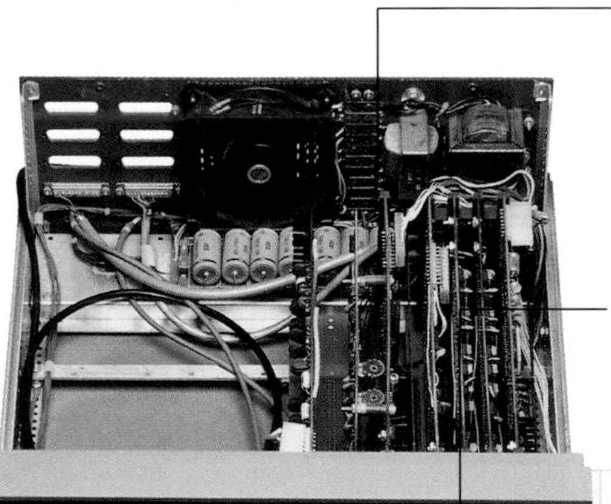

Limited Memory
The system unit offered a maximum 64 Kb of memory; today's average PC offers more than 100 times that amount.

Switchboard
Toggle switches on the front of the panel were used to program the machine.

Set in Wood
Keyboards of the time came without a case; this one has been enclosed in wood to protect it.

1975

MITS Altair 8800
The Altair, built around Intel's 8080 processor chip, usually came in kit form. The floppy disk drive shown here was added later; originally, data was stored on audiocassettes.

1977

Apple II
The Apple II came fully assembled and offered a built-in keyboard, sound, color graphics, and optional floppy disk drive. With a price tag of $1,298, it was the most expensive of the home computers, but this didn't stop Apple Computer from securing 60 percent of the education market in the United States by the end of the 1970s.

Software Development

With the success of Apple and the other all-in-one systems, the computer market expanded rapidly. Users were soon able to buy software packages off the shelf rather than writing their own, and could choose from a selection of primitive word processors, educational programs, and games.

The hardware and software market thrived. Personal computers had arrived – although initially they were still the province of home enthusiasts and the education market.

CP/M System

PCs arrived in the business market because of an operating system called CP/M (Control Program for Microprocessors). Most computers of 1980 vintage were operated by CP/M (Apples were a notable exception), so it became economic for software firms to write complex business applications for this installed base of CP/M machines. Despite not running CP/M, the Apple II still enjoyed widespread success in the business market, thanks to a program called *VisiCalc*, the world's first spreadsheet package (designed to help accountants process numbers).

Operating systems
For more on operating systems, see page 70

Xerox PARC

During the 1970s, personal computing history was also being made in the hills south of Cupertino, California. This was the home of Xerox Corporation's advanced research arm, PARC (the Palo Alto Research Center).

PARC researchers had been given a free hand to look at the future of office automation. Over the decade, Xerox spent more than $100 million on PARC, where many of today's computing standards originated – yet they never capitalized on their ideas by incorporating them into a cheap, marketable product.

Icons
By using graphic representations of commands, PARC aimed to make computing easy for beginners. A mailbox, for example, was used to send messages to other computers.

Windows
Multiple documents could be opened via a series of partitioned areas known as windows.

Graphics
PARC's adoption of a technology known as bitmapping enabled the screen to display very precise images.

Picturing the Future

The most significant of PARC's inventions was the GUI (pronounced "gooey"), which is an acronym for Graphical User Interface.

In a GUI system, a mouse or joystick is used to control small graphical images of objects on the screen. The PARC GUI used a "desktop metaphor," putting icons (small pictures) of familiar objects such as folders on the screen. Instead of typing in commands, the user selected an icon with the mouse; this called up a menu from which an option could be chosen.

PARC's influence on modern computing can be seen in the operating systems used by both PCs and the Macintosh.

Xerox PARC's GUI
It was the PARC team that invented the Graphical User Interface – using graphics and a mouse to simplify computing – something most computer users now take for granted.

1979

Popular Software
By the late 1970s, the floppy disk (a flexible, magnetic disk in a protective case) had become the common way to store data. Off-the-shelf software programs such as *WordStar* were an instant hit in the business community.

1980

Business PCs
By 1980, the typical business computer ran on an 8-bit processor chip. Most used the CP/M operating system and offered 64 Kb (kilobytes) of RAM, twin floppy disk drives, and a text-only green screen. Unlike Apple's operating system, CP/M could not cope with graphics in any form.

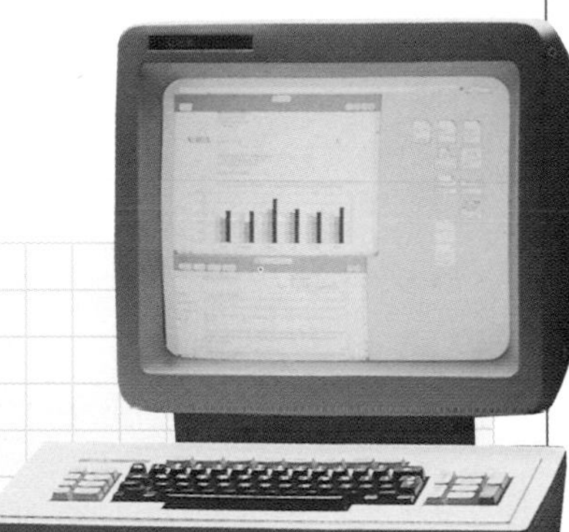

1981

Xerox Star
Despite inventing many of the technologies now standard in desktop computing, Xerox's research center was slow to market its inventions. The Xerox Star was released in 1981 – many years after the invention of the GUI. With a price tag of $16,000, the Star failed to find many buyers.

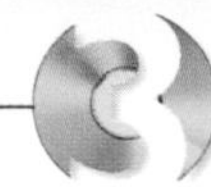

The IBM PC

By 1980, there were over 200 brands of desktop computers in the United States alone. Wary of losing its position in the business market, mainframe manufacturer IBM began designing a PC.

The IBM personal computer was launched in 1981, less than a year after its inception. Built around Intel's new 8088 processor, the PC was twice as fast as its rivals. It also offered expansion slots for the addition of devices such as hard disks and extra memory.

Expansion slots
For more on expansion slots, see page 73

Microsoft's Big Break

The new processor could not run the standard CP/M as its operating system, so IBM asked a Seattle-based software house, Microsoft, to make a new CP/M-type program for the PC. Microsoft named the new operating system MS-DOS (for Microsoft Disk Operating System). For a number of years, MS-DOS was the dominant PC operating system, and its position has only recently been usurped by Windows (a more recent Microsoft system).

Empire Builder
Microsoft cofounder Bill Gates was a billionaire by the age of 30, thanks to a contract to supply the IBM PC's operating system.

Although MS-DOS was similar to CP/M, it could not run CP/M software, so few applications were available for the IBM PC at its launch. In theory, this should have ensured the machine's failure; in practice, it was a huge success. Corporate America saw the IBM logo as a guarantee of quality and the PC (with MS-DOS) was soon setting the standards in personal computing.

MS-DOS
MS-DOS was controlled by typing in cryptic commands at the keyboard – this did nothing to endear it to beginners.

The Apple Macintosh

Anxious to keep the IBM PC at bay, Apple's next project found inspiration in the designs developed at Xerox PARC. Steve Jobs had visited the research center in 1979, returning to Apple with a head full of ideas (and a handful of Xerox employees).

Putting PARC's theories into practice would require a fast processor, and Apple's eye fell on the Motorola 68000. This chip processed data more efficiently than the Intel 8088 chip found inside the IBM PC, and it formed the basis of two new Apple machines, the Lisa and the Macintosh.

The Lisa arrived on the market in 1983, introducing the icons, menus, and mouse of Xerox PARC's GUI technology to the mass market – to no avail. The job of displaying graphics on screen made the Lisa much slower than the PC, yet at $10,000 it cost almost twice as much. Computer buyers remained indifferent to its charms.

The Macintosh was launched one year later. Despite an enthusiastic reception from the computer press, it seemed destined to follow the Lisa into obscurity, when a couple of factors conspired to keep it alive. The first was the launch of Microsoft *Excel* for the Macintosh, which rapidly became the most popular spreadsheet program of the time. The other factor was the release of a number of "desktop publishing" applications, which turned the Macintosh into a one-stop graphics and printing shop.

Monochrome Monitor
The IBM PC displayed green text on a black background, but a color graphics card could be slotted into an expansion slot to give extra colors.

Speaker
The PC offered a built-in loudspeaker that could do little more than bleep.

Floppy Disk Drives
Each of the two floppy disk drives could accommodate 160 Kb (kilobytes) of data.

1981

Original IBM PC

IBM launched two versions of its PC. The basic model came without a monitor and required a cassette player for data storage. The better model cost just over $4,300 and included a monitor, keyboard, and twin floppy disk drives.

Microsoft *Excel*
This spreadsheet program was hugely popular. Many people bought the Macintosh just for this program.

1984

First Apple Macintosh

The Macintosh was launched with a single floppy disk drive, tiny built-in monochrome monitor, and no expansion slots. Compared to the IBM PC it was less powerful but easier to use because of its GUI. Software developers used the GUI to dramatic effect, and when Aldus Corporation created *PageMaker* (a graphic design program for laying out pages of magazines and books), the Macintosh found a role that no other computer could play.

Multimedia Moves In

Throughout the 1980s, personal computers grew and developed. IBM's PC was cloned by hundreds of manufacturers, and add-on hardware such as sound cards began appearing, extending the PC's capabilities. The Macintosh was redesigned to accommodate color graphics. A new system of storing digital data – the compact disc – arrived. And every few years, a new generation of microprocessor chips came along that doubled computing power.

When Intel introduced the 80386 chip in 1985, PCs finally received the power required to shift large amounts of sound and graphics around. Still, it was only in 1990 that multimedia software for the PC really took off, with the release of version 3.0 of Microsoft's Windows operating system.

This version of Windows introduced a standard method by which programs could communicate with multimedia hardware such as sound cards. Software manufacturers could now be assured that their products would work on any PC running Windows. As a result, the market in multimedia software took a giant leap forward.

Sound cards
For more on sound cards, see page 77

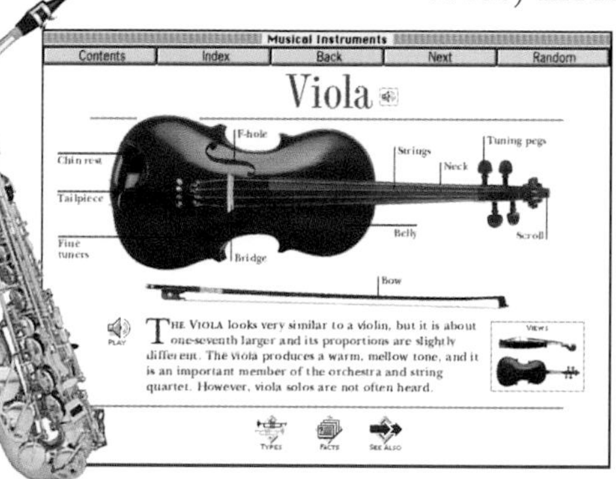

Multimedia Titles
CD-ROM-based software titles for the home, such as Microsoft's *Musical Instruments*, first appeared in the early nineties.

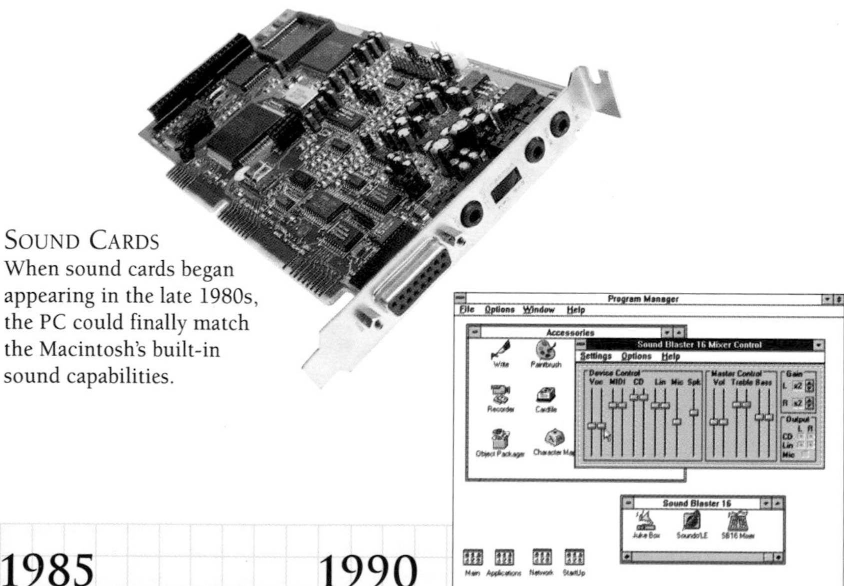

Sound Cards
When sound cards began appearing in the late 1980s, the PC could finally match the Macintosh's built-in sound capabilities.

Processing Advances

As software grows more sophisticated, processor technology is evolving to meet its demands.

PCs and Macs have traditionally been built around a family of processors made by a specific chip designer – Intel's 80... line for the PC (such as the 80386 and 80486) and Motorola's 68000 series for the Mac.

While they have different capabilities, both chip families are based on a technology known as CISC (pronounced "sisk"). CISC stands for Complex Instruction Set Computing, and it means exactly that – CISC processors are good at handling long, complex commands, and they can do so in large numbers. The drawback is that they do so at a leisurely pace.

RISC versus CISC

Recently, a new type of processor has arrived in the desktop computing world. Developed jointly by Apple, IBM, and Motorola, and known as the PowerPC chip, it is based on a processor technology known as RISC (Reduced Instruction Set Computing). RISC processors can handle short, simple sets of commands very quickly. They are also substantially cheaper to manufacture than CISC chips.

The first personal computers to use a PowerPC processor were Apple's Power Macintosh machines launched in 1994. Intel, meanwhile, has developed a chip that combines CISC and RISC technologies; this chip appears in the latest generation of PCs.

1985

CD-ROM
At the time of its arrival, a CD-ROM disc could hold about 20 times more data than the average hard disk.

1990

Windows 3.0
Version 3.0 of Microsoft's operating system was the first truly effective version of the Windows GUI; PCs were now user-friendly. By introducing special support for multimedia hardware such as sound cards and CD-ROM drives, Windows 3.0 also laid the foundation for the development of multimedia software.

1994

RISC Technology
Always eager to improve processor performance, manufacturers began moving toward using RISC processors in their machines. Apple's PowerPC range is RISC-based, and Intel's latest processors incorporate elements of RISC technology.

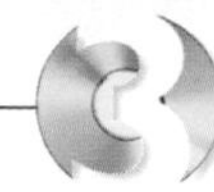

The IBM-Compatible

IBM launched its first desktop computer in 1981, adopting the already widely used term PC (personal computer) as the machine's brand name. Most IBM PCs were sold with Microsoft's MS-DOS operating system, and software companies began adapting their existing programs to work with IBM's computer and MS-DOS. Soon a massive selection of PC programs was available, which further increased the demand for IBM PCs.

The PC Clones

In 1981, it was common for one computer manufacturer to copy another's design. As most of the components used in IBM's PC were from independent producers, cloning the system looked easy. In addition, Microsoft's MS-DOS operating system was available to any computer manufacturer for a fee, and any machine that used MS-DOS as an operating system could in theory make use of all the software that had been written for the PC.

One essential part of the PC could not be bought, however: the BIOS (Basic Input/Output System). The BIOS, which is usually permanently encoded into a chip in the machine, is the instruction code that tells a computer how to perform basic functions such as loading the operating system from the hard disk into memory. Although IBM had published the BIOS code, the company had taken great care to retain the copyright.

Compatible Rivals

Undaunted, a new computer company called Compaq hit upon a strategy that would get around the copyright problem: reverse engineering. They hired programmers who had no knowledge of the PC's BIOS code to study its function and then – without ever looking at IBM's published code – to write new code that would imitate it exactly. By 1983, they had a new, legal BIOS code. The PC was joined on store shelves by the "IBM-compatible" Compaq Portable Computer; and dozens more PC clones followed.

At first commercial users saw the IBM brand as their only guarantee of quality, but before long they started buying the cheaper clones in great numbers. Over the next few years, IBM lost control of the PC market – most PCs sold today are clones.

The PC
Shortly after IBM introduced its personal computer, other manufacturers began cloning the machine. Today, a PC is any computer that can run the same programs as an IBM PC.

Colorful Display
Early machines were monochrome, although an optional graphics expansion card added pink, turquoise, and brown to the black-and-white display. These days, PCs can display millions of colors.

Mouse
Initially, PCs were operated by typing in commands from the keyboard, but the mouse is now an essential part of the machine.

CD-ROM Drive
Today, more than half of all PCs sold include a CD-ROM drive.

Sound
Until the late 1980s, the PC could only bleep through its single speaker. Today, however, multimedia-ready PCs include stereo sound capabilities.

Compaq Clone
The early clone makers were highly successful. Compaq, which built the first PC clone in a portable case, was the most successful American start-up of all time, with sales of over $110 million in its first year.

The Multimedia PC

The PC soon came to dominate the world of business computing, with two companies leading its evolution. The first of these was Intel, the chip makers, who launched a new processor on average every two years – the 286, 386, 486, and Pentium series – each of which is approximately twice as powerful as the one before. The other company was Microsoft, whose MS-DOS operating system was the one thing every PC had in common.

The PC became a multimedia machine in the late 1980s, with a processor (the 386) that was fast enough to handle moving graphics and the arrival of the sound card. The sound card, which plays back music and sound recordings, soon became a popular optional extra. When the price of the newly invented CD-ROM drives became affordable, the multimedia PC we know today had arrived.

Processor
For more on processors, see page 71

Sound card
For more on sound cards, see page 77

The Upgrade Kit

In the late 1980s, sound cards and CD-ROM drives became affordable. Soon, the two devices were sold together, with speakers, as a "multimedia upgrade kit" that could be added to a standard PC. These days, most PCs come with multimedia hardware already built in.

Speaker

Sound Card

CD-ROM Drive

Into the Home

Meanwhile, PCs were slowly creeping into people's homes. The workhorse computer was now being furnished with a wide range of educational software and games, and it soon became the most popular computer for home use. The problem for home users was choosing exactly which of the hundreds of different PCs, sound cards, and CD-ROM drives to buy to ensure that they could use the very latest multimedia titles. The other problem was that PCs, and MS-DOS in particular, were not very easy to use.

Multimedia Standards

Both problems were resolved in 1990. The introduction of the MPC (multimedia PC) standard gave buyers a set of exact hardware specifications to follow when choosing a multimedia computer. And Microsoft's new graphical operating system Windows 3.0 made PCs, and multimedia, far easier to use.

Since then all these trends have continued. Multimedia PCs are ever becoming faster and more powerful. The MPC standard has been revised twice – MPC2 and MPC3 – to reflect this. In 1995 Microsoft launched Windows 95, which has made using the PC and installing new multimedia software easier again. And today the PC is still the world's most popular multimedia machine.

Windows 95

Windows 95 is a "plug-and-play" operating system. It can automatically detect new hardware such as CD-ROM drives and will attempt to configure the PC to work with them immediately.

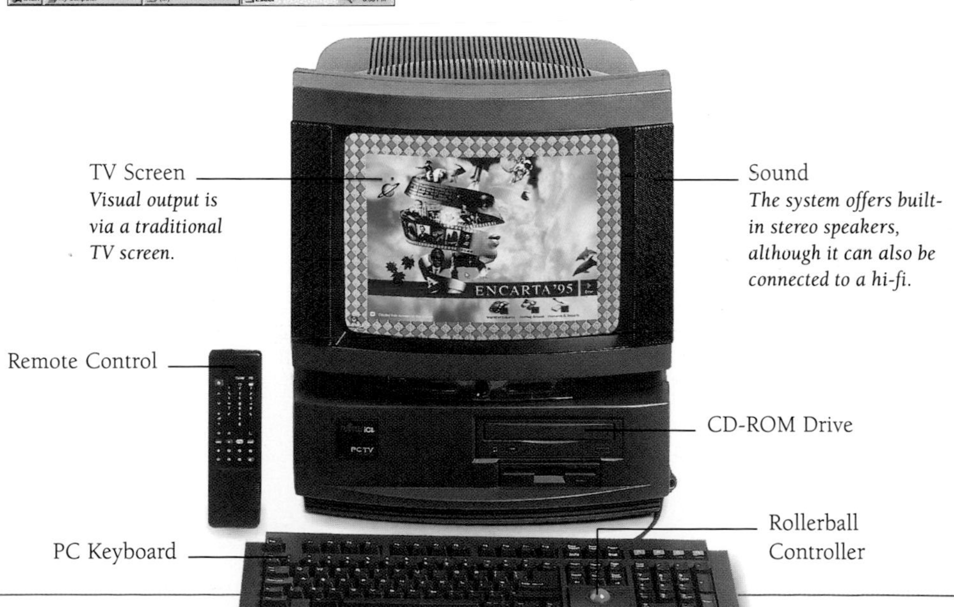

TV Screen
Visual output is via a traditional TV screen.

Sound
The system offers built-in stereo speakers, although it can also be connected to a hi-fi.

Remote Control

CD-ROM Drive

Rollerball Controller

PC Keyboard

PC/TV

Many computer makers are building all-in-one systems, such as the Fujitsu/ICL PC/TV shown here, that combine a television with a multimedia PC.

The Apple Macintosh

When Apple launched the Macintosh in 1984, they were confident that it would change the face of computing. The business community had bought wholesale into the IBM-compatible PC, with its text-based screens and complicated commands – but the Macintosh was a computer that had been designed to be user-friendly. With its easy to use GUI (Graphical User Interface), built-in sound, high-quality black-on-white graphics, and a new pointing device called a mouse, the Macintosh was a revolutionary machine, offering a number of features barely seen outside a research laboratory.

The First Macintosh
Often hailed as a design classic of the eighties, the Macintosh has evolved a long way from the 1984 model (right) to the way it looks today (below).

Computing Made Easy

Apple's aim was to take computers away from the experts and make them friendly enough for anyone to use – in the words of Apple's cofounder Steve Jobs, the Macintosh was a computer for "the rest of us." The GUI system, with its icons, menus, and mouse, made computing easy. New users could learn to work with the computer by following their intuition rather than a manual. Furthermore, the Macintosh looked different – its compact, all-in-one casing housed the computer, a small monitor, a speaker, and one of the first floppy disk drives to use today's plastic-cased disks. Many first-time computer users fell in love with the "Mac" immediately.

Business Rejects the Mac

If the Mac had caught on with business, it might have ruled the computing world. To commercial users, however, the Mac seemed too much like a toy to be capable of anything useful – the first Macs had no hard disk, were very short on memory, and were not cheap. More importantly, many firms had invested heavily in IBM-compatible PCs and the software to match, and Macs could neither run PC software nor read PC files.

Years later, PCs were to adopt many of the Mac's innovations, from GUIs and the mouse to built-in sound hardware and more. But for the time being, Apple and its ideas were locked out of the main market, and the Mac had to discover its following elsewhere.

Power Macintosh
Apple's latest machines are based on the speedy PowerPC chip and offer impressive multimedia performance. Add-ons range from a TV tuner to a card that lets you use PC software.

AudioVision Monitor
The Mac AV monitor has a built-in microphone and stereo speakers.

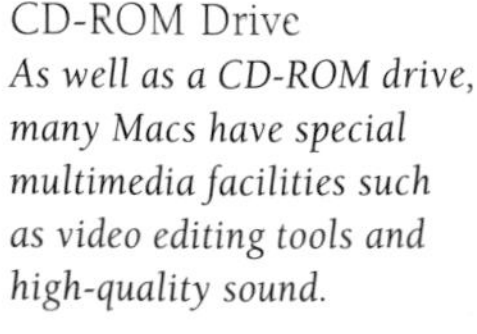

CD-ROM Drive
As well as a CD-ROM drive, many Macs have special multimedia facilities such as video editing tools and high-quality sound.

Publishing Hits the Desktop

The Macintosh brought about a completely new use for computers – DTP (desktop publishing). DTP programs allow document pages to be laid out in the same way newspaper and magazine designers once used layout pads, scissors, and glue. The book you are reading was produced on a Mac with the aid of a DTP program.

The Mac Makes its Mark

The Mac's graphical way with information had an impact in several areas. The first was publishing – DTP, or desktop publishing (see above), revolutionized the industry. The second area the Mac profoundly changed was education – the Mac's ease of use and obvious visual appeal was a big hit with children, their teachers, and their teachers' teachers, and Apple has successfully kept in touch with the needs of schools and universities to maintain its market lead.

From the start, Macs were natural multimedia machines, and teachers and enthusiasts began producing their own interactive multimedia with a Mac program called *HyperCard*. All that was missing from the multimedia mix was color – until the arrival in 1987 of the Mac II, which could display and manipulate photo-quality pictures. It was not long before the art of computer graphics switched from expensive workstations to the Mac, and designers rushed to use the powerful new tool. And because of its ability to handle graphics, the Mac still remains the machine of choice for making multimedia.

HyperCard

Apple's *HyperCard*, the first multimedia "authoring" tool, imitates a card filing system – but to each card you can add sound and graphics, as well as "buttons" that spring you to other cards.

Motorola Processor

Apple steered clear of Intel, and stayed with Motorola's 68000 series chips – until Apple, IBM, and Motorola later created the PowerPC.

Color Graphics Card

Apple added color to the Mac in great style, with cards that can show over 16 million colors.

RISC Ventures

While Apple now dominates the use of computers in publishing, education and graphics, fewer than 15 percent of all desktop computers are Macs – they remain in the shadow of the vastly popular PC. As a result, the market for Mac-based multimedia titles remains small, despite the Mac's long pedigree as a multimedia machine.

In recent years, Apple has tried hard to win ground. In 1994, the Mac became one of the first personal computers to make the move to RISC technology. RISC chips are very fast, and when Apple introduced the Power Macintosh line, with the RISC-based PowerPC chips at their core, multimedia titles were given an immediate performance boost. Apple's next step was to license Mac technology to other companies, and in 1995 the first Mac clones appeared. When in the same year Apple embraced its old enemy the PC – literally – by releasing a Mac with a whole PC on a card inside, it combined the best of both multimedia worlds.

RISC
For more on RISC technology, see page 87

Inside a Macintosh

With the Macintosh II, Apple left behind the all-in-one box design of the first Mac and added expansion slots, color, and a lot more power.

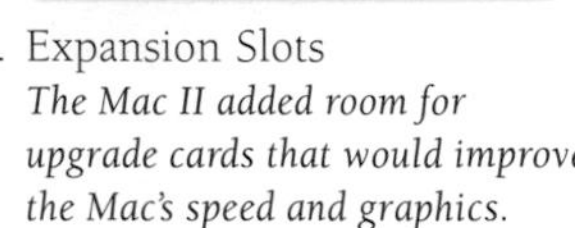

Expansion Slots

The Mac II added room for upgrade cards that would improve the Mac's speed and graphics.

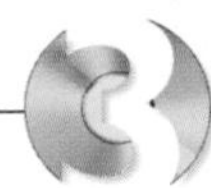

Home Consoles

A console is a type of computer used primarily for playing games. Home consoles cost a mere fraction of the price of a desktop computer, plug straight into a television set, and offer instant gaming without any computer know-how. Yet many computer experts dismiss them as machines for beginners that play only a trivial role in the multimedia revolution. In fact, their contribution is vital. Consoles have always been at the leading edge of home entertainment: the most exciting multimedia titles often appear first on a console, and many of today's consoles are more advanced than their desktop counterparts.

The First Consoles

In the early 1970s, video games started appearing alongside pinball machines in amusement arcades. The first games consisted of crude blocks of light that players moved around the screen in a rough approximation of tennis. Soon afterward, TV-based games systems started appearing in homes. Here too, all the games were based on the idea of a bat and ball. It was not long, however, before car racing simulations and tank battles were appearing on arcade screens. They were enormously popular, and developers such as Atari soon realized the potential of the TV-based systems for bringing arcade games into the home. This next generation of consoles offered crude color graphics and a range of different styles of games. By 1982, consoles were ensconced in homes all over the world. In the United States alone, an estimated 15 million homes had a TV-based games system.

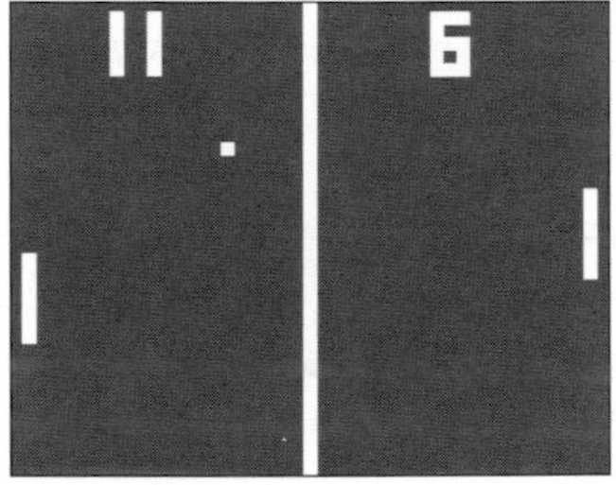

Innovations
Atari's 1978 tennis game *Pong* (above) was the first video arcade game, and its 1980 tank battle game *Battlezone* (left) was the first computer game to use 3-D graphics.

Video Game Fears

Within a year, however, the market had crashed. Two factors forced the closure of a number of console manufacturers: the steady fall in price of personal computers, and parental concern about the effects of video games on children. Stories were told of children who became obsessed, anti-social, or aggressive while playing video games, while doctors identified an early form of RSI (repetitive strain injury), called Space Invaders Wrist, which threatened players of video games.

Personal computers
For more on personal computers, see page 82

Atari 2600 Console
Atari announced their first venture into the home video market in 1977. It offered advanced sound and graphics.

Return of the Console

In the United States and Europe the games console market remained depressed for a number of years. In the East, however, the sun soon rose again for Japanese ex-toy manufacturer Nintendo, which in 1985 launched a home video system called Famicom. Encouraged by the machine's huge success in Japan, Nintendo turned to the United States, where it released the NES (Nintendo Entertainment System) in 1986. Soon afterward, another Japanese company, Sega, entered the American market with its Master System console.

Super Nintendo
Nintendo chose an Italian plumber, Mario, to champion its 16-bit Super NES console.

Head to Head

The two new machines each had an 8-bit processor (see box below), which offered a level of speed and range of colors never seen before on any competing system. Within a year, the United States and Europe were hooked, and the world console market was thriving once again.

In 1989, Sega launched the Genesis (known as the Megadrive in Europe). This 16-bit machine offered digital stereo sound and superior graphics. Nintendo's response was the Super NES in 1991. Other makers brought out 16-bit systems, but Sega and Nintendo were the only serious contenders. The rivals were championed by characters from their games – Nintendo by Mario and Sega by Sonic – who achieved worldwide fame comparable to that of Mickey Mouse.

Sega Genesis
Sega adopted a speedy hedgehog called Sonic as the mascot for its 16-bit Genesis console system.

Improving Bit by Bit

The increasing sophistication of console games is mainly due to improvements in the processor chips at the heart of the machines. The first console processors were 4-bit – they could only handle four bits of information at one time. The latest consoles have a 32- or 64-bit main processor, and extra processors that handle sound and 3-D graphics.

Atari's 4-bit *Space Invaders*

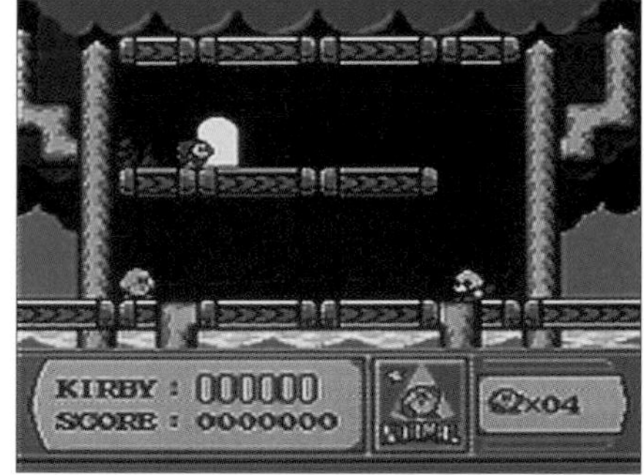

Nintendo's 8-bit *Kirby's Adventure*

Activision's 16-bit *X-Kaliber*

Crystal Dynamics's 32-bit *3D Baseball*

Atari's 64-bit *Highlander I*

The New Generation

Most of today's consoles are powerful 32- and 64-bit multimedia machines. Many console makers now crowd the arena, and the competition between them is fierce. As well as the games machines, there are several machines called "multimedia players." In addition to games, these play reference and educational multimedia titles, and some play audio, Photo, and Video CDs too. The first multimedia player, the 16-bit CD-i (Compact Disc Interactive) was also the first CD-based console. It was launched in 1991 by Philips, which, along with Sony, invented both the compact disc and CD-ROM.

Video CDs
For more on Video CDs, see page 81

Home Console

Modern consoles plug into a television set and a hi-fi system to provide high-quality graphics and stereo sound. Some consoles can be connected – either in the same room or over a telephone line – for multiplayer games.

Powerful Players

The 3DO Company followed suit, designing a 32-bit multimedia player technology, 3DO, that has been licensed to several console makers. In 1995, Sega responded with the Saturn, a 32-bit games console that aimed to outdo the 3DO. In the same year, Sony made its entry into the console market with the 32-bit PlayStation games machine. Then Nintendo controversially rejected the multimedia possibilities of the CD by launching the 64-bit Ultra 64 console as a traditional cartridge machine.

All of the other machines are CD-driven. Most of them have specialized hardware that delivers high-quality stereo sound, enhanced 3-D graphics, and full-screen video. Even with their superior multimedia performance, the consoles still cost only a third as much as a desktop computer.

Fingertip Control

Consoles are controlled using two-handed joypads such as the one shown here. Since joypads first appeared over ten years ago the number of buttons has increased, but the basic design has changed very little.

Direction Pad
This thumbpad controls the direction of movement in a game. It can also be used to control an on-screen pointer.

Option Buttons
These buttons are used to make choices outside the game action – for example, choosing game options and pausing the game.

Gameplay Buttons
These buttons control actions within the game, such as jumping, firing, and punching.

Alternatives to the Joypad

Dedicated gamesplayers can choose from a range of alternative ways of controlling their consoles. In the eighties, many different control devices came and went, from light guns, which were used for on-screen target practice, to data gloves, which recorded the movement of the player's hands in space. Today's control devices reflect the new trends in CD-based multimedia.
Most of the multimedia players, which play reference and educational titles as well as games, can be controlled with the keyboard and mouse of traditional computing. On the games consoles, the most popular titles are 3-D racing, flying, and fighting games, hence the control devices shown here: racing car steering wheels, airplane-style joysticks, and improved joypads with extra buttons for fighting moves.

Steering Wheel

Super Joypad

Joystick

Competing Standards

Games consoles have always been more popular than desktop computers in the home. Today, several console makers are competing with the computer companies and with each other to bring multimedia into the home. On the following pages, you can read more about each of the home consoles shown here.

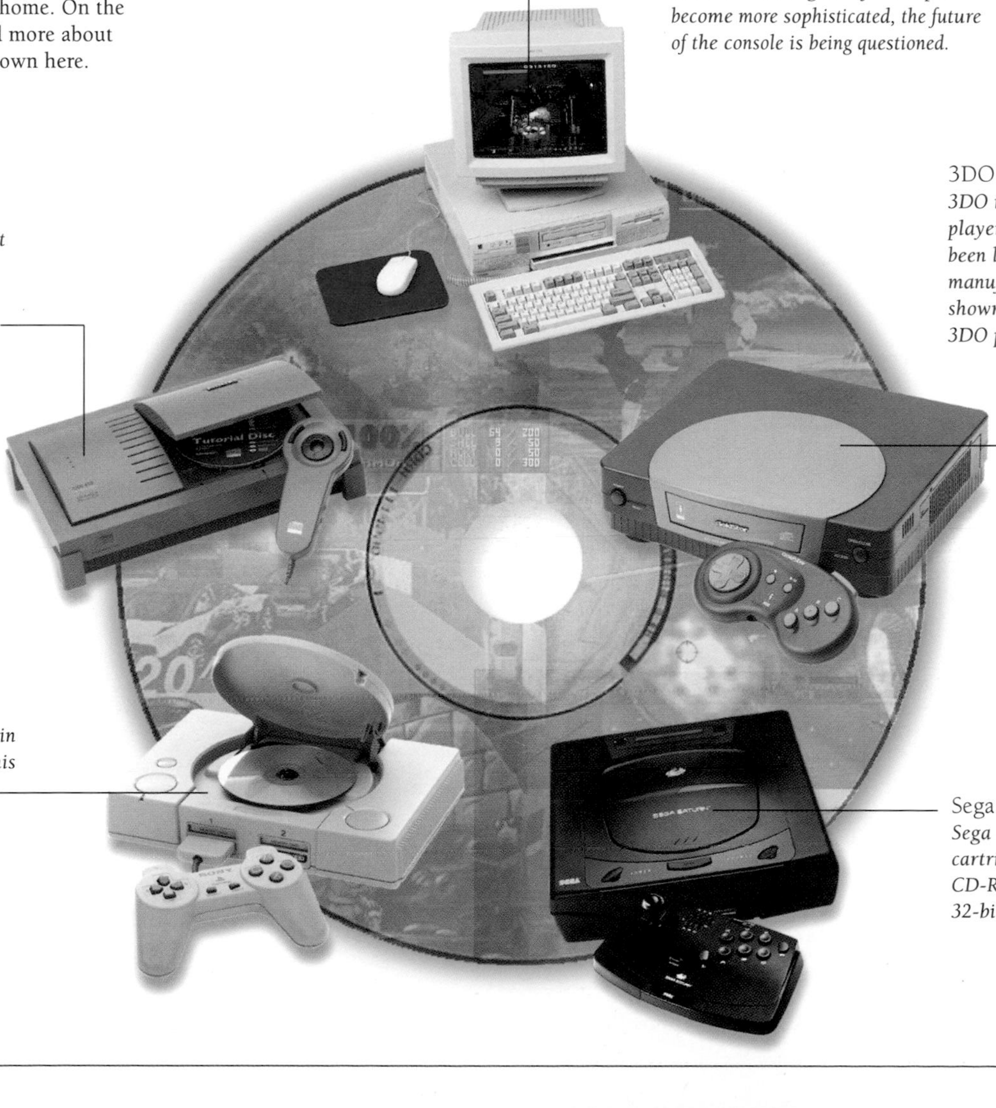

Multimedia PC
In the past, computers and consoles have occupied opposite ends of the market – but as games for computers become more sophisticated, the future of the console is being questioned.

Philips CD-i
The 16-bit CD-i was the first CD-based console. It was launched in 1991 as an all-round entertainment center.

3DO
3DO is a multimedia player standard that has been licensed to several manufacturers. The model shown here is GoldStar's 3DO player.

Sony PlayStation
Sony has made its debut in the console arena with this 32-bit games machine.

Sega Saturn
Sega moved from games cartridges to games on CD-ROM with their 32-bit Saturn console.

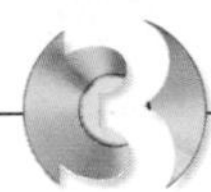

PHILIPS INVENTS CD-i

It is appropriate that Philips, a coinventor of the compact disc, was one of the first companies to attempt putting CD-based multimedia into homes. Using the CD-ROM standard it helped to create, the company began work in 1987 on a home multimedia system – CD-i (Compact Disc-interactive) – which eventually came out in 1991.

A COMPLETE SOLUTION

The other home entertainment systems at the time were cartridge-based machines such as the Sega Genesis. However, its CD-ROM format was not all that distinguished CD-i from its competitors. Philips designed its machine as a complete home entertainment system that would fit into a hi-fi stack and could be used to play audio CDs as well as games and educational and reference software on CD-ROM. Unfortunately for Philips, however, this concept did not catch on with consumers: most saw CD-i as just another games console – and one that cost nearly three times more than its competitors. Also, a CD-ROM is many times slower than a cartridge. However, over the years, the public has gradually caught up with the CD-i concept. Philips was proved to be ahead of its time, and all its innovations are incorporated into today's games consoles.

Internet Access
With an optional modem and software, a CD-i machine enables the user to access the Internet. A keypad enables users to type in e-mail messages.

THE ENTERTAINER
The Philips CD-i 450 Player is an all-around home entertainment center. As well as playing the full range of games available today, this and other CD-i machines can also play audio and Video CDs, and, with an optional modem, can be plugged directly into the Internet.

Top-loading CD-ROM Drive

Design Rethink
Philips's original design for their CD-i player resembled a videocassette recorder. Subsequent redesign placed the machine firmly in the mold of entertainment and games equipment.

Performance Matters

Processor
The Philips CD-i is powered by a 16-bit processor.

CD-ROM Drive
CD-i machines have a single-speed CD-ROM drive.

Sound
CD-quality stereo sound.

Graphics
No special graphics chips.

Software
Full range of software, from games to business applications. Also audio, Photo, and Video CDs.

Linking
CD-i players are designed to work as individual units.

Special Features
Internet access and a PC CD-i card to play CD-i discs through a PC.

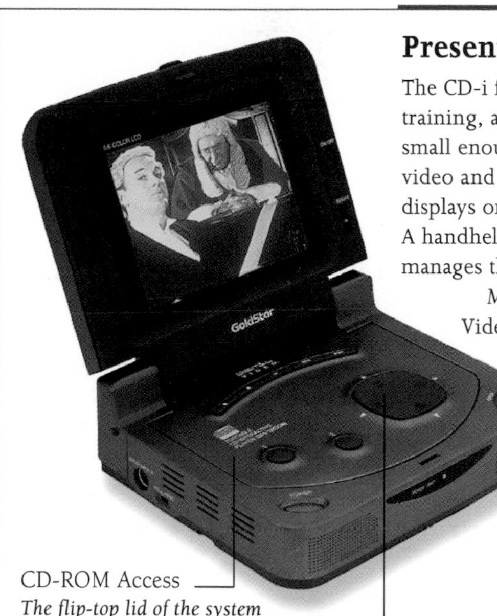

Presentation Matters

The CD-i format has proved to be ideal for business, training, and other presentations. The portable models, small enough to fit into a briefcase, offer full-motion video and CD-quality sound, and can provide full-color displays on any TV or conference room video system. A handheld point-and-click remote control unit manages the presentation.

Meetings, Bloody Meetings (shown here), from Video Arts, features British comedian John Cleese outlining the five essential disciplines for successfully chairing a meeting.

CD-ROM Access
The flip-top lid of the system unit provides access to the CD-ROM drive.

Direction Pad

MINISCREEN
The GoldStar GPI 1200 CD-i player includes a compact LCD (Liquid Crystal Display) screen, which enables the machine to be used for stand-alone presentations.

FURTHER INNOVATIONS

Philips began a second assault on the market when the Video CD standard emerged. It launched a Digital Video cartridge that enables the CD-i machine to play Video CDs. A number of feature films became available in this format; video sequences were included in CD-i games, and music began to be produced for Video CD. It is also possible to access the Internet by using a modem and CD-i software that displays an interface to the Internet. E-mail messages can be typed on a keypad and sent by using the software supplied. In addition, a PC CD-i card is available that enables CD-i discs to be played on a PC.

INTERNATIONAL TENNIS OPEN
This title from Infogrames was one of the first successes on CD-i. You can choose from grass, clay, and indoor surfaces.

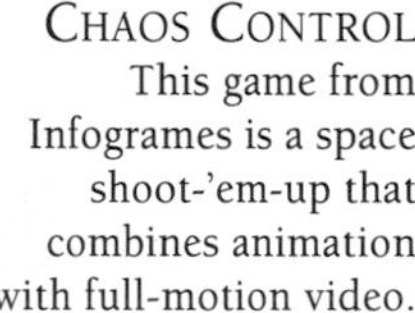

CHAOS CONTROL
This game from Infogrames is a space shoot-'em-up that combines animation with full-motion video.

BURN:CYCLE
The first CD-i title to reach number one in the CD-ROM charts was the interactive movie, *Burn:Cycle*, from Trip Media

In Control
The CD-i controller has a thumbpad in the center and a button on either side. Optional alternatives include a joypad and an infrared remote controller.

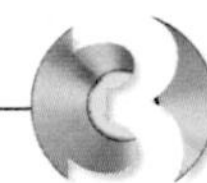

THE 3DO STANDARD

In 1993, Trip Hawkins, founder of the games software company Electronic Arts, launched 3DO as a hardware specification for a games machine. The intention was that 3DO machines would be accepted as the industry standard and bring some order into a chaotic market. But the first machines had three drawbacks: they were marketed as all-around multimedia players rather than games machines; their price was nearly three times that of their competitors; and there was no "must buy" games software available to stimulate sales of the machines.

3DO PLAYER
The GoldStar GDO 202P can play 3DO titles, audio CDs, Photo CDs, CD Plus, and, with an optional digital video cartridge, Video CDs. It can also be upgraded to the second-generation 3DO player standard known as M2.

HARDWARE

At the heart of the 3DO is a fast 32-bit RISC (Reduced Instruction Set Computing) processor supported by 3Mb of memory. Graphics are handled by two coprocessors that twist and spin images, generating special 3-D effects with ease. The 3DO's double-speed CD drive also acts as a CD-quality audio player, which, while a disc is playing, fills the screen with psychedelic patterns that match the music. Like CD-i, 3DO can also play Kodak Photo CDs. At first glance, the 3DO control pad looks like a standard console unit, but, uniquely, it features a connector allowing up to eight controllers to be "daisy-chained" together for multiplayer games. Another expansion option allows the connection of VCRs and camcorders for editing video. And the addition of an FMV (full-motion video) cartridge enables you to play Video CDs.

RISC
For more on RISC chips, see page 87

Front-loading CD-ROM Drive

Joypad

SOFTWARE

The reaction to the first 3DO machine, made by Panasonic, was disappointment. There were even stories of disgruntled buyers returning their new 3DO players for refunds – not because they were dissatisfied with the machine's performance, but because they were disappointed with the first batch of software produced. This did not represent the massive leap forward in quality that had been expected to accompany such a powerful machine. Nevertheless, the telephone company US West did select 3DO as the cable set-top box to be used in network trials in the United States. And about a year later the first really impressive software – mostly games – appeared, and 3DO was at last able to show its true strength. The most popular 3DO games were first developed for the Sega Megadrive – but 3DO's superior graphics hardware brings even more realistic and convincing animation to the titles.

Performance Matters

Processor
32-bit RISC processor; and in the M2 specification, a 64-bit accelerator card.

CD-ROM Drive
3DO machines have a double-speed CD drive.

Sound
CD-quality stereo; a 3-D Audio Imaging technique makes sound appear and fade from different directions.

Graphics
Twin coprocessors dedicated to graphics handling.

Software
Mostly games, but also some reference and edutainment titles. Can also play audio CDs, Photo CDs, CD Plus, and, with a special adapter, Video CDs.

Linking
Up to eight controllers can be linked for multiplayer games.

Special Features
Optional M2 upgrade for faster graphics and video, and a PC 3DO card to play 3DO titles through a PC.

ACTION-PACKED SOCCER
Electronic Arts has been mainly responsible for the evolution of 3DO software. One of its most widely praised titles has been *FIFA Soccer,* whose detailed graphics and fast processing speed show off the power of the 32-bit RISC processor.

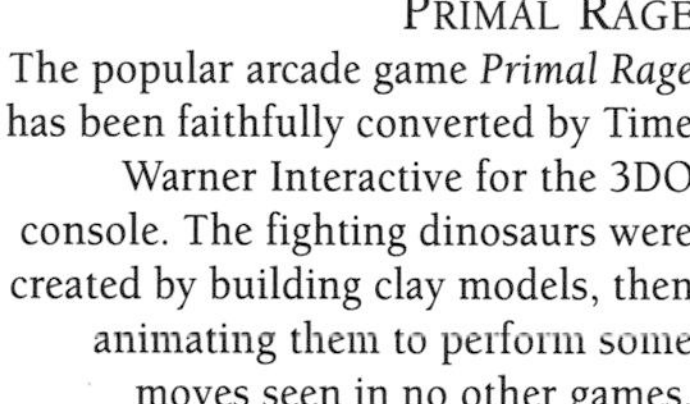

PRIMAL RAGE
The popular arcade game *Primal Rage* has been faithfully converted by Time Warner Interactive for the 3DO console. The fighting dinosaurs were created by building clay models, then animating them to perform some moves seen in no other games.

ROAD RASH
Electronic Arts has combined digitized video recordings of outlaw bikers and police officers in pursuit to make *Road Rash.* The mayhem is accompanied by a grunge sound track played by six bands, who can also be viewed on video.

Panasonic 3DO Console
Panasonic's FZ-1 Real 3DO Interactive Multiplayer, released initially in the United States at the end of 1993, was the first 3DO machine. Its appearance was greeted with considerable excitement.

M2 UPGRADE

Despite being the first 32-bit games platform, the 3DO format not only failed to become the industry standard – it was on its way to becoming a forgotten also-ran. This changed when machines were released that met the new M2 specification – the second-generation 3DO – which included massively enhanced processor power and graphics capabilities. The 3DO M2 is available both as a separate system and as an upgrade cartridge that plugs into the back of original 3DO systems. This cartridge takes the form of a 64-bit accelerator card, based on PowerPC technology, with built-in FMV hardware. The 3DO system is also available as an expansion card for multimedia PCs, enabling them to play 3DO software.

The Sega Saturn

Most games players think of the Japanese corporation Sega as the creators of Sonic the Hedgehog and longtime underdogs to Nintendo in the games console market. Sega actually began production in a different area of the interactive games sector – in video arcades, where its cutting-edge 3-D graphics technology has powered games far superior to any home video game. And now Sega's latest console, the Saturn, is powerful enough to bring their arcade games into the home.

Memory Cartridge Slot

The Sega Story

Sega's first major assault on the console market came in the form of the Genesis (known in Europe as the Megadrive), the world's first 16-bit home console system. Launched in the United States in 1990, it was a massive hit with the games-playing public. The Genesis was cartridge-based, but in 1993 Sega introduced the Sega CD, an add-on CD-ROM player.

When 3DO technology was announced in 1992, Sega began planning its next console. Based on a 32-bit processor and a double-speed CD-ROM drive, the new machine's specifications would, Sega hoped, put it beyond the reach of the competition. Then Sony announced the PlayStation console, and reports of its revolutionary performance reached Sega's ears. In response to this unexpected and powerful new rival, Sega delayed the Saturn development program. It was too late to make major alterations to the system, but Sega decided to take the time to equip the new machine with an extra graphics processor; arcade-quality 3-D imagery was to be the hallmark of almost all of Sega's future games.

Joypad Supplied

Processing Power

The Sega Saturn arrived in Japanese stores at the end of 1994, and proved to be as powerful as Sega had promised, thanks to a collection of seven specially designed main processors. The main processing power comes from two fast 32-bit RISC chips built by Hitachi. These perform the thousands of mathematical calculations that are needed every second to magnify and rotate two- and three-dimensional images at great speed. Specialized graphics tasks are handled by three separate graphics chips: a sprite chip, which moves flat animated characters around the screen, and two background chips, which share the task of drawing, rotating, and scrolling moving backgrounds. The two remaining processors are on the custom sound card – designed by audio experts at Yamaha – which offers sound performance superior to that of any other home multimedia player.

Optional Extras

The range of peripherals for the Saturn includes several alternative control devices for gaming enthusiasts and an adapter that enables up to six people (or 12 people when used in tandem) to connect their joypads for multiplayer games.

Joystick

Mouse

Six-player Adapter

Steering Wheel

What It Can Do

The Saturn is first and foremost a games machine – but as with most other consoles, it plays audio CDs and, with an adapter, Photo CDs. However, it is unique in that it also acts as a karaoke player, by removing the voice track from ordinary music CDs. With an optional digital video card, the Saturn can play Video CDs and games that have video sequences built in, such as interactive movies. And with an extra modem, Saturn owners can access the Internet.

Sega capitalized on its arcade game pedigree by launching a range of arcade-style control devices – for example, a racing steering wheel – that enable the Saturn to imitate Sega's multiplayer arcade machines. In addition, Sega has adapted most of its most popular arcade games so that they work on the Saturn. As the success of a games console can depend simply on the popularity of the two or three big-name titles that are available for it, this is a significant advantage in a home console market that is much more crowded than Sega had at first anticipated.

Sega Rally
The racing game that took the arcades by storm can now be played at home on the Saturn. Fast-moving and detailed scenery and multiplayer action add to the racing excitement.

Performance Matters

Processor
The Sega Saturn is powered by two main 32-bit RISC processors.

CD-ROM
The Saturn has a double-speed CD-ROM drive.

Sound
The Saturn's Yamaha sound card gives it 32 channels of CD-quality sound, MIDI music, and surround sound effects.

Graphics
The Saturn's three graphics processors produce fast and sophisticated 2-D and 3-D animation.

Software
Most Saturn titles are action games. The Saturn can also play audio CDs, CD+Graphics, and with extra adapters, Photo and Video CDs.

Linking
With extra adapters, up to 12 players can play together.

Special Features
An optional memory cartridge allows users to save game data. With a modem, users can connect to the Internet.

Virtua Fighter 2
Sega's 3-D hand-to-hand combat game involves hundreds of realistic fighting moves and a constantly changing point of view that accentuates the 3-D graphics.

Bug!
The Saturn's 3-D capabilities are used to bring a new dimension to the traditional platform game genre in Sega's *Bug!* The animated insect hero travels across a set of 3-D platforms, dispatching enemies along the way.

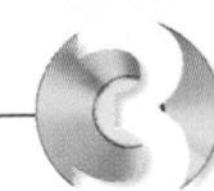

THE SONY PLAYSTATION

It is perhaps surprising that before the launch of the PlayStation, Sony, the largest consumer electronics corporation in the world, had barely involved itself in video games. Its many years of research into digital image manipulation technology had been mainly channeled into the production of television and video units. But in the late 1980s, special circumstances directed the fruits of this research, in combination with Sony's work in high-performance computer systems, into the development of the PlayStation games console.

Image manipulation
For more on image manipulation, see page 136

HOW IT ALL BEGAN

The genesis of the PlayStation occurred in 1988 when Nintendo asked Sony to create a CD-ROM drive for a new games platform that it was developing. Partnerships between giant corporations have a poor record in many fields, and the one between Nintendo and Sony was no exception – irreconcilable demands and conflicting interests drove the two companies apart. However, Sony continued alone and built on the research it had already carried out. Its approach was that high-quality graphics are as vital as the interactivity itself to the success of a game. Sony's experience with display technology ensured that the PlayStation's graphics were incomparable when it was finally released in Japan in 1994.

GRAPHIC QUALITY

The silicon responsible for the PlayStation's display is the Graphics Processing Unit, which can draw more than half a million flat triangular surfaces per second. Another dedicated graphics processor, the Geometry Transform Engine, performs the mathematical calculations necessary to build the simple triangles into realistic and fast-moving 3-D images. The PlayStation can also generate 4,000 sprites (small 2-D images), which can be individually rotated or scaled to any size to represent player-characters, missiles, enemies, and so on. In addition, it can play full-screen video clips between stages of the main game action.

Memory Card Slot

Direction Keys

Function Keys

UNASSUMING APPEARANCE

From the outside, the PlayStation is an unobtrusive, light gray box just slightly smaller than this page. Inside are powerful new display electronics that cost a reputed half a billion dollars to develop. The joypad has a total of 14 fire and control buttons. Optional controllers include a mouse and a steering wheel.

Guaranteeing the Software

Having developed hardware more powerful at displaying graphics than the PC's Pentium processor, Sony set about ensuring that matching software would be available. They bought the English games developer Psygnosis, which first achieved fame as the publisher of *Lemmings*, one of the most popular computer games of all time. Additionally, Sony demonstrated the PlayStation's capabilities to the world's largest software developers. The enthusiastic reception virtually guaranteed that the PlayStation would not be short of games when it was finally released.

Designed to Play

Sony had no interest in making the PlayStation a complete information-retrieval system, such as the Philips CD-i machines. The PlayStation was always intended to be a very advanced games console, one that uses CDs as if they are extremely large cartridges.

Philips CD-i
For more on the Philips CD-i, see page 96

Performance Matters

Processor
The PlayStation is powered by a 32-bit RISC chip.

CD-ROM
The console has a double-speed CD-ROM drive.

Sound
The PlayStation can play 24 channels of CD-quality sound.

Graphics
The PlayStation's graphics processors are designed for real-time 3-D animation using textures and shading.

Software
The PlayStation is dedicated to games but can also play audio CDs.

Linking
With optional cables, several consoles can be linked. A separate adapter allows up to eight players to play on one console.

Special Features
Can play audio CDs while you play games. Optional memory card to save game data.

Demolish 'em Derby
A feature of this game by Psygnosis is that the damage caused by collisions is shown on the model car in the lower right corner.

Discworld
Psygnosis has converted Terry Pratchett's *Discworld* book series into a spectacular cartoon adventure, which itself plays games with space and time.

Wipeout
Racing takes off into the third dimension with this Psygnosis hover-racing title. If cornering in midair fails to burn off your opponents, you can always use some formidable weaponry to complete the job.

Battle Arena Toshinden
Tamsoft's martial arts game has been built around the PlayStation's superb graphics technology. The title is the most richly textured of the genre.

Virtual Reality

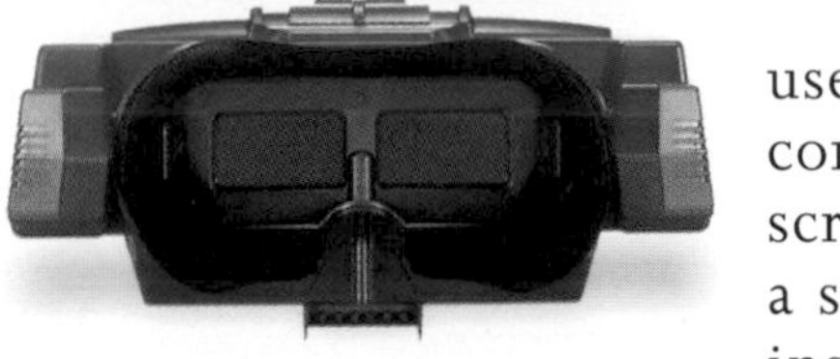

VIRTUAL REALITY IS ONE of the most talked about developments in multimedia. Essentially, it is a form of technology that lets the user enter and move around inside a computer-generated, interactive, three-dimensional environment, often called a virtual world. Instead of looking at a window on a computer screen, the user wears a headset that contains two small video screens – these provide a sense of actually being inside the virtual world. New uses are constantly being found for virtual reality. They range from the ultimate in interactive entertainment to advanced car simulators and systems that let doctors practice "virtual" surgery.

Early Development

Virtual reality may seem like a new technology, but it is descended from the flight simulators that have been used by the military for over 40 years. The biggest boost to its development came from NASA, which in the mid-eighties created the Virtual Interface Environment Workstation for planning missions into space. This was the first system to combine the elements of virtual reality that we now consider essential, such as computer graphics, video, stereo sound, and a head-mounted stereoscopic display. Even more significant was that the system was created using readily available parts. For example, the two screens in the headset were miniature television sets purchased at Radio Shack. As a result, research into virtual reality dramatically increased.

Immersive Virtual Reality

Using virtual reality is a unique experience. Computer graphics can look impressive, especially when they consist of rendered three-dimensional images, but they still appear on a two-dimensional computer screen. With virtual reality, instead of looking at a computer-generated world, you feel as if you are actually inside one. You enter a scene, and interact with it as if it were real. For example, you can pick up an object, or open a door, or use an elevator to move to a different floor of a building. If you tilt your head backward you see what is above you, and if you turn around you see what is behind. This is called "immersive" virtual reality.

Virtual Reality Games
Popular games, such as *Dark Forces* by LucasArts (above) and *Magic Carpet 2* by Bullfrog (left) can be played using a virtual reality headset.

Virtual Reality Kit
Virtual reality kits, such as this one from Virtuality and IBM, may soon become common accessories for personal computers and consoles.

Virtual Reality in the Home

For many years, virtual reality was confined to research laboratories and would only run on expensive workstations. However, with the increase in power of personal computers, it is now possible to experience virtual reality technology using an ordinary desktop computer or games console. Low-cost headsets are widely available, and an increasing number of software applications have been written to take advantage of them. Many observers predict that virtual reality will be the next big consumer craze, and that the stereoscopic headset will become as common as the joystick is today.

Workstations
For more on workstations, see page 70

Control Devices

In addition to a headset, a control device is needed to allow the user to interact with the virtual world. Such devices range from a standard keyboard or mouse to more specialized pieces of equipment such as the dataglove. This is lined with fiber-optic strands – when you point a finger or make a fist, the strands send signals to the controlling computer, which translates your movements to the screen. A dataglove enables you to see your hand in front of you and to use it to point to things or touch objects. Finally, a computer system acts as the "engine" at the heart of any virtual reality system. It generates the graphics and acts upon information received from the user via the control devices.

Stereoscopic Headset

The stereoscopic headset is the most recognizable piece of equipment in a virtual reality setup. The first, crude head-mounted display was built by an American academic, Ivan Sutherland, in 1968. For years such headgear was limited to specialized uses. Today, however, they are widely available, and are increasingly found in the home.

Tracking Sensor
A tracking, or motion, sensor is built into the headset. It detects horizontal and vertical movement and sends this information to the controlling computer.

Earphones
These provide stereo sound that adds to the immersive experience.

Display
The headset contains a small screen in front of each eye to provide stereoscopic vision. This gives a sense of depth and realism.

Inside a Virtual Game
Players of virtual reality games are completely surrounded by a virtual landscape – this adds to the sense of realism and excitement.

Our Virtual Future

The next few years will almost certainly bring great advances in virtual reality technology. The computers that run the controlling software will become faster, and capable of displaying higher-quality graphics with more realism. Today's head-mounted stereoscopic displays will evolve into smaller, lighter "glasses" linked to the computer by infrared beams, and tracking sensors may become small enough to be built into clothing. We may also see devices that can simulate the sensations of movement, and even smell and touch.

Human-Computer Interaction

As virtual reality technology improves, it will doubtless play an ever-increasing role in our everyday lives, both at work and in the home. It will certainly change the way we interact with computers. For example, a virtual reality database might allow the user to walk through corridors and into virtual rooms that contain information on different subjects, and then "pick up" the desired document from a virtual filing cabinet. Such applications could make computers far more intuitive and easier to use.

ARCADE MACHINES

Over the last few years strange new machines have been appearing in games arcades. These are virtual reality arcade machines, designed to give the ultimate interactive entertainment experience. In a typical setup, the user steps into a pod and is surrounded by a protective barrier. Then, wearing a headset and using a pointing device, the player begins the game. Arcade machines contain a powerful computer that controls the game – far more powerful than the average personal computer.

GAME PODS
Playing a virtual game can be a disorienting experience. These Series 2000 game pods, from Virtuality, surround the player with a cushioned barrier for added safety.

DEGREE OF REALISM

Generally, the more powerful the computer running the virtual reality game, the more realistic the visual effect of the 3-D graphics. Top-of-the-range systems display environments in smoothly blended color, complete with curved, textured surfaces and realistic lighting and shading effects.

3-D graphics
For more on 3-D graphics, see page 138

Reaction time is also crucial in achieving a realistic effect: any perceived timelag between the user performing an action and it actually taking place in the virtual world can ruin the immersive effect. The very best systems can run in "real-time," meaning that the user's actions are executed without any noticeable delay. They can also create advanced graphical effects, such as motion blur (which imitates the blurred look of fast-moving objects), and warping (where an image is stretched or exaggerated).

Quickshot Carnival

Trap Master

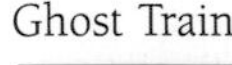

Ghost Train

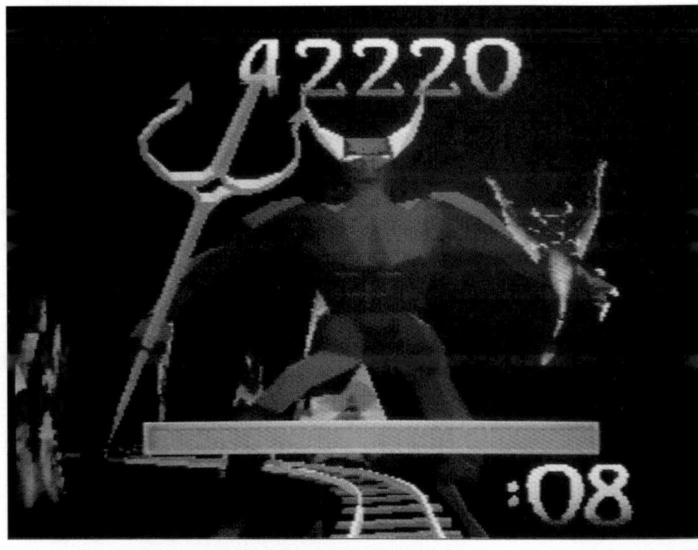

VIRTUAL REALITY ARCADE GAMES
Virtuality has produced a range of games for their virtual reality game pods. In *Trap Master* and *Quickshot Carnival*, players use an exact replica of a Winchester 101 shotgun to shoot at clay pigeons or fairground-style ducks. *Ghost Train* takes the player on a white-knuckle roller coaster ride through a virtual world populated by monsters and skeletons.

Spatial Information

Battle Simulation
Virtual reality that simulates battle situations is widely used by the military to train pilots and soldiers.

Studies have proved that it is far easier to solve a problem when information is presented spatially instead of in words and numbers. With its simulation of three-dimensional space, virtual reality is ideal for displaying information and has many practical applications in this respect. For example, an aircraft designer working on a new wing would traditionally have checked its performance by studying a printout of data from a wind tunnel test, whereas, using a virtual reality system, the designer can watch a more useful visual display of air flowing over a three-dimensional wing.

Real-world Applications

Virtual reality provides a cheap and safe way of simulating environments that would be either expensive or dangerous to replicate in real life. For example, combat pilots can be trained initially on a relatively inexpensive flight-simulation system rather than in a multimillion-dollar jet fighter.

Practical Uses

The number of uses for virtual reality technology is growing every day, in both the public and the private sector. The military, pioneers in virtual reality, use it to simulate battle environments for training purposes. Soldiers can use it to practice firing a new weapons system, pilots to prepare for flying in battle situations, and officers to improve planning and strategy.

Another major commercial use is CAD (Computer-Aided Design). An example of this is the architectural walk-through: an architect's data relating to a proposed new building is used to create a 3-D design, a virtual construction. By wearing a headset, clients can "tour" the building, gaining a much more realistic idea of its character than would be possible from viewing drawings or models. Similar techniques are used by engineers to plan the construction and maintenence of nuclear power plants.

Virtual Car
It may soon become common to "test drive" a car using virtual reality. To try out a new model, the driver sits in a car simulator and wears a headset. Such systems are also used to test drivers and to simulate car crashes.

Virtual Reality Headset

Architectural Walk-through
Virtual reality is used by engineers and architects to visualize complex structures, such as a nuclear reactor (above), or to "walk around" a house before it is built.

4 How Multimedia is Made

Multimedia-making is a young, dynamic, and fast-paced industry. This chapter shows how a multimedia encyclopedia and an interactive movie were made and then examines each multimedia element – authoring, text, sound, graphics, animation, and video – in turn to reveal the secrets behind some of today's best games and reference titles.

Making a CD-ROM

From first idea to final product, most CD-ROM titles are between one and two years in the making. The multimedia production process combines the ideas and efforts of dozens of skilled individuals: designers, editors, animators, video and sound engineers, programmers, and producers. The industry is young, rapidly changing, and very competitive. As a result, multimedia companies are always looking for technological improvements and new title areas to explore that will give them the edge over their rivals. In this section, we show how two CD-ROM titles – an encyclopedia and an interactive movie – were made.

Making History

Dorling Kindersley's *Eyewitness History of the World* is one of the company's series of award-winning multimedia encyclopedias. The multiple challenge for its creators was to encompass a vast subject while keeping the information accurate, interesting, and interactive. Each of the encyclopedias in the *Eyewitness* series is based on an elaborate central console that offers different ways to explore a set of illustrated articles. What needed to be established initially for *History* was exactly how the information would be arranged and how the console would work. In multimedia production, thorough planning is vital, and so management put together a small team of editors and designers and gave it two months to generate and discuss ideas for the title.

Project Proposal

After trying out and rejecting many possibilities, the team reached its final proposal. The main console would enable the user to travel between ten themed periods in history – for example, the Age of Conquerors, (1100–1492), and Nations and Empires (1825–1900). A globe in the center of the console would make it possible to travel through the world history of each period. Arranged around the console would be a collection of artifacts (such as pieces of art, weapons, tools, and so on) that would change to reflect each period – the user would be able to choose any artifact to find out more about it. A small bookshelf would contain a Who's Who and guides to the history of Innovations, Everyday Life, and Culture, and a quiz machine would test the knowledge the user had acquired.

Planning Meeting

Once the overall structure of the title has been established, the team leaders meet to discuss the project in detail, to establish a production schedule, and to determine what the workload will be for each team.

Design
The design team is responsible for designing the title's interface and producing all the 2-D and 3-D graphics.

Production
The production team coordinates the different strands of the project and is responsible for keeping the title on schedule and within the budget.

Resources
The resource teams produce sounds, animations, and videos for the title.

Editorial
The editorial team structures the information content of the title.

Flowchart
The team leaders discuss a proposed flowchart of the title's interactive connections.

Interface
This designer works on the structure and design of the main console.

Prototypes and Preparation

Once management accepted the proposal, the next stage was to build a series of working prototypes. The editorial and design teams used the early prototypes to test and refine the way the title worked and looked, and the final version was used both to establish a design template for the rest of the project and to provide a means of demonstrating the product to the multimedia industry.

With the template for the CD-ROM established, preparation for the main production began. Each historical period had its own editor and designer. Working with a history expert, the editor began detailed research into the key events, inventions, and personalities of the period, at the same time gathering archive pictures and video footage. The designer worked on rough screen layouts for every article.

Prototyping

The design and editorial teams coordinate words, images, sounds, and moving pictures to build a prototype version of the CD-ROM.

Design Ideas
The design leader discusses the screen layout with an editor and a designer.

Authoring
The design and editorial teams use authoring software to build all the multimedia elements into one interactive program.

Early Prototype

Early prototypes are used to test the interactivity of the product. The multimedia elements are represented by sketches and placeholders.

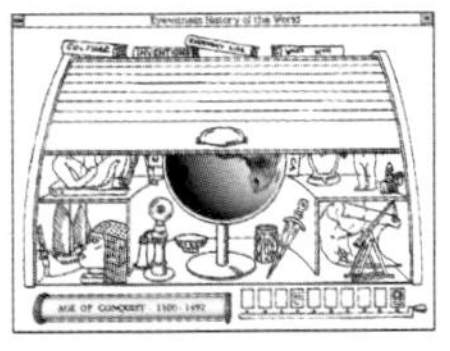

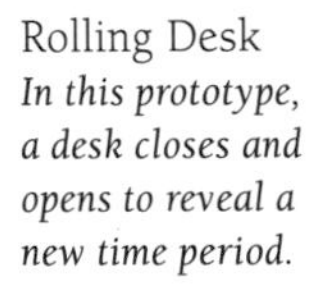

Rolling Desk
In this prototype, a desk closes and opens to reveal a new time period.

Everything on Paper First

Before work on the multimedia elements begins, the editor-designer pairs prepare everything on paper – detailed plans that show exactly what text, still pictures, sounds, animations, and video clips are needed, and exactly where they belong.

Editor
The editor researches every topic and decides which multimedia elements to use.

Designer
The designer experiments on paper with design ideas for each screen.

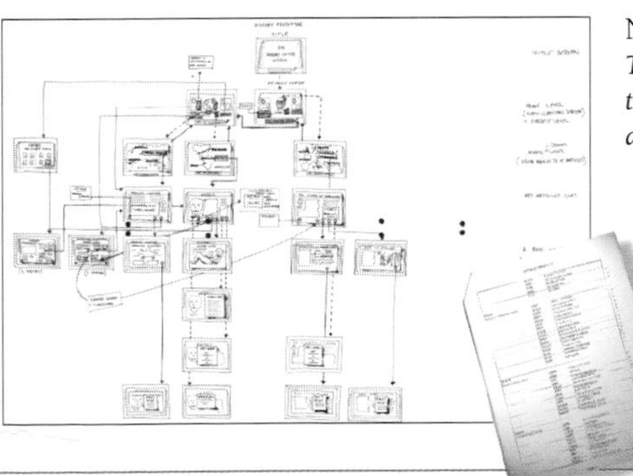

Navigation Blueprint
This is a template of how the user can navigate around the title.

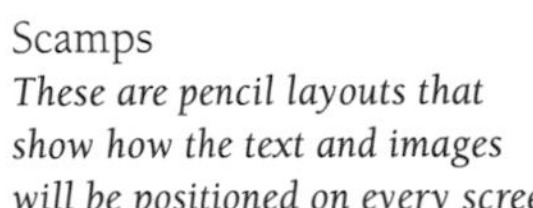

Headword List
This is a list of every topic to be covered. Each will become an on-screen article.

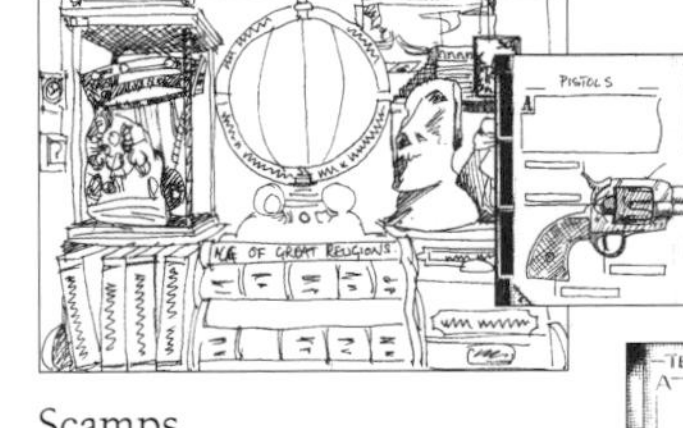

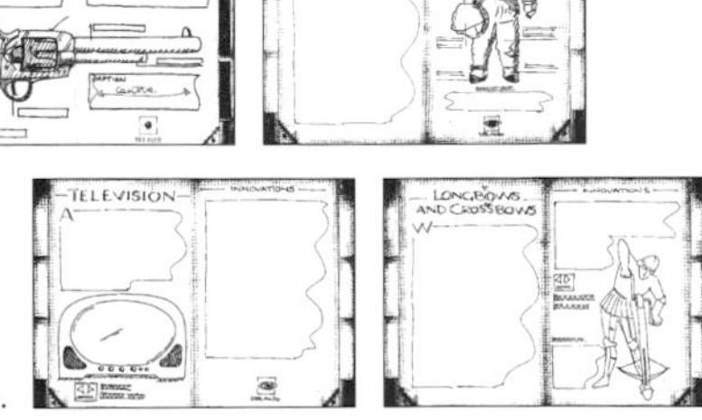

Scamps
These are pencil layouts that show how the text and images will be positioned on every screen.

Multimedia Resources

After planning each screen, the editorial team's next task was to research and commission the article text for it. Writing for a CD-ROM history of the world was not always straightforward – the writers had to present all the key information while keeping the articles short enough to allow space for screen images. The editors then edited each article and wrote quiz questions, index entries, and cross-references to other articles.

Meanwhile, the other teams set about creating their multimedia resources. The designers switched from paper to the computer screen to create the graphics; and the sound, video, and animation teams began work. By now, the combined development team had grown to 20 people, all of whom had new ideas and ways to improve the title they were working on.

Sound

The sound team records a spoken narration of every article, as well as voice-overs for animations and video footage, and sound effects to accompany the user's progress through the title.

Sound File

Studio work takes up less than a third of the sound engineer's time. Most of the work is in editing and mixing digital sound files.

Graphics

The designers build up the graphics for the console and all the articles by combining existing artwork and archive photographs with original 2-D and 3-D computer graphics.

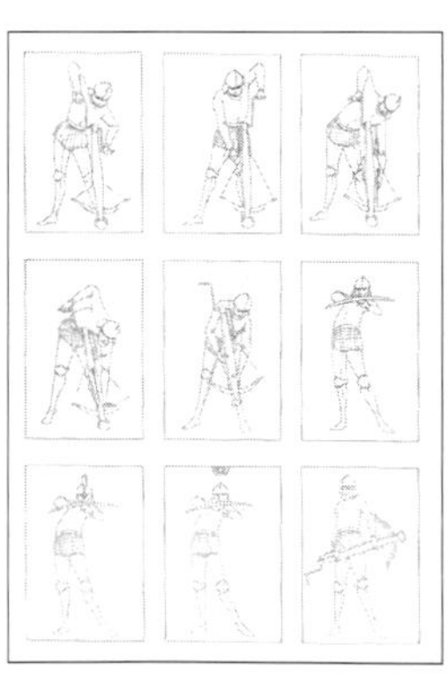

Animation Frames

The pencil animation frames are first digitized, then colored in using computer paint software.

Animation

To produce the animations for the title, the animators combine the techniques of traditional hand-drawn cartoon animation with computer image manipulation and 3-D graphics.

Video

The video engineer produces the clips to be used by editing together archive documentary footage. The computerized video clips need to be of high quality if the product is to succeed.

Digital Video

The video team uses computer video-editing software to digitize and edit the footage.

Building the Title

While the resources were being prepared, the programming team worked on the company's "run-time engine" – the software that would play the finished title. The engine had been developed for earlier titles, to play them faster and more smoothly than authoring software can. The task now was to expand and adapt the engine to meet the specific interactive needs of the history encyclopedia.

As the required multimedia elements materialized, the editor-designer pairs began creating the final screens. To do this, they used specially modified page-layout software (which is normally used to put books and magazines together). This enabled them to lay out the images, cut the text to fit, and add hotspots and interactive links all at the same time. It also meant that the finished screens could be plugged directly into the run-time engine.

Final Stages

The final months involved repeatedly testing and fine-tuning the title. As the programmers finished each new section of software code, the development team would test it to identify any bugs. The whole team also worked on refining the title's multimedia elements, functionality (the different ways a user can interact with it), and performance.

In the last month, a series of test releases of the title were burned onto gold master CD-ROMs and sent to a team of professional testers for checking. When the last gold master was declared bug-free, it was sent to the pressing plant for mass production.

Layout and Authoring

The designer and editor use modified page-layout software to compose the graphics and text for every screen, building in hotspots and interactive links at the same time.

Page File
This is an authored page. It can be plugged directly into the run-time engine (the software that will play the title).

Testing

Computers as well as human beings are used to test the product. Here, a computer is clicking randomly on the screen and recording what happens.

Programming

The programmers work on adapting the existing run-time engine for *History*. This involves adding new kinds of functionality and fine-tuning the program for optimum performance.

```
DKBOOL DKCProductData::Load (DKCInStrStream&  in )
{
    DKLONG lCurrPos = (DKLONG)in.tellg();

    in >> m_XrefDataOffsetStart;
    in >> m_XrefDataOffsetEnd;
    in >> m_IdxDataOffsetStart;
    in >> m_IdxDataOffsetEnd;

    m_XrefDataOffsetStart += lCurrPos;
    m_XrefDataOffsetEnd += lCurrPos;
    m_IdxDataOffsetStart += lCurrPos;
    m_IdxDataOffsetEnd += lCurrPos;
```

Debugging
When the test program crashes or performs badly, the programmers often have to search through hundreds of lines of programming code to isolate the instructions that are causing the problem.

Burning the Master

The final program is burned onto a gold master disc from which every marketed CD-ROM will be produced.

Creating a Game

Back in the days of *Space Invaders*, when computer games were little more than bleeps and flashing lights, it was common for a successful game to be invented and produced by a couple of friends working from a garage. Today's generation of computer games, however, has more in common with a Hollywood blockbuster movie than with the kind of video game found in most arcades. These new multimedia games require hundreds of people to produce and distribute them, and have budgets that run into millions of dollars. Fun and games are serious business these days.

The Darkening

Today's games inventors have to be more than just someone with a good idea: they also need to be a combination of salesperson, personnel manager, and diplomat. For Aaron Roberts, the inventor and director of Electronic Arts's *The Darkening*, it was not enough to have come up with an original concept – he also had to prove it would make enough money to justify the cost of producing and marketing it. The first step was to write up a brief outline of the game, called a "concept document," to take to the marketing department of the games company. Since the games market is now a truly global business, the discussions involved the company offices in the United States, Canada, and Europe. They were conducted by videoconferencing, so that the different offices could not only talk to one another but also show one another how they imagined the finished product would look.

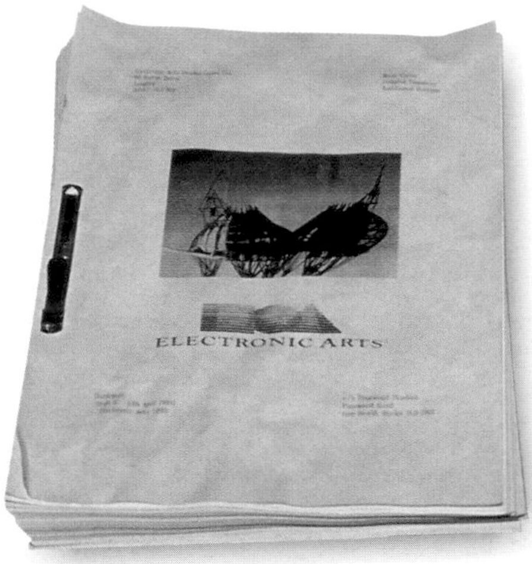

Extended Script
Unlike a regular movie, *The Darkening* enables the player to choose his or her own route through the story. As a result, the script must contain several different versions of each scene.

Branching Storyline

After the green light is given to a game, the next step is to work out the fine details of the story. For an interactive game, this is a far more complex process than it is for a conventional book or movie – because the game has to allow the player to choose how to react to an event, where to go, and even what sort of person to be. That means that the storyline keeps forking at various points, ramifying into a mass of different paths that could be followed. In the case of *The Darkening* the alternatives include different planets and cities, with different inhabitants, and even different types of personalities. For example, one type of character, when confronted by the police, might obey them; another might choose to fight his or her way out of the situation.

Mapping the Story
Because players can take so many different paths through *The Darkening*, any mistakes in planning them could lead to a player simply running out of game. Therefore, a team of designers has to draw up a detailed map of all the different possible routes.

Storyboarding
As well as a map of the branching storyline, the design team creates a picture storyboard of every action in the game, like a giant comic strip. This forms the basis of the designs for locations, costumes, and action sequences.

Wireframe Models
Many of the scenes in *The Darkening* are designed using 3-D modeling software.

Game Engine

An important part of every successful game today is the "game engine," the fast-reacting computer program that controls the player's actions on the screen. When, for example, the player presses a button to turn to the left, it is the game engine that has to move all the pictures on the screen to give the illusion of turning. The game engine also controls the movement of on-screen objects, such as spacecraft: it sets the speed of these, sends them in to attack you, and decides whether their shots hit you or your shots hit them. Building a fast, efficient game engine takes weeks of software programming; it is particularly important for action sequences, such as fighting and flying. In view of all the effort that is put into it, it is not surprising that a good game engine is often used for more than one game, and improved over time to make it even faster.

Evolutionary Design

After the initial wireframe design has been created, a scene is built up in a process called rendering to produce the finished effect.

Initial Wireframe Scene

Partially Rendered Scene

Fully Rendered Scene

Creating 3-D Models

Once the storyline is fixed, work can start on designing the game itself. *The Darkening* contains nine different planets to explore, each one with its own inhabitants, airports, bars, and spaceships. Many of these were created entirely by using computers running 3-D modeling software. Each of the planets has its own kind of society, ranging from the post-apocalyptic to the highly advanced. A designer created appropriate cities for each type of society, with a little guidance from architecture books. The spaceships started off as designs on paper, each design suggesting different qualities of speed and armor. They were then given a "skin" consisting of metallic textures, bolts, and even rust streaks. The inspiration for their insignia came from photographs of World War II planes and tanks.

3-D modeling
For more on 3-D modeling, see page 138

Checking Perspective
Computer-generated rooms are peopled with software "mannequins" in long lines fading away into the background. This ensures that any detail in the background that is out of scale can be spotted before the video of human actors is added.

FILMING AT PINEWOOD

Pinewood Studios, home to the James Bond films, was chosen for the shooting of *The Darkening*, which took place over several months. The entire technical team normally required for a full-length movie was hired – assistant directors, cameramen, "sparkies" (electricians), and lighting engineers suddenly found themselves working for a computer games company. From their point of view it was business as usual, with one exception: in an interactive movie each scene has to be filmed several times with different endings, to allow for the different choices the user might make when playing it. Because the player can choose to befriend or betray characters, the actors have to enact the same scene four or five times, with endings that vary from joyful triumph to painful death. According to John Hurt, one of the stars of *The Darkening*, such variations are, in fact, very rewarding because the actor is able to explore a role more thoroughly than is possible in a traditional movie.

POSTPRODUCTION

During filming, many scenes are shot against a blue background. Later on, in the post-production stage, a technique known as chromakeying is used to replace these blue backgrounds with computer-generated images, such as those created using 3-D modeling techniques. Also during post-production, many video sequences are made interactive: they are programmed to react when the player moves the cursor to a particular position. In some sequences, for example, the programmers will enable the player to talk to a character in the scene by moving the cursor over that character.

Chromakeying
For more on chromakeying, see page 153

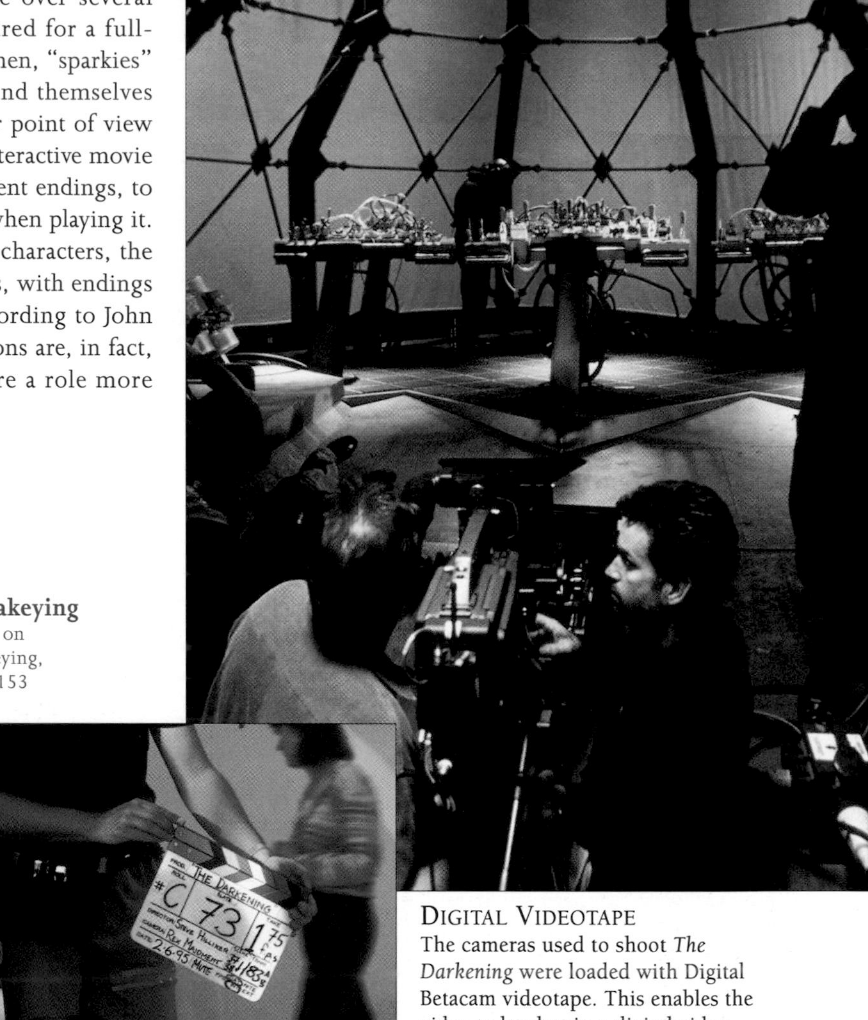

DIGITAL VIDEOTAPE
The cameras used to shoot *The Darkening* were loaded with Digital Betacam videotape. This enables the video to be shot in a digital video format that computers understand.

BUILDING THE SET
A set designer from Pinewood Studios was called in to plan, then physically build, the sets for the filmed scenes.

Set Construction

Construction Team

Plan of the Set

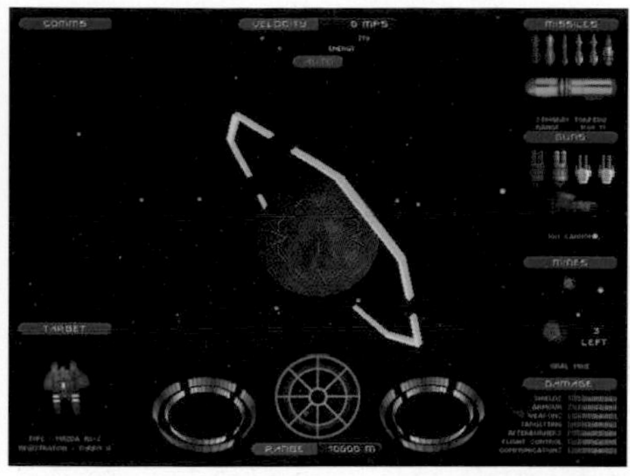

CUSTOM DATA
Players can choose how much data is displayed on their screen; for example, they can choose to view their current missile count or damage status.

SOUND AND MUSIC

Sound as well as video has to be added to the computer game. The actors' voices are recorded at the time of filming; voice-overs and sound effects are recorded later, onto DAT (Digital Audio Tape). One problem is that most multimedia computers play sound through accompanying small plastic speakers, so game developers go to great lengths to optimize the sound quality possible with these speakers. They use sound editing software to look for waveforms that expand to the point where they distort – any waves that go over the distortion limit are electronically corrected or smoothed out.

Sound editing
For more on sound editing, see page 128

TESTING AND PUBLISHING

In the final stage of production, a multimedia game has to go through weeks of testing. Playing *The Darkening* through just once from start to finish can take nearly 50 hours. Even if there were no mistakes to correct, it would still take one person several weeks to check all the possible variations. Instead, a team of youngsters is drafted for the dream job of being paid to play games all day. The testers note down any misspelled words, any hitches in gameplay, any sounds that crackle, and so on. The entire process is then repeated for each different foreign language version. Finally, when everyone is satisfied, the master discs are created (the game fills six CD-ROMs) and sent for pressing, packaging, and distribution.

Sister Maria

Talk to Sister Maria

Exit to Customs

Alternative Actions

PLAYER CHOICE
During interactive scenes, players can choose a course of action. In this scene, moving the cursor over Sister Maria causes her to turn toward you. Move the cursor over the exit door, however, and she turns away. The choice is yours.

TRADING
Successful trading is an essential part of *The Darkening*. Here a player can buy or sell a variety of spaceships.

Hiring the Cast

With a budget of around five million dollars, Electronic Arts was able to hire leading actors. In addition, 500 extras were chosen from photographs sent in by agencies specializing in striking and bizarre-looking characters.

Christopher Walken

John Hurt

Clive Owen

4

Authoring Multimedia

Multimedia is created by incorporating all the different elements – sound effects, text passages, video clips, and so on – into one program, and then defining how the user can interact with them. This process, known as authoring, begins early on in the production of a multimedia title, when the development team builds a working prototype to demonstrate how the title will work. During the main production stage, the team refines the prototype to improve the interactivity; and when all the multimedia elements are ready, the team builds them into the final interactive framework. Ten years ago, this would all have required the skills of a programmer, but it is now possible to buy those skills off the shelf in the form of multimedia authoring software.

Programming Made Easy

Most authoring software replaces the complex text-based world of programming with a graphical one where multimedia elements can be moved around on-screen and every decision can be made by selecting from menus of simple commands. Many authoring programs, such as Macromedia's *Director*, use the analogy of directing a movie or a play to simplify the process – and they even refer to a multimedia production as a movie. Authoring software can be used to create sound, video, text, graphics, and sophisticated animations from scratch, as well as providing the links that join these elements and make a title interactive. These multimedia elements are then used as "cast members" to produce the movie.

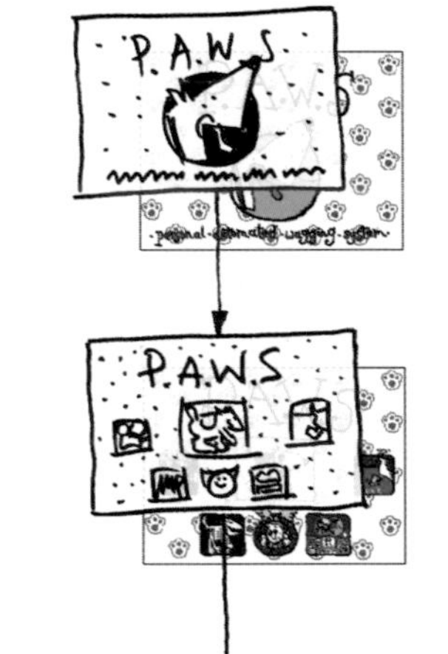

Planning
The first stage in authoring a multimedia title is detailed and careful planning. The design team storyboards every scene and prepares a route map of all the interactive connections in the title. The flowchart below shows the main interactive framework of *P.A.W.S.*

Cast Members on Stage

The blank screen onto which the cast members are placed is known as the stage. The designer selects the visual cast members – which include graphics for the background, on-screen buttons, animated icons, and so on – and uses the mouse to place them in position on the stage. Cast members that represent events, such as video clips and sound effects, are placed in a timing grid called the score, which synchronizes their entrances, movements on stage, and exits. For instance, if the designer wants a cast member to move around the stage, he or she can simply drag it across the stage with the mouse, and the score will automatically keep track of when and where it should move. The example on this and the following three pages shows how two sequences from the humorous "dog simulator" *P.A.W.S* by Domestic Funk Products were put together.

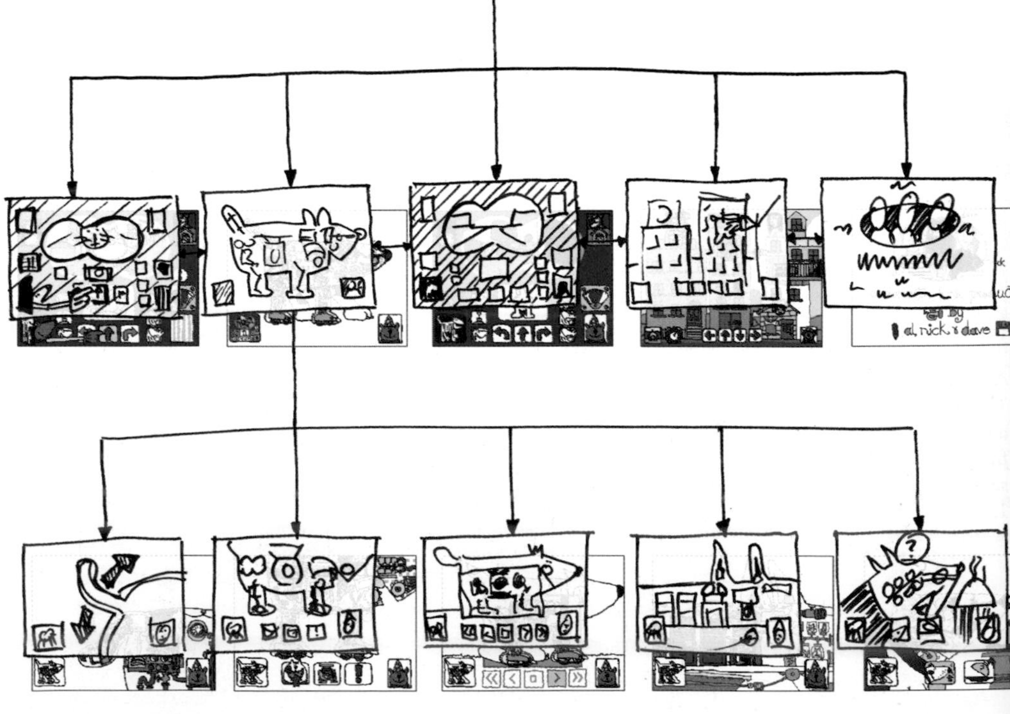

Canine Welcome

The noninteractive introductory sequence of *P.A.W.S* features the opening credits and then this title screen, where the animated dog hero greets the user with a plaintive howl. Building the sequence involves creating sounds, graphics, and an animation, and then combining them using Macromedia's *Director* authoring software.

Set Building

The designer first creates the background graphics for the sequence. This is the fixed set on which the other cast members will perform.

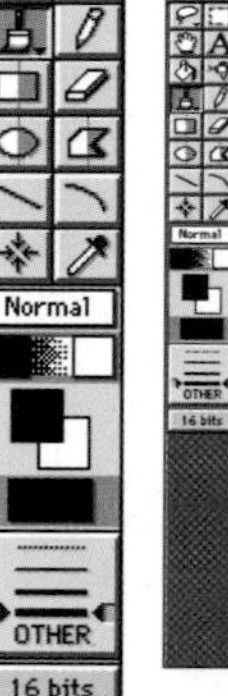

Painting Tools

Here, the designer uses Director's painting tools to create the cartoon background. For more sophisticated graphics, the designer uses specialized graphics software.

Sound Effects

The designer brings in sound files of the background music and the dog howl. These have been recorded, digitized, and edited by a sound engineer working in a multimedia sound studio.

Cast Window

The multimedia elements, or cast members, all appear as thumbnail-sized icons in the cast window, a sort of backstage area. Once here, they are ready for positioning on the stage.

Animation

The animator creates the howling dog animation by painting each frame individually using specialized animation software.

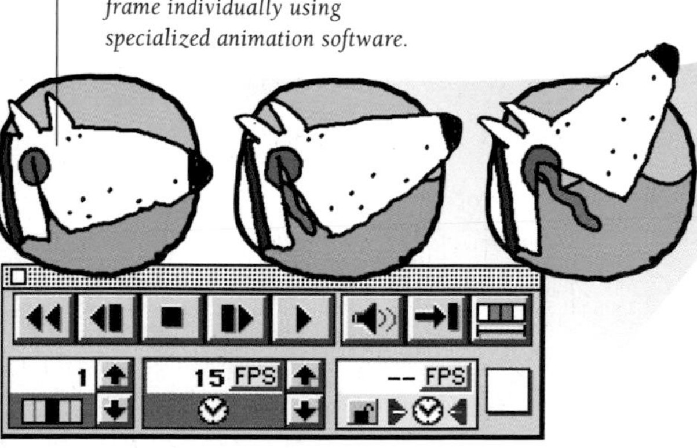

Stage

The stage is the empty set to which the cast members are introduced. The designer simply drags the background graphics, music, howling sound, and animation from the cast window onto the stage to build the scene.

Animation Controller

This is used to preview animations and video clips – it works like the front panel of a tape recorder. It also shows the playing speed (here set to 15 FPS – frames per second).

Score

The designer puts cues for the animation, sound effects, and music in a timing grid that keeps track of what happens when.

Adding Interactivity

To make a sequence of multimedia interactive, the designer has to add controls for the user and instructions that tell the program how to respond. The designer adds controls by defining certain areas of the screens as on-screen buttons, or hotspots. The next step is to attach a set of instructions – a script – to the hotspot. When the hotspot is activated, the script will initiate the response – a video sequence, for example, or a jump to another part of the program. The script is written in Lingo, a simplified programming language that approximates English. For instance, the instruction to respond to a mouse click by jumping to a contents screen could be written as follows: On MouseUp go to movie "Contents."

Contents Page

In the anatomy section of P.A.W.S, a mechanical dog is used to explain the workings of a dog's anatomy. This screen is to act as a graphical contents page – the user will be able to click on any part of the dog to jump to a detailed view. To achieve this, the designer adds hotspots to the screen.

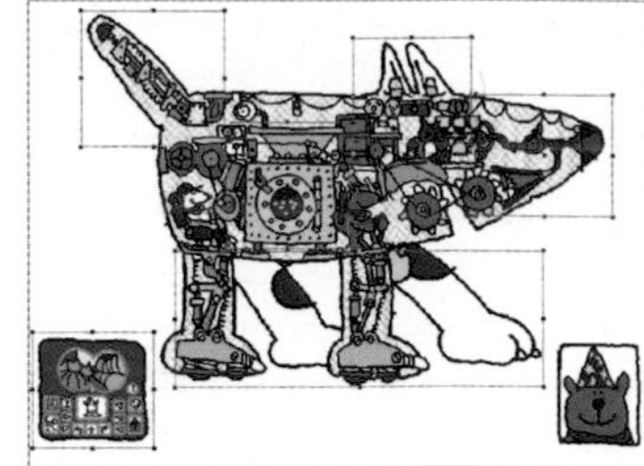

Invisible Buttons
Each of the rectangles shown here is an invisible hotspot that will take the user to another screen.

Projecting the Movie

The prototype multimedia movie usually includes simplified versions of all the sounds, graphics, and so on, used as placeholders. Once final versions of all the elements are ready, the designer builds them into a new version of the movie.

The final stage, before the movie can be put on a CD-ROM, is to convert it into a "projector." A projector is a program made up of two parts – the movie and a version of the authoring software that can play movies (but cannot be used to create them).

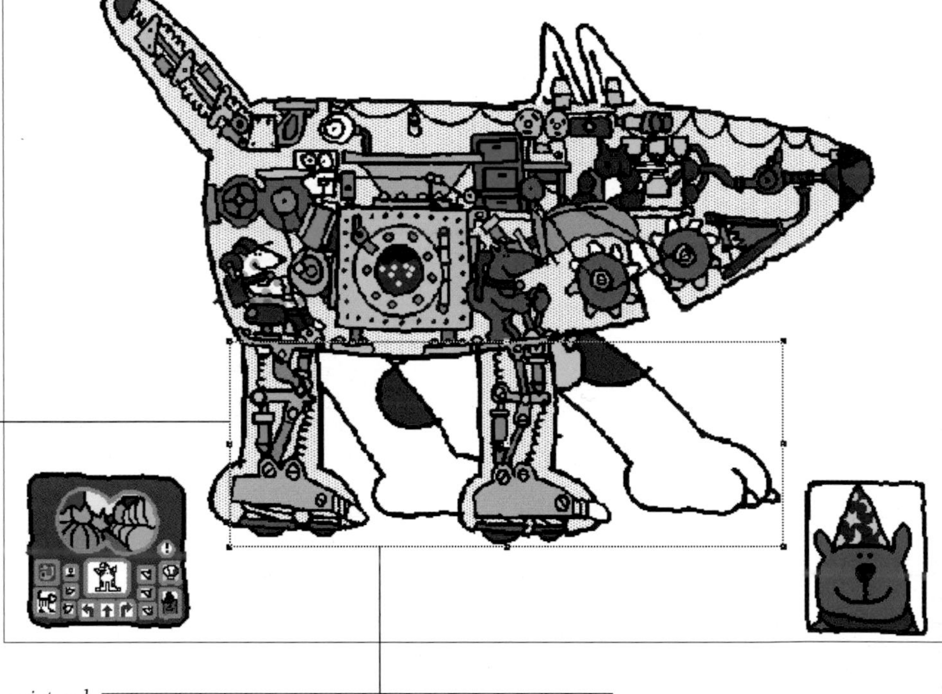

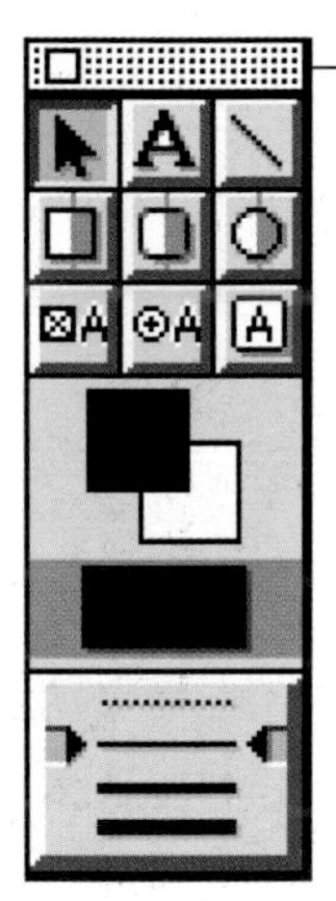

Creating Hotspots
The hotspot tools can be used to create a variety of different hotspots. Here, the designer creates a rectangular hotspot that covers the dog's legs.

Script
The designer writes a script and attaches it to the hotspot. This script tells the program to jump to the Legs screen when the user clicks on this hotspot.

Legs Screen

Visible Hotspots

As well as using invisible hotspots, the designer can employ a range of visible hotspots. Below are some of the types that are commonly used.

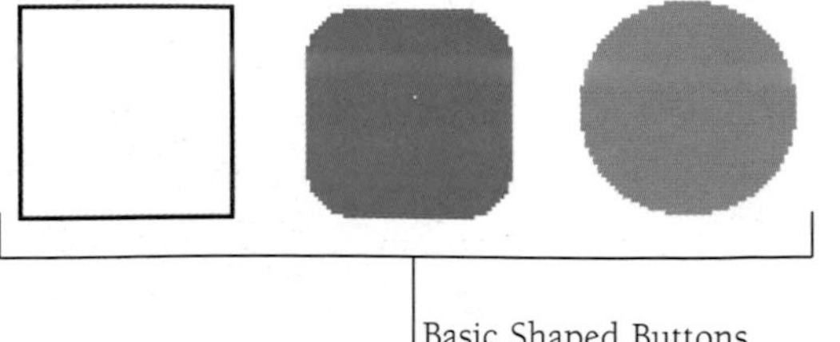

Basic Shaped Buttons

☐ off
☒ on

Checkboxes

○ off
◉ on

Radio Buttons

To find out more, click **here**.

Hot Text

OK

Text Button

ANIMATED LEGS
The close-up of the legs shows how a dog walks. The user will be able to control the animation of the moving legs with five buttons. To make them work, the designer must create a combination of animations, hotspots, scripts, and a complex score.

Cast Member 11

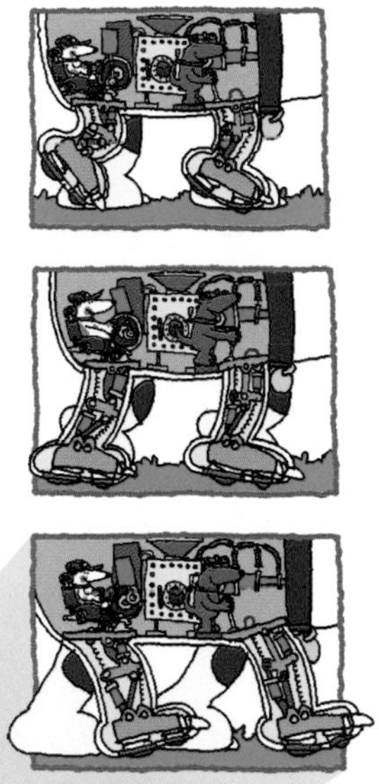

Animation Hotspots
The designer first makes a hotspot for each of the control buttons on the screen.

Scripts
The designer attaches scripts to the rewind, backward, stop, play, and fast forward buttons.

Score
Each script points to a different loop in the score; each loop contains a separate animation. These animations have their sound tracks built in.

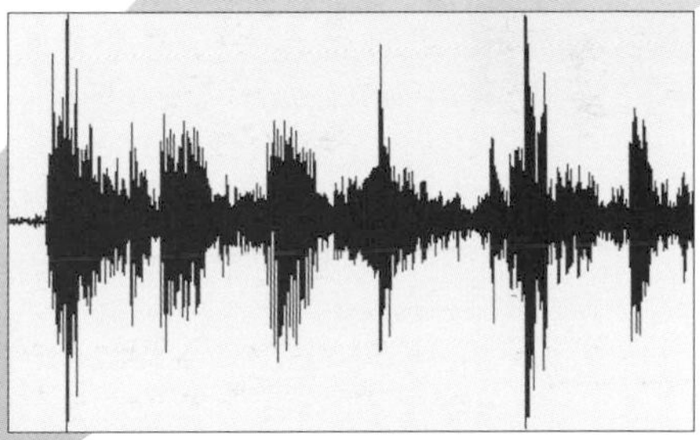

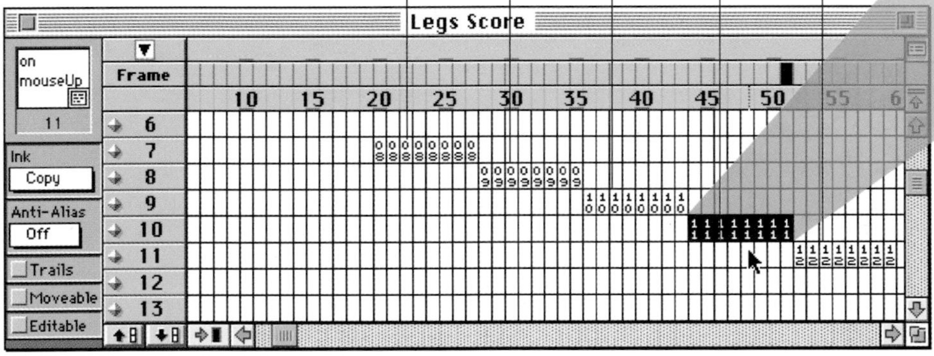

Legs Score

Play Cast Member 11
When the user presses the play button, the program will play cast member 11: an animation of the dog walking forward at normal speed accompanied by the loud noise of machinery.

The Programmer's Art

Authoring software is easy to use, but titles that are produced with it tend to run slowly. As a result, most multimedia companies employ teams of programmers to write a "software engine" – in a complex text-based programming language – that will run a title as quickly as possible.

Multimedia titles that go beyond a point-and-click style of interface, such as action games, need to be programmed from scratch. The programming team develops two programs: the main game software and a game editor. At the heart of the game software is the graphics engine, the software which moves 2-D or 3-D images around the screen during gameplay. The game editor is an authoring program that makes it easier for designers to build the different graphic environments for the game.

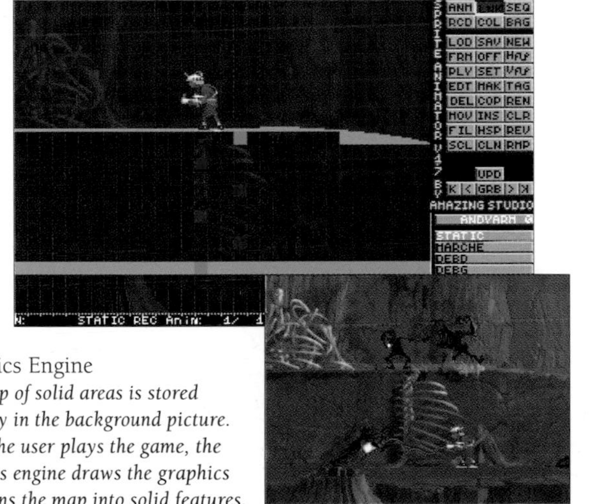

Game Editor
The game editor for Amazing Studio's Heart of Darkness gives the designers a graphical way to program in information about the game environment. Here, the designer is coloring in the areas that represent platforms (green) and ladder steps (blue).

Graphics Engine
The map of solid areas is stored invisibly in the background picture. When the user plays the game, the graphics engine draws the graphics and turns the map into solid features.

TEXT AND TYPE

AFTER BINARY NUMBERS, TEXT was the first medium to appear on a computer. And, generally speaking, it is the most straightforward element to deal with in the making of multimedia titles. Sounds, pictures, animations, and videos all require extensive processing before they can be used in multimedia software, but text can be typed in at a keyboard or even digitized straight from the pages of a book. It also takes up only a fraction of the disc space that the other media occupy. Even so, multimedia text does make its own demands – editors and designers have to pay very careful attention to how it is written, how it appears on screen, and how the reader will interact with it.

WRITING FOR MULTIMEDIA

The simplest way to generate text for multimedia is to take it from a book. This is common practice – most large book publishers have branched into multimedia, and many of their titles are conversions of popular reference or children's books. Each page of the book is digitized with a scanner, which feeds a faxlike electronic picture of the page into a computer. The editor then uses OCR (Optical Character Recognition) software, which converts the pages into electronic text that can be edited with a word processor.

Scanner
For more on scanners, see page 136

If the text is being created from scratch, it is usually written in short, self-contained chunks: this is because most people do not like to read large amounts of text from a screen. (The exception to this is "live" scrolling text – see below.) As a result, the editorial team has to plan the structure of the text very carefully. The team tries to establish what kind of text will fit on each screen – its subject matter, length, and so on – and will often make rough sketches of each screen before the text is commissioned from an author.

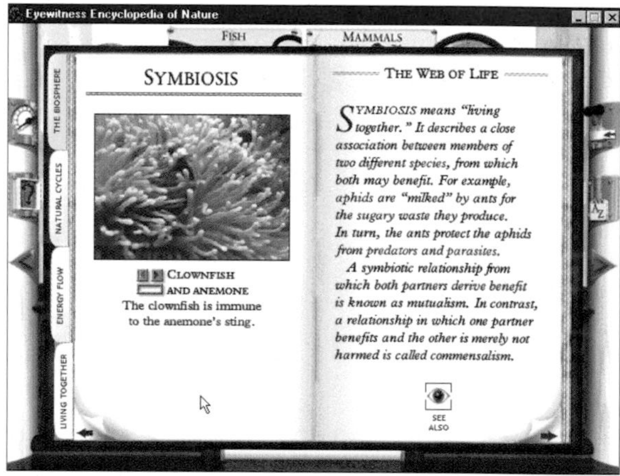

STATIC TEXT
The text in Dorling Kindersley's *Eyewitness Encyclopedia of Nature* is built into the graphics rather than being stored as a text file. This enables it to be well laid out and easy to read.

TYPES OF TEXT

There are two radically different ways to include text in a multimedia title. One way is to build it into each screen as "static" text. Here, the words are designed to look their best on screen and laid out to fit in well with their graphical surroundings. Static text has one major drawback: design considerations are paramount, and the text is always limited to a single screenful. "Live" text, however, overcomes these limitations. Live text takes the form of a database of linked articles, offering a wealth of information, from which you can access related subjects. On-screen, it appears as a word processor file, through which the user can scroll for page after page, clicking on any word to obtain further information, to pursue an associated topic, and so on. In this way, it is much more interactive than static text.

LIVE TEXT
The text entries in Microsoft's *Encarta* are live text. This enables the production team to fit large amounts of text into the encyclopedia, every word of which responds to a mouse click.

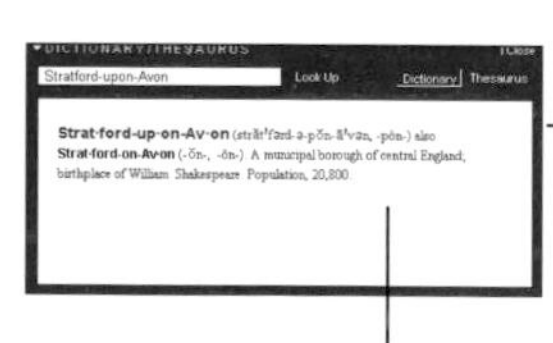

Instant Definition
Choosing any word in the entry takes you straight to a definition of or further information on that word.

Scrolling Text
Only a small portion of the large text entry fits onto the main screen. To read the entry in its entirety, you have to scroll through it.

Designing Type

The print quality of the type you are reading now is more than thirty times better than it would appear on a computer monitor. Reading poorly defined type on a screen is tiring, so multimedia designers give careful consideration to the use of typefaces, or lettering styles. Most book designers use serif typefaces – such as this one – which have small cross-lines (serifs) at the end of each stroke of a character. Serifs generally make text on the printed page easier to read.

On-screen, however, sans serif typefaces – **such as this one** – are much easier on the eye, and many screen designers opt for them. This is because pixels, the small elements that make up a screen, are square, which makes curved or elaborate letter shapes appear blocky. In the industry terminology, such letters have the "jaggies," and serif typefaces are especially prone to the jaggies.

Some designers combat the jaggies by using a technique known as antialiasing, which blends the jagged edges into their surroundings. If, say, the type is black on white, the designer fills in the pixels surrounding each letter with shades of gray, which gives the edges of the letters a much softer appearance. However, antialiasing can only be used for larger type sizes.

Color Palette
The designer uses a palette of 16 shades of blue to smooth the edges of the letter.

Drawing Tool
The designer uses a pencil tool to modify the outline of the letter one pixel at a time.

Page versus Screen

The basic principles of type design change when text is transferred from page to screen. In print, serif typefaces give each letter a more distinctive outline, making text easier to read at speed. On the screen, designers often use simpler, sans serif typefaces.

On the Page
This is how a sample of serif text appears on the printed page.

On the Screen
For the computer screen, the designer has used a sans serif typeface. It still appears blocky, but it is easier to read than serif type.

Smoothing Type

Even the plainest typeface appears jagged on-screen – the solution is to use smoothed, or antialiased, type. Antialiasing involves using type design software to blend the edges of every letter into its surroundings. It is painstaking work, but it improves the appearance of type enormously.

Jagged Type

Antialiased Type

Localization

Most multimedia titles are made in only one language, but increasingly developers are adapting their titles for other countries. This process is known as localization. It is rarely as straightforward as simply translating the original words into another language, however: voiceovers need to be rerecorded, and the new text needs to be adapted to the available space (German text, for instance, generally takes up about a quarter as much space again as its English equivalent). Some titles present even greater problems: in a child's illustrated dictionary, for example, a picture of an apple would illustrate the letter A in English, but M in Spanish, P in French, and so on, which could make it necessary to restructure the whole title.

Localization Difficulties

Often localization teams have to produce new graphics, as is shown by the title screens from the English and French versions of Dorling Kindersley's *The Way Things Work*.

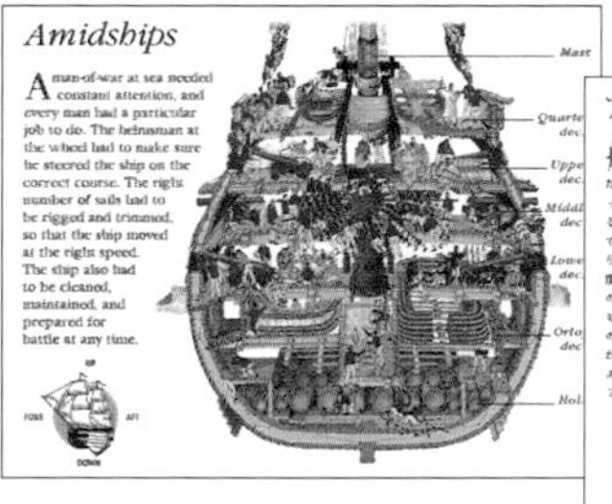

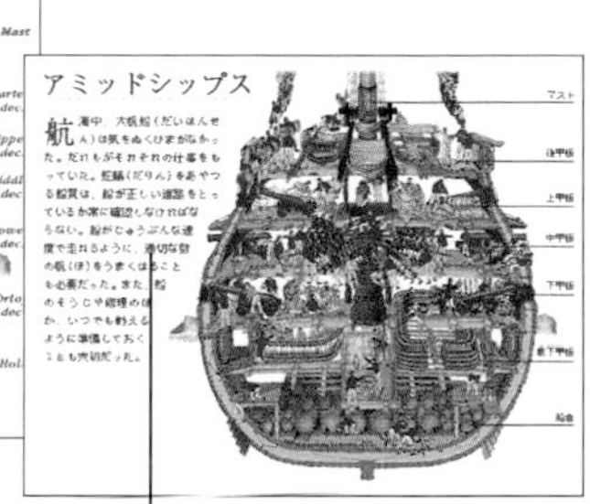

New Text for Old

Most of the work in adapting Dorling Kindersley's *Stowaway* for Japan involved inserting translated text and rerecording the voiceovers.

Copy Fitting
The Japanese text has been antialiased, laid out, and cut to fit around the existing graphics.

THE ART OF SOUND

THE ENTERTAINMENT INDUSTRY has long appreciated that sound can enhance visual experiences. Even before the invention of a sound track on celluloid turned silent films into the talkies, the screening of movies was often accompanied by a piano or an orchestra. In today's multimedia titles, music and sound effects are used, as in the movies, to enhance the drama and realism of what the user sees – but now multimedia sound professionals are having to rise to a new challenge, one that is unique to the industry. Multimedia puts the user in control of the action, so it needs an interactive sound track.

ENHANCED ACTION
Interactive sound effects add realism to 3-D action games such as Psygnosis's *Novastorm*.

LISTENING PLEASURE

Until recently, multimedia developers were all too concerned with how their titles looked and not enough with how they sounded. In the rush to exploit the new possibilities of 3-D graphics, animation, and video, developers failed to realize the full potential of the audio track. Poor sound quality, music that stopped abruptly at the press of a mouse button, or even screens that were totally silent all betrayed a lack of attention to the user's listening pleasure. But this is changing. As TV, film, and record companies move in on the multimedia act, they are bringing higher sound production values with them.

MIXING MUSIC
Jump, the David Bowie Interactive CD-ROM, by Ion, puts you in control of the mixing desk for one of his songs.

INTERACTIVE SOUND

In the best multimedia, music, dialogue, and sound effects are used not only to accompany the visual experience, but also to enhance interactivity. In many information titles, mouse clicks are confirmed audibly and the transitions between screens are accompanied by music. As well as adding to the experience, this fills the gap while the CD-ROM drive reads a new chunk of data. Entertainment titles use sound in a different way. In 3-D games, for example, the flyby of an enemy jet or the footsteps of an alien creeping up behind you are re-created with stereo sound effects to reinforce the sensation of moving in three dimensions.

For the multimedia sound team, the challenge is always to make the sound track the most exciting part of the experience.

How Multimedia Sound is Made

Making sound for multimedia titles involves several distinct stages. This example follows the creation of a sound track to accompany an animated sequence.

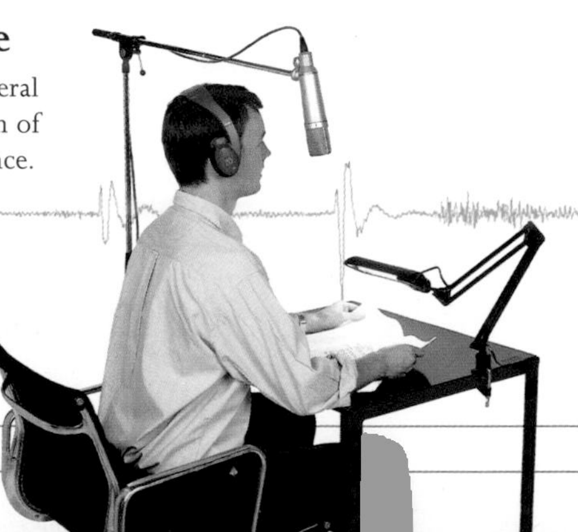

Recording
In the studio, narration, dialogue, and sound effects are recorded with a microphone.

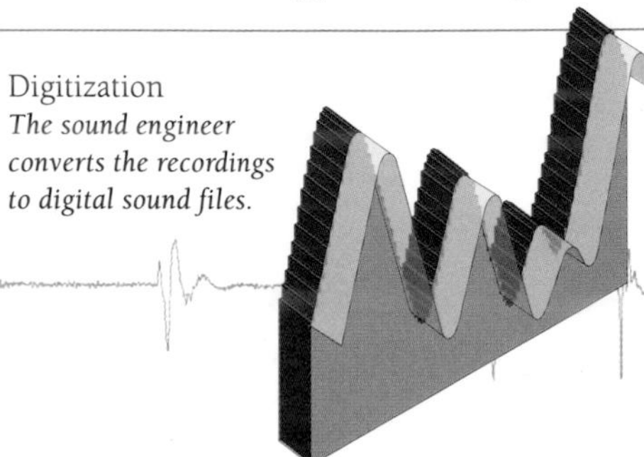

Digitization
The sound engineer converts the recordings to digital sound files.

How Sound Works

Sound is produced when an object vibrates – for example, a spoon when it is dropped or a guitar string when it is strummed. These vibrations produce sound waves – waves of pressure which move through the air in all directions. When the sound waves reach your ear, they are converted into signals that are interpreted by your brain.

Recording for multimedia involves converting sound waves into two other types of signal – first into an analog electrical signal, and then into digital information that can be stored and manipulated by a computer. Eventually, when the sound is played back, the process will be reversed, and the digital sound converted back into sound waves.

From Sound Waves to Digital Sound

To record sound for multimedia, sound waves are converted first into an analog electrical signal, and then into digital sound. The three types of sound, and how they relate to one another, are shown here.

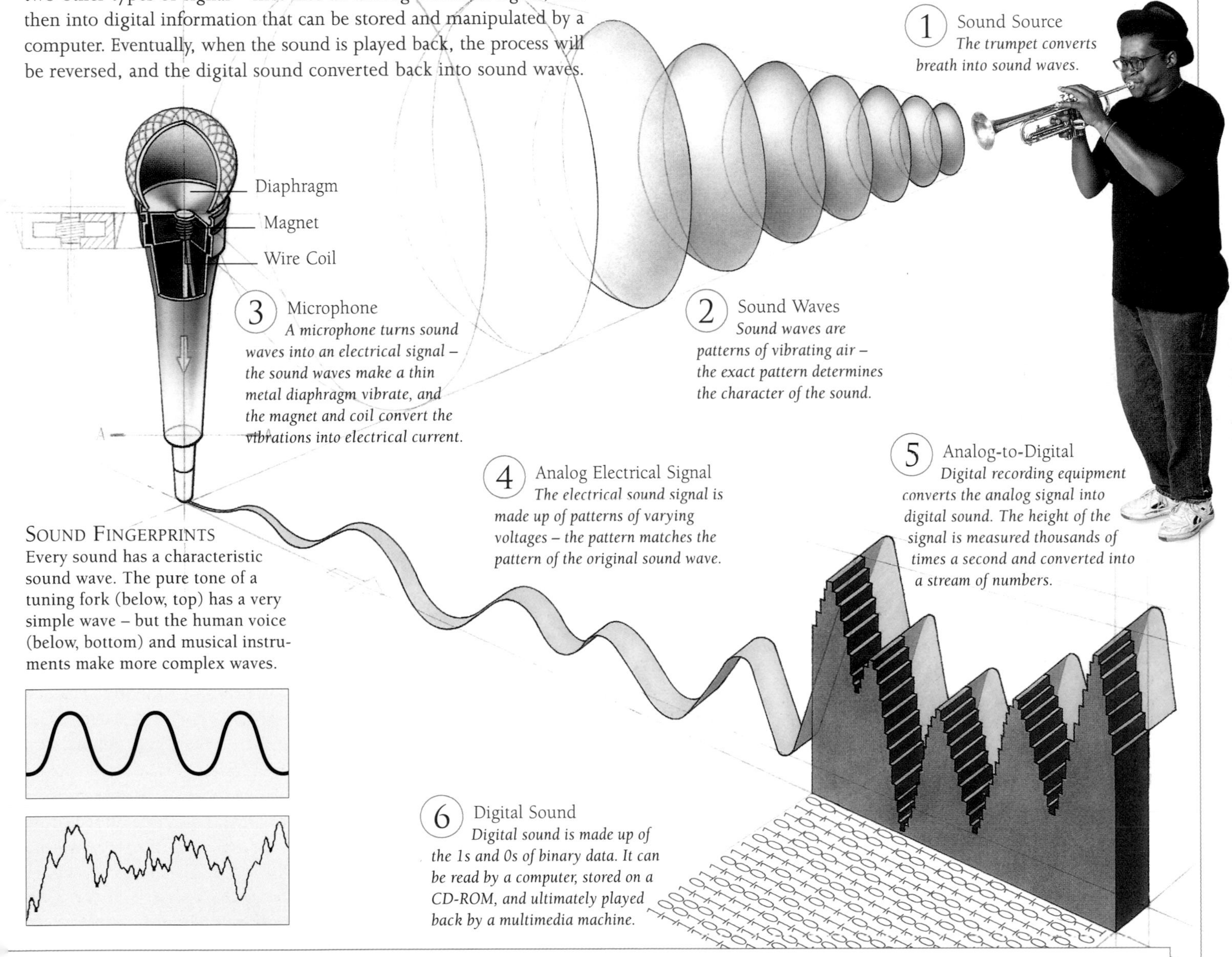

1 Sound Source
The trumpet converts breath into sound waves.

2 Sound Waves
Sound waves are patterns of vibrating air – the exact pattern determines the character of the sound.

Diaphragm
Magnet
Wire Coil

3 Microphone
A microphone turns sound waves into an electrical signal – the sound waves make a thin metal diaphragm vibrate, and the magnet and coil convert the vibrations into electrical current.

4 Analog Electrical Signal
The electrical sound signal is made up of patterns of varying voltages – the pattern matches the pattern of the original sound wave.

5 Analog-to-Digital
Digital recording equipment converts the analog signal into digital sound. The height of the signal is measured thousands of times a second and converted into a stream of numbers.

6 Digital Sound
Digital sound is made up of the 1s and 0s of binary data. It can be read by a computer, stored on a CD-ROM, and ultimately played back by a multimedia machine.

Sound Fingerprints

Every sound has a characteristic sound wave. The pure tone of a tuning fork (below, top) has a very simple wave – but the human voice (below, bottom) and musical instruments make more complex waves.

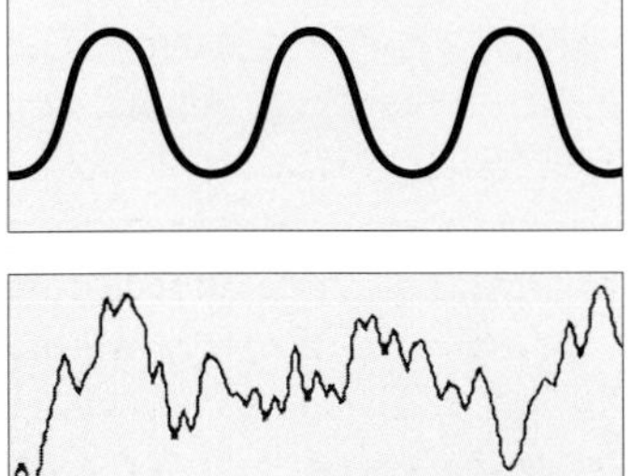

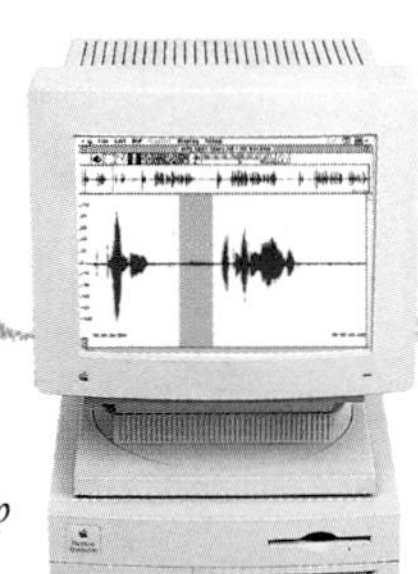

Editing
Next, the sound engineer cleans up and edits the files on a computer.

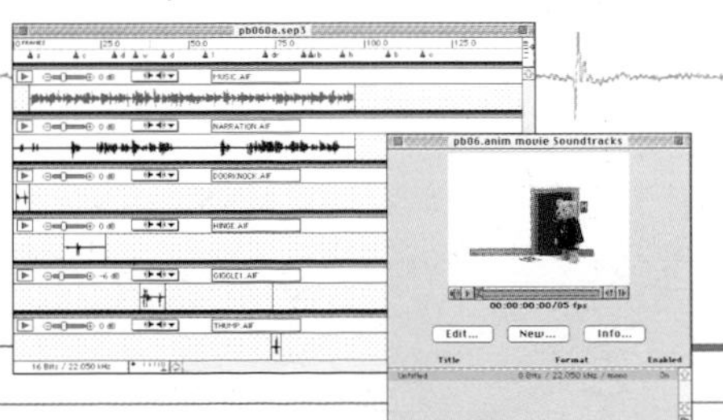

Mixing
The sound engineer adds the different sounds to the animation and mixes them into a final sound track.

Onto the CD-ROM
The sound track is stored on the CD-ROM, not as a CD audio track but as a computer sound file.

The Recording Studio

Step into a recording studio sound booth and the first thing you notice is the total silence – the background hum of everyday life is gone. The booth is not only completely soundproof, it is also "dead" – the walls and ceiling are built to absorb sound instead of reflecting it, so no echoes distort the recording. Even the furniture in the booth is kept to a minimum, because every surface affects the character of the recorded sound. This careful attention to the finer points of sound quality runs through the whole process of recording for multimedia.

The Voice Artist

Until recently, many multimedia titles used the vocal talents of the development team for their narration and dialogue, with predictably poor results. Sensibly, most multimedia makers today use professional voice recording artists, and even well-known actors such as Christopher Lee and Dennis Hopper are being enticed onto CD-ROM. Voice artists come in two varieties – narrators and character actors. Narrators are skilled at making documentary information punchy and clear, while character actors can breathe life into an animated character or dub a filmed performance.

Professional Voices

A good narrator must have a "clean" voice, with little or no trace of an accent. A clean voice is free from sibilance (hissing s sounds), loud breaths between words, and mouth noise (the tiny sounds of tongue touching palate). For a character actor, however, irregularities such as these can lend an interesting individuality to the voice.

Good timing is critical, too. A narrator should be able to time the delivery of a paragraph to within half a second, while making subtle changes to the emphasis and tone of the script. Character actors need even better voice control to synchronize their performance to lip movements on video or animation.

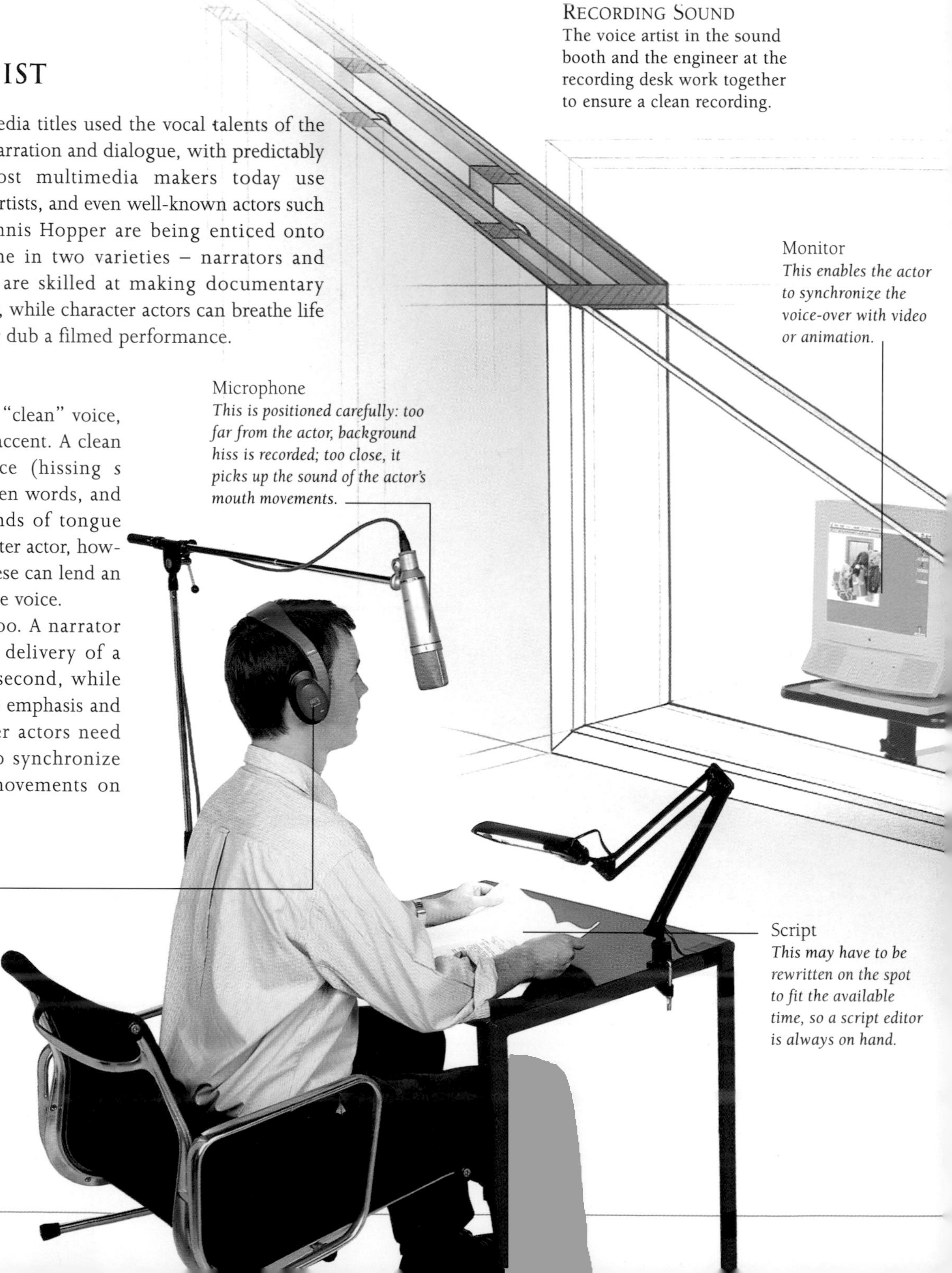

Recording Sound
The voice artist in the sound booth and the engineer at the recording desk work together to ensure a clean recording.

Monitor
This enables the actor to synchronize the voice-over with video or animation.

Microphone
This is positioned carefully: too far from the actor, background hiss is recorded; too close, it picks up the sound of the actor's mouth movements.

Headphones
These allow the actor to hear his or her voice as the microphone hears it.

Script
This may have to be rewritten on the spot to fit the available time, so a script editor is always on hand.

Sound Effects

Every multimedia studio has its sound effects library – thousands of clips on CD ranging from cartoon bangs, whizzes, and pops to earthquakes and police cars. But to get exactly the right effect the sound team often has to record the sound from scratch. However, it is not always as simple as staging events in front of a microphone. For example, when the sound team at Broderbund (makers of the adventure game *Myst*) recorded a crackling fire, the result just did not sound like the real thing. To get the sound they wanted, they ended up driving a station wagon over the gravel driveway outside the studio, and then slowing the recording down. For the sound engineer, this sort of ingenuity is called for every day. With a little bit of remixing, falling bags of sugar become footsteps, a flapping pair of leather gloves turns into an eagle taking off, and a box of vigorously shaken rocks is transformed into a marching army.

CRUNCHING SNOW
Engineers simulate the crunching noise of footsteps in soft snow by teasing a ball of cotton apart.

WRITING
For the sound of a quill pen writing on parchment, a plastic spoon is scratched against rough paper.

The Sound Engineer

The bulk of the sound engineer's work happens after the recording session, when the sound files are edited and laid down as a sound track. At the recording stage, however, the engineer still has a vital task to perform: to capture the sound at the best possible quality. The engineer listens carefully for background hiss and distortion, and uses a range of tools to eliminate them. The analog electrical signal from the microphone is fed first into a mixing desk, then through a series of electronic filters that clean up the sound. Finally, the analog sound signal is converted to digital data.

Mixing Desk
At the mixing desk, the analog electrical signal from the microphone is equalized (sounds of different pitches are boosted or dampened).

Monitor
The engineer can see the sound levels of the recording on screen.

Peak Limiter
This electronic filter tones down the loudest sounds for a more even recording.

De-esser
This filter reduces the high-pitched whistle in sibilant s sounds.

Effects Processor
Effects such as echo or concert-hall acoustics can be added to the recording.

DAT Recorder
The Digital Audio Tape recorder converts the sound signal to digital data and stores it on tape.

Sound Insulation
Beneath a thin cloth covering are layers of insulating material: sound-absorbing foam, wooden supports, an air cushion, rock wool, and plasterboard.

Direct-to-Disk Recorder
The sound signal can also be saved right onto a computer hard disk as digital sound files.

Sound Craft

After the recording session, the engineer listens to the sound files and decides which takes will go into the final sound track. Then the painstaking work of further cleaning up and enhancing the sound files begins. The engineer identifies individual problems and corrects each one using sound-editing software. The digital sound waves are shown directly on the screen, so flaws can be seen as well as heard – background hiss, mouth noise, and breaths between words all have distinctive shapes. The software's editing tools make manipulating the sound and correcting mistakes straightforward.

Cleaning Up Sound Waves

Every sound file is edited to remove mistakes and improve sound quality. Here the engineer is using Digidesign's *Sound Design* editing software to work on part of a recording – the words "cobweb" and "special laws" – that highlights many of the problems involved.

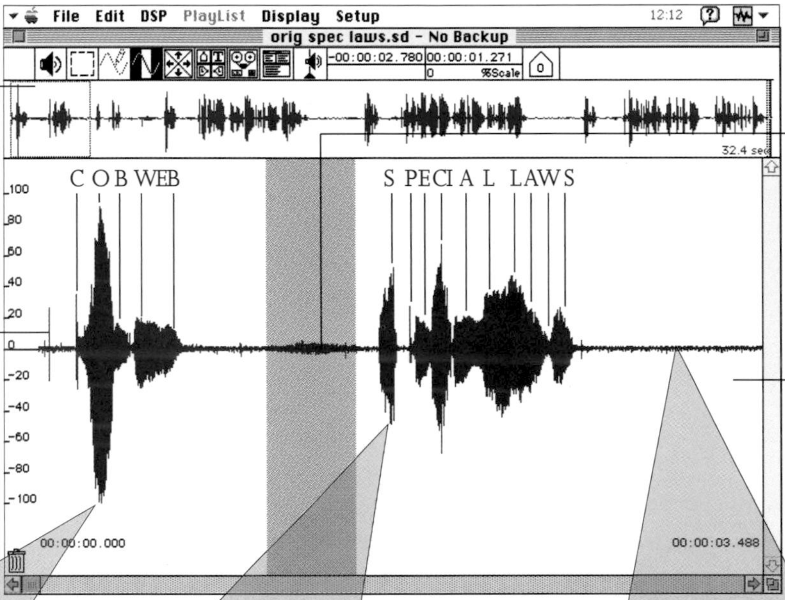

Zooming In
The whole sound file shows across the top – the engineer will zoom into problem areas to work on individual words.

Breath
Here the narrator has breathed in sharply. The engineer selects and dampens this sound, or cuts it completely, just like cutting text in a word processor.

Mouth Noise
These sharp peaks are tiny clicks made by the narrator's mouth – the engineer removes them from the file.

Sound Wave Display
Three seconds of sound are shown in detail – the engineer can zoom in by any amount to correct even the tiniest of flaws.

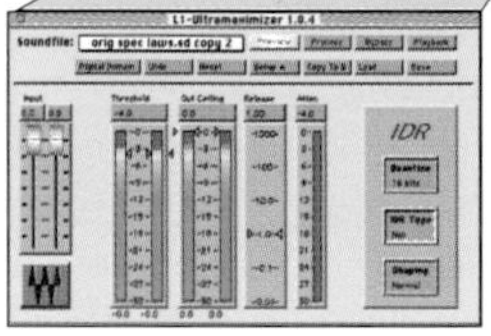

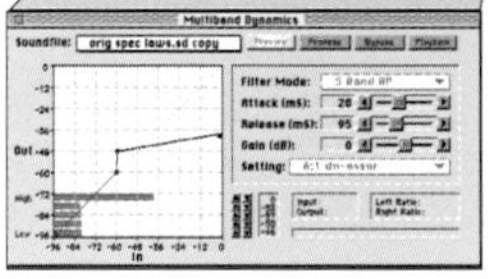

Sibilant S Sounds
The three s sounds in the words "special laws" are made softer with "de-essing" software.

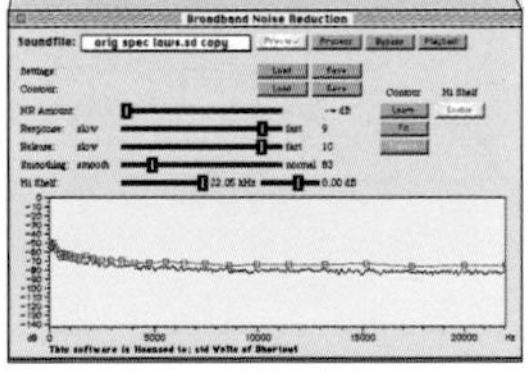

Background Noise
The background hiss in a quiet moment is analyzed by noise reduction software, which then removes hiss from the whole file.

Sound Peak
The "co" in "cobweb" is much louder than the rest of the word. Peak limiter software is used to tone down the loudest sounds so the overall volume is more even.

Cleaned-up Sound

Once the sound file is free of unwanted noise and the volume has been evened out (below), the engineer boosts the volume of the whole file (right).

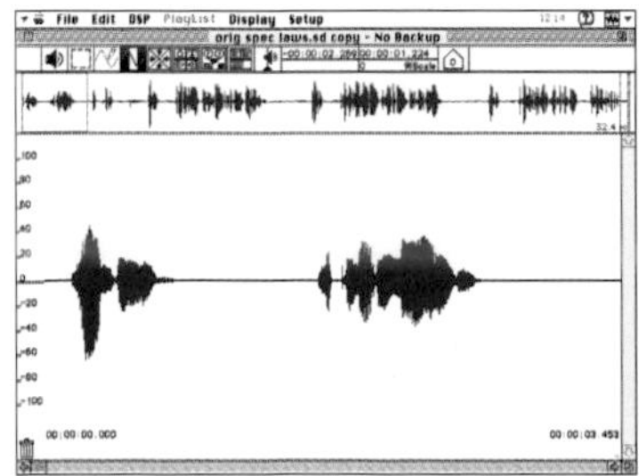

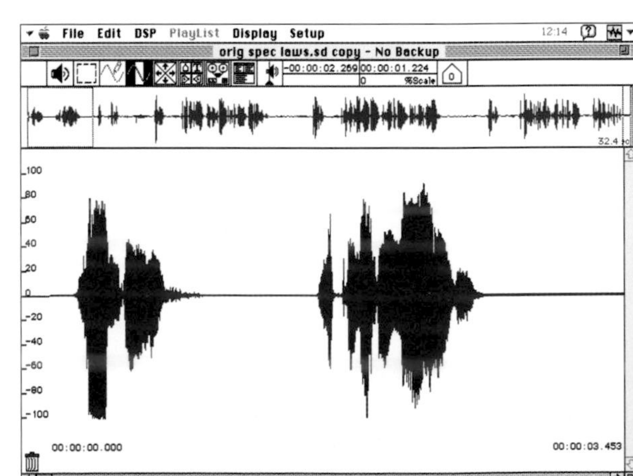

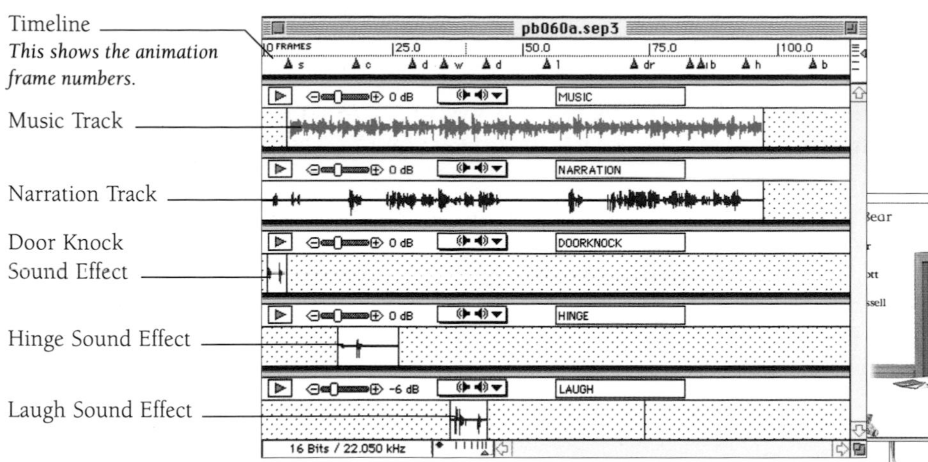

Laying Tracks

The sound track is built up from the separate sound files – in this case, music, narration, and sound effects are being added to an animated sequence from the Dorling Kindersley title *P.B. Bear's Birthday Party*.

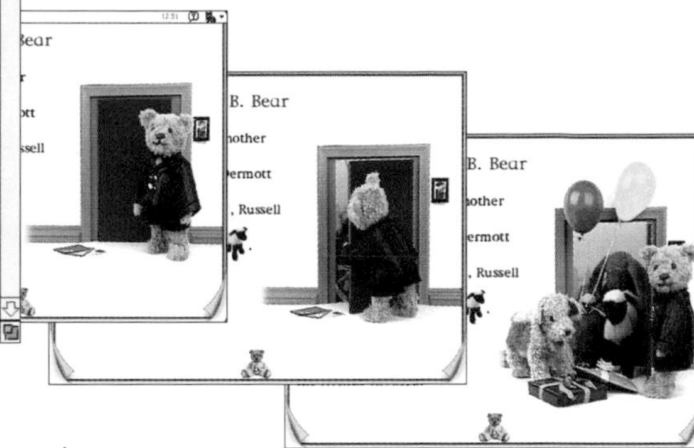

Animation Frames
Each sound effect is cued into a different frame in the animation.

Cuing in Sound

Once all the voice-over and sound effects files have been edited, the engineer uses mixing software to put the final sound track together. At this point, specially recorded background music is also added to the mix. If the sound track is for video or animation, the first step is to watch the moving images frame by frame, deciding when to cue in each sound recording. The engineer then arranges all the sound files along a timeline, balancing the volume of each one. After checking that the finished sound track fits the moving images exactly, the engineer saves it as a single sound file.

Shrinking Sound
This illustration shows how a CD-quality sound file can be made smaller. Each of the steps shown here halves the size and the quality of the sound file.

Making Sound Files Smaller

While most multimedia machines can play stereo CD-quality sound, many titles use lower sound quality. This is for two reasons – first, because poorer sound takes up less room on the CD-ROM; and second, because playing high-quality sound slows the computer down. Sound files can be made smaller by a factor of 16 or more, but unfortunately the quality drops too.

1 CD-quality Stereo Sound
At its best, multimedia sound uses 44,100 samples a second (each sample is shown here as an upright block), and uses 16 binary digits, or bits, to measure each sample.

2 Stereo to Mono
The simplest way to shrink sound is to combine the two stereo channels, left and right, into one mono channel.

3 Half the Bits
By using eight bits instead of 16 to measure each sample, the sound file is made smaller still – but the result is less precise, grittier sound.

4 Half the Samples
To shrink the sound file even further, half as many samples are used every second. This makes the sound muddier.

Measuring Differences
The difference between one sound sample and the next (shown here in red) is often very small.

Compressing Sound

Sound files can be squeezed further with compression. Compression works by measuring only the small differences between successive sound samples, instead of measuring the whole height of every sample. With compression, 16-bit sound files can be made four times smaller, and the quality barely suffers. When the sound files are played back, the processor decompresses them to almost their original quality.

The Digital Orchestra

Although the compact disc was invented to carry high-quality recordings of music, ironically the music featured in multimedia is often of poor sound quality. This is because still and moving images take up so much space on most CD-ROMs that it is hard to find enough room to fit in music without sacrificing either quality or amount. The exception is music-based titles, in which only a small amount of multimedia interactivity is added to what is basically a musical album. Fortunately for multimedia software, there is a solution to the problem: a technology called MIDI, which allows hundreds of hours of music to be stored on one CD-ROM.

Music-based titles
For more on music-based titles, see page 56

Music by Numbers

MIDI (Musical Instrument Digital Interface) is a code that gives musical instructions. In the same way that the notes on sheet music tell musicians what to do, MIDI code gives instructions to synthesizer keyboards, drum machines, and other electronic instruments. For multimedia, MIDI is perfect – not least because almost every multimedia machine contains a synthesizer on a chip. A whole symphony can be converted into MIDI and the chip can play it back, taking on all the parts of the orchestra. Unlike traditionally recorded sound, MIDI takes up very little room and does not slow down the rest of multimedia's activity; the synthesizer chip does all the work. It may not sound quite like the New York Philharmonic, but with today's synthesizer technology it can come surprisingly close.

How MIDI Works

MIDI is very similar to sheet music. The basic message simply says: play this note, this loud, for this length of time, on this instrument. It is one thing, however, to see a saxophone solo written as music notation, and quite another to hear a skilled saxophonist perform it. So MIDI also includes detailed information about how the music must be played, from the minute variations in pitch and volume of every chord to special effects that imitate the smooth slide between notes of a fretless bass guitar.

Most of the MIDI synthesizer chips inside games consoles and on the sound cards of multimedia computers can play up to 16 instruments at one time from an orchestra of over 120 prerecorded sounds – everything from a harpsichord to a marimba.

Sound cards
For more on sound cards, see page 77

MIDI music can be recorded without a real harpsichord or marimba in sight – all it takes is a talented musician and a setup like the one shown here.

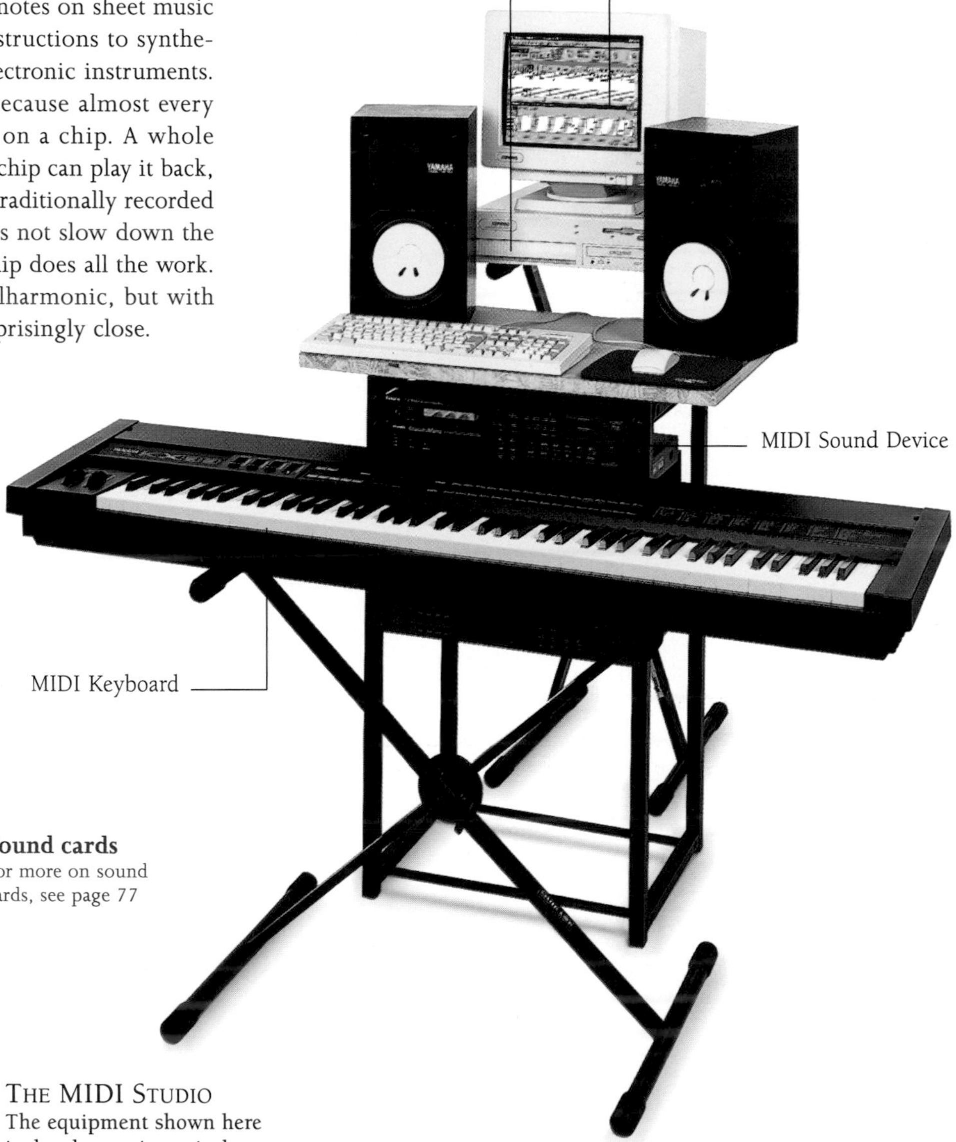

Sequencer
A computer running MIDI sequencing software is used to record and edit MIDI music.

MIDI Sound Device

MIDI Keyboard

The MIDI Studio
The equipment shown here is the electronic equivalent of a composer's piano, a full orchestra, a recording studio, and a sound-editing suite.

Recording MIDI

Using sequencer software – the musical equivalent of a word processor – the multimedia composer records an electronic score, playing the part of one instrument at a time on the keyboard. The performance does not need to be perfect: the musician can edit any mistakes afterward, and the sequencer automatically corrects notes that are not exactly in time. Absolutely perfect timing may make the recording sound too clinical, so the sequencer can then add subtle computer-generated variations – oddly enough, this is called "humanizing." The composer can then edit the recording, by playing new notes into a section or by rewriting the score.

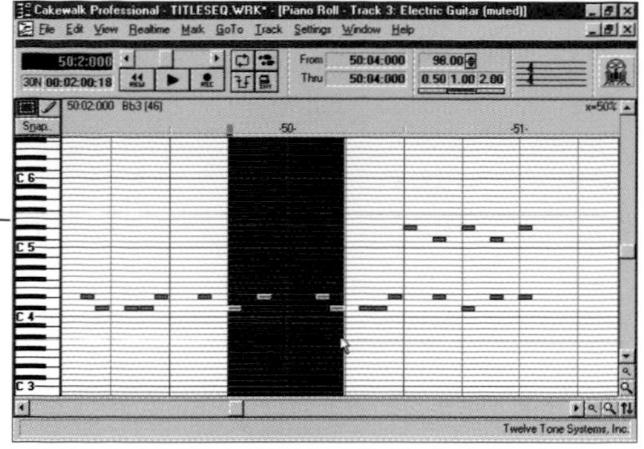

Piano Roll Display
As the composer plays each instrumental part, the notes are recorded on a grid that mimics a piano roll.

Score Display
Meanwhile, the sequencer keeps track of the score – classically trained musicians may prefer to edit the music by moving notes around staves.

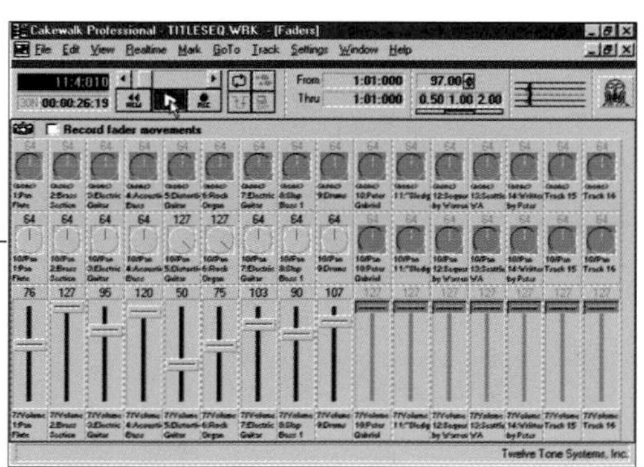

Mixing Desk Display
Finally, the different tracks are combined and the whole piece is mixed at an on-screen mixing desk.

Flexible Score

MIDI music is most often used to accompany fast-paced action games and interactive adventures, where the music has to change to reflect the often unpredictable events on screen. To achieve this, many multimedia composers will record loops of music that can be repeated over and over – one for each scene, say. The composer may also record a set of tailpieces and musical links that can be played if the action is cut short or as a bridge from one scene to another. The end result is a flexible score – a toolkit of musical parts that is composed into a seamless flow every time the title is played.

The only drawback to MIDI has been the varying quality of the synthesizer chips used in multimedia machines to play MIDI back – at worst, the full sweep of the digital orchestra can sound like a great mass of electric organs. Today's newer multimedia computers and games consoles, however, boast increasingly sophisticated sound hardware that can do justice to MIDI music.

MIDI Instruments

It is possible to record the sounds of an entire orchestra with a sequencer and a keyboard. However, a piano performance cannot reflect the intricate playing patterns of a saxophone or a guitar – to do this, musicians can use specialized instruments designed for recording MIDI. None of the tools shown here makes sound directly – instead they all make MIDI data.

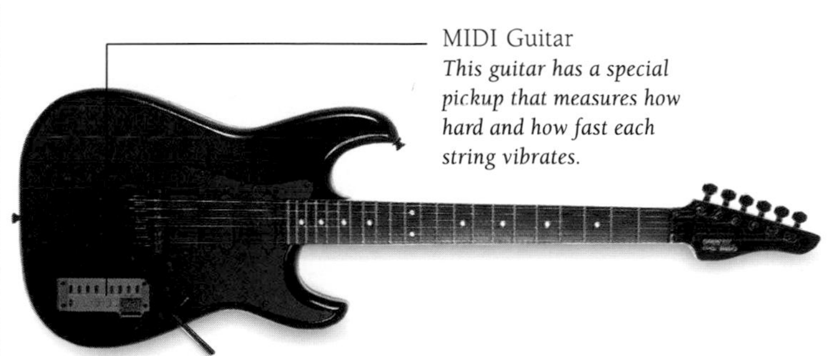

MIDI Guitar
This guitar has a special pickup that measures how hard and how fast each string vibrates.

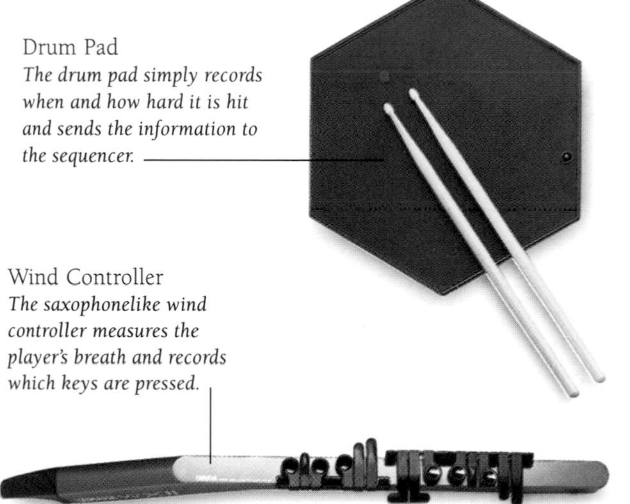

Drum Pad
The drum pad simply records when and how hard it is hit and sends the information to the sequencer.

Wind Controller
The saxophonelike wind controller measures the player's breath and records which keys are pressed.

Graphic Designs

Superb graphics is one of the keys to multimedia's appeal, and developers are well aware that the success of a title depends largely on the visual impact it makes. The multimedia industry attracts highly talented artists, who combine traditional skills as designers, illustrators, fine artists, and photographers with computer expertise. Each specialized area in the traditional arts is reflected in the computer graphics world by a different type of graphics software – powerful tools limited only by the artist's imagination. Here, a screen from Dorling Kindersley's *Eyewitness History of the World* shows how an artist can combine a range of techniques in creating a single image for the screen.

History of the World
For more on this title, see page 110

Art and Technology

A decade ago, computer graphics were more a science than an art – graphics for computer games were mostly left to the programmers, while graphics for film and television were produced by a small number of designers using expensive, specialized computers. Since then, two things have happened. One is that graphics technology has made great progress. Designers now use desktop computers such as the Macintosh, which are powerful enough for all but the most intricate 3-D graphics work. The other development is that the software has become easier to use and is packed with tools and tricks that give designers infinite room for experiment and expression.

Macintosh
For more on the Macintosh, see page 90

Back to the Drawing Board

Accompanying this technological progress has been a return to more traditional design values – for, although computers make it easy to produce graphics, it takes a good designer to produce them well, instead of merely showing off what the software can do. As a consequence, the design team puts a lot of work into planning the overall look and feel of a title to make sure that the images are clear and consistent and do not swamp the rest of the information.

There are four main types of graphics software, three of which imitate equipment already familiar to traditional designers: the technical illustrator's drawing board, the photographer's darkroom, and the artist's easel. Many designers also prepare artwork by hand. The fourth type of software – and the only uniquely electronic art form – is 3-D graphics, which began as a tool for engineers and architects but is now at the heart of many of the most creative and exciting multimedia projects.

Graphic Techniques
The historian's console shown here was created using a combination of all the main computer graphics techniques: drawing, painting, 3-D graphics, and image manipulation.

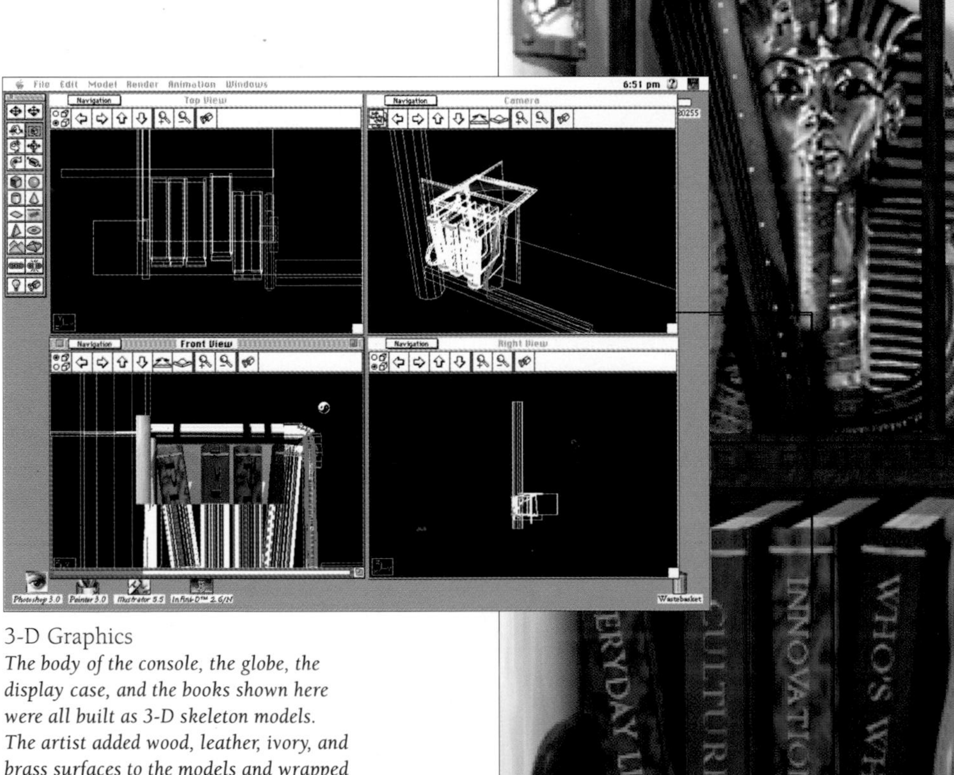

3-D Graphics
The body of the console, the globe, the display case, and the books shown here were all built as 3-D skeleton models. The artist added wood, leather, ivory, and brass surfaces to the models and wrapped the world map around the globe using the same 3-D graphics software.

Drawing
To create the surface of the globe, the artist first drew an outline map of the world on the computer using drawing software, which imitates the tools of a technical illustrator or draftsman.

Painting
The artist used paint software to color the map and to give it the texture of aging parchment. Paint software mimics the paper, brushes, and painting styles of traditional artists.

Image Manipulation
The skull and all the other artifacts on the console came from photographs. The artist used image manipulation software to resize and retouch the picture of the skull, adding highlights and shadows to make it blend into its surroundings.

Drawing & Painting

The multimedia artist's canvas is the grid of over 30,000 tiny squares – digitized picture elements known as pixels – that make up the picture on a computer screen. Instead of a pencil or a paintbrush, the artist draws or paints with light. But the fundamentals of creating original two-dimensional graphics for multimedia are similar to those of the traditional arts of technical drawing and painting. Drawing software enables artists to construct mathematically precise technical illustrations, while paint software allows for experiment with brush strokes, color mixing, and painting styles.

The Digital Easel

Most multimedia artists create images for the screen by using paint software – a range of artificial paintbrushes, paints, and other equipment that the artist can use to color in the pixels on the screen. Some paint programs, known as "natural media" programs, specialize in re-creating exactly the subtle effects of traditional media such as charcoal, watercolors, oil paints, and so on. The advantages of painting digitally are: every idea can be tried out, because mistakes can be corrected instantly; and many tasks are automated, as the main illustration on this page shows.

Technical Drawing

Some artists use drawing software instead of paint software to create images. Drawing software is close in principle to technical drawing, but more colorful. With it, the artist creates shapes not with strokes of the brush but by building up geometric outlines. The artist can choose a color and line style for every shape either before or after it has been drawn. Because every shape is mathematically constructed, any line can be singled out and reshaped at any stage, no matter how many other lines overlap it. This flexibility with shapes makes drawing software especially useful for creating diagrams, line drawings, and stylized illustrations.

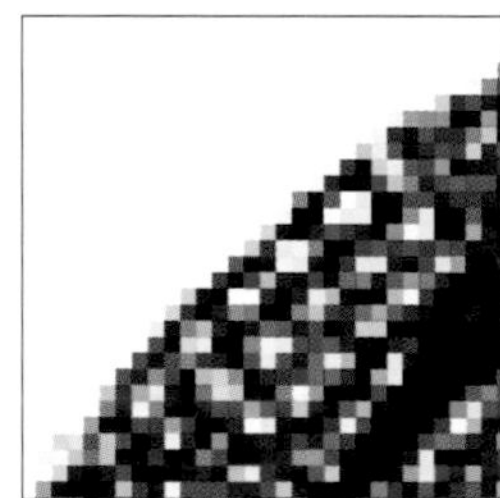

Painting with Pixels
The artist's brush paints the screen by coloring a swathe of pixels. If necessary, the artist can use a magnifying tool to zoom in and color each pixel individually.

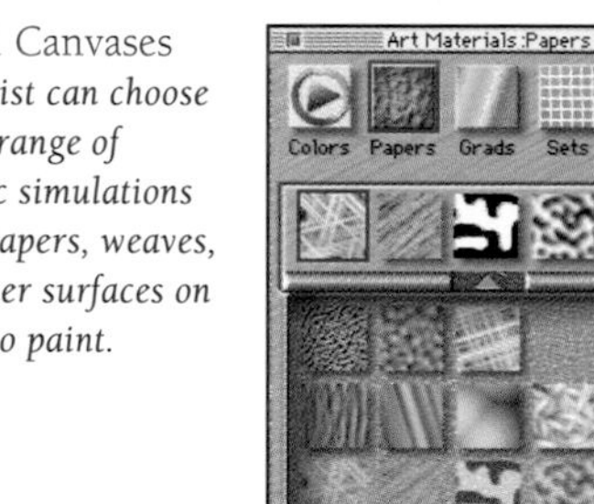

Digital Canvases
The artist can choose from a range of realistic simulations of art papers, weaves, and other surfaces on which to paint.

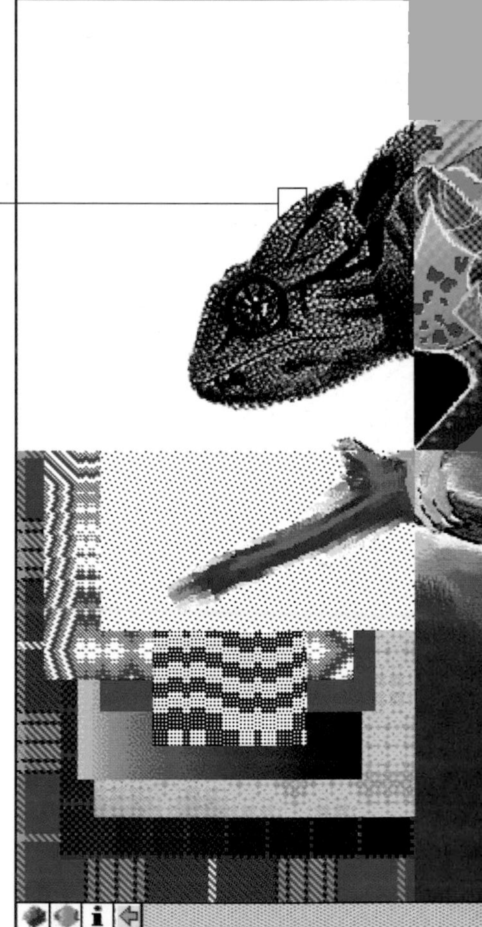

Painting with Light
This chameleon was created using Fractal Design's natural media paint program *Painter*. Each of the six segments has been painted using a different combination of "paper" and painting tools.

Graphics Tablet

Some multimedia artists draw and paint with a mouse, but many prefer to use a graphics tablet attached to their computer. The artist draws or paints with a stylus, and the tablet exactly re-creates every move of the pen on the screen. Most tablets are also pressure-sensitive, which enables the artist to thicken or darken a line or brush stroke by applying more pressure to the pen.

Instant Patterns
A traditional artist creates patterns by building up brush strokes, but for a multimedia artist the patterns are ready-made. They can be painted on with a brush, or flooded in to fill the space enclosed by an existing outline.

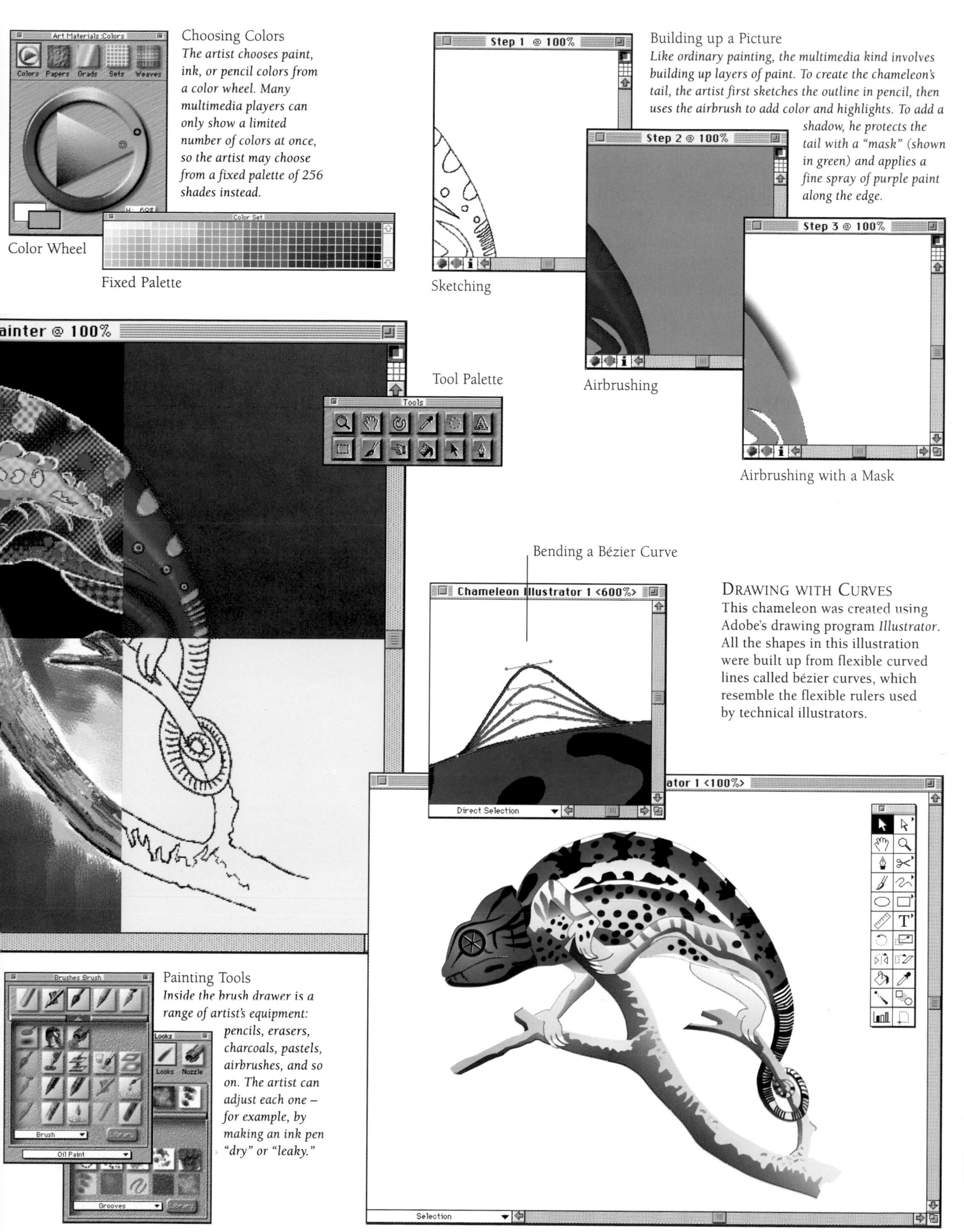

Choosing Colors

The artist chooses paint, ink, or pencil colors from a color wheel. Many multimedia players can only show a limited number of colors at once, so the artist may choose from a fixed palette of 256 shades instead.

Color Wheel

Fixed Palette

Building up a Picture

Like ordinary painting, the multimedia kind involves building up layers of paint. To create the chameleon's tail, the artist first sketches the outline in pencil, then uses the airbrush to add color and highlights. To add a shadow, he protects the tail with a "mask" (shown in green) and applies a fine spray of purple paint along the edge.

Sketching

Airbrushing

Airbrushing with a Mask

Tool Palette

Bending a Bézier Curve

Drawing with Curves

This chameleon was created using Adobe's drawing program *Illustrator*. All the shapes in this illustration were built up from flexible curved lines called bézier curves, which resemble the flexible rulers used by technical illustrators.

Painting Tools

Inside the brush drawer is a range of artist's equipment: pencils, erasers, charcoals, pastels, airbrushes, and so on. The artist can adjust each one – for example, by making an ink pen "dry" or "leaky."

Image Manipulation

Multimedia designers do not always create graphics from scratch on the computer – they often use photographs and hand-drawn artwork as the starting point for screen images. With a digital camera, a photographer can take electronic photos and feed them through a cable into a computer. More commonly, existing pictures are digitized with a scanner, which reads them in the same way as a color photocopier but creates digital copies instead of paper ones. Getting pictures into the computer is only the start of the process. With image manipulation ("imaging") software, the designer can use cameralike filters and all the tricks of a photographic darkroom to transform the original images into something totally new.

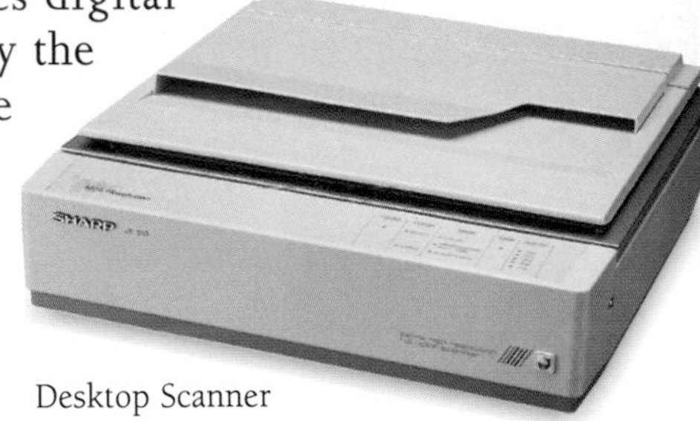

Desktop Scanner

The Electronic Darkroom

The first step in image manipulation is to improve the quality of the scanned image. A professional photographer may spend hours in the darkroom adjusting the brightness, contrast, and color balance of a single print, but with imaging software such as Adobe's *Photoshop* it can be done instantly with on-screen controls. With painting tools, the designer can also imitate the specialist techniques of hand finishing or retouching. For example, he or she can use an airbrush to paint over blemishes in the scanned image and add extra shading.

Making the Camera Lie

Imaging software has a range of powerful tools called filters, which the designer can use to completely transform an image. Some of these imitate traditional camera effects, such as distortion with a fish-eye lens, while others do things that normal photography never could, such as making an out-of-focus picture sharper. By combining elements from different photos, and using filters and retouching tools, the designer can build a realistic scene that never actually took place. The coral reef from Dorling Kindersley's *Eyewitness Encyclopedia of Nature* on the opposite page shows how imaging software was used to create an underwater montage.

Effects Filters
Designers can transform an image dramatically and instantly by using a range of software filters.

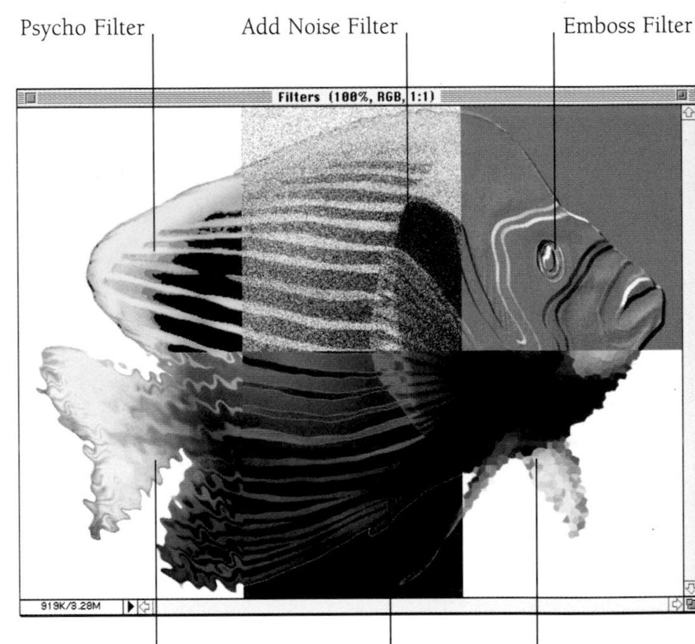

Encyclopedia of Nature
For more on this title, see page 22

Picture Quality

Most multimedia players cannot show photo-quality images, so the designer has to downgrade each screen picture in two ways. The first is to reduce its resolution – the number of pixels it contains. The second is to reduce its color depth – the number of different colors each pixel can have. The resulting image takes up a fraction of the storage space of the original.

Photomontage

This coral reef is a montage of over 30 illustrations and photos, assembled using Adobe's *Photoshop* image manipulation software.

Cut-out Shark

Placing Images
Each image is cut out from its original photo and placed into the montage.

Background Layer
The montage is made up of many layers, one for each image. The background layer sits behind the others.

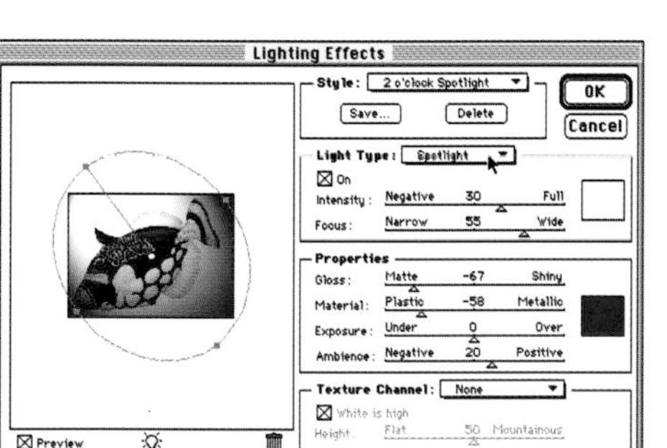

Lighting Filter

Underwater Lighting
Using an automatic lighting filter, the designer adds highlights to this picture of a fish. The fish is on its own layer of the montage, so it can be manipulated individually without affecting the background.

Color and Shading
To make this fish blend into its surroundings, the designer first adjusts the colors in the image with a filter, and then uses the airbrush tool to add realistic shadows.

Original Artwork

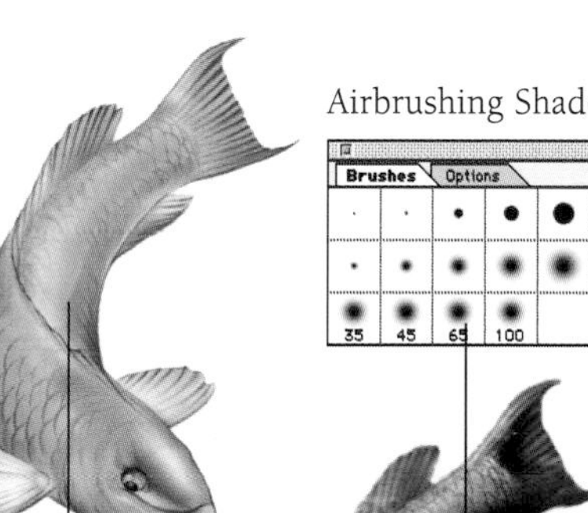

Adjusting Colors

Hue/Saturation
Master
R
Y
G
C
B
M
Hue: +30
Saturation: -15
Lightness: -40
Sample:
OK
Cancel
Load...
Save...
Colorize
Preview

Airbrushing Shadows

Modeling in 3-D

Many of the most spectacular multimedia titles immerse the user in an artificial 3-D world that is as complex and richly detailed as it is beautiful, but creating an alternative reality is not as difficult as it seems. Even so, sometimes it takes a while for designers who are used to flat images to become accustomed to working in three dimensions – in fact, multimedia developers often employ trained architects to create 3-D designs, because architects are better able to visualize spatially. Imagination is allowed free rein, because the artificial world is not constrained by the laws of the real world; the software used to make 3-D models is powerful enough to turn almost anything the designer can think of into an almost tangible artificial reality.

3-D Console
This information console from a prototype of Dorling Kindersley's *Eyewitness Virtual Reality Cat* was built as a 3-D model, using modeling software.

Wireframe Models

Modeling software creates an imaginary three-dimensional space for the designer to work in. Every object in the space is represented as a set of points, which are joined to make an outline framework of straight lines. This is known as a wireframe (see opposite page). The whole 3-D world and all the characters in it are built up as a series of wireframes, to which the designer can add artificial surfaces, textures, and lighting to make a realistic final scene.

Making a Wireframe

The first step is to build a wireframe model. The example shown here is a console from a prototype of Dorling Kindersley's interactive 3-D "museum" *Eyewitness Virtual Reality Cat*. To construct the console, the designer used Specular International's *Infini-D* modeling software. Building a simple model is easy because the designer can choose from a set of basic shapes – spheres, cylinders, cubes, and so on – which can be placed on the screen, moved, and joined, or stretched and reshaped to create new shapes. By combining several basic shapes with a few more complex techniques, the designer can build up the wireframe of the console.

Virtual Reality Cat
For more on this title, see page 28

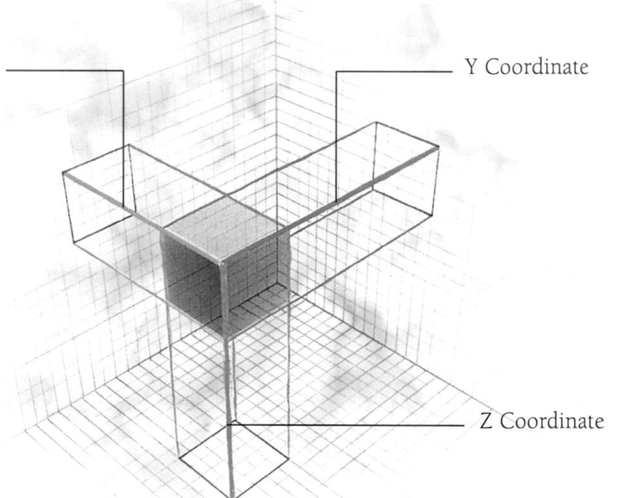

3-D Coordinates
A 3-D model consists of many points in imaginary space. This cube is defined by where its corners are – the position of every corner is measured in each of the three dimensions X, Y, and Z.

Modeling Made Easy

Building 3-D models from scratch is time-consuming, but there are short cuts. Some 3-D graphics companies sell ready-made wireframes, which the designer can adapt. The alternative is to use a 3-D digitizer to take a wireframe from a real object – the designer touches the object repeatedly with the stylus on the end of the digitizer arm, and the computer measures the position of the stylus in space. With enough points, the designer can build a whole model.

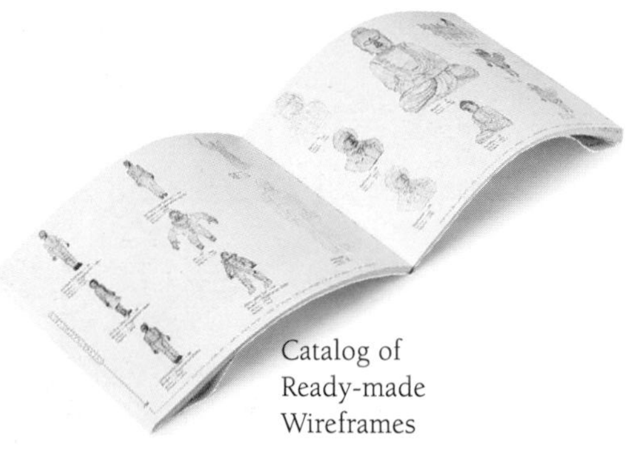

Catalog of Ready-made Wireframes

3-D Digitizer

Basic Shapes

The designer uses 3-D modeling software to create the wireframe for the console (left). Working with a tool kit of basic shapes, the designer can move and reshape each object in the 3-D space of the program. Each of the building blocks below corresponds to the same-colored shape(s) in the model.

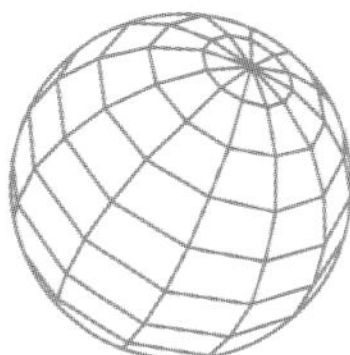

Sphere Tool

The sphere tool creates a globe of any size. Inside the computer's 3-D world, a perfect sphere is stored, but on the screen it is drawn with straight lines as a wireframe outline.

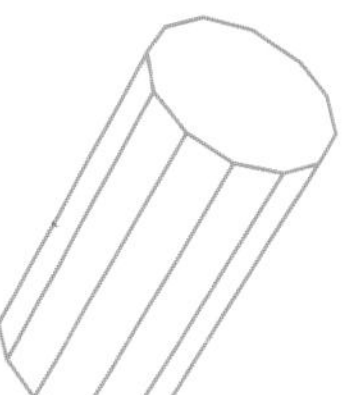

Cylinder Tool

The designer uses this tool to create the fluting on the side of the console and the struts that support the top. Once a cylinder has been placed, it can be stretched to the right dimensions and then moved into position.

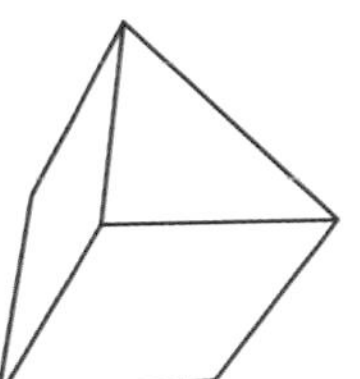

Extrude Tool

This tool adds simple depth to any flat shape. To make the top of the console, the designer draws a triangle and then stretches it into three dimensions with the extrude tool.

Lathe Tool

This tool makes a flat shape three-dimensional by rotating it in space. Here, the designer uses a circle as the starting point to make a doughnut ring.

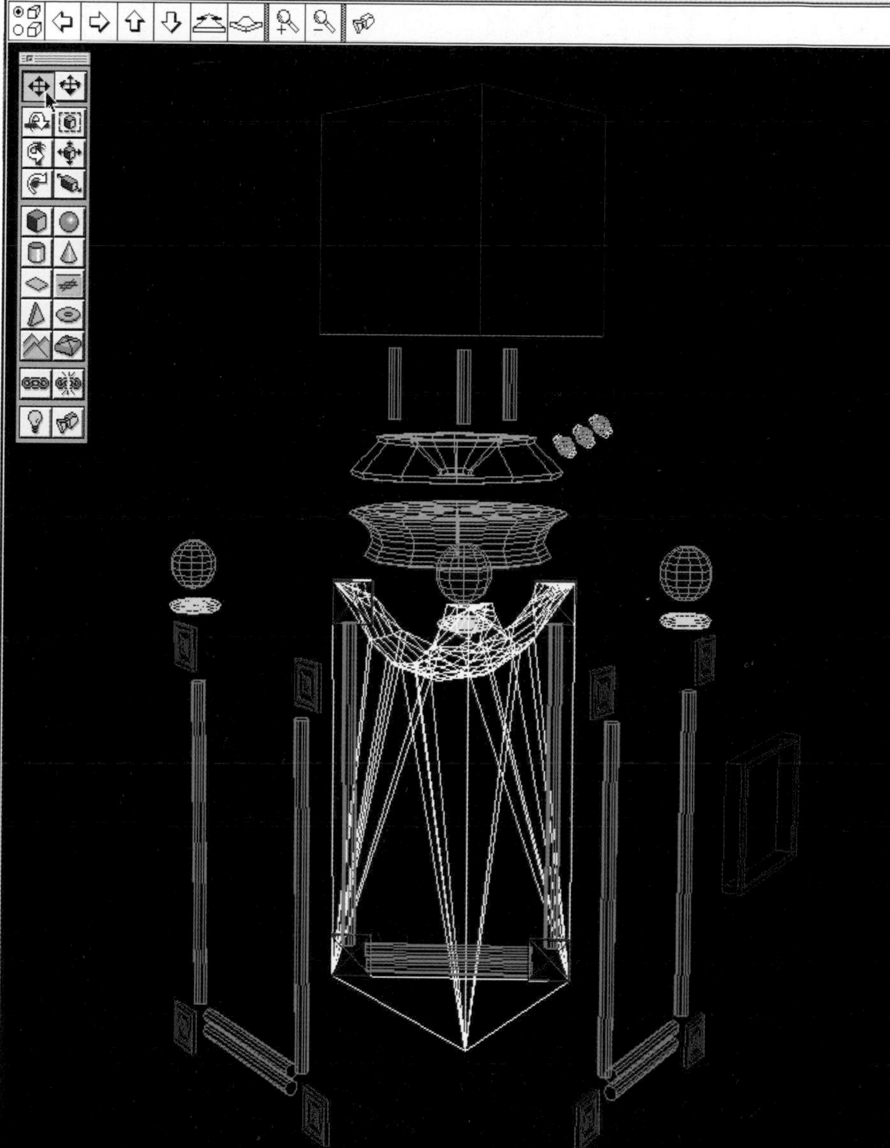

Complex Shapes

As well as combining simple building blocks, the designer can use some advanced modeling techniques to create the more complex shapes in the console.

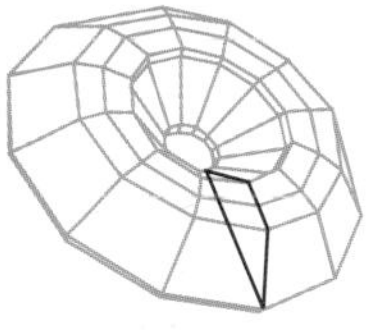

Lathe Tool

To make the console's pivoting center, the designer uses the lathe tool again, this time changing the starting point to the shape shown at right.

Freeform Tool

The designer can create a new shape from scratch by drawing cross-sectional blueprints on the screen. Here, the designer is working on a sideways view (right).

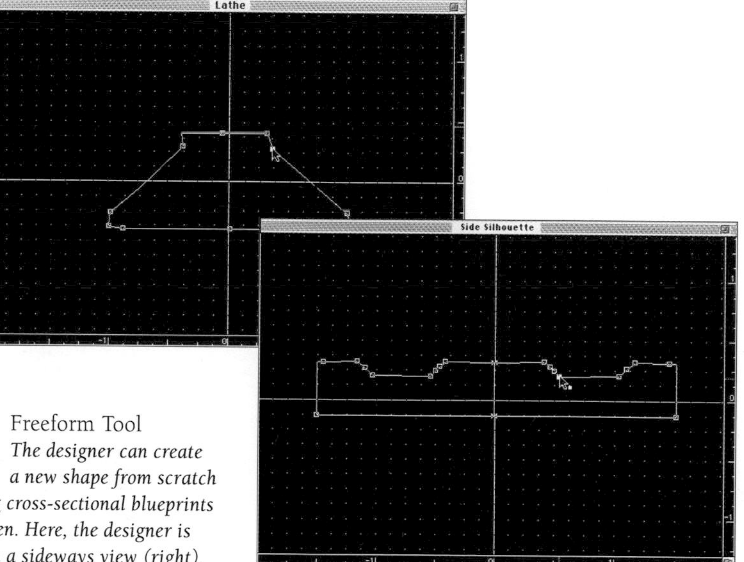

LIGHTS, CAMERA...

Once the model of the console is ready, the designer turns the computer's 3-D space into a photographer's studio by adding lights and a camera. These are small wireframe models that behave like the real thing. The position of the camera will determine the viewing point for the final image, and the light sources will illuminate the scene – they can imitate anything from the warm glow of a bedside lamp to the focused beam of a searchlight.

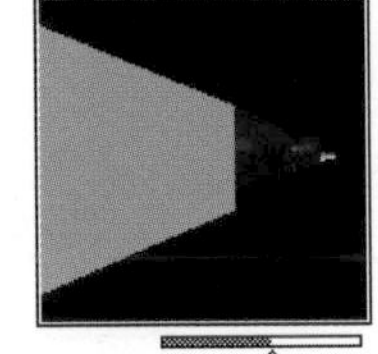

Light Angle

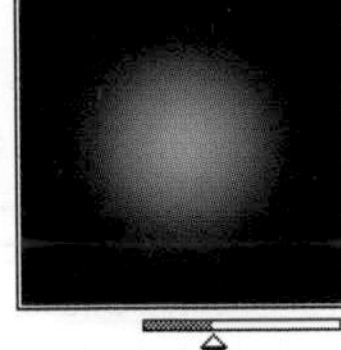

Light Focus

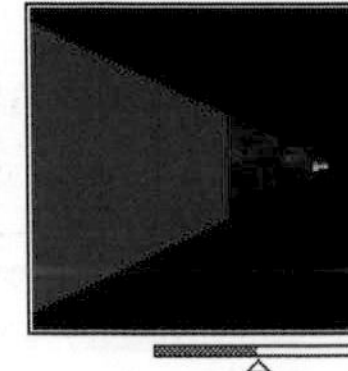

Light Color

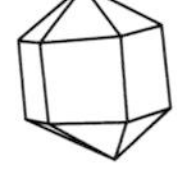

SPOT LIGHTING
The designer places one or more light sources in the 3-D space. By adjusting the angle, focus, and color of each light, it is possible to re-create almost any real-world lighting effect.

Light Source

RENDERING

The wireframe model still only shows an outline. To see the solid console under the lights, the designer takes a picture with the camera. This is called rendering. Seeing the rendered image enables the designer to try out different surface textures – such as ivory, wood, or concrete – on the model, and to adjust the wireframe and lighting.

There are three ways to render the object (see below). Flat shading is the fastest but crudest method – it treats every surface on the wireframe as a flat shape and fills it with a block of color. Curved shading goes a step further by blending the colors at the edges of each shape to make the surfaces appear smoother. Once the designer is happy with the model, surfaces, and lighting, the whole scene is rendered using the best (and slowest) method of all – ray tracing.

Raytracing retraces the exact path of every single ray of light that hits the camera, following each one in turn as it bounces off the surfaces of the object. As a result, the final image is highly detailed and very realistic, but on average it involves tracing the paths of over 300,000 rays. This can take a desktop computer days – so designers either use a powerful workstation computer or link several desktop computers together.

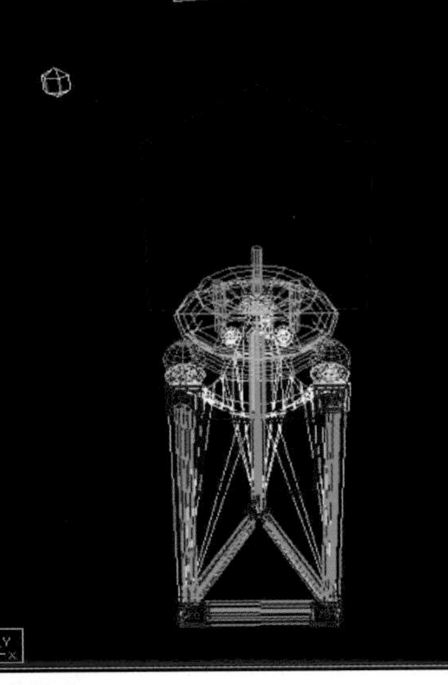

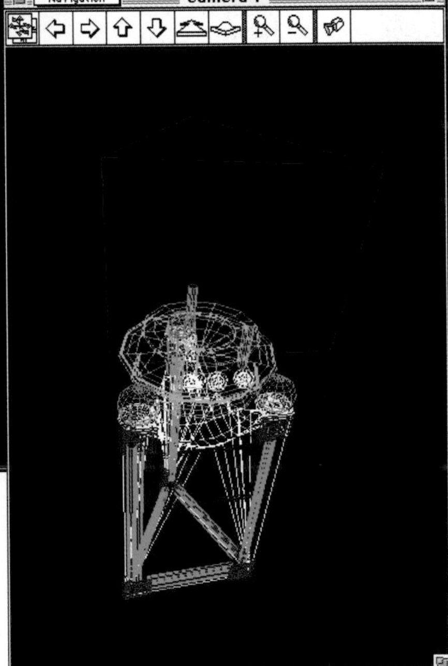

Camera View

CAMERA ANGLES
The designer places a camera into the 3-D space (above) and then looks through it at the wireframe console (right) to check the camera's position.

Camera

Flat Shading

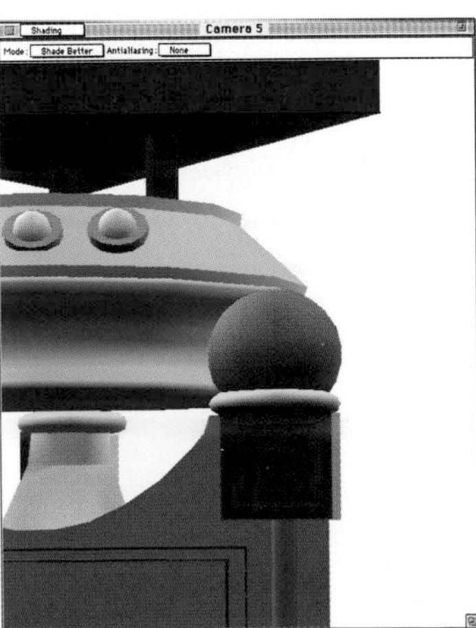

Curved Shading

Ray tracing

THREE WAYS TO RENDER
The three main rendering methods are flat shading, curved shading, and ray tracing. The first two methods are quick ways to test the wireframe, camera position, and lighting. They also give the designer an opportunity to experiment with colors and surface textures. Ray tracing is used to create the final image – it is by far the slowest technique, but it accurately draws in all the shadows, reflections, and highlights in the scene

Adding Surfaces

The designer can attach realistic surfaces to any part of a model. Each different surface has its own coloring, texture, transparency, and reflectivity, and each of these properties can be adjusted. To try out new surfaces on the model, the designer has to render it again.

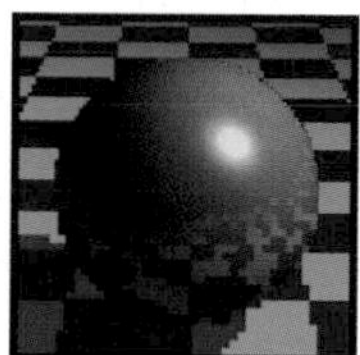

Brass

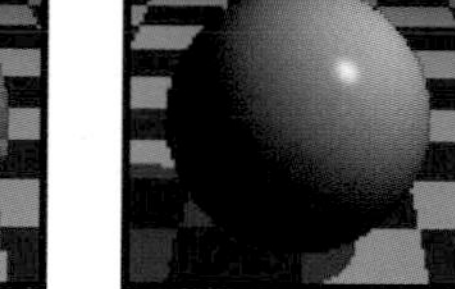

Eggshell

Blue Plastic

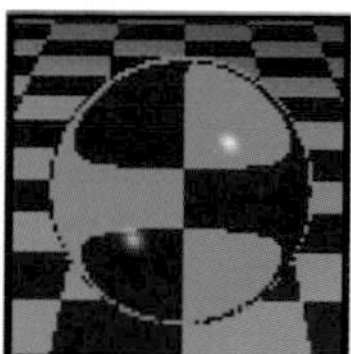

Glass

Strawberry

Spruce

Water Ripple

Coral

Emerald

Ball Bearing

Concrete

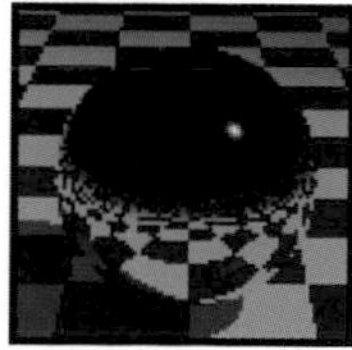

Mirror

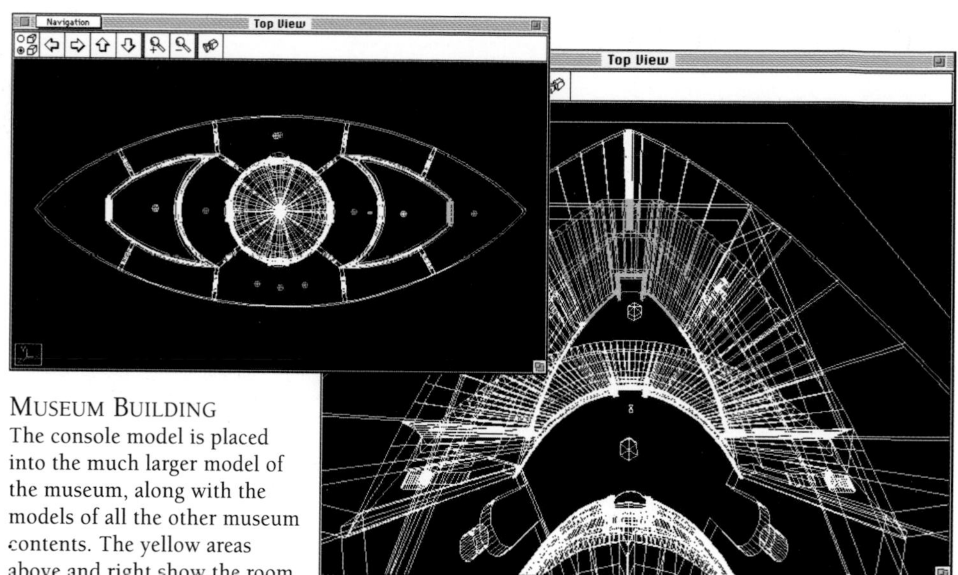

MUSEUM BUILDING
The console model is placed into the much larger model of the museum, along with the models of all the other museum contents. The yellow areas above and right show the room in which the console belongs.

Wireframe of Room from Above

THE FINAL RENDER
The completed scene is ray traced. Because this is so time-consuming, designers often link several desktop computers together; each one renders a fraction of the image at a time.

Rendering in Squares
Each of these squares is being rendered by a different computer. When a computer has finished one square, it moves on to another.

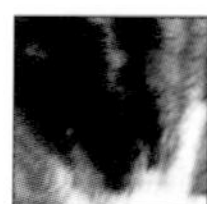

Cat Fur
This is a photograph of a real piece of fur. The designer has digitized the photograph, made it into a new surface type, and applied it to the top of the console.

Lynx
This picture is a 3-D model of a frame, in which hangs a flat digitized photograph of a lynx.

Inside Animation

Multimedia combines two very different animation techniques, one old and one new. First, there is the hand-drawn animation of cartoons – Disney-style animated characters are used in multimedia software as everything from friendly on-screen teachers to the heroes of interactive cartoon adventures. The other, far newer, technique is computerized 3-D animation, which is used to create most of today's fast-moving action games. Between these apparent extremes of art and technology, however, multimedia animation encompasses a wide range of other techniques, all of which demand creativity, ingenuity, and skill.

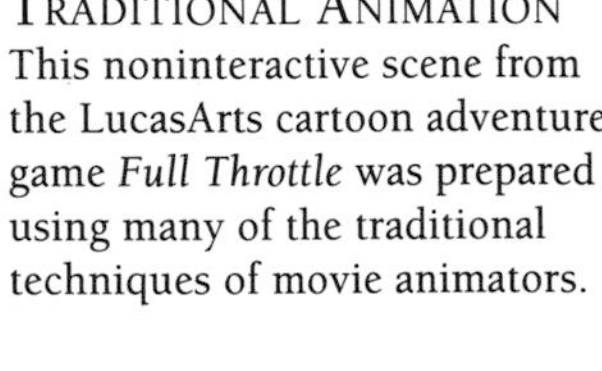

Traditional Animation
This noninteractive scene from the LucasArts cartoon adventure game *Full Throttle* was prepared using many of the traditional techniques of movie animators.

Cartoon Animation

The most straightforward type of multimedia animation is the cartoon, which is produced in a very similar way to a cartoon for the movies. First, a team of animators draws every frame of the action by hand – this can mean as many as 25 frames for every second of animation. The next step is to trace and color in each frame. While many traditional animation companies still use armies of artists to do this, multimedia animators digitize their drawings with a scanner and use paint software to color them.

Interactive Cartoons

Many multimedia titles, especially animated adventure games, have cartoon characters that the user can control. These titles use a technique called sprite animation. A sprite is an animated cut-out character (or object) that is moved over a stationary background. Each sprite consists of a tool kit of all-purpose animation sequences – running, jumping, fighting, for example – that are played in response to the user's actions.

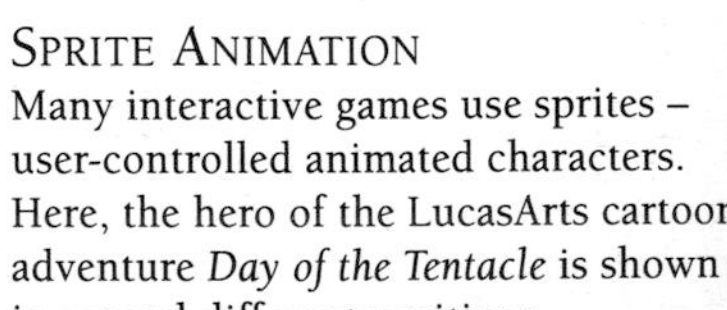

Sprite Animation
Many interactive games use sprites – user-controlled animated characters. Here, the hero of the LucasArts cartoon adventure *Day of the Tentacle* is shown in several different positions.

Background
While the sprite moves, the cartoon backdrop stays fixed.

Sprite
Only the sprite is animated.

Moving in Three Dimensions

Creating high-quality 3-D graphics requires a lot of computing power – and making them move requires even more. When the animator has built all the 3-D models for an animation and programmed in the movement, it can take a computer hours, or even days, to render (draw) every frame. Despite these enormous time demands, this sort of "prerendered" 3-D animation is often used to create the spectacular opening sequences of action games. It cannot, however, be used for the action itself. This requires another style of animation that a multimedia machine can draw very quickly in response to the player's actions – real-time 3-D.

3-D graphics
For more on 3-D graphics, see page 138

Prerendered 3-D Animation
This footage from Mirage's *Rise of the Robots (The Director's Cut)* shows the high level of detail that can be used in noninteractive animated sequences, where the 3-D animation frames have been prepared in advance.

Real-time 3-D

To make real-time 3-D animation possible, animators have had to develop many new techniques. Most 3-D action games are built around specially written software called a graphics engine that speeds up the animation. Many multimedia players, most notably consoles, include extra hardware designed to accelerate 3-D animation even more.

3-D action games
For more on 3-D action games, see page 46

Consoles
For more on consoles, see page 92

But producing real-time 3-D graphics also means taking shortcuts with the animation; these include using far simpler 3-D models and cruder rendering techniques. Although this makes the graphics appear more blocky, the movement is much more realistic.

Drawing 3-D Quickly
The space combat simulator *X-Wing* from LucasArts draws the 3-D view from the pilot's cockpit several times a second. The spacecraft shown flying past is built from fairly simple 3-D shapes so that the game can draw the pilot's view quickly.

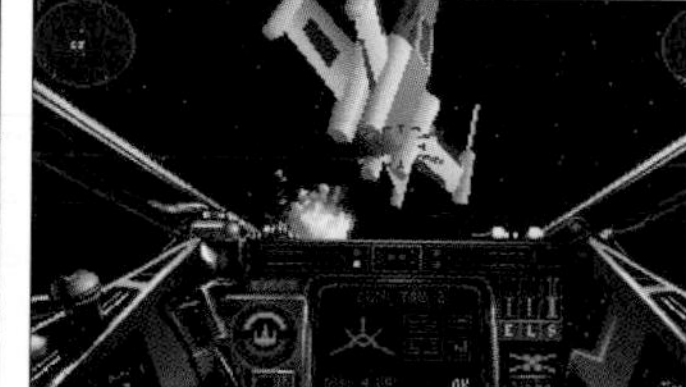

Mixing 2-D With 3-D
Dark Forces, by LucasArts, uses a combination of 3-D graphics and flat cartoon sprites – the player moves through a 3-D environment that is drawn in real time, but the characters in the game are all flat cutouts.

3-D World
As the player moves around the 3-D world, the game constantly redraws the player's view.

2-D Sprite
Here, the sprite of the enemy soldier is simply enlarged as it gets closer to the player.

CARTOON ANIMATION

Many of the traditional functions of cartoon animators can now be performed using computers – teams of animators slaving away, tracing and coloring frames by hand, can be replaced with just a few skilled computer artists; this makes the process of creating an animation much quicker and easier. Even so, animators still prefer to use the old methods and materials – for example, they would rather draw on paper than on a screen. Titles such as Houghton Mifflin's *American Heritage Children's Dictionary* shown here demonstrate the blend of long-practiced human artistry and computerized assistance that is unique to multimedia animation.

CREATING A CHARACTER
The animated dolphin in Houghton Mifflin's *American Heritage Children's Dictionary* was created using cartoon animation techniques.

OLD AND NEW TECHNIQUES

The first step in producing an animation of any kind is planning: the animator produces a storyboard of the sequence and a set of rough sketches of the characters. Then he or she begins drawing the actual animation frames as pencil outlines. To ensure that the movement is accurate, the animator first draws the "key frames" – every fourth frame, say – to fix the overall movement, and then draws all the frames in between.

A traditional animator would then hand over the pencil frames to an army of junior animators, who would first trace every frame in ink onto a sheet of clear plastic called a cel, and then color in every cel in paint. In multimedia animation, these stages can be carried out in a fraction of the time with the help of computer paint software.

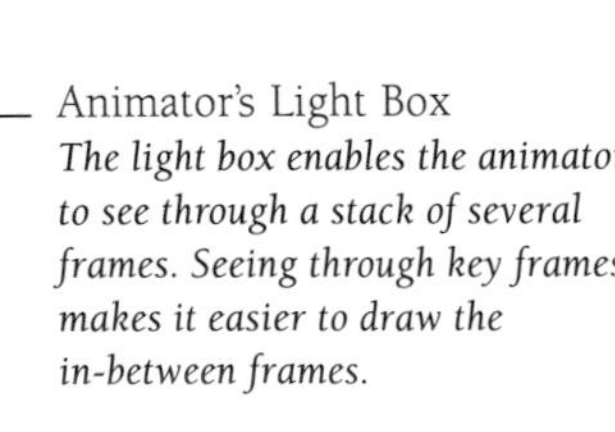

SCANNING IN
Once the pencil frames are ready, the animator digitizes them with a scanner and feeds them into the computer.

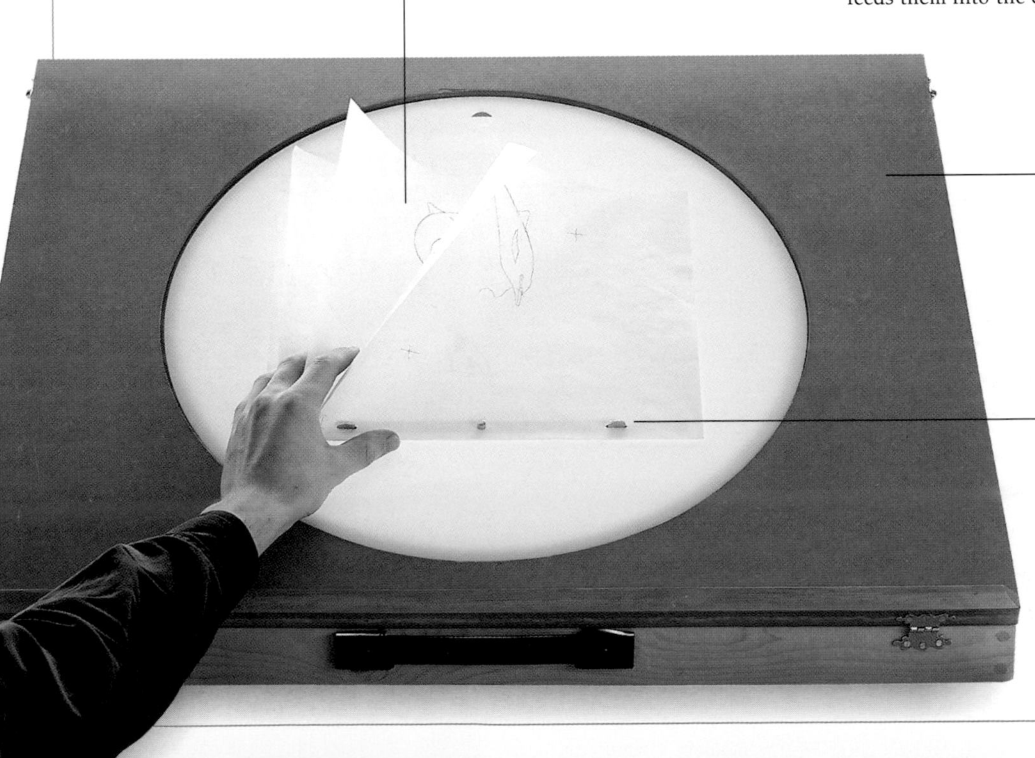

Animation Paper
The animator uses special translucent paper that is sometimes called onion skin.

Animator's Light Box
The light box enables the animator to see through a stack of several frames. Seeing through key frames makes it easier to draw the in-between frames.

Pins

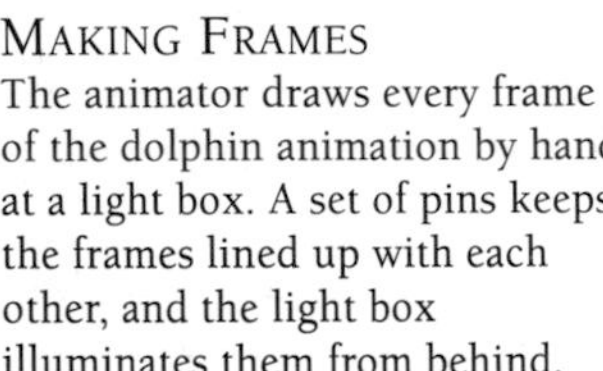

MAKING FRAMES
The animator draws every frame of the dolphin animation by hand at a light box. A set of pins keeps the frames lined up with each other, and the light box illuminates them from behind.

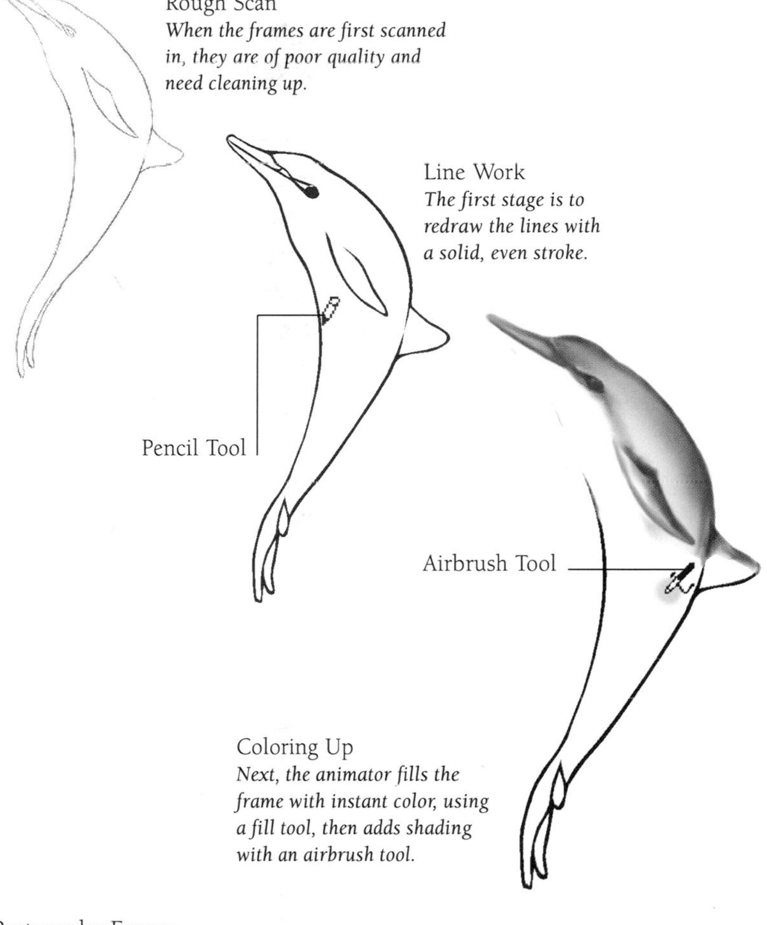

Rough Scan
When the frames are first scanned in, they are of poor quality and need cleaning up.

Line Work
The first stage is to redraw the lines with a solid, even stroke.

Pencil Tool

Airbrush Tool

Coloring Up
Next, the animator fills the frame with instant color, using a fill tool, then adds shading with an airbrush tool.

Painting the Frames

The animator does all the line work and coloring in using the paint tools in Adobe's *Photoshop* image-manipulation software. When all the frames are finished, the animator cuts the dolphin out of each one and places it into a rectangular cutout of the background.

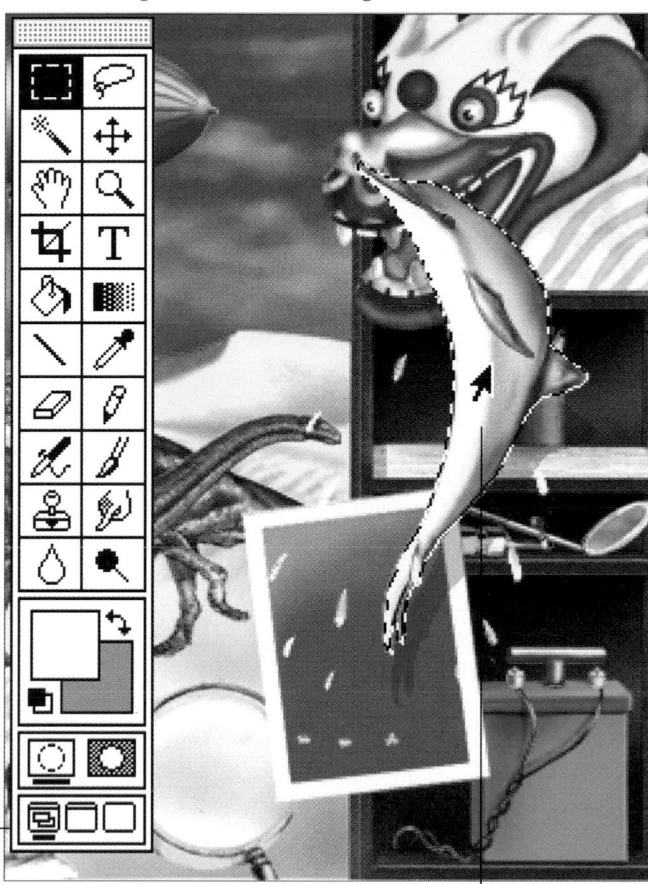

Painting Toolbar

Rectangular Frames
The finished frames are now ready to be included in the title.

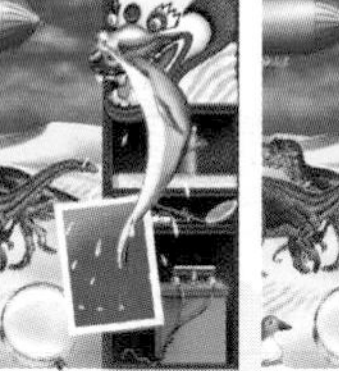

In Position
The final stage in preparing each frame is to position the dolphin in an area of the background.

Authoring

Finally, the animator uses Macromedia's *Director* authoring software to place the set of rectangular frames as a single animation into the title and create a hotspot that will launch the animation.

Animation Frame
The first frame of the dolphin animation is put into place on the screen.

Hotspot
The animator draws a hotspot around the card. When the user clicks here, the animation will be activated.

Animating 3-D Models

For cartoon animators, making drawings move well is a straightforward matter, the essence of their art – but animating in three dimensions presents major problems. To create a moving character, the animator starts by building it as a 3-D model. The next step it to animate it, but getting a 3-D jointed skeleton on a computer screen to follow natural movement patterns is not easy. The second problem is making 3-D models in such a way that the game software can draw them from scratch several times a second. Fortunately, both problems have their solutions, as Argonaut/GTE's martial arts combat game *FX Fighter* shows here.

3-D model
For more on 3-D models, see page 138

Capturing Motion

Some 3-D animators are very successful at re-creating the subtleties of human motion purely from their own observations. Others use a shortcut – a technique called motion capture. Instead of watching human movement, these animators film an actor going through a set of choreographed moves while wearing a special motion capture suit: each of the actor's joint's – shoulder, wrist, knee, and so on – is represented on the suit by a large white dot, and when the actor moves, the positions of the dots show the key stages in the movement. The animators then use a computer to analyze the movements and fit them to the 3-D models.

Actor
The actor is filmed going through one of the hundreds of martial arts moves that will be used in the game.

Motion Capture Suit
This highlights each of the actor's joints.

Fighting Moves
Each of the characters in Argonaut/GTE's *FX Fighter* has a unique set of fighting moves. To make these realistic, the animators film real martial arts experts in action, then use a computer to re-create the same motion with a jointed 3-D skeleton.

White Dots
The computer first re-creates the position and movement of the white dots on the motion capture suit.

Wireframe Skeleton
The computer then joins the dots together to form a crude 3-D wireframe skeleton.

Matchstalk Moves
The skeleton's movements accurately reflect the original fighting sequence.

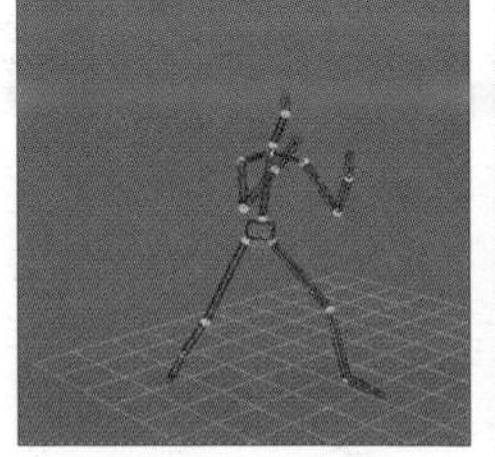

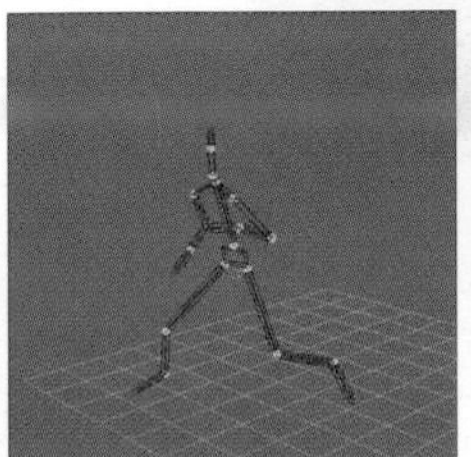

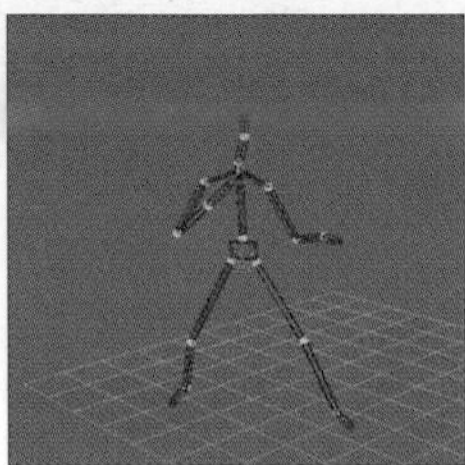

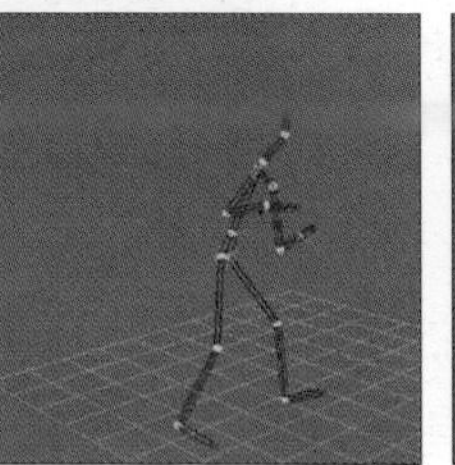

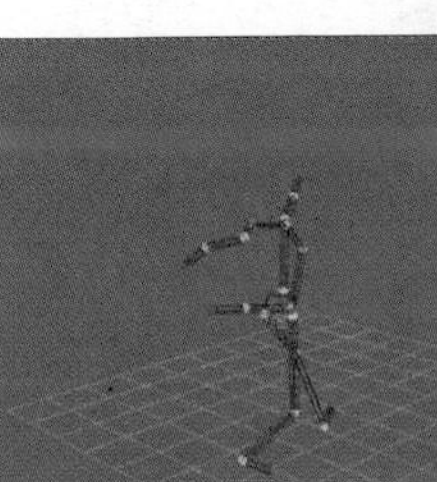

Simple Models

The next step is to fit the moving skeletons to 3-D character models. For every character, two models are built. The first is highly detailed and is used for the game's noninteractive title sequence; each frame of animation undergoes high quality rendering (which adds highlights and shadows and so on). The second model is the one used during the game proper. This is much simpler, because the software has to be able to animate the character very quickly in response to the game player's commands.

Rendering
For more on rendering, see page 140

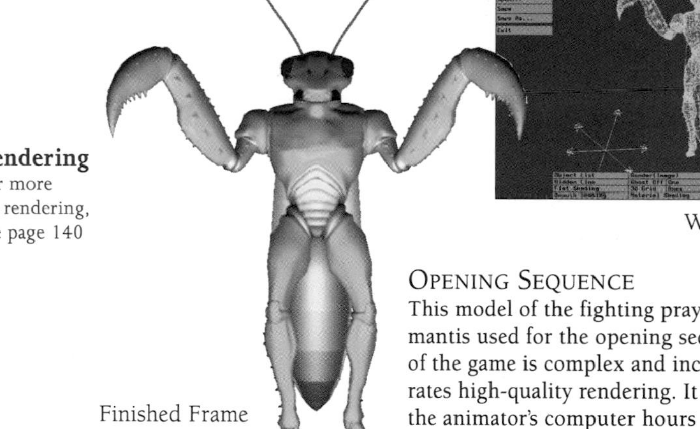

Finished Frame

Wireframe Model

OPENING SEQUENCE
This model of the fighting praying mantis used for the opening sequence of the game is complex and incorporates high-quality rendering. It takes the animator's computer hours to draw each frame.

ACTION MODELS
The model used in the game is much simpler than the one used for the introductory sequence. During the game, the software can draw the model in three ways, which range from least detailed and fastest to most detailed and slowest.

Simple Wireframe
This model has less than a third of the surfaces of the opening sequence model.

Quick Draw
The fastest way to draw the character is to fill every surface with flat color.

Better-looking
A slower way is smoothing each area of color to give a less blocky look.

Surface Patterns
The most sophisticated technique, and the slowest, adds surface patterns to the model.

PLAYING THE GAME
In the game, the software animates the two fighters and their 3-D surroundings, redrawing the whole scene up to 25 times every second.

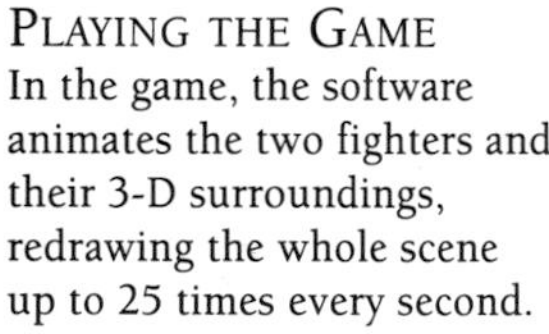

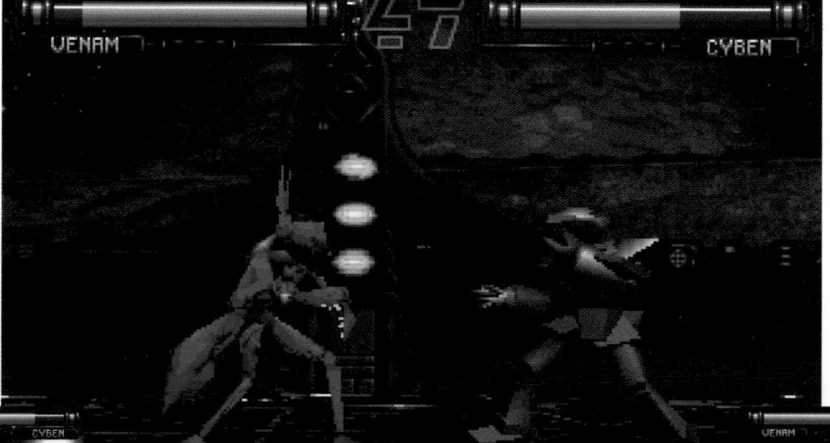

Camera Angles
During the bout, the game changes the player's viewpoint. This also heightens the 3-D effect.

Faster but Cruder
To speed up the animation, the player can make the software use one of the simpler drawing techniques.

ANIMATING WORLDS

Many action games animate three-dimensional worlds that you can move through and explore in real time. This sort of 3-D animation requires two things – a powerful multimedia player and some very clever animation shortcuts. Titles such as Bullfrog's strategy game *Dungeon Keeper* use two techniques that make animating worlds possible. First, instead of drawing complex 3-D characters in real time, the game uses sprites – flat cutouts of the characters. And second, the richly detailed game world is in fact built entirely from very basic 3-D shapes – patterned cubes.

Multimedia player
For more on multimedia players, see page 80

BUILDING CHARACTERS

The first stage in creating the characters who will inhabit the dungeon is to build a 3-D model of each one, using modeling software. Some games animate the 3-D models in real time, during the game. Here, however, the models are animated in advance, and converted into a series of sprites. Because the sprites are 2-D, they can be animated very quickly during the game.

MAKING MONSTERS
The monsters in the Bullfrog game *Dungeon Keeper* are first built and animated as 3-D models. It took a powerful workstation computer several hours to render this image of a troll – during the actual game, the software has to use images it can draw more quickly.

Character Sketch
The troll begins its life as a pencil sketch.

Building the Wireframe
The animator constructs the troll and its weapons as 3-D wireframe skeleton models.

ANIMATED SPRITES
The 3-D animation frames are created in advance and converted into flat sprites. Because the game is set in a moving 3-D world, there are several versions of each animated character, each seen from a different angle.

Textured World

Once the characters have been completed, the animator uses software known as a game editor to create a three-dimensional world for the characters to inhabit. The dungeon interior is built up entirely from simple, cube-shaped building blocks: the animator first creates a selection of decorative patterns – called textures – for the blocks and then constructs the dungeon by piling the patterned blocks on top of each other.

Animating the 3-D world is left to the graphics engine, the part of the game software that draws the player's view. Because the dungeon is built from very basic shapes, the graphics engine can draw the player's 3-D view several times a second during the game. First, it calculates the shape of the room from the player's point of view, warping the shape of every block as it does so – this makes the walls appear crooked and more dungeonlike. Then it draws the view of the room, applying realistic lighting effects at the same time. Finally, it draws in all the object and character sprites in the room.

Interior Decorating

The animator adds realism to the dungeon interior by creating a range of different building blocks – each one has a unique surface pattern.

Texture Map
The animator uses paint software to create a flat, cross-shaped texture map. This map will cover all six sides of a cube.

Building Blocks
The animator wraps each texture map around a cube. One by one, the animator builds up a large selection of building blocks.

Creating a World

The designer uses a special piece of software – the game editor – to build and populate the dungeon.

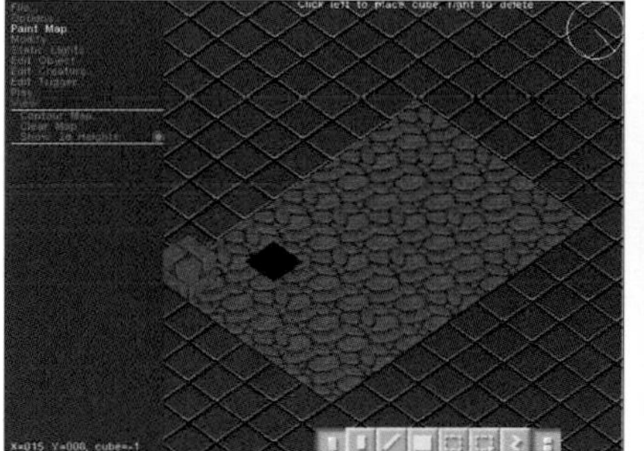

Building Walls
The animator builds walls by placing blocks one by one onto a map of the dungeon floor.

Lighting
Once the walls have been built, the animator adds the flaming torches that will later provide realistic lighting for the scene.

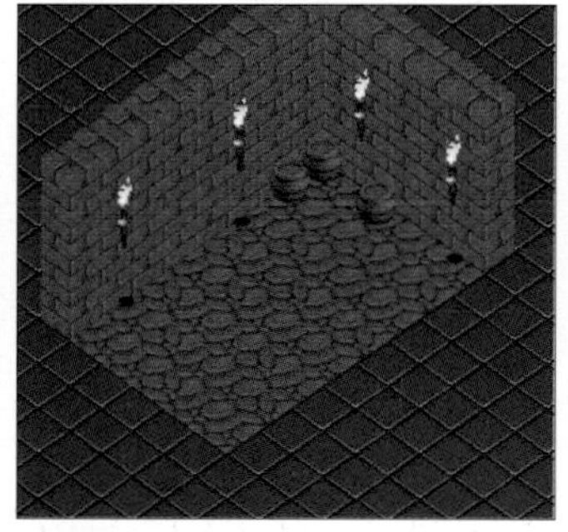

Barrels
The animator adds to the scenery by scattering sprites of barrels and other objects around the dungeon.

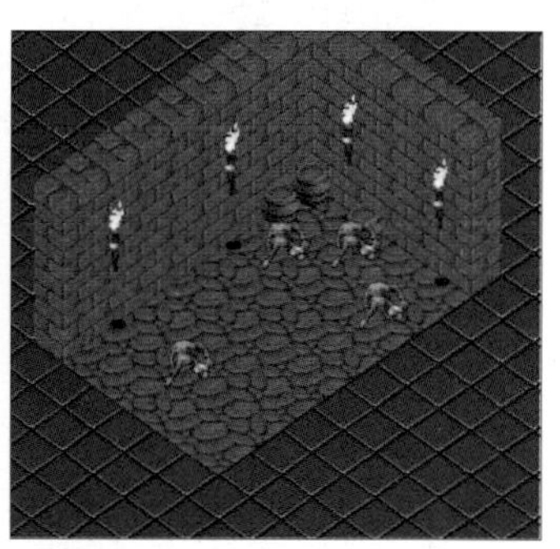

Monsters
Then the animator populates the dungeon with monsters. Here, he has placed several troll sprites in the room.

The Graphics Engine

Finally, the animator switches on the graphics engine, which can draw the room from any angle in real time.

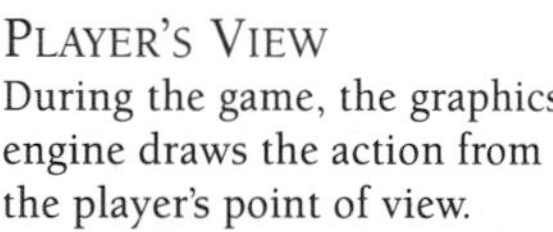

Special Effects
The graphics engine warps the walls as it draws them and adds realistic torch lighting to the scene.

Player's View

During the game, the graphics engine draws the action from the player's point of view.

Scaled-up Sprite
As the player draws nearer to the troll, the graphics engine simply enlarges the troll sprite. This speeds up animation, but sometimes results in blocky sprites.

Digital Video

Text and still pictures are often inadequate to depict complex actions such as a cheetah running or a mechanical loom in motion, so many multimedia titles use digital video for these sequences. However, digital video is still a young technology and some see it as a weak link in the multimedia chain – the main problem is that playing back video files from a CD-ROM takes a great deal of computing power. But, as new ways are found to speed up playback, digital video is now beginning to mature into one of the most exciting areas of multimedia today.

Uses of Video

Video is used in multimedia titles in a number of different ways. Educational titles, such as multimedia encyclopedias, usually include short clips to illustrate important historical events, such as the first man landing on the moon, or the Berlin Wall being torn down. Reference titles may show video clips of a city's well-known buildings or streets, or of animals in their natural habitats. The video for these titles is normally taken from stock analog footage, which is then digitized and inserted into the product.

Educational Video
Dorling Kindersley's *Eyewitness Encyclopedia of Nature* includes video clips such as this one of a hummingbird in flight.

Plot Control
The interactive movie *Wing Commander III*, by Origin, lets the player determine how the story unfolds. Players can choose different paths of action at key moments in the plot.

Interactive Entertainment

By contrast, the latest interactive movies use high-quality video that has been specially shot, often at a cost of millions of dollars. The video footage is combined with computer-generated graphics to create spectacular scenes and settings. Players can control the plot of the movie by selecting various options, so each scene must be shot to cover every possible path a player might take. These titles are often based on feature films and use extra footage that was specially filmed for use in the CD-ROM.

From Storyboard to CD-ROM

Creating video for multimedia is a long and often expensive process. Methods vary, but most developers follow the steps shown here.

Planning
Video sequences are carefully planned by drawing rough sketches of each scene on storyboards.

Filming
The sequences are shot in analog video. A blue background is often used and removed during editing.

Rough Edit
Using an analog video editing desk, the footage is reviewed. A list of editing decisions is made.

Problems with Video

Seeing digital video for the first time can be a disappointing experience. Many early multimedia titles had video clips in them that were jerky, black-and-white, and shown in a window not much bigger than a postage stamp. Compared to watching analog video on a television set, digital video seemed like a giant leap backward. The situation has improved since then, but digital video is still a long way from matching broadcast-quality standards.

The problem is that video files are extremely large. A technique called compression can make files smaller, but even compressed video files are big compared to text or sound files. The only practical medium with a large enough storage capacity to contain them is CD-ROM – but CD-ROM drives are slow at transferring data compared to a computer's hard disk or RAM (memory), so playback can become jerky. Another factor is that the processor in the multimedia player has to decompress the video as it plays, slowing things down even further.

Compression
For more on compression, see page 156

Video in a Window
Digital video rarely fills the whole screen, as shown by this example from *The Daedalus Encounter* by Mechadeus – but the size of the window is increasing as technology advances.

Anatomy of a CD-ROM
By far the largest amount of space on a CD-ROM is taken up by video files – often more than half the disc. Multimedia developers make constant efforts to squeeze more and more video into their titles.

Hardware Bottleneck

The quality of video playback in a multimedia title is directly dependent on the hardware being used to play the CD-ROM. The faster the CD-ROM drive and the more powerful the processor, the bigger the video window can be, and the better the playback quality. Multimedia companies have to consider all these factors before making video for their titles. They have to take into account that PC hardware can vary enormously. The problem is that if the user's machine is a low-powered computer with little RAM and a slow CD-ROM drive, the video clips will only be able to play in a relatively small window, if at all. Clearly the audience for a title may be limited if it will perform only on the latest high-specification computer with a fast CD-ROM drive. As a result, multimedia developers have to think carefully about their target audience and the average level of computer hardware they own. Most developers then decide on a minimum specification of computer on which their title will run, and make sure that their video clips play back fast enough on that machine.

Digitization
The analog video is played into a computer, which creates digital files of each frame – these can now be manipulated by computer software.

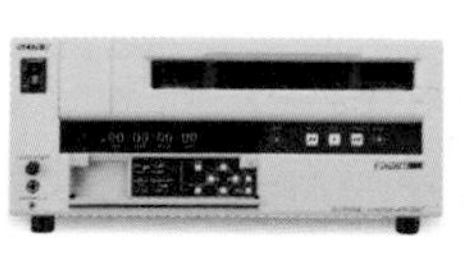

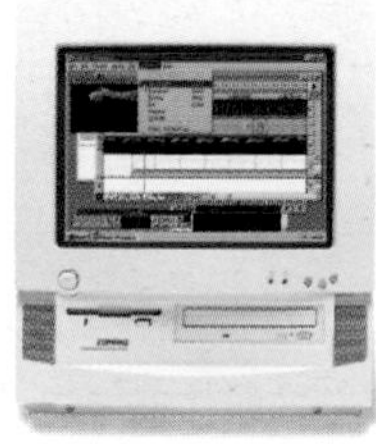

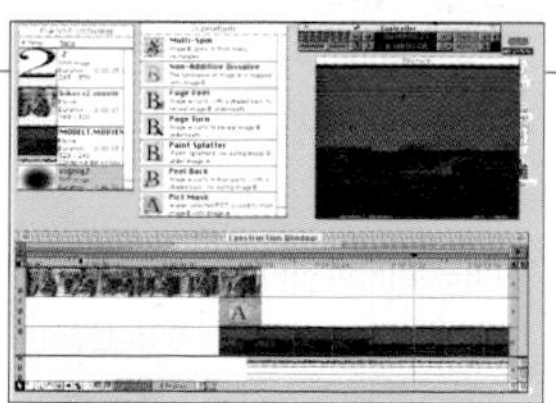

Final Editing and Special Effects
Special effects, such as computer-generated backgrounds, are added, and a final edit is produced.

Compression
The completed video clips are compressed into smaller files so that they fit onto a CD-ROM.

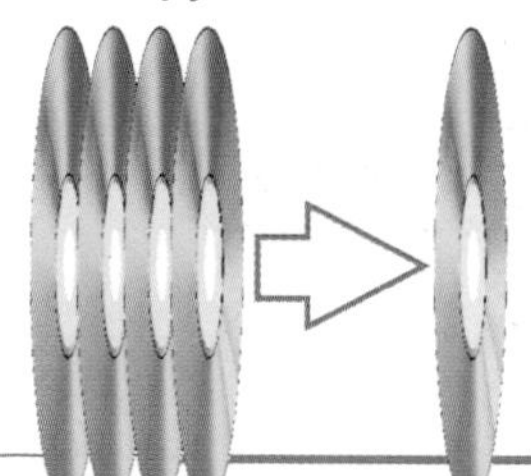

Authoring
The compressed video files are incorporated into the multimedia title using authoring software.

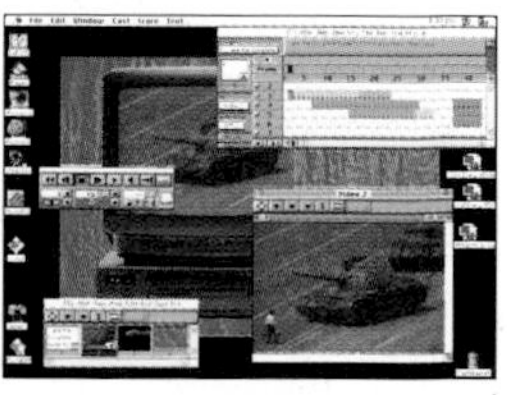

Video Production

Shooting video for multimedia requires traditional video production skills combined with an understanding of the special demands of multimedia and CD-ROM. Unfortunately, such skills and understanding have not always been in evidence. The video in early titles was often shot by inexperienced staff who knew little about the process. Most multimedia companies now employ highly experienced professionals with backgrounds in film or television.

Professional Approach

Most of the rules of traditional television production also apply to shooting video for multimedia. Hiring a studio with high-quality equipment is expensive, so shoots are planned well in advance and scenes are storyboarded. Good lighting and good camerawork are essential to producing professional results.

The difference is that the material being shot will be played back from a CD-ROM instead of a television set. In order to place video in a multimedia title it first has to survive the effects of digitization and compression – and this creates special problems.

Picture Quality

Digitization involves feeding analog video footage into a computer to create digital files of the sequence. Compression reduces these files in size so they can be played from a CD-ROM drive at an acceptable speed. The problem is that both processes discard data from the original images, causing a loss in picture quality. To keep this loss to a minimum, developers always try to shoot high-quality original footage, because the higher the quality of the source material, the more chance there is of obtaining good results once digitization and compression have taken their toll. With this in mind, the best possible camera equipment is used, and special attention is paid to areas such as lighting, background texture, and use of color.

Special Requirements
Analog video footage for use in multimedia is later digitized and compressed. Certain tricks and techniques help to reduce the loss of picture quality that this process entails.

Camera Stand
Any unwanted camera movement, such as shaking, will produce film that digitizes badly. A stand ensures rock-steady images.

Camera Mobility
Close-ups are shot by placing the camera nearer to the subject, not by zooming in with the lens. Zooming in would cause the whole picture to change every frame, which increases the amount of data that needs to be compressed later on.

Storyboarding

Producing video footage within time and budget restraints requires good planning. Storyboards are used to plan each scene shot by shot, so that fewer directing decisions have to be made while time is ticking away in an expensive studio. Storyboards consist of a series of rough sketches, drawn by an artist, which help to guide the production team through the actual filming process.

Color and Texture

The process of digitization normally reduces the number of colors that can be shown on video footage. For example, the original video frames may contain millions of colors, but the digitized frames typically show only 256 colors. Because of this, video producers try to use strong, solid colors that will contrast well on a limited palette. Each actor usually wears a costume made from a single color, without a reflective belt or buttons. Complex color images, such as those of horizontal blinds, crowds of people, or patterned clothes, are particularly avoided because their pattern changes as the camera moves. This increases the amount of data in each image, resulting in larger video files, slower playback, and lower image quality.

Blue-screening
Chromakeying will remove everything blue on a film later in the editing process, so costumes must not contain any blue color. Blue-eyed actors and actresses must wear tinted contact lenses.

Lighting
Particular attention is paid to lighting a set. Well-lit subjects survive digitization and compression without too much loss of picture quality.

Chromakeying

Putting an actor into an interactive movie, such as *The Daedalus Encounter* by Mechadeus (shown here), is relatively simple. It involves filming the actor in front of a blue screen. Later on in the editing and digitizing process, a technique called chromakeying removes all the blue color from the film, allowing the actor to be cut out and placed onto a computer-generated background.

Removing the Background
Chromakeying removes the original blue background of the film set, leaving the actors alone in the frame.

Computer-generated Set
A new background is generated, often using a combination of 3-D computer graphics and traditional illustration.

Finished Scene
Finally, the actors are superimposed on the new background, creating the desired illusion.

POSTPRODUCTION

After the shoot, the video tapes are taken into an editing suite for post-production, where they are edited down to size and digitized. The order in which these steps are taken varies between developers. Some companies digitize all the original video footage and then edit the entire production using digital editing software. Others prefer to use a traditional analog editing desk to create a rough edit of the required scenes, which are then digitized and finely tuned by computer.

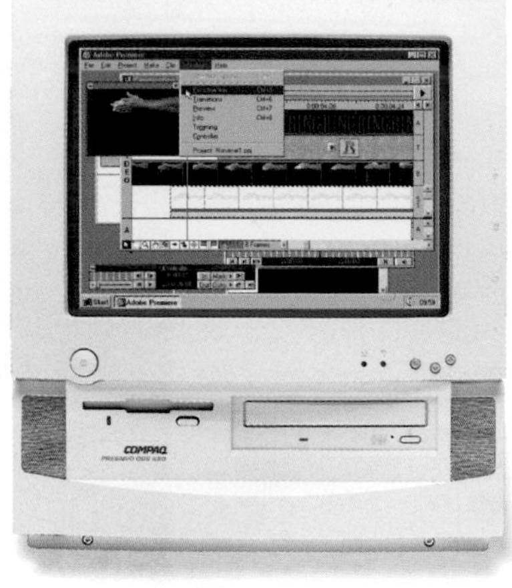

DIGITIZING VIDEO

Video must be be digitized before it can be played on a computer. This is because video is an analog medium, whereas computers are digital – therefore the analog video must be converted into the binary code that computers recognize. This is done by connecting a video source, normally a broadcast-quality video player, to a computer, using a special cable. Inside the computer is a video-capture card, that, along with video-capture software, receives the analog video signals, converts them into digital video files, and sends these to a hard disk for storage.

Binary code
For more on binary code, see page 69

VIDEO CAPTURE
Video is digitized by connecting a VCR to a computer with a special digitizing card.

VIDEO QUALITY

The quality of the digitized video will largely depend on the performance of the video-capture card – the higher the picture resolution it can capture, the closer the digitized images will be to the footage on the original video tapes.

However, video in multimedia titles never looks as good as the original broadcast-quality material. Three factors affect how video eventually appears on screen. The first is the size of the window in which the video will appear. The second is how many times per second the video image is updated – television runs at 30 frames per second, but most multimedia video runs at only 10 to 15 frames per second. And the third factor is how many colors are used to draw the images – most video playback reduces video from millions of colors to only 256.

During the digitization process the video editor selects the window size, frame rate, and number of colors that best suit the power of computer at which the title is aimed. Titles designed to play on powerful computers with fast CD-ROM drives can play video in larger windows with more frames per second and more colors than systems with slower performance.

BROADCAST QUALITY
This is how an analog video frame would look on a normal television screen.

FEWER COLORS
Color quality drops if the color palette is reduced to 256 colors, (often the case with digital video).

BLOCKING
If the original frame size is enlarged, the computer will pixelate images (enlarge the tiny picture dots).

COLOR BANDING
After compression, colors often band together, which reduces picture quality.

Editing Digitized Video

The main advantage of digital video is that it can be edited and manipulated just like text in a word processor package. Each frame can be copied, deleted, or moved, all with the click of a mouse button, and sequences can be played back at any point to see how they look. This ease of use gives video editors a great deal of freedom to experiment and create several versions of a sequence, because different edits can be saved as separate files without affecting the original digitized material.

In digital editing it is also easy to access different parts of a video sequence. This is because the video files are stored on a hard disk and the editor can retrieve them very quickly, instead of having to rewind or fast-forward, as with analog video tape. Another advantage of digital video is that there is no loss of image quality during editing. Traditional analog editing involves copying video from one tape to another – but each time analog video is copied it loses picture quality. Digital editing avoids this because each video frame is stored as binary data, which can be duplicated any number of times without deterioration.

Transition Effects

Digital transitions, such as the "band wipe" shown here, are simply a visual way to link video clips. In this example, the two clips are divided into strips or bands which intertwine as they "wipe" across the screen.

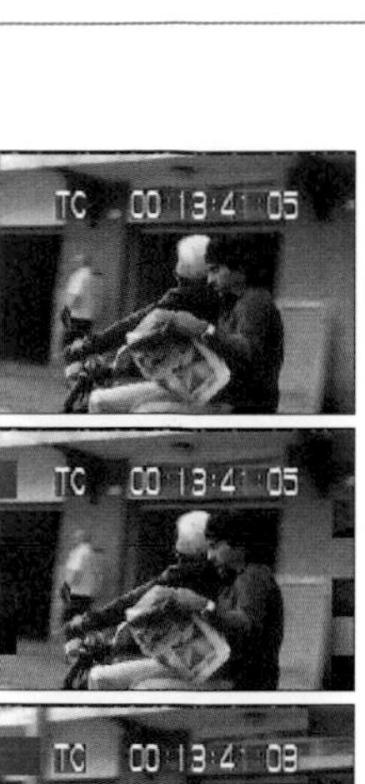

Navigation Controls
Video playback is controlled with VCR-style buttons.

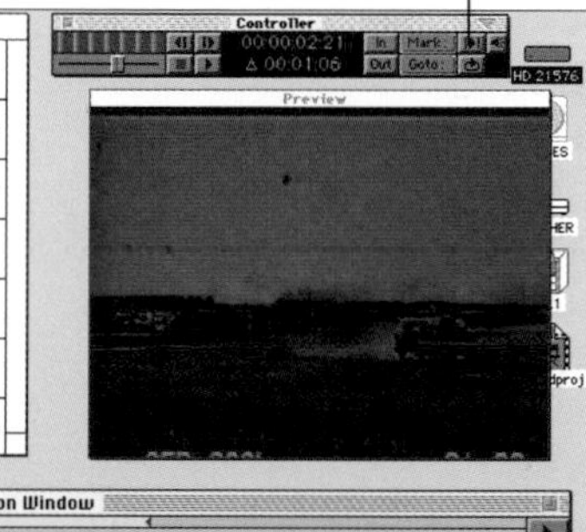

Editing Software

Popular digital-editing packages, such as Adobe's *Premiere*, show each video frame as a separate image, as on a strip of film. These frames can then be dragged to new positions, copied, deleted, and so on.

Construction Window
This window shows each frame of video in sequence.

Transition Menu
Transitions can be dragged from this menu and used in video clips.

Audio Track
The audio track is shown in a separate channel.

Frame Transition
This icon shows that a transition is taking place between two clips.

The Ripple Filter

The right side of this video frame has had a ripple filter applied to it, which creates a waterlike ripple effect. The left side has been left untouched.

Special Effects

Before the arrival of digital video, some of the special effects used in multimedia titles would have taken days, even weeks, to develop. And many would have been impossible. Today, most effects can be produced in a matter of minutes by using the filters and transitions in digital-editing software. Filters mimic conventional photographic effects, such as that produced by a fish-eye lens or a soft-focus lens filter. Most digital-editing software packages come with a built-in range of filters, and it is normally possible to add even more from third-party specialists. They can be applied to a single frame or to a whole sequence, simply by choosing from a menu. Although special effects can be extremely impressive, most multimedia developers use them sparingly because too many can be distracting or even irritating.

Video Compression

Without compression there would only be enough space on a CD-ROM for approximately 20 seconds of broadcast-quality video. Furthermore, the speed at which an average CD-ROM drive transfers data means it would take about three seconds to display each frame. The only way to achieve an acceptable level of playback is to compress video files down to a practical size.

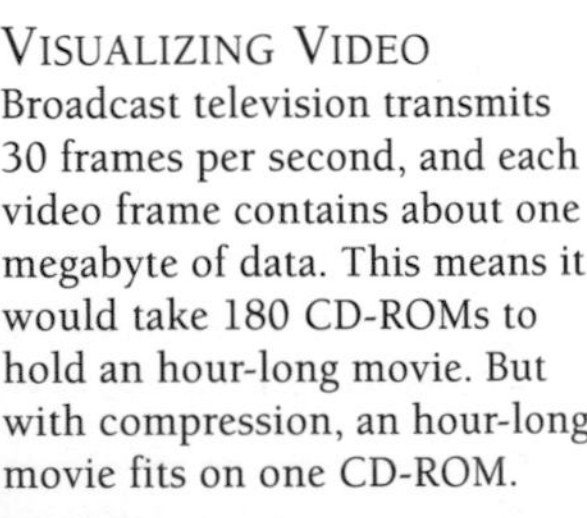

Visualizing Video
Broadcast television transmits 30 frames per second, and each video frame contains about one megabyte of data. This means it would take 180 CD-ROMs to hold an hour-long movie. But with compression, an hour-long movie fits on one CD-ROM.

How Compression Works

Most video compression formats can be played back using Apple's *QuickTime* or Microsoft's *Video for Windows*. Once installed, these programs engage automatically whenever a CD-ROM contains digital video. The compression process is usually carried out by the software developer, with the user's computer simply decompressing the original image for playback. Although a great deal of processing power is needed for the compression stage, a relatively small amount is required for decompression.

In most cases, compression can remove 95 percent of the original data contained in an analog image. This is acceptable because most moving pictures contain information that can be removed without greatly affecting the overall image quality. Compression systems use complex mathematical codes called algorithms, which analyze a picture and discard surplus information.

Image Distortion

Compression techniques are improving all the time, but it is still difficult to match the quality of broadcast television. Compression works best if the original video material is of high quality – but if the source material is poor the pictures suffer. Factors such as flashing lights, fast movement, or distortion on the original footage can confuse compression software and produce unwanted effects. A common problem, called pixelation or blocking, can sometimes be seen during fast-moving sequences. If a person suddenly starts to run, the compression system cannot keep up, and images may break up into tiny colored blocks.

Data Reduction
Compression software uses a "key frame" to draw a video sequence, such as this one from Origin's *Wing Commander III*. Subsequent frames only contain data about the changes to the key frame, greatly reducing the amount of data needed for playback.

Key Frame
The opening image of a compressed video sequence contains all the data relating to the image.

Selected Data
Subsequent frames only contain data relating to the actor's new position, and the area he previously occupied. Data for the rest of the image is not needed.

The Result
The result is that subsequent frames can be drawn using a fraction of the data contained in the key frame.

MPEG Compression

The compression system currently causing the most excitement in the multimedia industry was developed by MPEG (Motion Picture Experts Group). It is very powerful, offering compression ratios of up to 200:1 – in other words, the compressed video files are just half a percent of their original size. There are two ways to play back MPEG-compressed video. One way is to use a special accelerator card or module – these contain special hardware, entirely devoted to processing MPEG video. They give impressive results, and many computers and consoles now have MPEG cards included as standard. The other way is to use a software-only MPEG player, although this requires a powerful computer to achieve acceptable playback quality.

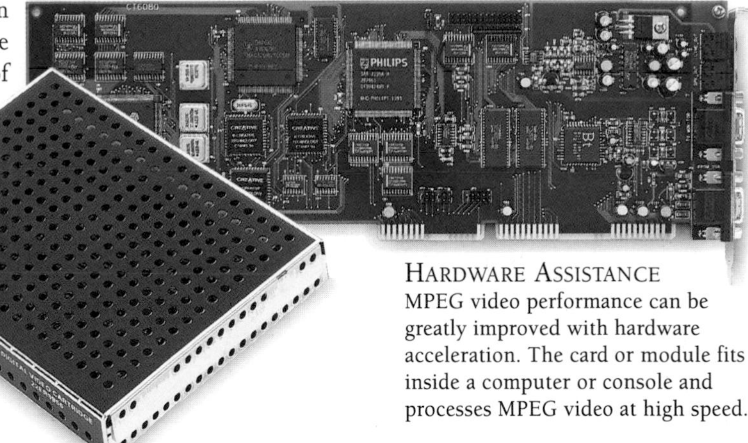

Hardware Assistance
MPEG video performance can be greatly improved with hardware acceleration. The card or module fits inside a computer or console and processes MPEG video at high speed.

Blending
The video clips in Wienerworld's *Bob Dylan: Highway 61 Interactive* are integrated into a larger image to disguise their small size. In this scene, a video clip of an interview with Eric Clapton plays in a dressing-room mirror.

Putting Video into a Title

Authoring software
For more on authoring software, see page 118

The final stage in creating video for multimedia is to incorporate the video clips into a title, using authoring software. Developers have come up with various ways to hide the fact that most video clips play in small windows rather than taking up the full screen. One way is to blend the video clip into a larger image that acts as a border – the overall effect makes the video look bigger than it really is. Another technique is called pixel doubling. This takes the video data for one pixel and spreads it over four instead, creating a much larger image – but with less definition. Pixel doubling can turn video from quarter-screen to full-screen size, but only on more powerful computer systems. Some titles have optional "enlarge" buttons that will play larger video clips on more powerful systems, either by using pixel doubling, or by storing two different versions of the video file, one large, one small.

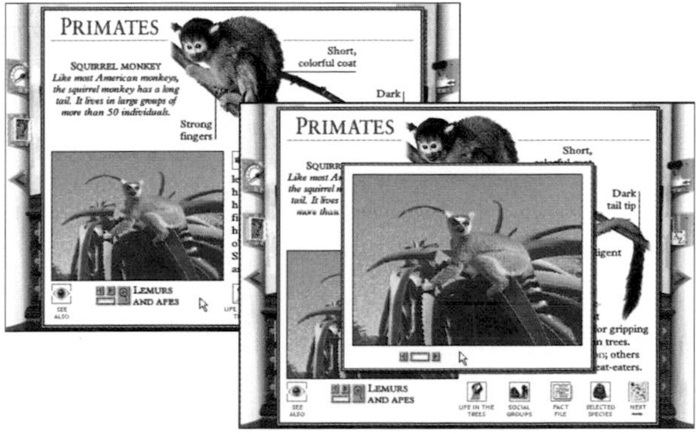

Enlarging Windows
Dorling Kindersley's *Eyewitness Encyclopedia of Nature* stores two different files for some video clips. On a sufficiently powerful system, users can click a button to watch the larger version.

Pixels Up Close
This enlargement shows how pixel doubling spreads data for one pixel over a group of four.

Pixel Doubling
Blown Away, by Imagination Pilots, uses pixel doubling to increase the apparent size of the video on the screen.

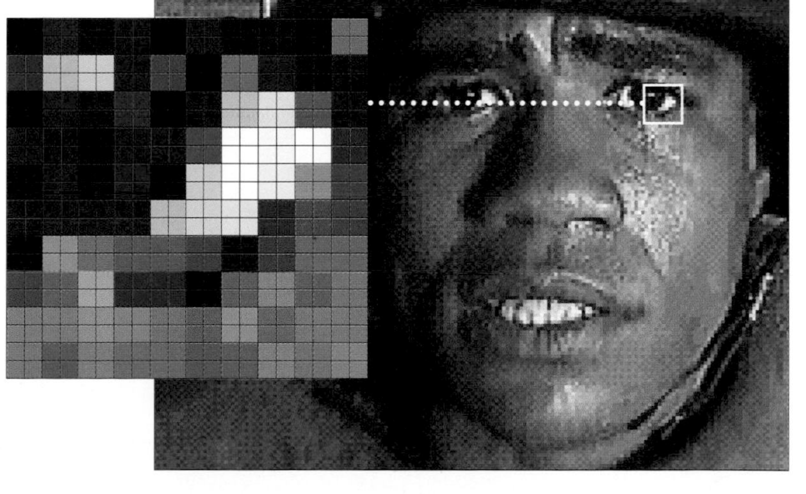

M
R/S
1
ABC
2
DEF
3
GHI
4
JKL
5
MNO
6
PQR
7
STU
8
VW
9
XYZ
*
0
#

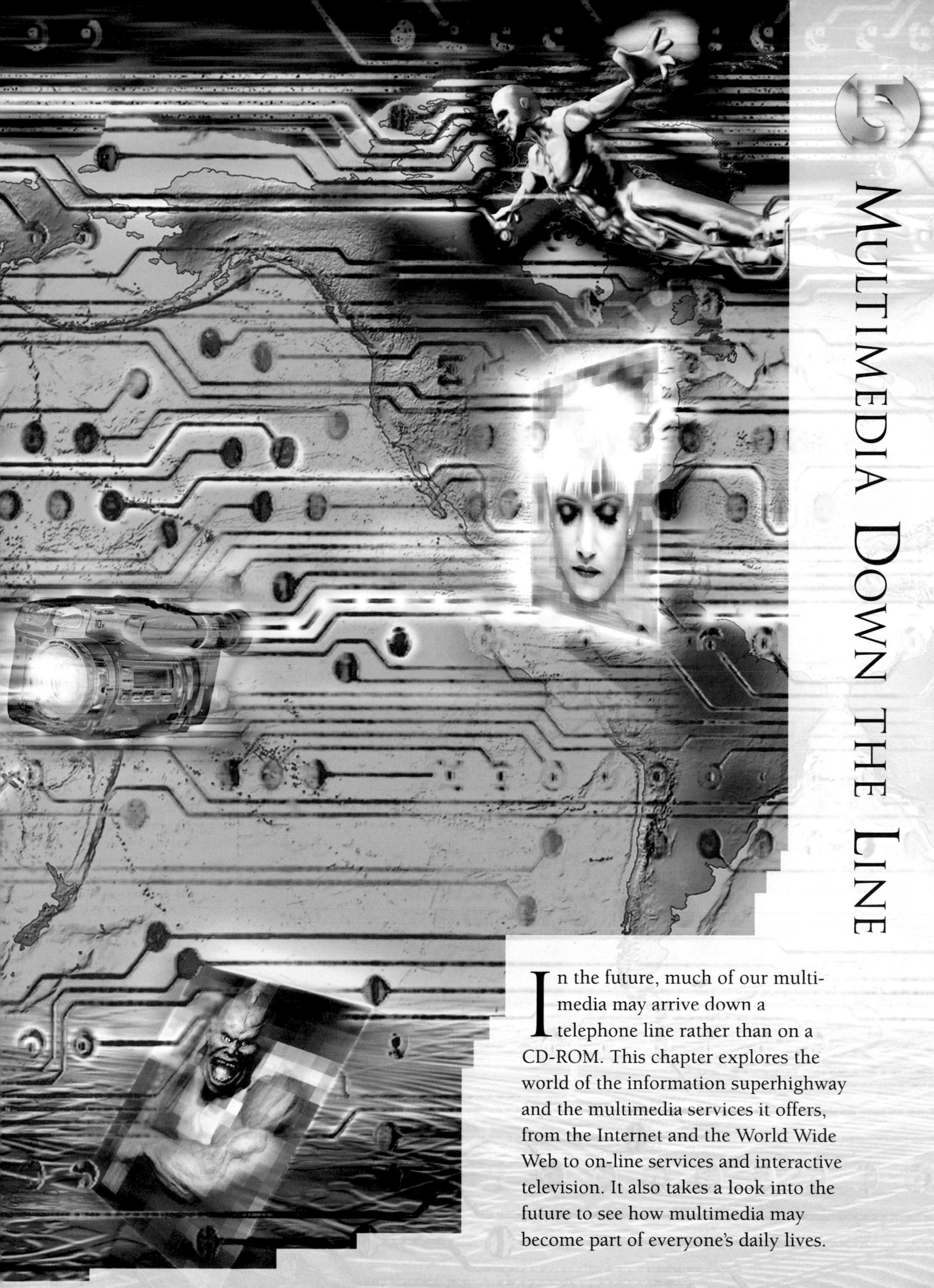

5 Multimedia Down the Line

In the future, much of our multimedia may arrive down a telephone line rather than on a CD-ROM. This chapter explores the world of the information superhighway and the multimedia services it offers, from the Internet and the World Wide Web to on-line services and interactive television. It also takes a look into the future to see how multimedia may become part of everyone's daily lives.

The Superhighway

For all its sophistication, the multimedia CD-ROM is seen by many people as a stepping-stone to an even more exciting future. That is because anything that can be stored on a CD-ROM can also be sent over a telephone line or television cable. The CD-ROM player may be replaced by a computerized junction box, giving us access not to just one CD but to thousands or even millions of sources of information and entertainment from around the world. Multimedia will no longer be just an innovative new form of technology – it will be a force for social change as great as the car or the telephone once was. At least, that is what its proponents say.

The Superhypeway?

The superhighway has attracted much comment, reflecting a variety of opinions:

"We will socialize in digital neighborhoods in which physical space will be irrelevant..."
Nicholas Negroponte, Director of MIT Media Lab

"A global and highly competitive tele-economy will be born within a generation."
The World Bank

"[We are] committed to the goal of connecting every classroom, every library, every hospital, and every clinic to the national and global information infrastructures by the end of this decade."
Al Gore

"The full information superhighway is 15 to 20 years away in the United States and Europe – 50 years in the rest of the world."
Rupert Murdoch, Chairman of News Corporation

What Is the Superhighway?

Just before the 1992 American presidential election, vice-presidential candidate Al Gore declared that he wanted an "information superhighway" to be built across the country. By that he meant a high-capacity telecommunications network (sometimes called a "broadband" network) that would carry vast amounts of digital binary data – training programs, educational material, and so on – in and out of every American home.

Binary data
For more on binary data, see page 69

He believed that such a network would give a boost to the American economy in much the same way the railroads had in the nineteenth century, or the freeway system had in the middle of this century. It would bring people closer together, not physically but electronically – and that would mean they could do more business together, thus generating greater wealth.

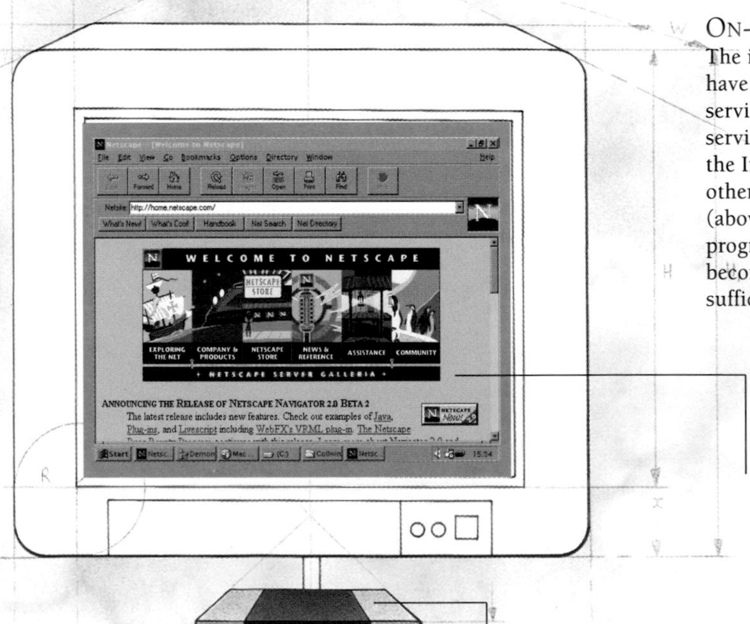

On-line Multimedia
The information superhighway will have the capacity to bring a host of services into our homes. Some of these services are already available, such as the Internet and on-line services (left); others, such as interactive television (above right), are being tested in pilot programs around the world, and may become widespread if there is sufficient public demand.

The Internet
The Internet, a global computer network, contains a wealth of services, including World Wide Web pages such as this one.

Modem
A modem lets you access on-line services and the Internet from a computer.

Will the Highway Be Built?

National broadband networks are already at the early planning stage. US West, which provides telephone services to the Rocky Mountain region, aims to have a fiber and coaxial network in place by 2003. And in Japan the government has said it wants a broadband network built by 2010. But whether these and other projects come to fruition depends principally on public demand. If enough people want the services that a broadband network can bring, and are prepared to pay enough for them, it will make economic sense to build a network.

Bandwidth

The superhighway has been made possible largely by advances in cable technology. There are three basic types of cables, each with a maximum data-carrying capacity, or "bandwidth."

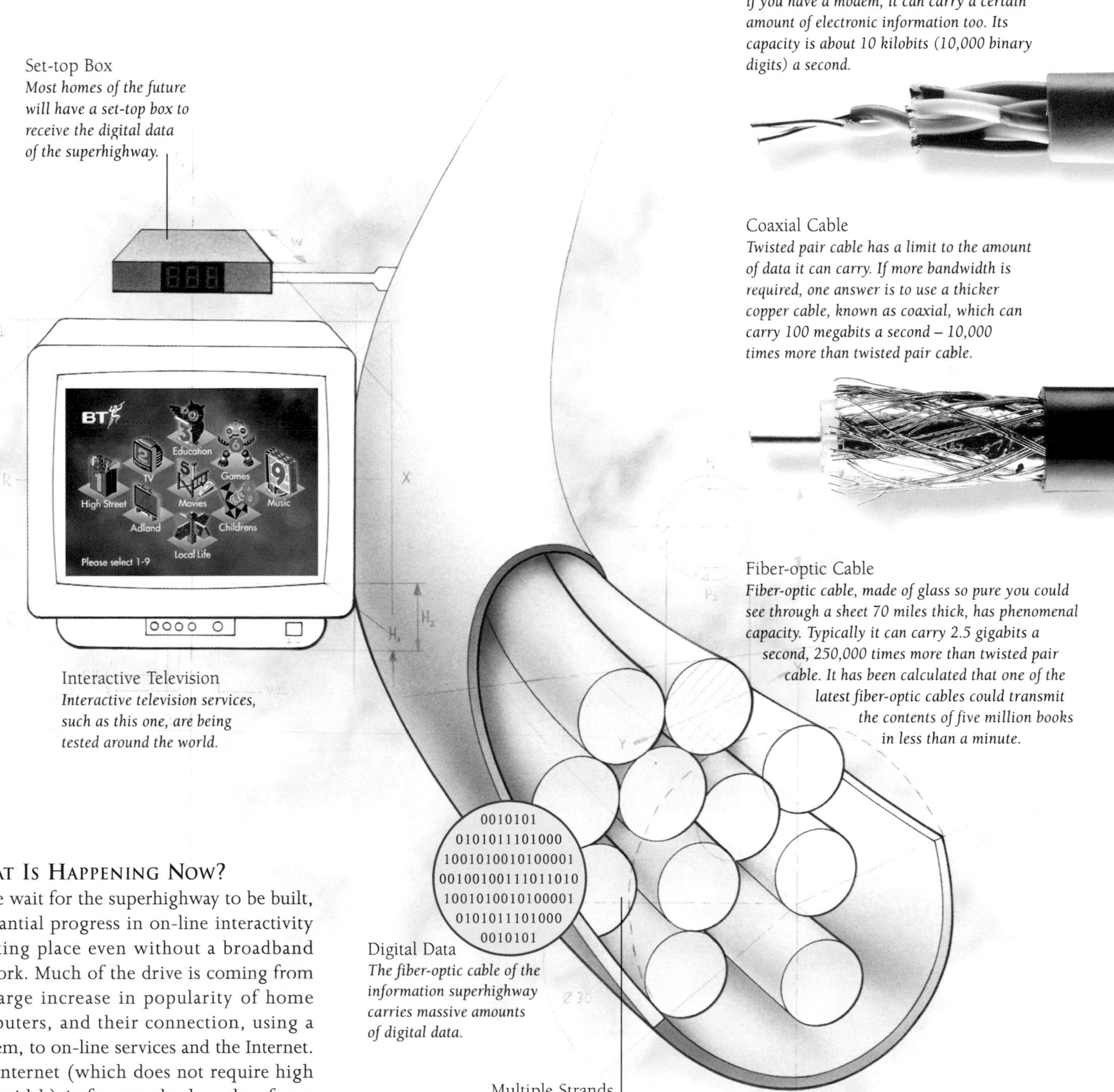

Twisted Pair Cable
The ordinary phone line into a house consists of two pieces of thin copper cable, known as a twisted pair. It can carry telephone calls, and if you have a modem, it can carry a certain amount of electronic information too. Its capacity is about 10 kilobits (10,000 binary digits) a second.

Set-top Box
Most homes of the future will have a set-top box to receive the digital data of the superhighway.

Coaxial Cable
Twisted pair cable has a limit to the amount of data it can carry. If more bandwidth is required, one answer is to use a thicker copper cable, known as coaxial, which can carry 100 megabits a second – 10,000 times more than twisted pair cable.

Fiber-optic Cable
Fiber-optic cable, made of glass so pure you could see through a sheet 70 miles thick, has phenomenal capacity. Typically it can carry 2.5 gigabits a second, 250,000 times more than twisted pair cable. It has been calculated that one of the latest fiber-optic cables could transmit the contents of five million books in less than a minute.

Interactive Television
Interactive television services, such as this one, are being tested around the world.

Digital Data
The fiber-optic cable of the information superhighway carries massive amounts of digital data.

Multiple Strands
Most fiber-optic cables consist of many strands of fiber bound together in a casing.

What Is Happening Now?

As we wait for the superhighway to be built, substantial progress in on-line interactivity is taking place even without a broadband network. Much of the drive is coming from the large increase in popularity of home computers, and their connection, using a modem, to on-line services and the Internet. The Internet (which does not require high bandwidth) is frequently thought of as a prototype of the information superhighway. It has many of the services we can expect to find on the superhighway in the future.

THE INTERNET

THE INTERNET (COMMONLY known as the Net) is a network that links many computer networks across the globe. It is used mainly as a communications channel for electronic messages (e-mail), but it also holds an enormous amount of useful information (much of it consisting of multimedia), stored by individuals, governments, educational and research establishments, and by commercial organizations. The Internet uses a standard language (called a protocol) so that anyone using a computer, a modem, and a phone line can access sites on the Internet to send e-mail, join discussion groups, or experience the graphically rich pages of the World Wide Web. The number of Internet users can only be guessed at, but today's estimates put it at 40 million people worldwide.

HISTORICAL BACKGROUND

In the late 1960s, the United States Department of Defense was worried that its computer network was vulnerable to nuclear attack. If one link was broken, the whole system might collapse. So the Advanced Research and Projects Agency developed a set of computer protocols called TCP/IP (Transmission Control Protocol/Internet Protocol), and created a military network called ARPANET. TCP/IP could send data from one computer to another via several alternative routes, so if one site was destroyed the data would still arrive safely.

In the early 1980s the military traffic on ARPANET was split off, leaving what was to become known as the Internet. Its growth was initially fueled by the academic community, who saw it as a wonderful way of moving data. Universities built broadband links between one another so they could swap data using TCP/IP. Government agencies such as NASA and the Department of Energy linked their own networks into the Internet, and were joined by hundreds of others, inside and outside America. By 1990, businesses and private individuals were beginning to use the Net to exchange e-mail and transfer computer files, and ever since then the trend toward commercialization has been relentless.

PACKET SWITCHING
Computers on the Internet communicate using a common language, or protocol, called TCP/IP. A message on the Internet is divided into sections, called packets. TCP (Transmission Control Protocol) puts these packets in secure "envelopes." IP (Internet Protocol) adds the address of the destination computer.

Data Transmission
The message is divided into packets of data.

How Modems Work

The modem, or modulator/demodulator, was first used in the 1950s to allow computers to communicate via the telephone line. Modems convert the digital data used by computers into the analog audio signal used by the telephone line. When we have all-digital networks, modems will no longer be needed: they will be replaced by a simple "data card" that transfers information from the computer straight onto the digital telephone line. Until then, modems remain a necessity. They can be external (sitting between the computer and telephone point) or internal (a modem card plugged into the motherboard of a personal computer).

Sending E-mail
A computer in New York sends an e-mail message to a computer in London.

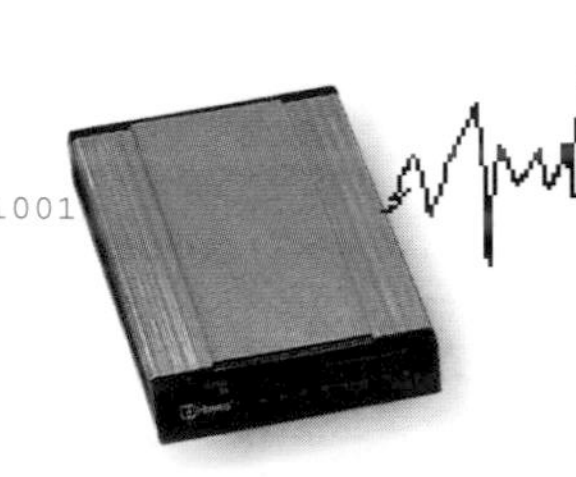

Modem
The modem translates the computer's digital signal into an analog audio signal that can be sent over a telephone line.

Internet Service Providers

Until recently, the Internet was difficult to use because most of the mainframe computers on it use the UNIX operating system. Only those who understood UNIX could take advantage of it. Now, software has been developed that will allow anyone using the DOS, Windows, or Macintosh operating systems to tap into it. Service providers have also sprung up to act as "gateways" to the Internet. They run powerful computers that are linked directly to the Internet by permanent high bandwidth connections. Subscribers hook up to these computers by a dial-up connection.

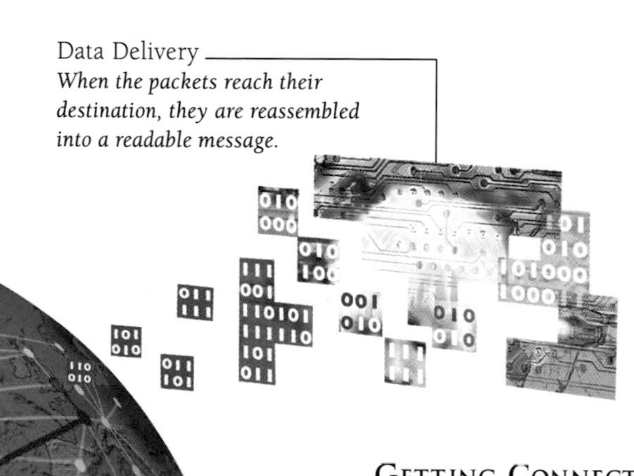

Data Delivery
When the packets reach their destination, they are reassembled into a readable message.

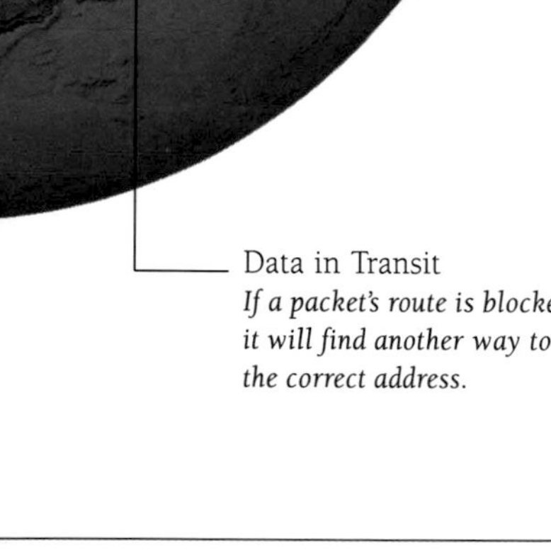

Data in Transit
If a packet's route is blocked, it will find another way to the correct address.

Getting Connected

Subscribers usually pay a monthly or an annual fee, in return for which they receive a password, an e-mail address, and access to the necessary software. They may need to "download" this software (import it to their computers via a modem) or they may receive it on a disk. The software contains a dialing program, which dials the service provider's number, checks the password, then gives access to the Internet. It is also likely to have programs for using e-mail, FTP (File Transfer Protocol), Newsgroups, and the World Wide Web.

People use the Internet in many ways and for many purposes. Many use the World Wide Web simply for browsing; others use newsgroups for sharing information on hobbies and interests with other enthusiasts. Many use e-mail, FTP, newsgroups, and the World Wide Web primarily as part of their daily professional life, or as an essential tool in the fields of education and research. Whatever these users are looking for, the information is almost certainly available somewhere on the Internet.

What You Can Use on the Internet

E-mail
Most traffic on the Internet is electronic mail (e-mail), a convenient and cheap way of sending messages. An e-mail message can be sent to the other side of the world in seconds.

Newsgroups
Electronic bulletin boards, allowing computer users to ask questions or "chat" to others, have existed for many years. There are now over 11,000 bulletin boards, called newsgroups, in an area of the Internet called Usenet. Newsgroup topics range from politics to Star Trek *and the stock market.*

FTP (File Transfer Protocol)
FTP is a method of transferring files from one computer to another. Free or public-domain software can be downloaded from a variety of FTP sites.

World Wide Web
For many people, the most exciting part of the Internet is crisscrossing the globe to browse the multimedia pages of the World Wide Web.

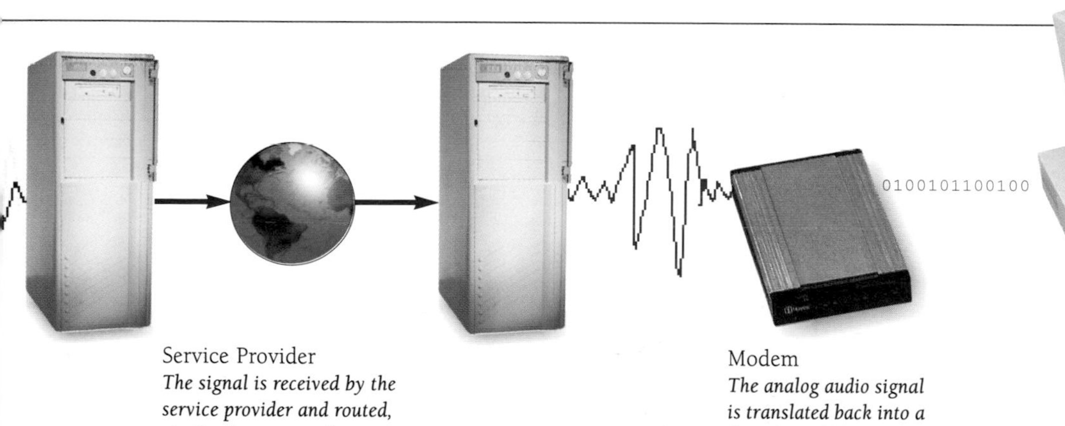

Service Provider
The signal is received by the service provider and routed, via the Internet, to the correct electronic address.

Modem
The analog audio signal is translated back into a digital signal by a modem.

Receiving E-mail
The e-mail message is received by the computer in London.

The World Wide Web

The Web is the finest example of multimedia on the Internet, and the one that has tempted millions of nontechnical people to try out the network. The Web consists of tens of thousands of "pages," many of which use rich graphics and photographs mixed with text. These can be viewed by a "browser," a program that provides a window in a computer screen on which the pages are displayed. By clicking on any word that is highlighted, users are transferred to another linked page. The Web has no complete index, but it is ideal for "surfing," or wandering from page to page.

Origins of the Web

In the early 1980s, a young Englishman named Tim Berners-Lee was working at CERN, the European high-energy physics research facility near Geneva. He developed a hypertext program that allowed him to link academic documents electronically. This program made it possible for CERN's researchers to tap into a "web" of information, jumping from one document to another at the touch of a key.

The program sparked a lot of interest. It soon became clear that a standard format for Web pages would be needed, and academics were asked to write browser programs that would make the system easy to use. The first came out in 1991, but the Web took off only when the National Center for Supercomputing Applications, in Illinois, produced the Mosaic browser in 1993. This rapidly made the Internet very easy to use – it had two million users within a year.

Hypertext Mark-up Language

World Wide Web pages can be constructed by anyone with a little programming knowledge, and now cover a very wide range of subjects – from the CIA Fact Book and the Hungarian budget to a guide to Dublin pubs and a tour of the Electronic Zoo. The Web's language, HTML (Hypertext Mark-up Language), is used to create documents for the Web.

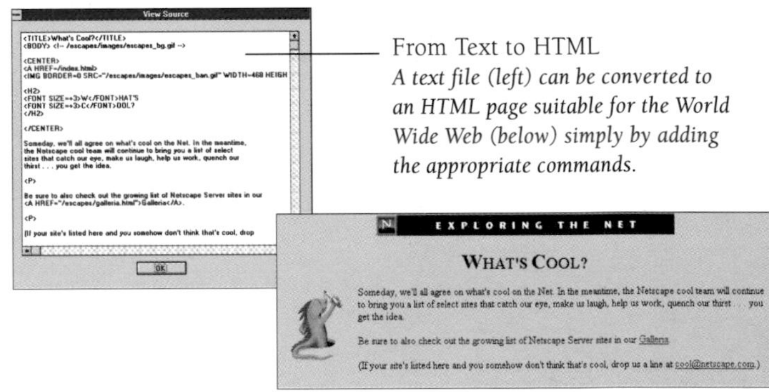

From Text to HTML
A text file (left) can be converted to an HTML page suitable for the World Wide Web (below) simply by adding the appropriate commands.

Netscape Web Browser

The Netscape Web Browser is one of the most popular of the browsers currently available. Some test versions are available free.

Site Address
The address of the current Web site is displayed in this box. Users can type in new addresses to access other sites and pages.

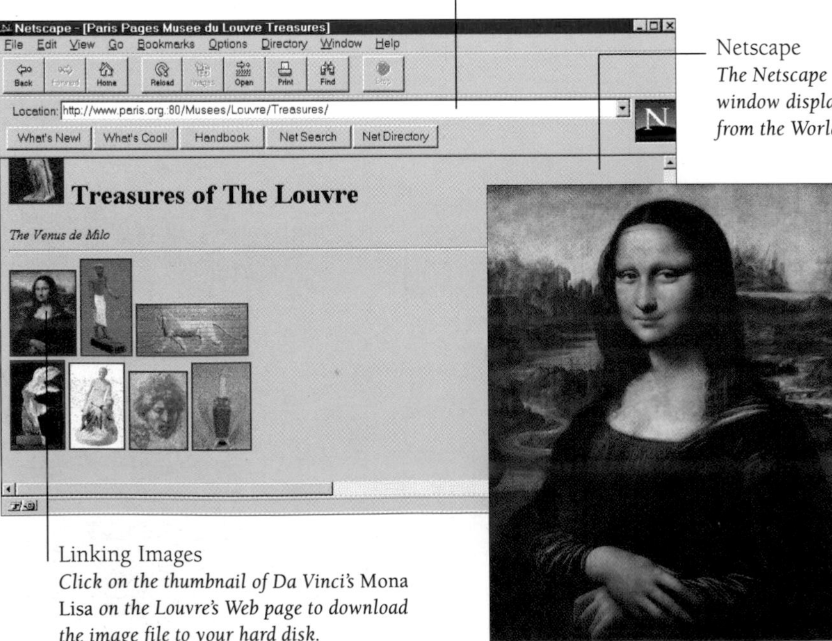

Netscape
The Netscape browser window displays a page from the World Wide Web.

Linking Images
Click on the thumbnail of Da Vinci's Mona Lisa *on the Louvre's Web page to download the image file to your hard disk.*

Web Browsers

Originally Web pages carried just text, but the arrival of the Mosaic browser in 1993 made it possible to view graphics in fine detail. Since then, the most popular pages have included multimedia elements such as images, sound files, video and animation clips, and so on. Some artists have even started creating specifically for the World Wide Web. Web browsers are becoming increasingly sophisticated by the month and some now incorporate features such as 3-D graphics and advanced encryption systems for protecting personal details you may want to send to someone across the Internet. Test versions of some Web browsers can be downloaded free by private users, but these test versions often have a 30 day time limit, so many users now purchase the full commercial versions.

Hypertext Links and Hotlists

When you click on a hypertext link (usually text that is underlined on the page), you move directly to the computer that stores the page, wherever it may be in the world. If you need to find specific information (rather than just surf around), you can access one of the many "search engines," such as the Lycos Catalog search tool, available on the Internet.

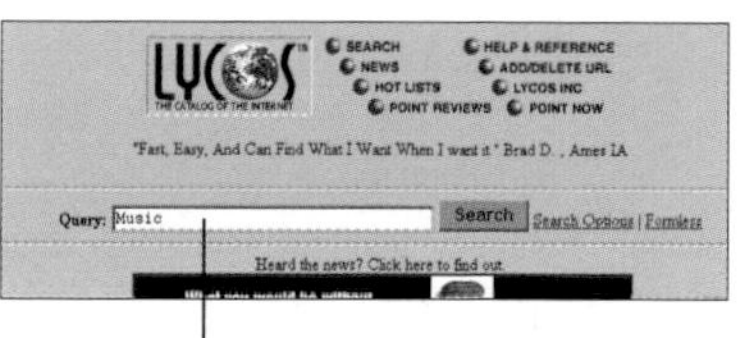

Lycos Search Engine
Search for a single word or use the options menu to narrow the field.

Video and Sound on the Web

Video clips can now be downloaded from many Web sites, and can be viewed on a computer equipped with video playback software such as Apple's *QuickTime*. Because these clips comprise a great deal of data, they can take some time to download to a hard disk, and they can occupy a considerable amount of disk space when they get there. For this reason, video clips are likely to be brief and are usually shown in a small window on the screen. The same problem affects the length of sound files available on the Web. However, with the development of new compression techniques, downloading lengthier video and sound files will become common practice. Compression will also increase the volume of cheap telephone calls made on the Web. Kits that include a microphone and software are already available.

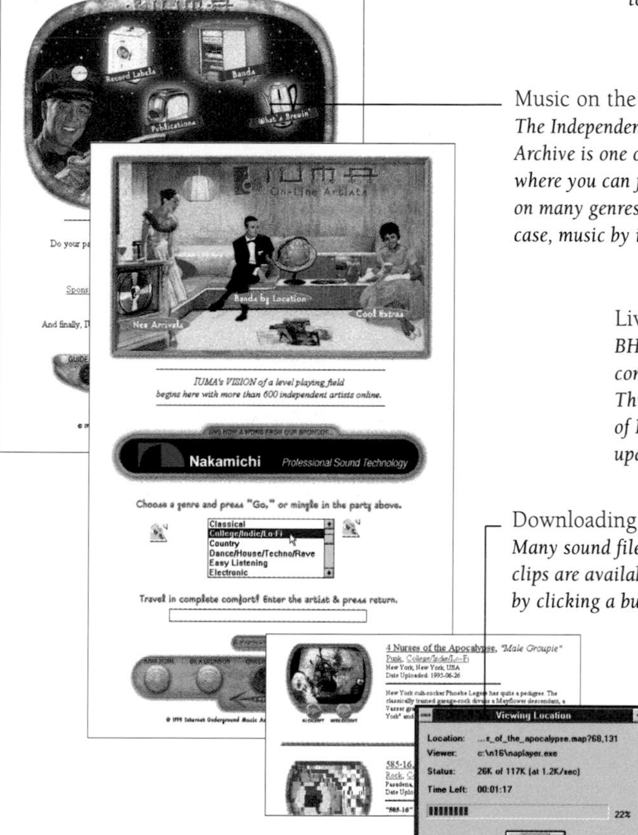

Music on the Web
The Independent Underground Music Archive is one of many Web sites where you can find multimedia files on many genres of music – in this case, music by independent artists.

Downloading Sound
Many sound files and video clips are available simply by clicking a button.

Live Video Links
BHI's Hollywood page contains live video links. This picture of the corner of Hollywood and Vine is updated every 20 seconds.

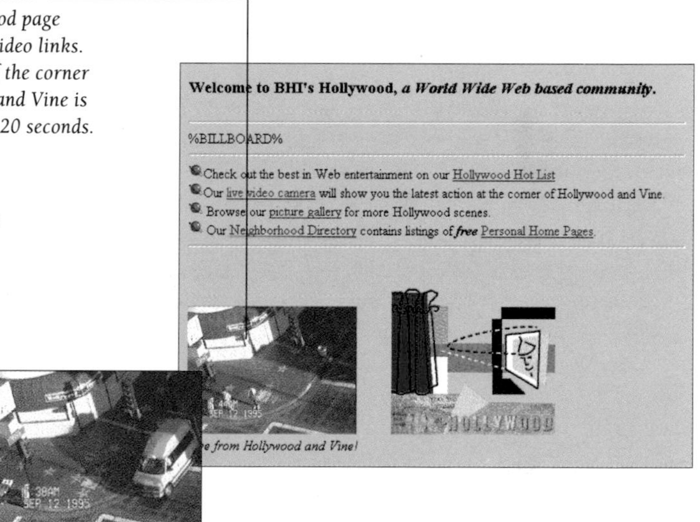

Around the World from Your Desk

Using a Web browser, it is so easy to jump from one site (and subject) to another that you may be unaware that you are traveling across the globe and back in only seconds. These pages give a flavor of the Web's global nature.

Hardware and Software
Most major software and hardware developers, such as Apple Computer, have a World Wide Web presence.

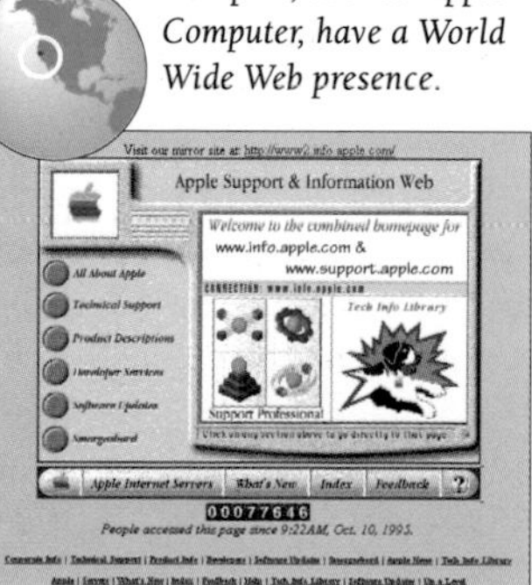

Travel and Tourism
This page holds a wealth of information on all types of vacations in New Zealand, and provides links to travel operators.

The White House
Many government departments in many countries can now be accessed via the Web. You can hear a message from the President at this site.

Electronic Press
Many newspapers and magazines, such as the UK's Daily Telegraph, *now have regularly updated on-line editions.*

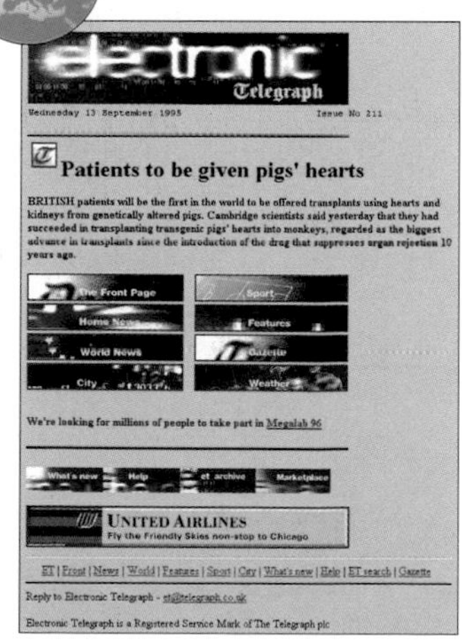

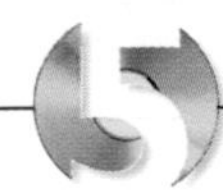

ON-LINE SERVICES

While the Internet grew up without any real parents, privately run on-line services were set up by their owners as a commercial concern. On-line services may not be as big or as full of surprises as the Internet, but they do have advantages. They usually have easy-to-use interfaces, making them more attractive to beginners, and information is clearly categorized, enabling subscribers to access the information they need quickly and simply. On-line services also carry a wide range of useful databases (often unavailable on the Internet) that include encyclopedias, airline and train timetables, and press clippings; subscribers usually pay extra for this information. Finally, most private services offer a gateway to the Internet, and many also provide a way into the World Wide Web.

THE PIONEERS

In the 1970s, commercial organizations realized that they could offer information via a phone line and a modem. One of the first attempts to set up a public on-line service was made by state-owned France Telecom, which set up its Minitel service in 1982. In a bold move aimed at upgrading the country's technological culture, the company gave every phone subscriber in France a terminal, free. France thus had its own on-line service years before most other countries.

The first American on-line service was CompuServe. It was originally the data-processing department of an insurance company, but in the early 1980s it started using its spare computing capacity to offer services to personal computer users. It has been joined by America Online, Prodigy (which belongs to IBM and Sears), and a number of smaller services such as Delphi (belonging to The News Corporation), GEnie (General Electric) and eWorld (Apple). In 1995, Microsoft launched its own service: The Microsoft Network. All these services offer a similar mix of products, although the level of Internet access and the degree of internationalism vary.

Minitel

In the early 1980s, France Telecom's Minitel was providing an on-line telephone directory, as well as a route through which companies could advertise or provide information: there are now 24,000 such information providers.

Text-based Service
Minitel's text-based interface is typical of many of the earlier on-line services.

Choosing Menus
The nature and cost of Minitel's services are clearly indicated on each menu.

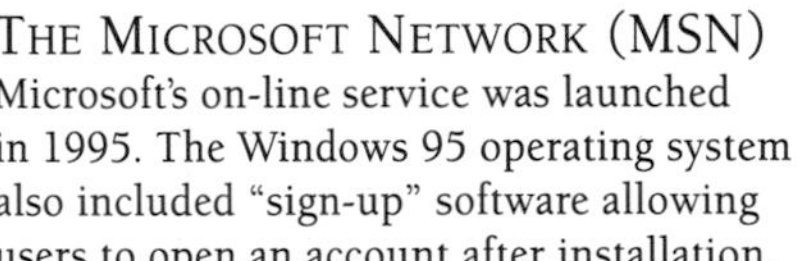

THE MICROSOFT NETWORK (MSN)
Microsoft's on-line service was launched in 1995. The Windows 95 operating system also included "sign-up" software allowing users to open an account after installation.

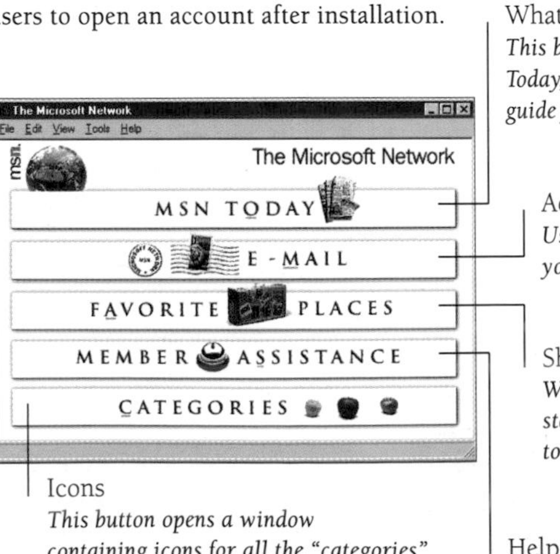

What's On
This button opens MSN Today, a daily "what's on" guide for the network.

Accessing E-mail
Use this button to access your e-mail messages.

Shortcuts
With this button you can store and access shortcuts to your favorite locations.

Help
Use this button to obtain help.

Icons
This button opens a window containing icons for all the "categories" on the MSN – for example, Education and Reference, or Business and Finance.

EWORLD
Apple Computer's eWorld was launched in 1994. The simple graphical organization of information is typified by the "town square" interface used on the opening screen. Choosing one of the buildings will lead you to a wide range of services.

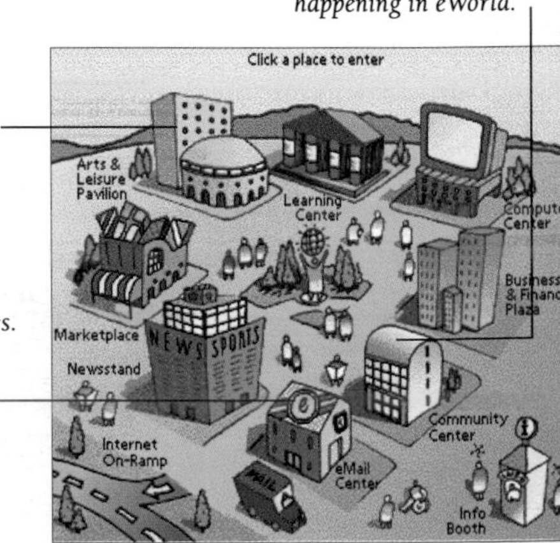

Community Center
Choosing the Community Center keeps you informed of what is currently happening in eWorld.

Arts and Leisure Pavilion
From the Arts and Leisure Pavilion you can access services such as Hollywood Online, from which you can download full-motion video clips from your favorite movies.

EMail Center
Mail a message or check your mailbox by calling into the eMail Center.

What They Offer

On-line services usually provide a clear, user-friendly interface for accessing up-to-date information from reliable sources, including well-known providers of news, reference, and shopping services. Services such as CompuServe and America Online offer custom-made software for Windows or Macintosh. Most services offer "on-line chat rooms" or conferencing – like a huge conference call, although the contributions are currently written rather than spoken. Conferences are formal, covering a specific topic, while chat is unstructured – more like a ham radio or Citizens Band conversation. Most services also offer forums (bulletin boards). Unlike Internet newsgroups, they are carefully controlled, and usually have their own elaborate introductory screen. Although on-line services have fewer forums than the Internet, they are considered by many users to be better organized and more friendly.

Internet Access

Many on-line services now offer Internet access, and some, such as CompuServe, supply a World Wide Web browser.

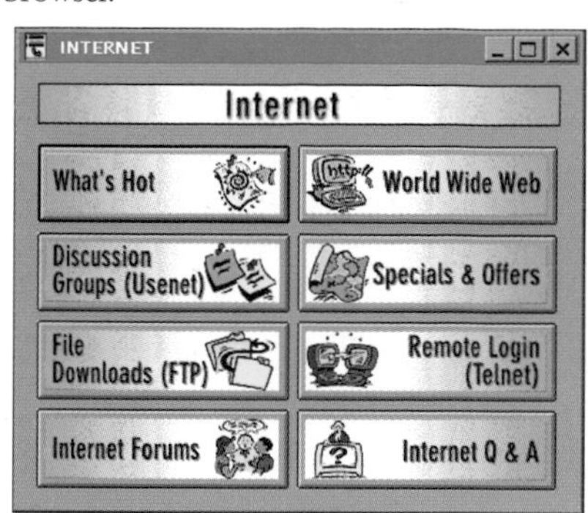

CompuServe
CompuServe added Internet services in 1995, providing access to many newsgroups, file transfer sites, and other features that were previously unavailable to its members.

How an On-line Service Works

CompuServe is an on-line service that is used around the world. By choosing one of the twelve buttons in the main window, members access the main services. Each service is presented in a window that contains more buttons and a menu of further services. The toolbar is present on every subsequent screen. From the toolbar, users can save and transfer files, send e-mail, request their current billing statement, and so on.

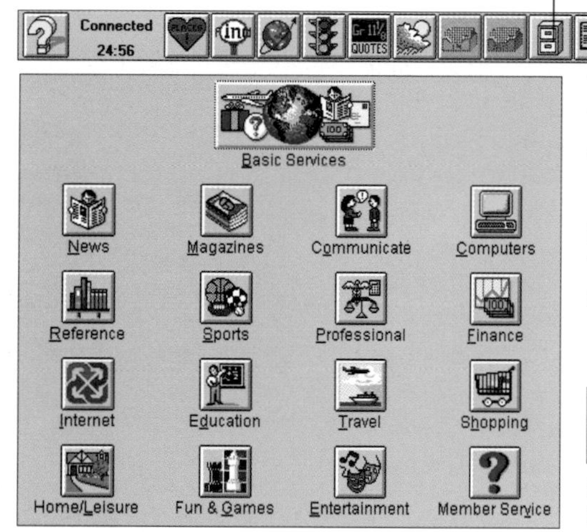

Toolbar
The toolbar appears on every CompuServe screen.

Filing Cabinet
The toolbar buttons provide many useful features. This button, for example, opens the "filing cabinet" where text can be stored for reading or printing off-line (when disconnected from the service).

Main Screen
This shows the main services and the toolbar.

Shopping Services
If you know where to look, you can shop on the Internet, but on-line services make things easy by providing "electronic malls."

On-line News
This service offers up-to-the-minute information from news services such as CNN.

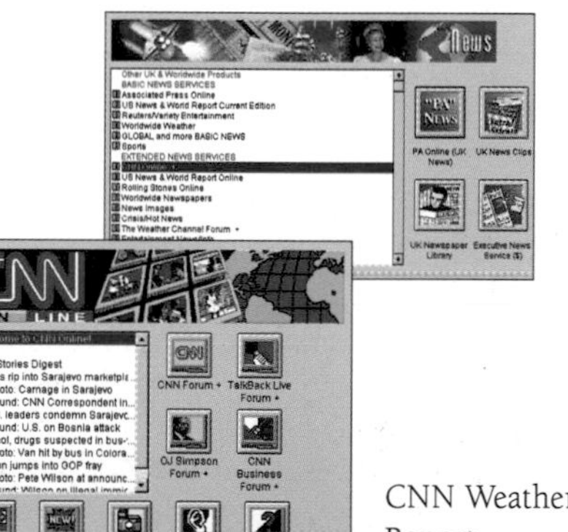

Reference Works
Most on-line reference works and databases include a powerful search facility.

Search an Encyclopedia
On-line reference works such as The Hutchinson Encyclopedia *can be searched for pictures or text.*

CNN Weather Report

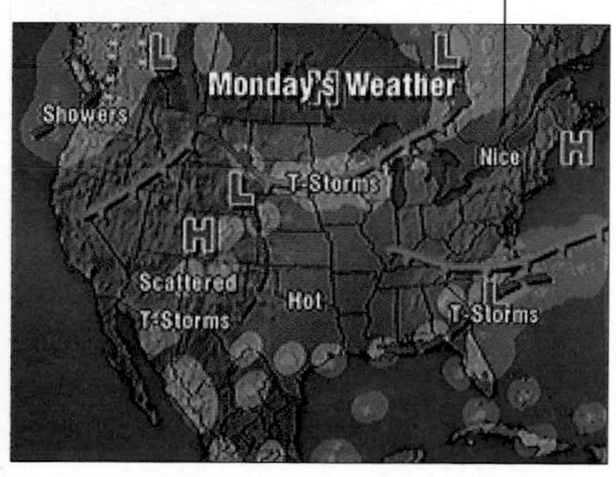

Downloading Images
After you have searched for and found the image you want (in this case Greta Garbo) you can view it and then save it on your hard disk.

View Before Buying
By accessing the Interflora "store," you can choose your flowers from the pictures and descriptions provided. You then simply enter the relevant billing, payment, and delivery information.

Interactive Television

Pilot programs around the world are testing interactive television systems and finding out which features their customers enjoy the most. Systems such as Time Warner Cable's Full Service Network in Orlando, Florida, offer a variety of different services that we may one day regard as commonplace, from video-on-demand to home shopping and interactive video games. The technology needed to provide such services now exists. Which services, if any, are finally adopted will depend less on technological ability than on public demand. The pilot programs are designed to find out which service will be the so-called "killer application" that customers are prepared to pay for, in order to justify the huge financial investment needed to install interactive television systems in our homes.

Video-on-demand

The arrival of the VCR in the 1970s meant it was possible for the first time to watch a movie when you wanted. But you first had to tape it or rent it. Video-on-demand, however, provides the movie instantaneously. Using a remote control supplied by the service provider, you choose a movie category, such as drama, comedy, or action. An "electronic rental store" then presents an extensive list of movies in that category. With the press of a button, you select one, and seconds later it appears on the screen. You can then stop it, pause it, rewind or fast-forward it, just as though it were a video in a VCR machine. Many commentators believe that video-on-demand will be the killer application of interactive televison.

Near Video-on-demand

A cheaper alternative to video-on-demand, known as "near video-on-demand," has been adopted by some satellite television services. It is a development of the "pay-per-view" systems already widespread on cable television. The movies it offers each start every 15 or 30 minutes. After selecting a movie you are then told how long to wait before it starts to play.

Satellite
For more on satellites, see page 173

List of Movies

Lethal Weapon 3
Made in America
Malcolm X
The Neverending Story
Point of No Return
Robin Hood Prince of Thieves
The Secret Garden
Sommersby
This Boy's Life
Under Siege
A to Z
Batman Returns

Movie Choice
Time Warner Cable interactive television customers can choose from an extensive list of popular movies.

Remote Control
BT's interactive television service is controlled by a multipurpose remote control unit.

Direction Button
This gamepad-style button enables you to navigate through options and menus.

OK Button
This unit has an OK button for making selections.

Function Buttons
These buttons enable you to select different options on the screen.

Video Controls
Video-on-demand can be paused, rewound, or fast-forwarded at will.

Home Shopping

Many people have experienced a form of home shopping through mail-order catalogs or television shopping channels, but these services can offer only a limited range of goods. The home shopping service offered on interactive television systems is far more flexible. Viewers can enter virtual stores and examine goods by revolving them in three dimensions on the screen. They can read the details on a product's packaging, and make a purchase simply by pressing a button on their handset. This debits their credit card, and the goods are then delivered to the home.

Virtual Supermarket
Time Warner Cable's ShopperVision shows a 3-D graphic view of the products on the shelves.

Games and News-on-demand

Most interactive television trials are offering games to their customers. These games are sent to the set-top box in the same way as video-on-demand. They can then be played either alone or with friends. Another option is to play against someone else linked up to the network: once the player has selected a game, he or she can compete against other opponents who are playing at the same time.

Games
For more on games, see page 44

Another significant service is news-on-demand. Instead of watching news bulletins when they are scheduled by a broadcast television company, users of interactive television can call up the latest bulletin from major news networks, such as CNN, at any time. A sports-on-demand service is also possible. This system can be applied to any category of television program, and could theoretically do away with the entire concept of television schedules.

Services on Trial

Both the Time Warner Cable trial in the United States and the BT trial in the UK are experimenting with a wide range of services such as video-on-demand, home shopping, and on-line games.

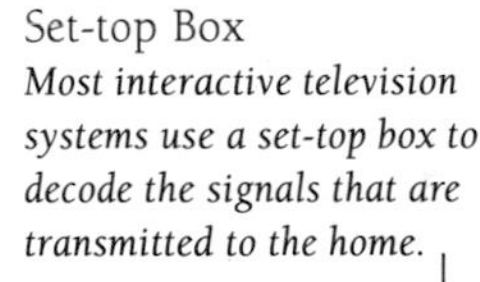

Set-top Box
Most interactive television systems use a set-top box to decode the signals that are transmitted to the home.

Graphical Interface
The Time Warner Cable trial uses an interface called Carousel, a revolving visual display of the services available to the viewer.

Main Menu
Participants in the BT pilot program are presented with a main menu in the form of numbered icons.

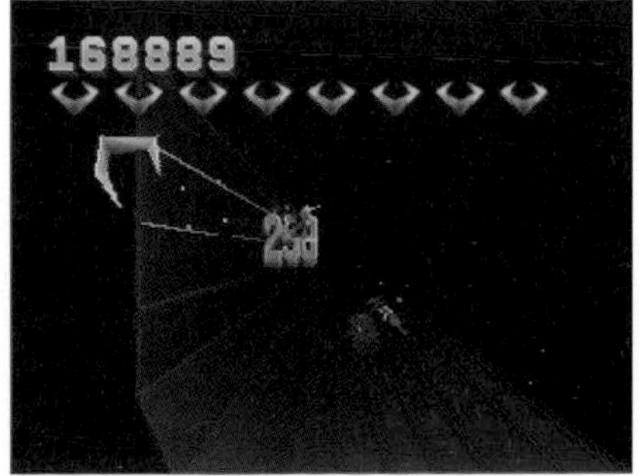

Video Games
Time Warner Cable offers a range of 64-bit action games with three-dimensional color images and CD-quality sound.

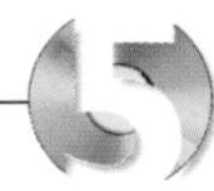

How Interactive Television Works

Participants in interactive television pilot programs, enjoying the range of services available, may not appreciate the technical difficulties in bringing these services to the home. Unlike broadcast television, an interactive service allows the customer to decide which service to use at any given time. Therefore, not only does the service provider have to manage the task of sending massive amounts of digital data over a cable, but it must also set up a system for receiving signals back from the customer. For example, if a customer decides to watch a movie, he or she chooses it from an on-screen list, using the remote control. This signal then travels to a computer in the operations center, where it is interpreted and acted upon. The right movie is located, and sent back to the appropriate home. All this takes place in less than a second, and there may be thousands of similar requests every minute, presenting the service provider with an enormous technical challenge.

Optical Fiber

Fiber-optic cable is made up of fibers of extraordinarily pure glass. Instead of transmitting data in electrical impulses as copper wires do, the glass fibers transmit it in pulses of light. Traveling at great speed, these are internally reflected throughout their journey from one end of the cable to the other.

Providing an Interactive Service

Providing an interactive television service is an impressive feat of modern engineering. Different pilot programs use different techniques. The example shown here – supplying video-on-demand – is based on Time Warner Cable's Full Service Network program in Orlando, Florida.

1 Operations Center
The operations center is the nerve center of an interactive TV service. It receives requests from customers, locates the relevant material, and sends the digital data back to the customer's home.

2 Storage Vaults
Data such as digital video is held in compressed form in large storage devices called vaults. A typical vault houses up to 100 magnetic hard drives – enough to store more than 500 movies.

3 Digital Server
The server is a powerful computer that acts as the central brains of the system. When it receives a request, it locates the correct movie and divides the data into packets; it then adds the address of the destination to each one, and sends them to the ATM switch.

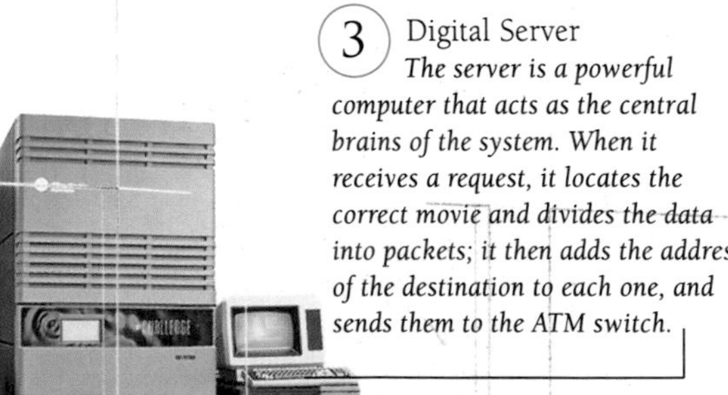

6 Fiber-optic Cable
The digital data is transmitted from the operations center to the neighborhood node along a fiber-optic cable.

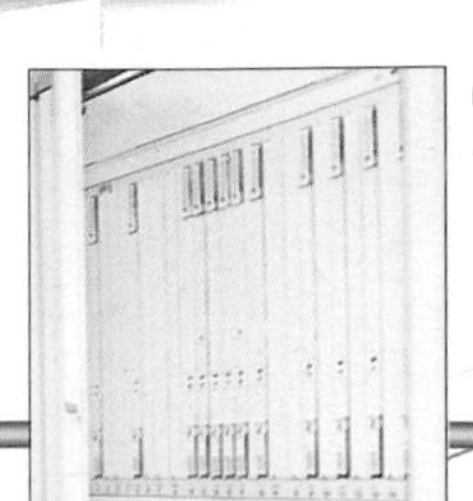

4 ATM Switch
ATM (Asynchronous Transfer Mode) is an advanced version of the packet switching used by the Internet. The ATM switch sends the packets of data coming from the server to the modulator at great speed.

5 Modulator
The modulator places the information it receives at the correct frequency for transmission through the network. This signal is then sent to the neighborhood node.

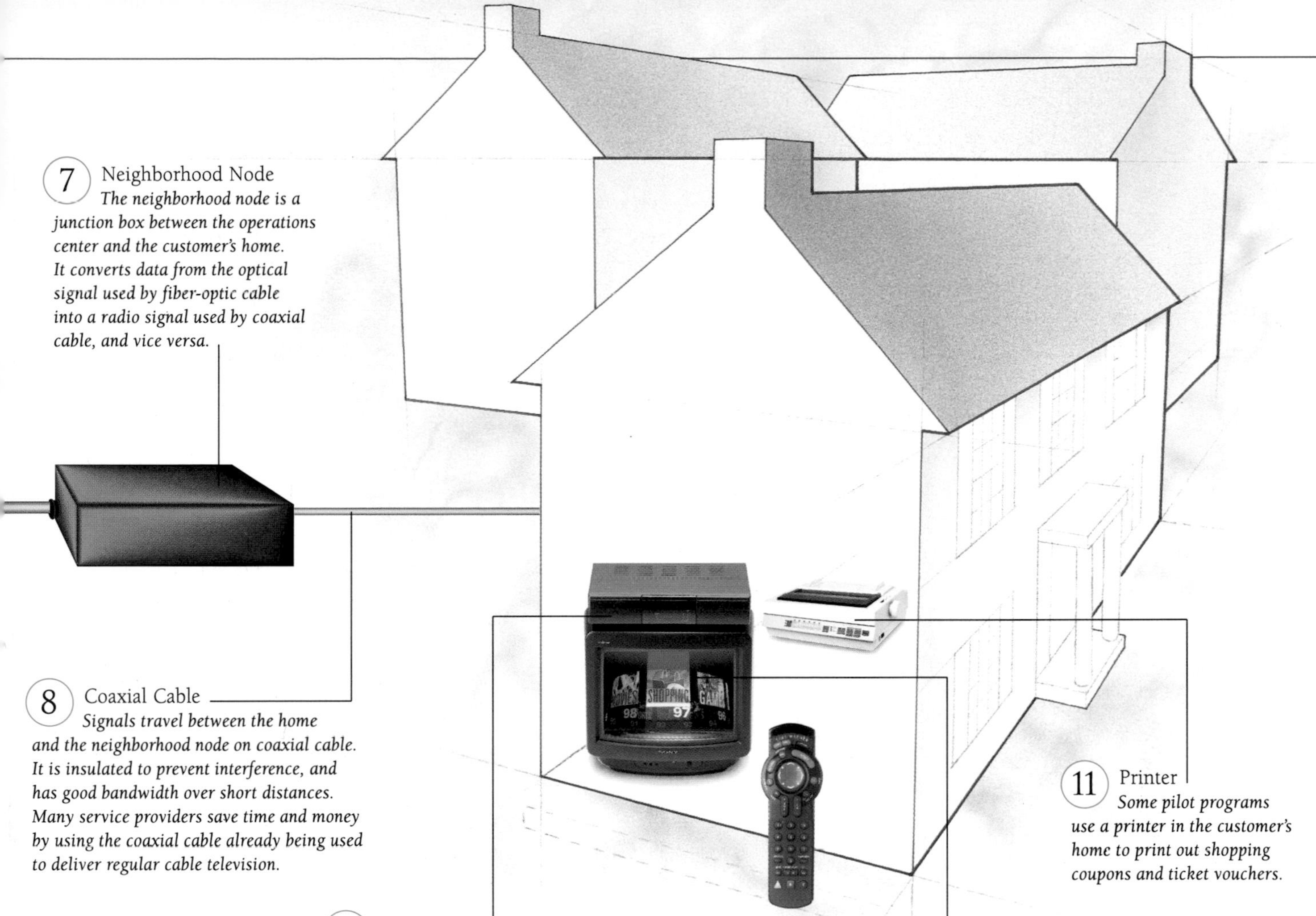

7 Neighborhood Node
The neighborhood node is a junction box between the operations center and the customer's home. It converts data from the optical signal used by fiber-optic cable into a radio signal used by coaxial cable, and vice versa.

8 Coaxial Cable
Signals travel between the home and the neighborhood node on coaxial cable. It is insulated to prevent interference, and has good bandwidth over short distances. Many service providers save time and money by using the coaxial cable already being used to deliver regular cable television.

9 Set-top Box
The set-top box receives data from the neighborhood node, and vice-versa. Inside, it is a powerful computer – often more powerful than many desktop models.

10 Video into the Home
When the video signal arrives, the set-top box reassembles the packets, decompresses the picture, and sends it to the television. It also separates this data from the regular television signal. The set-top box will never display a movie meant for another house because it reads the address on the packets, and will not decode data addressed to another house.

11 Printer
Some pilot programs use a printer in the customer's home to print out shopping coupons and ticket vouchers.

Digital Production Center

Before movies or television programs are sent for storage at the operations center, they have to be compressed, so that they will occupy as little storage space and bandwidth as possible. This compression is carried out by powerful computers at a digital production center, often located away from the main operations center. The production center also creates items such as logos, animated promotional sequences, and the visual interface from which the customer navigates the interactive television service.

Animation Suite
The production center houses a digital animation suite for creating animated sequences and for 3-D modeling. It uses powerful workstations, such as the Silicon Graphics Indigo 2 Extreme system shown here.

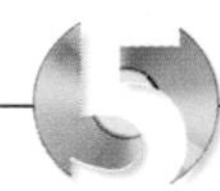

Into the Future

The future for multimedia looks dynamic: the quantity of digital information in our lives is ready to increase substantially over the next few decades, and it will improve dramatically in quality. Multimedia is evolving rapidly and in unexpected ways, but the broad trends all point toward a convergence of today's new technologies: CD-ROM, the Internet, and interactive television. This convergence is at the heart of a much broader revolution, which not only affects the way information is packaged and how we interact with it, but also looks ready to transform the way we communicate with one another. Multimedia is now becoming both personal and portable, as our new technologies demonstrate.

Personal Multimedia

The multimedia that we receive on CD-ROM is mass-produced, and sites on the World Wide Web are open to a mass audience, but current trends are all toward making multimedia more personal. Videophones, multimedia e-mail, and videoconferencing are bringing personal multimedia into one-to-one communication. Portable computers now make it possible to play multimedia titles and access the Internet while on the move. And PDAs (Personal Digital Assistants), the handheld electronic pocketbooks that started out as simple digital diaries, are fast becoming wireless communication stations. At the same time, the computer industry is working to remedy the problem that after twenty-five years of extremely rapid technological progress, computers are still impersonal objects that many people find hard to use. The move toward computer recognition of handwriting and speech and toward new computer interfaces suggests that the future of multimedia is to be a lot more human.

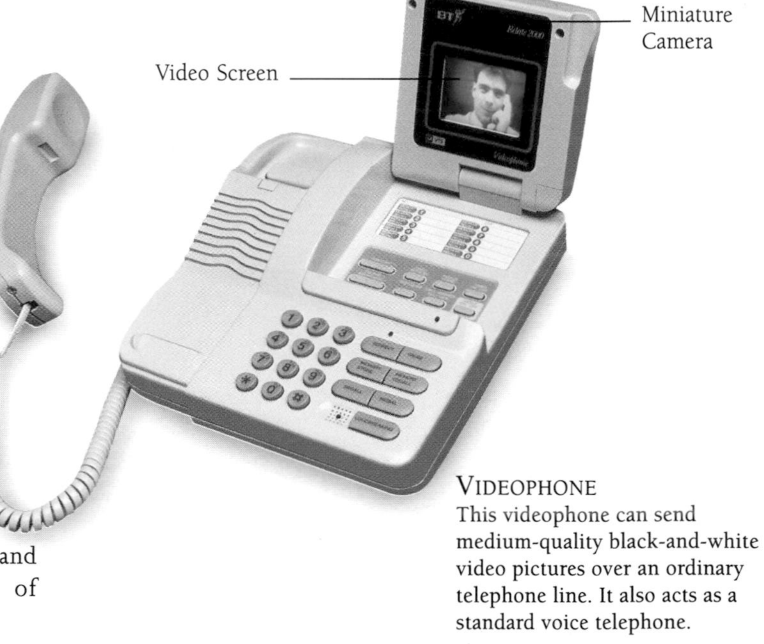

Videophone
This videophone can send medium-quality black-and-white video pictures over an ordinary telephone line. It also acts as a standard voice telephone.

Face-to-Face Communication

Multimedia messages can already be sent by computer users linked to a broadband network. In Berlin, where a fiber-optic ring has been installed, city architects can send their colleagues in the traffic department e-mail that might include a text message, a plan of a bridge to be repaired, and a video clip showing the volume of traffic at the bridge at rush hour. Also in the workplace, videoconferencing is enabling companies to set up international meetings without the expense or delay of travel. The other prime site for videoconferencing is in remote areas, where schools and medical centers can benefit from remote lessons and long-distance diagnosis. Videophones for the home, however, are proving slow to catch on. Research shows that, while family and friends may enjoy seeing some sort of image of each other while they talk, the small picture does not break the ice between strangers.

Videoconferencing
Broadband computer networks and digital cameras enable long-distance business meetings to take place in videoconference rooms (above left) and ordinary office environments.

Multimedia on the Move

Satellites already carry much of the world's long-distance telephone traffic. Organizations such as Intelsat, owned by a group of telecommunications companies, are steadily increasing their constellation of satellites to make digital communication even easier. Before the end of thc century, it will be possible to send multimedia e-mail or access the Internet from almost anywhere on the globe – even the middle of the Gobi desert or the top of Mount Everest. Most industry insiders predict that as mobile multimedia becomes more common, mobile telephones will be replaced by PDAs that function as telephones, fax machines, and e-mail stations. Some also predict that radio broadcasts will start to include multimedia information that can be picked up with a handheld PDA: traffic maps, say, or information about local events, or interactive advertisements.

Satellite
Mobile multimedia relies on an expanding network of satellites and ground transmitters that relay information around the world.

Color Screen
The flat LCD (Liquid Crystal Display) color screen can show almost photographic-quality pictures.

World Wide Web
The mobile telephone enables the user to explore multimedia on the Internet.

Multimedia in Your Lap

Wireless multimedia communication is already possible, thanks to the latest generation of laptop computers. The model shown here, a Toshiba 2150CD, has a color screen and a built-in CD-ROM drive. It also connects to a mobile telephone.

Mobile Telephone
A plug-in modem the size of a credit card connects to a mobile telephone for fax communications, e-mail, and access to the World Wide Web.

CD-ROM Drive

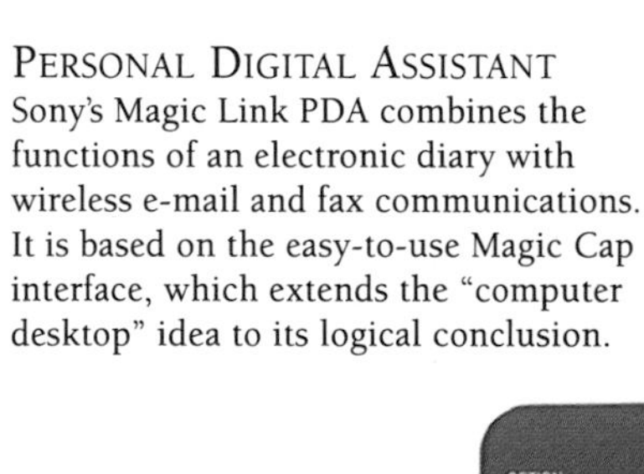

Personal Digital Assistant

Sony's Magic Link PDA combines the functions of an electronic diary with wireless e-mail and fax communications. It is based on the easy-to-use Magic Cap interface, which extends the "computer desktop" idea to its logical conclusion.

Screen
The user operates the PDA by pressing on the touch-sensitive screen with a plastic stylus.

Hallway
Activities outside the office are represented by doors to different rooms.

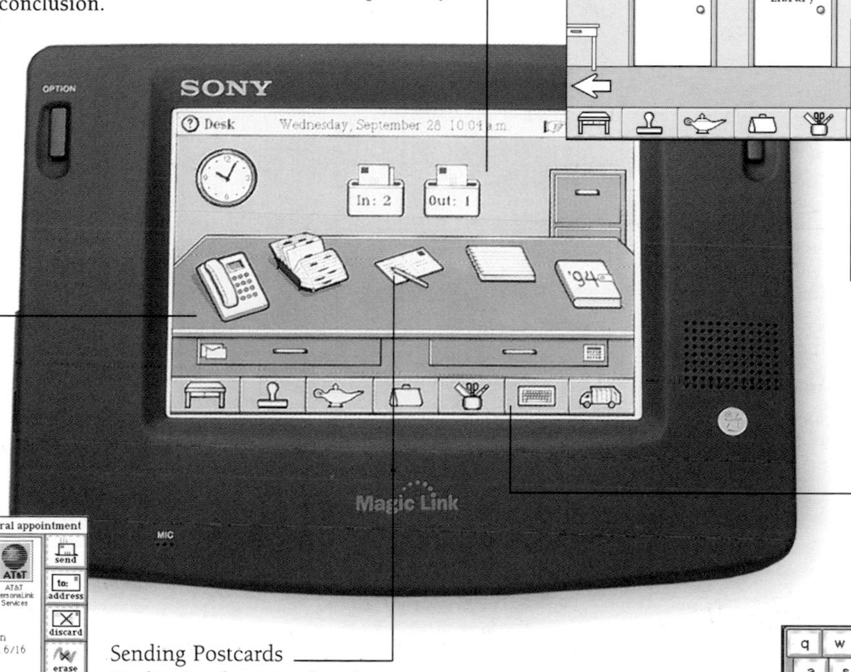

Desktop
The desk screen closely resembles an actual office or study.

Downtown
Commercial services are symbolized by main-street buildings.

On-screen Keyboard
The user types in messages by tapping an on-screen keyboard. Handwriting recognition is available as an optional extra.

Sending Postcards
By choosing the postcard on the desk, you can write a short message and e-mail or fax it instantly.

The Home of the Future

Predicting the future is a dangerous business – just think of all those 1950s comic strips that had us buzzing around in hover cars and spending our vacations on the moon. Such predictions have yet to come true, but by examining the technological developments we have seen in recent years, it is possible to paint a credible picture of the multimedia services that will be available to an ordinary home in, say, 2010. Naturally, we cannot say for certain that all homes will resemble our scenario; but we can say that there is no technological reason why they cannot be like this. A characteristic feature of the new services will almost certainly be their transformation of certain activities, such as shopping and attending conferences, that have always involved travel: in the future, on-line and virtual reality equipment will probably give us the option of pursuing much of our business without stirring from our home.

Convergence

The future will bring a convergence of different technologies, particularly of television, the telephone, and the computer. At present, the three remain physically separate in interactive television pilot programs and need to be connected by a cable – but this is changing: several companies have combined a television with a computer. Some of these machines, such as the Fujitsu/ICL PCTV, have full double function, changing from television to computer at the press of a button; others are predominantly computers that provide a television "window" on-screen.

PCTV
For more on the PCTV, see page 89

Virtual Reality in the Home

Within a few years, virtual reality computer games for the home will be in general use. As personal computers and games consoles become more powerful, they will be able to generate a quality of image comparable to that found in today's virtual reality arcade machines. Initially, these games will be supplied on CD-ROMs, but before long they will be generally available from on-line services and the Internet. Technically, this is already possible: a virtual reality game can be downloaded just like any other file – but virtual reality programs use up such an immense amount of data that few people would bother to download them without a high-speed broadband connection. Once they become easy to download, however, Arthur C. Clarke, the science fiction writer, predicts that virtual reality will "eat television alive." Many observers agree.

Multimedia House

From the outside, the home of the future will probably not look very different from a typical home of today. But on the inside, we will have access to many new services. To illustrate this, each room of the house below contains a member of the family engaged in a different multimedia activity, explained in more detail on this and the next page.

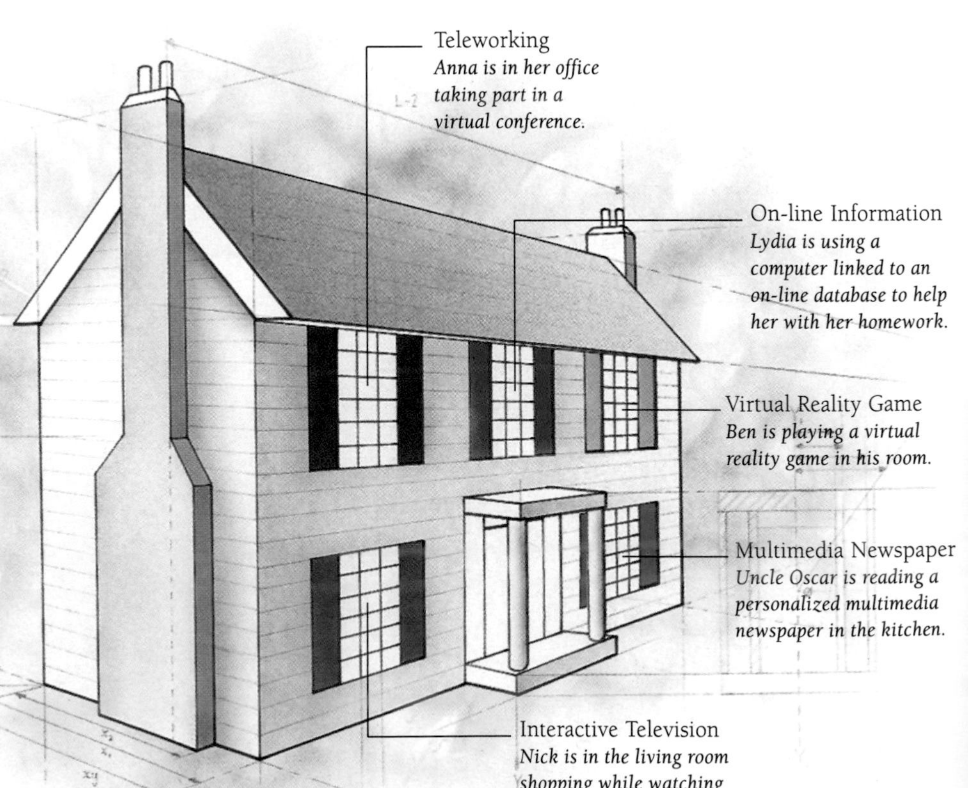

Teleworking
Anna is in her office taking part in a virtual conference.

On-line Information
Lydia is using a computer linked to an on-line database to help her with her homework.

Virtual Reality Game
Ben is playing a virtual reality game in his room.

Multimedia Newspaper
Uncle Oscar is reading a personalized multimedia newspaper in the kitchen.

Interactive Television
Nick is in the living room shopping while watching an interactive movie.

Interactive Television Services

In the living room, Nick, father of the family, is watching an interactive film while doing the shopping. He does this on a very large screen that hangs like a painting on the wall. Most of the screen shows a mountain with a climber on it. A question is displayed: "Do you want to take the North Col route or go straight up the West face?" But Nick has put the movie on hold, and is concentrating on his shopping.

Interactive Movie
The video-on-demand service that Nick subscribes to holds over 25,000 movies, from old black-and-white classics to the latest interactive blockbusters.

On-line Shopping
A window on the screen shows a range of olive oil bottles, each labeled with price, origin, and dietary information. Nick selects one with the handset, and a voice says: "You have selected one quart of Oliva. The price is ten dollars. This amount has been debited from your account. Thank you."

Remote Control
Nick uses the remote control to choose items on the screen, as well as to regulate other devices in the room, such as the air-conditioning.

"Flat Screen" Shopping
Nick could have gone to a virtual supermarket, where he can walk up and the down the aisle as in a real store, but he finds this "flat screen" shopping less of a strain. He does not like virtual reality, saying it gives him a headache.

Virtual Conference
When she first took part in a virtual conference, Anna found the experience strange – not least because she could put her hand straight though her colleagues. But she is now used to it.

Broadband Network
Anna's computer is linked directly into a fiber-optic broadband network, with enough bandwidth to handle her virtual conference.

Home Office

In her office, Anna, the mother of the family, is involved in a virtual conference with her colleagues in Paris and Tokyo. She wears a pair of virtual reality glasses, connected by infrared link to her computer. Through her headset she sees a virtual meeting with several people sitting around a table. Disembodied hands pass around documents, which are then stored on her computer. The faces and bodies are realistic, but not yet perfect likenesses.

Infrared Link
An infrared link connects Anna's keyboard to her computer. She uses the keyboard to control the documents that appear on her screen and to call up her own files.

Smart Appliances

The house of the multimedia future will be "smart" – most devices will probably be interconnected, and controlled and coordinated by a central computer. This means that the toaster will automatically switch on a certain number of minutes after the electric toothbrush has been switched off, and the washing machine will diagnose its own faults and automatically call the service engineer. Although all this is not strictly multimedia, it will be a direct consequence of technology that has been established as a result of the multimedia revolution. Furthermore, the social changes implicit in this new technology will be far-reaching. Governments, businesses, and the general public will be faced with many more choices – and with some perplexing questions.

Freedom of Information

The arrival of the photocopier in the 1970s made it simple to produce copies of printed information for distribution. Today, a similar phenomenon is taking place on the Internet. Anyone with a computer and a modem can tap into the Internet and access and publish vast quantities of information – and there is little a government or regulatory body can do to prevent it. No one can yet say whether this total freedom of access to information is a good thing or not, and the issue is likely to remain controversial for years to come.

Internet
For more on the Internet, see page 162

Controlling Computer

Underneath the stairs in the home of the future is a powerful computer. Although hidden from sight, it acts as the central nervous system of the house. Its functions range from sending out video signals to the various screens in the home to controlling the temperature and humidity in each room.

Communication Links
The controlling computer can communicate in several ways. It is linked directly to the information superhighway by fiber-optic cable. It is also linked to the other computers in the house by coaxial cable, and to many of the smaller appliances via radio signals and infrared links.

Intelligent Searcher

Each member of the family has a personalized newspaper (it is still called this, even though most people no longer print it out). The newspaper is multimedia – a mix of text, still pictures, video, and sound. It was created by an automatic "intelligent searcher" – a program that looks through hundreds of electronic newspapers, assembling what it believes to be the most suitable collection of stories for each member of the family.

Portable Screen
Oscar's screen is linked to the house's controlling computer by a radio link. The screen can be moved anywhere in the house and will still display images. It can even be taken outside, although the signal starts to fade at the bottom of the garden.

Personalized Newspaper
In the kitchen, Uncle Oscar is reading his newspaper on a portable screen placed on the breakfast counter. He has asked the intelligent searcher to look for football, traffic, and general political news, as well as a randomly generated selection of stories. At present, the screen is displaying a clip of last night's football game, while an article runs alongside it giving the sportscaster's opinion. Oscar's nephew, Ben, prefers to look at baseball reports, the computer games pages, and his favorite cartoons.

On-line Database

While doing her homework, Lydia has been distracted by news of an earthquake in Eastern Europe, so she is downloading video clips of it, and comparing the damage with that caused by other earthquakes. The clips are stored on a central educational database to which her school subscribes.

Interactive Education

In her bedroom, Lydia, age 10, is doing her homework, learning Spanish. She watches an episode of a Spanish soap opera; it stops regularly and asks her questions to test her comprehension. She speaks the answer out loud, and is immediately told if she is right. If she makes a mistake, an electronic "tutor," a cartoon character, appears on the screen to tell her what she has done wrong. If she needs to look up a word, she calls up the on-line dictionary; and if she is completely baffled, she can dial up her teacher at home and be given help via a videophone link.

Serious Questions

What will all these multimedia services mean for people who enjoy going out to shop, simply for a change of scene or because it is their only chance to meet people? What will they do if the shopping streets and malls have closed down through lack of demand? And what will the people who used to work in those shops do then? How will white-collar workers, who were used to meeting and working with colleagues at the workplace, feel when teleworking (or telecommuting) enables them to do the same job in physical isolation at home? Will the freedom from the hassle of commuting compensate enough for the loss of social interaction that most of us take for granted today?

Empty Cities

The idea of teleworking also raises concerns about the future of our cities. What will happen to cities – already suffering from the exodus of middle-class residents – when, as a result of teleworking, the office blocks become deserted because their former inhabitants are now working from home? These are critical questions, which show that great technological changes such as the multimedia revolution cannot meaningfully be considered in isolation but must also be seen in the light of their probable social and political consequences.

Headset

Mass-produced virtual reality headsets are becoming more common in people's homes.

Controller

Depending on which game is being played, the controller can represent a lance, a light saber, or a sword.

Remote Opponent

Ben's opponent is another child, who wanted to play at the same time and has, the computer says, about the same level of skill as Ben. The child lives on the other side of the world.

Virtual Reality Games

In his bedroom, 12-year-old Ben is wearing virtual reality gear. He is holding a stick, which he is prodding toward the window. In his virtual world he is a medieval knight, jousting (the stick is his lance). He is taking part in a global *Knights of the Round Table* tournament. Ben has gotten through to the fifth round, but since there are a million entrants his chances of winning the tournament (and the hand of the king's daughter) are remote.

Reference

HUMMINGBIRDS
Star Wars (1977)
One Flew Over the Cuckoo's Nest (1975)
Platoon (1986)
Silence of the Lambs, The (1991)
Son of the Sheik (1926)
THE WAY THINGS WORK
HUMMINGBIRD HOVERING
DETECTION BOX
ELECTRON GUN

List of Titles

Business

Classroom in a Book
This title and accompanying training manual teach graphic designers how to use Adobe's image manipulation program *Photoshop*.

Producer/Publisher .... Adobe
Platforms .... Mac, PC
Page 60

EasyTutor Learn Windows 95
A guide for beginners and intermediate users to Microsoft's operating system Windows 95, which combines step-by-step demonstrations with practical exercises.

Producer/Publisher .... CRT Multimedia
Platforms .... PC
Page 61

Leading Teams
Designed for trainee managers, this title presents simulations of work situations and asks the trainee to make management decisions, which it then evaluates.

Producer/Publisher .... Xebec
Platforms .... PC
Page 60

Meetings, Bloody Meetings
A training title in which the British comedian John Cleese explains how to chair business meetings successfully.

Producer/Publisher .... Video Arts
Platforms .... CD-i
Page 97

Education

Apprenez le Français avec le Fils d'Astérix
This title teaches intermediate French reading and aural comprehension skills through panels from the Asterix® cartoon book *Son of Asterix*.

Producer/Publisher .... EuroTalk
Platforms .... Mac, PC
Page 41

Counting on Frank
An animated adventure game for children that involves solving real-world math puzzles that exercise and develop math skills at the same time.

Producer/Publisher .... Electronic Arts
Platforms .... Mac, PC
Page 37

Creative Writer
An introduction to writing that encourages children to mix sounds and pictures into their writing to create stories, poems, greeting cards, and newsletters.

Producer/Publisher .... Microsoft
Platforms .... Mac, PC
Page 38

Freddi Fish and the Case of the Missing Kelp Seeds
An animated adventure game for young children that mixes problem solving, games, and math exercises into the adventure.

Producer/Publisher .... Humongous Entertainment
Platforms .... Mac, PC
Page 36

French Vocabulary Builder
A multimedia language lab that uses voice recognition software to evaluate the learner's command of spoken French.

Producer/Publisher .... The Learning Company
Platforms .... Mac, PC
Page 41

Isaac Asimov's Science Adventure II
A science tutor that uses 3-D exhibits, experiments, movies, virtual tours, and dual-level written explanations to teach science to children and adults.

Producer/Publisher .... Knowledge Adventure
Platforms .... PC
Page 42

Freddi Fish and the Case of the Missing Kelp Seeds

Reference

Jeux d'Images Multimédia
An interactive flash card system for learning basic French that also includes language games and a speech-recording facility.

Producer/Publisher .... **EuroTalk**
Platforms .... **Mac, PC**
Page **40**

Jumpstart Kindergarten
This preschool learning title uses a kindergarten environment to present games and exercises that develop simple learning, problem solving, and creativity.

Producer/Publisher .... **Knowledge Adventure**
Platforms .... **PC**
Page **32–33**

Klik & Play
A games creation title that enables users with no programming knowledge to create sophisticated computer games.

Producer/Publisher .... **Europress**
Platforms .... **Mac, PC**
Page **39**

Math Workshop
An activity center for children that presents math exercises as a series of puzzles and games.

Producer/Publisher .... **Broderbund**
Platforms .... **Mac, PC**
Page **36**

Spider-man Cartoon Maker
A creativity tool for children that enables them to design their own animated comics based on the popular Spider-man cartoon series.

Producer/Publisher .... **Knowledge Adventure**
Platforms .... **PC**
Page **39**

The Tortoise and the Hare
Aesop's classic fable presented as an entertaining animated storybook.

Producer/Publisher .... **Broderbund**
Platforms .... **Mac, PC**
Page **34–35**

The Way Things Work
An introduction to the science of machines that explains how they work and the scientfic principles on which they are based.

Producer/Publisher .... **Dorling Kindersley**
Platforms .... **Mac, PC**
Page **43**

3D Atlas
In addition to three-dimensional maps, this world atlas includes statistical, environmental, physical, and political information.

Producer/Publisher .... **Multimedia Corporation**
Platforms .... **3DO, Mac, PC**
Page **24–25**

American Heritage® Children's Dictionary
Words are brought to life by thousands of pictures, sounds, and animations in this dictionary designed for children aged 7–12.

Producer/Publisher .... **Houghton Mifflin**
Platforms .... **PC**
Page **144–145**

Blender
A bimonthly style magazine published on CD-ROM, which includes reviews, fashion, horoscopes, and electronic cartoons.

Producer/Publisher .... **Dennis Publishing**
Platforms .... **Mac, PC**
Page **31**

Body Works
The anatomy of the human body presented through fully rotating 3-D graphics.

Producer/Publisher .... **Softkey**
Platforms .... **PC**
Page **19**

Cinemania
An encyclopedia of the movies, containing clips, dialogue, music, reviews, and other information about thousands of movies and the people associated with them.

Producer/Publisher .... **Microsoft**
Platforms .... **Mac, PC**
Page **26**

Complete Baseball
An "all you ever wanted to know about baseball," which features an on-line service that provides information about the current season.

Producer/Publisher .... **Microsoft**
Platforms .... **PC**
Page **27**

Encarta
A general encyclopedia that offers great flexibility in finding information, animations, video, and illustrations on all subjects.

Producer/Publisher .... **Microsoft**
Platforms .... **Mac, PC**
Page **20–21**

Eyewitness Encyclopedia of Nature
A naturalist's desk is the starting point for a multimedia exploration of the natural world.

Producer/Publisher .... **Dorling Kindersley**
Platforms .... **Mac, PC**
Page **10, 22–23, 136–137**

Eyewitness History of the World
World history is presented in the form of an interactive encyclopedia divided into ten themed time periods.

Producer/Publisher .... **Dorling Kindersley**
Platforms .... **Mac, PC**
Page **110–113, 132–133**

Eyewitness Virtual Reality Cat
This title combines a realistic 3-D museum interior with interactive exhibits of the cat family to re-create the experience of visiting a museum.

Producer/Publisher .... **Dorling Kindersley**
Platforms .... **Mac, PC**
Page **28–29, 138–141**

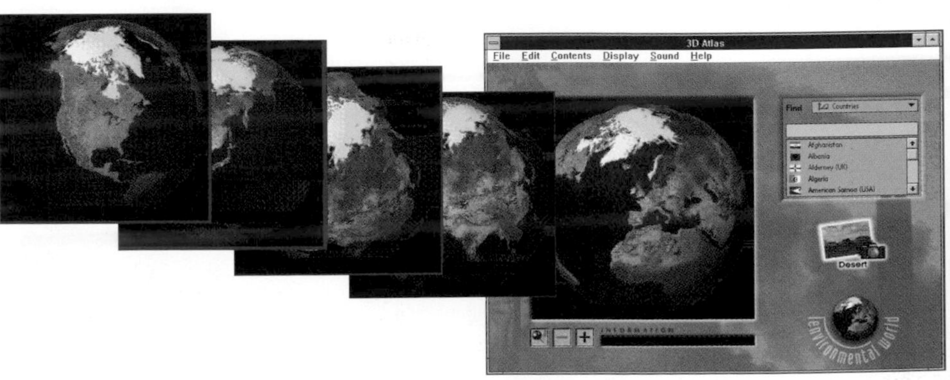

3D Atlas

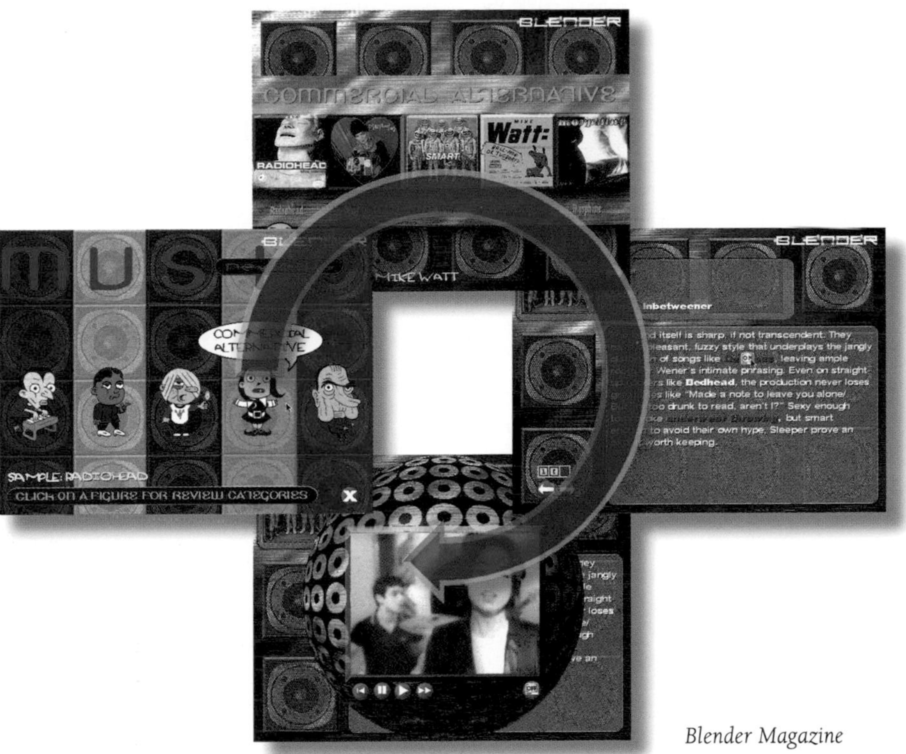

Blender Magazine

Le Louvre

An interactive tour that includes the *Mona Lisa* and 99 other famous paintings from the Louvre museum in Paris, France.

Producer/Publisher .... BMG
Platforms .... Mac, PC
Page 29

Making Maus

An interactive account of the making of the *Complete Maus* comic books – the documentary story of a survivor of the Holocaust.

Producer/Publisher .... Voyager
Platforms .... Mac
Page 19

Musical Instruments

A presentation of the world's instruments – their history, where they are played, their sounds, and the music they are used for.

Producer/Publisher .... Microsoft
Platforms .... Mac, PC
Page 87

Newsweek Interactive

An interactive news magazine, published quarterly, which contains the previous 13 issues of Newsweek magazine, as well as extended articles and features.

Producer/Publisher .... Newsweek
Platforms .... PC
Page 30

The Total Heart

This title covers the function and well-being of the human heart, as well as diseases related to it and their treatment.

Producer/Publisher .... Mayo Clinic
Platforms .... PC
Page 19

The Ultimate Human Body

Human anatomy is explored by zooming into an annotated human body and peeling away the organs one by one.

Producer/Publisher .... Dorling Kindersley
Platforms .... Mac, PC
Page 19

What Is a Bellybutton?

A cartoon-style introduction for young children to the basics of human anatomy.

Producer/Publisher .... IVI Publishing
Platforms .... PC
Page 19

Wine Guide

A comprehensive reference work for wine-lovers, which includes a general overview, an atlas, an encyclopedia, and a wine-tasting guide.

Producer/Publisher .... Microsoft
Platforms .... Mac, PC
Page 27

Entertainment

3D Baseball

A 3-D game that combines realistic human movement and changing camera angles to re-create the experience of playing baseball.

Producer/Publisher .... Crystal Dynamics
Platforms .... Saturn, PlayStation
Page 93

7th Guest

A mystery adventure game classic that involves solving tricky puzzles in a richly textured 3-D haunted house.

Producer/Publisher .... Trilobyte
Platforms .... CD-i, Mac, PC
Page 19

Battle Arena Toshinden

A fast-moving 3-D martial arts combat game.

Producer/Publisher .... Tamsoft
Platforms .... PlayStation
Page 103

Bioforge

A 3-D action adventure game in which the half-man, half-robot hero has to escape from a futuristic prison.

Producer/Publisher .... Origin
Platforms .... PC
Page 19

Bug!

A 3-D variant of the traditional platform game in which the player runs and jumps around a series of platforms, dispatching enemies along the way.

Producer/Publisher .... Sega
Platforms .... Saturn
Page 101

Burn:Cycle

An interactive movie that combines an adventure game plot with shoot-'em-up action in a nightmarish, futuristic setting.

Producer/Publisher .... Trip Media
Platforms .... CD-i, Mac, PC
Page 97

Chaos Control

A space shoot-'em-up that combines 3-D animation with full-motion video.

Producer/Publisher .... Infogrames
Platforms .... CD-i, PC
Page 97

Doom

Full Throttle

The Daedalus Encounter
An interactive movie, set in the future, in which the player works with two filmed accomplices to explore an abandoned space station.

Producer/Publisher .... **Mechadeus**
Platforms .... **3DO, Mac, PC**
Page 54

Dark Forces
A 3-D armed combat game in the *Doom* tradition set in the *Star Wars* universe.

Producer/Publisher .... **LucasArts**
Platforms .... **Mac, PC**
Page 47, 143

The Darkening
An interactive movie involving interplanetary trading, exploration, and 3-D space combat.

Producer/Publisher .... **Electronic Arts**
Platforms .... **PC**
Page 114–117

Demolish 'em Derby
A 3-D car racing game which involves causing maximum damage to your opponents and forcing them off the road.

Producer/Publisher .... **Psygnosis**
Platforms .... **PlayStation**
Page 103

Discworld
A vast cartoon adventure game set in the strange universe described in Terry Pratchett's *Discworld* series of novels.

Producer/Publisher .... **Psygnosis**
Platforms .... **Mac, PC, PlayStation**
Page 103

Doom
The multiplayer 3-D armed combat game in a hellish prisonlike setting that ushered in a new generation of action games.

Producer/Publisher .... **id Software**
Platforms .... **PC**
Page 46–47

Dungeon Keeper
A combat game in the tradition of *Doom*, but with a strategy twist: instead of fighting monsters the player designs the dungeon and coordinates the monsters that inhabit it.

Producer/Publisher .... **Bullfrog Productions**
Platforms .... **PC**
Page 148–149

FIFA Soccer
A smooth-flowing soccer simulation that uses changing camera angles to add to the realism and excitement of the game.

Producer/Publisher .... **Electronic Arts**
Platforms .... **3DO, PC**
Page 99

Flight Unlimited
A 3-D flying title in which the emphasis is on performing aerobatic stunts over a photo-realistic landscape.

Producer/Publisher .... **Looking Glass Technologies**
Platforms .... **PC**
Page 49

Formula One Grand Prix 2
This 3-D racing simulation includes customizable cars and accurately modeled Grand Prix race tracks. It also attempts to re-create the driving styles of famous Formula One drivers.

Producer/Publisher .... **Microprose**
Platforms .... **PC**
Page 49

Full Throttle
A cartoon adventure game set in the world of bikers and accompanied by a rock sound track and explosive action sequences.

Producer/Publisher .... **LucasArts**
Platforms .... **Mac, PC**
Page 50–51

FX Fighter
The first 3-D martial arts combat game for multimedia PCs, with realistic fighting moves.

Producer/Publisher .... **Argonaut/GTE**
Platforms .... **PC**
Page 46, 146–147

International Tennis Open
This tennis simulation, which offers a choice of playing surfaces, was one of the first successful games for the CD-i.

Producer/Publisher .... **Infogrames**
Platforms .... **CD-i, PC**
Page 97

Jump, the David Bowie Interactive CD-ROM
Explore Bowie's virtual skyscraper to discover photographs, interviews, and video clips, and enjoy the chance to remix songs and videos.

Producer/Publisher .... **Ion**
Platforms .... **Mac, PC**
Page 57

Magic Carpet 2
A 3-D flying and combat game with a twist: the game involves flying around a mystical world on a magic carpet and casting spells to complete a magical quest.

Producer/Publisher .... **Bullfrog Productions**
Platforms .... **PC**
Page 48

Marathon II
A multiplayer 3-D armed combat game in the *Doom* tradition but with a more involved plot and the chance to cooperate with the other players.

Producer/Publisher .... **Bungie**
Platforms .... **Mac**
Page 47

Monty Python's Complete Waste of Time
An anarchic mix of archive materials from the Monty Python television series and bizarre interactive activities such as "Spot the Loony."

Producer/Publisher .... 7th Level
Platforms .... Mac, PC
Page 59

Myst
The classic 3-D adventure game in which you awake on a surreal island and, through exploration and by solving puzzles, begin to understand why you are there.

Producer/Publisher .... Broderbund
Platforms .... 3DO, Mac, PC, PlayStation, Saturn
Page 44–45

P.A.W.S
This animated cartoon title tells you everything there is to know about a dog's life, from the inside out.

Producer/Publisher .... Domestic Funk Products
Platforms .... Mac, PC
Page 58, 118–121

Phantasmagoria
This adult interactive movie is a story of ghosts, possession, and murder that includes rich graphics, movie clips, and a dramatic ending.

Producer/Publisher .... Sierra OnLine
Platforms .... PC
Page 54–55

Primal Rage
A game of fighting dinosaurs that appeared originally on arcade machines, but has been successfully transferred to the 3DO format.

Producer/Publisher .... Time Warner Interactive
Platforms .... 3DO, PC
Page 99

Road Rash
A street race and chase game fought out between motorcyclists and law enforcement officers, featuring digitized video characters.

Producer/Publisher .... Electronic Arts
Platforms 3DO
Page 99

Rock 'n Roll Your Own
An interactive music title that lets you mix music tracks using prerecorded (and your own) sound samples.

Producer/Publisher .... Compton's NewMedia
Platforms .... Mac, PC
Page 56

Sarah McLachlan, The Freedom Sessions
An audio CD with an added multimedia track that contains song samples, photographs, and a biography and video clips of the artist.

Producer/Publisher .... Arista
Platforms .... Mac, PC
Page 57

Sega Rally
This 3-D racing game has been transferred to the Saturn console from the Sega arcade machines on which it first appeared.

Producer/Publisher .... Sega
Platforms .... Saturn
Page 101

Star Trek: The Next Generation "A Final Unity"
Based on the classic television series, this adventure game allows you to assume full control of the USS Enterprise and beam down to strange planets.

Producer/Publisher .... Spectrum Holobyte
Platforms .... PC
Page 52–53

Take Your Best Shot
This titles combines scenes of animated cartoon violence with surreal games to provide relief from stress.

Producer/Publisher .... 7th Level
Platforms .... PC
Page 58

Virtua Fighter 2
The floating camera view of this 3-D hand-to-hand combat game shows every angle of the many authentic fighting moves that it contains.

Producer/Publisher .... Sega
Platforms .... Saturn
Page 101

Wipeout
A murderous 3-D racing game in which the cars hover above the race track and are better armed than the average space battle cruiser.

Producer/Publisher .... Psygnosis
Platforms .... PlayStation
Page 103

Zen and the Art of Motorcycle Maintenance; Lila
This "expanded book" on floppy disk contains the full text of two novels by Robert Pirsig, and makes full use of hypertext.

Producer/Publisher .... Voyager
Platforms .... Mac
Page 18

Myst

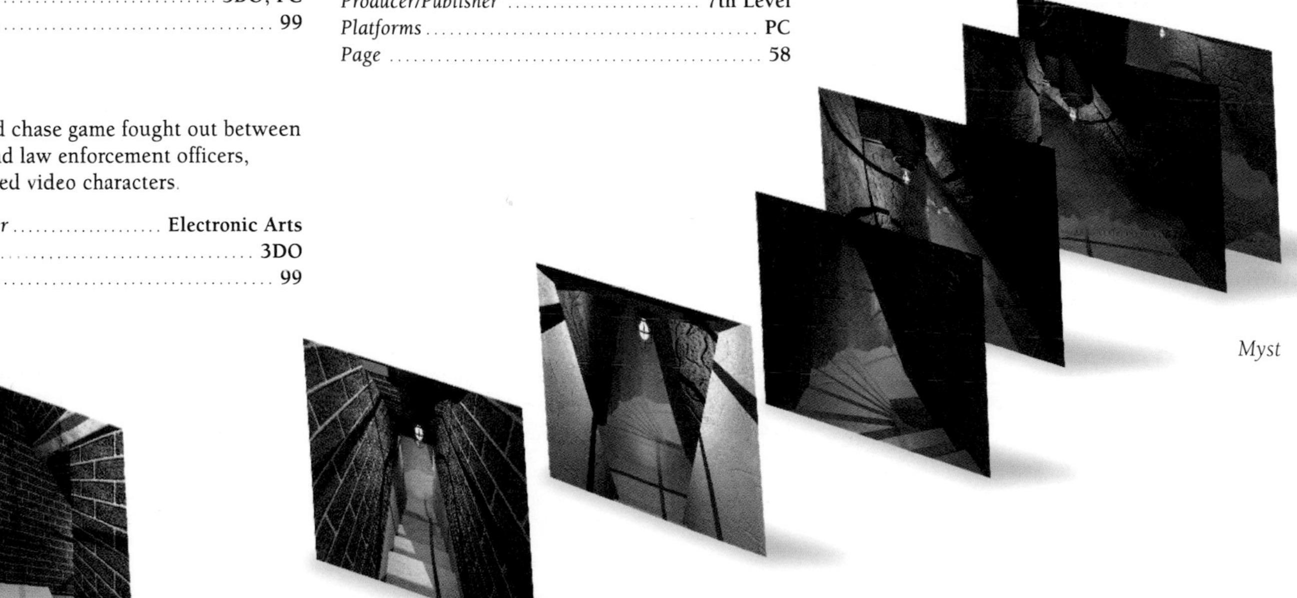

Myst

GLOSSARY

A

Acceleration Card
A card that slots into a computer or console to speed up activities such as video playback or graphics drawing.

Analog
A method of storing information as varying electrical voltages, rather than electronic code. Today's television sets, video recorders, radios, and telephones are analog devices.

Animation
The display of a sequence of still images to give the illusion of continuous motion.

Antialiasing
A technique used to reduce the jagged edges that appear around text and graphics when displayed on a screen; antialiasing blends the edge of every letter and image into its surroundings.

Authoring
The process of combining various elements, such as text, sound, video, and animation, to produce a multimedia title.

Authoring Software
A computer program that links the different parts of a multimedia title together.

B

Binary
A counting system based on only two digits, 1 and 0 (or on and off). Computers store and manipulate all data and information in binary code.

Bit
Short for binary digit, a bit is the smallest unit of information a computer can understand. Eight bits make a byte.

Broadband Network
A high-speed, high-capacity digital network that is gradually replacing conventional analog telephone networks. The information superhighway will be a broadband network.

Expansion Card

Bus
A pathway of thin metallic tracks along which data travels to different parts of a computer. A PC contains several different buses that each connect different parts of the computer.

C

Cartridge
A removable storage device that plugs into a games console.

CAD (Computer-Aided Design)
Computer programs for designing objects, usually in the fields of engineering, product design, and architecture.

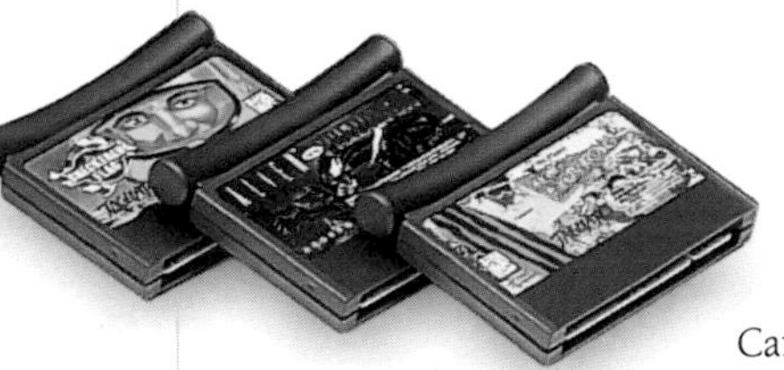

Cartridges

CD-ROM
The abbreviation for Compact Disc Read-Only Memory. A compact disc containing data that can be read by a computer. Often used for multimedia titles, CD-ROMs can hold large amounts of data; an entire encyclopedia can be stored on one disc.

CD-ROM Drive
A piece of hardware that uses a laser to read data from a CD-ROM. This data can then be interpreted by a computer.

Cel
Part of an animation sequence where individual drawings are made on transparent plastic sheets, each one recording a different position of a moving object. They are then photographed by a camera.

Chip
A tiny piece of silicon with miniature circuits imprinted on it. Often used as a CPU or as memory.

Click
To press and immediately release a mouse button. To click on something is to position the pointer above it and then click.

Clock Speed
This refers to the speed at which the computer's CPU operates, normally given in megahertz. The higher the clock speed of the computer, the faster it can process information.

Command
An instruction that a user gives to the computer, such as to print a document.

Compression
A technique that reduces the size of computer files, so that, for example, more of them will fit onto a CD-ROM.

Console
A type of computer that plugs directly into a television set and is used mainly for playing games. The Sony Playstation and the Sega Saturn are examples of consoles.

Convergence
A word used to describe the growing tendency of the new technologies to merge, such as combining a computer with a television.

CPU (Central Processing Unit)
The main chip in a computer that interprets commands and instructions.

D

Data
Information that is stored in a digital form that computers can understand.

Database
A database is simply a collection of related pieces of information, such as a list of addresses. The easiest way to think of a database is as a set of records stored in computerized form, much like a set of electronic index cards.

Data Transfer Rate
The amount of data that can be read from a hard disk or CD-ROM, usually expressed in kilobytes per second.

Desktop Publishing
A software program that lets you arrange a document's text and pictures on-screen. It can be used for laying out the pages of a magazine or a book.

Digital
Information that is stored as numbers (using the digits 0 and 1), as opposed to analog information. All data on a CD-ROM is stored in digital form whether it is sound, text, or video.

Digitize
To convert information into digital form. For example, scanners are used to digitize pictures, and sound is digitized by a process called sampling.

Download
To transfer files to your computer from another computer via a modem. The opposite term is upload.

E

Edutainment
Used to describe educational multimedia titles that combine education with entertainment.

E-mail (Electronic Mail)
Documents and messages you can send or receive directly on your computer.

Expansion Card
A card that sits inside a computer and adds extra capabilities, such as high-quality sound.

Expansion Slot
A slot inside a computer where you can insert an expansion card.

Sony PlayStation Console

F

Fiber-optic Cable
A type of cable consisting of very thin strands of glass. It carries enormous amounts of information in the form of light pulses.

File
A grouping of information, such as a document or program, normally stored on a disk, that can be read by a computer.

Frame
Multimedia animation and video consists of a series of frames or pictures, as many as 25 frames every second.

G

Game Editor
Software used to build graphical environments for multimedia games.

Graphics
Pictorial information that is displayed on a computer screen.

Graphics Engine
Games software that can draw rooms and other objects from any angle to give the illusion of a three-dimensional world.

Graphics Card
Controls the display of pictures on the monitor. Also known as a video card.

GUI (Graphical User Interface)
A way of controlling a computer by choosing from a selection of windows, icons, and menus, rather than by typing in lines of code and commands. Microsoft's Windows and Apple's System 7 are examples of graphical user interfaces.

H

Hardware
The physical parts of the computer, such as the monitor, printer, modem, and so on.

Hard Disk
A disk drive that can store a great deal of information, such as copies of all the documents or files you create. Hard disks are normally located inside a computer's casing, unlike a floppy disk which can be removed and easily transported.

Highlight
If you select a word from a menu it becomes highlighted – the word normally becomes white on a dark background.

High-density CD
A CD-ROM that can hold many times more data than the original CD-ROM.

Home Shopping
A service offered on interactive television systems. It enables customers to view a graphical display of products for sale and make purchases simply by pressing a button on a handset.

Hot Spot
An on-screen button or picture in a multimedia title that reacts when you select it, often transporting you to another part of the title.

Hot Text
Hot text is highlighted on-screen text that, when selected, calls up related information or links you to another part of that title.

Hypermedia
A collective term that describes the interactive elements of multimedia software, such as hot text and hot spots.

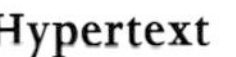

Hypertext
A body of text where some or all of the information is linked; so that when you, for example, click on a word you can find out more about that word or be transported to another area of the document that contains related information.

CPU Chip

I

IBM-compatible PC
A PC (personal computer) that can run the same software as a PC from the IBM corporation (inventors of the original IBM PC). Often simply called a "PC."

Icon
A pictorial representation of a computer file, program, feature, or function within a computer program or graphical user interface.

Image Manipulation Software
Used by multimedia designers to alter the appearance of images, such as photographs, once they have been scanned into a computer. Also known as imaging software.

Information Superhighway
A worldwide communications network that promises to bring multimedia services into the user's home via high-capacity fiber-optic cable. The Internet is sometimes seen as a prototype for the information superhighway. Also known simply as the superhighway.

Input Device
A device with which the user can transmit commands to the computer – a keyboard, mouse, trackball, and joystick are just a few examples.

RAM Chip

I/O (Input/Output)
Input means to feed information into the computer; output is both the process of getting information out of the computer and the information that comes out, such as a printout or the information displayed on a monitor.

I/O Port
A connector that lets you attach cables to a computer in order to connect it to external devices such as a printer, a scanner, or an external modem.

Interactive
A computer program, game, or any other product is interactive when the user can control what is displayed on-screen.

Interactive Television
A service that offers digital multimedia content on a television set, such as video-on-demand, on-line games, and home shopping.

Interface
The way two things work together. For example, the user interface refers to the way the user works with a computer, whereas the hardware interface describes the connectors that allow a computer to work with other hardware devices.

Mouse

Internet
A worldwide network of computer networks, linking universities, research institutions, commercial organizations, and private individuals. It offers access to the World Wide Web, e-mail, and a variety of services. Also known as the Net.

JK

Joypad
A handheld controller with a number of control buttons and a directional pad that is used mainly for playing multimedia games.

Joystick
A simple controller used mainly for playing games that controls the movement of objects on the screen.

Keyboard
An array of alphabetic and numeric keys that enables the user to type information into the computer.

Keypad
Any small group of keys used for a special purpose. For example, the numeric keypad, located to the right of a standard keyboard, is used for entering long lists of numbers.

Kiosk
A computer system, often found in retail stores or museums, that provides information and/or helps sells something.

M

Menu
A menu is usually a drop-down list of commands or functions. Choosing one of the items on the list will activate the command, such as opening a file or printing a document.

Microprocessor
A chip that processes commands.

MIDI
Stands for Musical Instrument Digital Interface. It is a code that gives musical instructions, allowing a computer to create, record, and play back electronic music.

Modeling Software
Used by multimedia designers to create three-dimensional objects and images.

MPEG Compression
A compression standard developed by the Motion Picture Experts Group, designed for compressing digital video files.

Modem
A device that enables computers to communicate with each other over a telephone line.

Monitor
A piece of equipment that houses the computer screen. Also known as a display, or a VDU (Visual Display Unit).

Motion Capture
A technique used to record human movements in order to create lifelike animation.

Mouse
A hand-controlled input and pointing device. As the mouse is moved, it moves a cursor or pointer on the computer screen.

Joystick

N

Navigation
The process of finding your way around the contents of a multimedia title.

Network
A situation in which two or more computers (and perhaps other devices, such as printers) are linked by means of cables, or by a modem over a telephone line. A network may be in the same room, or it may be a larger system that connects computers all over the world.

Modem

O

On-line
Generally this refers to communication with other computers via a modem or a network. The Internet provides on-line multimedia. A CD-ROM, by contrast, delivers multimedia off-line.

On-line Services
Commercial services that can be accessed over a telephone line using a modem. They normally offer services such as e-mail, on-line encyclopedias, electronic newspapers and magazines, and hotel and airline reservation systems. Users normally pay for the time they are connected to the service.

OS (Operating System)
This is the control software that runs the essential operations of a computer, such as the on-screen display, organization of files, and communication with devices such as CD-ROM drives and sound cards. All computers need an operating system in order to function. UNIX, Apple's System 7, and Microsoft's DOS and Windows are examples of operating systems.

OCR (Optical Character Recognition)
A system of translating scanned text into a form that can be edited by a computer.

P

PC (Personal Computer)
A small computer designed for a single user. Technically, a PC refers to any brand of personal computer – however, many people use the term to refer to an IBM-compatible PC.

Pixel
Short for picture element, a pixel is one of the little dots of light that make up the picture on a computer screen. The greater the number of pixels in a given area, the higher the resolution.

Platform Game
A computer game where players have to jump from platform to platform, collecting various items, or fighting an enemy.

Pointer
The shape that moves on the screen when you move the mouse. Some common shapes are the arrow, the hand, and the "I-beam."

Printer
An output device that prints information onto paper.

Program
A list of computer commands that perform a specific function. A multimedia title is a type of program, as are word processing and image manipulation applications.

Plug-and-play
Something is "plug-and-play" when it can be plugged in and used immediately, without a complicated set-up procedure. For example, a plug-and-play CD-ROM drive can be connected to a compatible computer and used right away. A plug-and-play operating system is one that can automatically recognize and set up external devices that are attached to a computer. The Apple Macintosh and some PCs are plug-and-play computers.

QR

RAM (Random Access Memory)
Memory chips that store information that can be easily read from or written to.

ROM (Read-Only Memory)
A storage device that can be read from but not written to. The most common examples are CD-ROMs and certain memory chips.

Rendering
The process in which a computer calculates a final image of a three-dimensional wireframe model, drawing in the surfaces, textures, and lighting chosen by the designer.

Resolution
The density of pixels that are used to make up an image on a computer.

RISC
An abbreviation for Reduced Instruction Set Computing – a new generation of processor chips that only carry a limited number of commands for faster operation.

S

Scanner
A device, similar to a photocopier, that creates electronic versions of photographs, drawings, and text. To store a picture on a computer, a scanner divides the image into a series of small dots and then processes them into digital bits of information.

Seek Time
The length of time it takes to access data on a hard disk or CD-ROM. The lower the seek time, the faster the information can be located.

Service Provider
A company that offers access to the Internet or an on-line service. Customers use a modem to connect to the service provider's computer, which has a permanent connection to the Internet or on-line service.

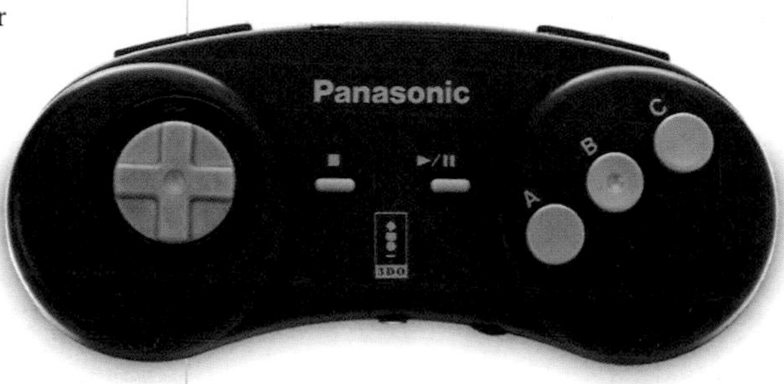

Joypad

Software
A series of instructions for a computer that tell the computer what to do. For example, a multimedia title consists of software stored on a CD-ROM. A program is a piece of software.

Sound Card
An expansion card that allows the user to hear high-quality sound playback. It can also take sound from a microphone and convert it into a sound file for storage.

Sprite
An animated cut-out character or object that can be moved independently of the background in computer animation.

Stereoscopic Headset
A headset worn by users of virtual reality that helps to create the illusion of being in a three-dimensional world. The headset contains a small screen for each eye.

T

Telecommuters
A term used to describe people who work from home by connecting their home computer to their office computer via a modem or network. Also known as teleworkers.

Trackball
A device that lets you control the cursor by rolling a stationary ball around with your fingers. Often used on portable computers where there is no desk space for a mouse.

Transfer Rate
The rate at which data is transferred from one computer to another, or from a disk drive or CD-ROM drive to the computer.

UV

Virtual Reality
A situation in which a computer is used to create an illusion of reality by simulating a three-dimensional environment.

Voice Recognition
A computer system designed to recognize and act upon the human voice.

W

Window
A rectangular frame on the screen that contains specific information. For example, one window might contain a multimedia program, while another might contain a list of files.

Wireframe
A way of representing three-dimensional shapes when designing computer graphics. Objects are drawn as if they were built out of wires, without complex shading or textures.

Workstation
A computer that is far more powerful and much more expensive than a personal computer. Most workstations contain special-purpose graphics hardware and are used for animation, software development, and computer-aided design.

World Wide Web
A hypertext-based system for finding and accessing information on the Internet. The World Wide Web consists of a series of "pages" of information, many of which contain text, color graphics, and even sound and video clips.

INDEX

ACKNOWLEDGEMENTS

The publisher would like to thank the following copyright holders for their kind permission to reproduce their screengrabs, all of which are trademarks.

l left; *r* right; *a* above; *b* below; *t* top; *c* center.

Activision 93bl; Adobe 60br,133t,br, 135br,bra,137cl,bca,bl,145tr,151bcl,bc, 154tr,155cr,r; Apple Computer Inc. 90tr,cb,91ca,165br; Argonaut Software Ltd, London 46bc,br,95c,146-147; Atari 8bl,br,92c,cr,br,93clb,br; Boosey and Hawkes Music Publishers Ltd 131tc,ca, cb,bl,br; Brøderbund Software Ltd 17tcb,17cr,34-35,36b,44-45,142tc; BMG Interactive 17crb,29br,57,93bc,124clb; Bullfrog Productions Ltd.48,104cb, 148-149; Bungie Software 17clb,47bc; Cakewalk Music Software 130cra,131tl, cl,cla; CCTA 63tr; CD Online 96tr; Comptons NewMedia 56,75c; CompuServe 167; CRT Multimedia 61; Dennis Publishing 31; Digidesign 125bl, 127c,128; Disc Manufacturing Inc. 81cr; Division Ltd. 105clb107tl,cl, bl; © 1994/1995 Domestic Funk Products 58cl,b,br,118-119,120tr,c,br, 121t,tr; Electronic Arts 16crb,17tr,19trb, 24-25, 37,99t,cr,cb,114-115,116-117, 150cb, 156br; EuroTalk/Heinemann International 40bl/© Les Editions Albert René, Goscinny-Uderzo 40-41c,41t; Europress Software 39c,bc,br; Fractal Design Corporation 133cra,134-135 *Painter /Natural Media* ™ ; France Telecom Intelmatique 166cr; General Magic 173bl,br,bc; Humongous Entertainment Inc. 36tr; id software 12bl,46c,95b; Infogrames 95b,97cr,bra; IVI Publishing 13cr,19bcr,br,157br; Knowledge Adventure 17tc,ca,32-33, 39t,42; *French Vocabulary Builder* © The Learning Company 1995. All Rights Reserved 17tcb,41b; © 1994 Lucasfilm Ltd. 12br,47c,ca,tr,cr,cra104cr,143b/ © 1994 LucasArts Entertainment Company.17c,50tr,c,r,51,142c,cr/© 1993 LucasArts Entertainment Company. 142b/© 1992 Lucasfilm Ltd. 143cb All Rights Reserved. Used Under Authorization; Macromedia 112cra, 119bc,120cl,bc,b121c,ca,123cl,c,125bc, 129tc,145bl,151br; MicroProse 49cl,c, cr,br/Spectrum Holobyte 52-53; Microsoft Corporation 13cr,16cr,20-21,26-27,38,70cra,cl,80bc,86c,br,87ca, crb,88ca,89cb,122bc,br,123tr; Mirage Technologies (Multimedia) Ltd 143tr,cr; Muze Inc. 64tr; Netscape Communications Corporation 160bc, 164cr; Newsweek Inc./Software Toolworks Inc. 30; Nintendo 65c,93tr, cb; Philips Interactive 94ca,97br; Pixsys/Image Guided Technology 138br; Quark Inc. 91tr,113tr; Sega 92tc,93ca, 95b,100-101; 7th Level 58tr,59; Sierra On-Line 17cl,50bc,54-55; Softkey International 19bl; Sony Interactive, Europe/Psygnosis 70cr,95b,103c,bc, crb,124cl/Tamsoft br; Specula International 132cb,139,140-141; Time Warner Cable's Full Service Network, a division of Time Warner Entertainment Co.,L.P. 168tc,bc,169tr,crb,bc,170bl, 171,11cr,bl,12tcr,168tc; Time Warner Interactive 99cra; Turner Music Publishing Inc. 127tl; Video Arts 97tl; Virgin Interactive Entertainment 19cra,121br/Looking Glass Technology 49t/ © Virgin Interactive Entertainment, Inc. All Rights Reserved. Created by Mechadeus 54bl,151tr,153tc,b; Virtuality Entertainment 106c,clb,br; Voyager 18bl,cr,br,19c,cl,cr,crb; Wienerworld Interactive/Graphix Zone 157cl; Xebec Multi Media Solutions 17bc,60bl.

The publishers would like the following for their kind permission to reproduce their photographs.

Bridgeman Art Library 9tr; British Airways 17bcl,64cr,br,bc,65b; British Telecom 13bl,161cr,168br,169clb,172; Compaq Computer Corporation 88bc; The Computer Museum, Boston 84bl, 84cr; Encyclopaedia Brittannica 9br; IBM 82cb,83tc,bl,86bl; Microsoft Corporation/Text 100 86cla; Science Photo Library 71bc,74tr,83cb; Smithsonian Institution 17bcr,62; Telegraph Colour Library 122t; Woodfin Camp/Jim Wilson 84ca; Xerox PARC/ Brian Tramontana 85br.

Every effort has been made to trace the copyright holders and we apologise in advance for any unintentional omissions. We would be pleased to insert the appropriate acknowledgement in any subsequent edition of the publication.